For Judy Goldsmith,

who to *lieves in

the great tradition

Fanny Wright

began.

Best,

Celia Eckhardt

August 14, 1985

Fanny Wright

Fanny Wright

Rebel in America

Celia Morris Eckhardt

Harvard University Press
Cambridge, Massachusetts
London, England
1984

This book is printed on acid-free paper, and its binding materials
have been chosen for strength and durability.

Publication of this book has been aided by
a grant from the Andrew W. Mellon Foundation

Library of Congress Cataloging in Publication Data

Eckhardt, Celia Morris, 1935–
Fanny Wright, rebel in America.

Bibliography: p.
Includes index.
1. D'Arusmont, Frances Wright, 1795–1852.
2. Feminists—United States—Biography. I. Title.
HQ1413.D2E25 1984   303.4'84 [B]   83-8571
ISBN 0-674-29435-1

For Martin and David
who made it possible

Acknowledgments

Along with her own richly demanding presence, Fanny Wright has graced my life with the friendship of four other women who became, over the years, my sister sleuths. The late Cecilia Payne-Gaposchkin was almost as eager as I to know the woman who had been her great-grandmother's best friend, and she trusted me with her transcripts and only copies of the letters that passed between them 150 years ago. Josephine M. Elliott of New Harmony, Indiana, shared my excitement as she led me through the Workingmen's Institute archives in pursuit of the Owenses, the Maclures, and their amazing colleagues in the wonderful attempt they made to discover new dimensions to human community and thereby remake the world. Linda Pike, formerly of the Lafayette Project at Cornell University, introduced me to the great French hero of the American Revolution and helped me puzzle out his strange and touching relationship with Fanny Wright. Jill Liddington of Halifax in Yorkshire proved my unerring guide to the Jane Austen world of Fanny's childhood as well as to the radical Britain of her middle age.

I am indebted to people in three countries for their knowledge, their patience, and their laughter: to John Egerton of Nashville, Tennessee, who called one memorable day in 1974 and said, "I've just run across the most dazzling woman: her name is Frances Wright"; to Richard Strassberg of the Martin P. Catherwood Library at Cornell, who helped me sort out the Theresa Wolfson Papers there; to Aline Cook, archivist of the Workingmen's Institute at New Harmony, who insisted that I come there to read one letter, and who proved right; to many men and women in the Library of Congress, but especially to David Kresh, who found answers to the most unlikely questions; to Susan Moore of Edinburgh, Scotland, whose genius lies with genealogy; to the late Henry Morgan, chairman of the Dawlish Museum Society, who knew the people who lived in Dawlish in the 1810s as though they were his contemporaries and who discovered for me the world in which Fanny came of age; to Edward Royle of the University of York, who shared his understanding of Fanny's radical contemporaries in Great Britain. To Karl J. R. Arndt, who helped me know the Harmonists and those who dealt with them.

To the National Endowment for the Humanities I owe my thanks for a year to do research. To Bob Eckhardt I am deeply indebted for enduring many drafts of the manuscript and for providing the financial support that kept me while I wrote the book. Alan Zients's cheerful midwifery lasted far longer than either of us expected. Shirley Nelson Garner, Claire Foudraine, and Catherine Breslin read each version and gave without measure of their love and their confidence in me and my writing. Gerda Lerner, Edward Pessen, Irving Howe, and Ronnie Dugger brought their insights and impeccable standards to bear on the book. Frances Gray was my expert typist and patient companion in the manuscript's last stages. With breathtaking generosity, Lawrence Goodwyn became my most creative editor and colleague in making this book the fittest tribute I can give to one of the great women in the American past.

Contents

Illustrations

xi

Fanny Wright

Jane Austen
and the Rebel

1

On the sixth of September, 1795, a child was born on the southeast coast of Scotland whose life proved as vital as any could be in the nineteenth century, and almost as full of pain. Her name was Frances Wright, and John Stuart Mill would call her one of the most important women of her day.[1]

She was important because she dared to take Thomas Jefferson seriously when he wrote, "All men are created equal," and to assume that "men" meant "women" as well. She was important because she made of her life a determined search for a place where she could help forge the institutions that would allow that principle to govern society. She was important because she had the integrity and courage to renounce the upper middle-class world to which she was born—a world whose prizes and comforts were hers for the taking—and to risk her health, her fortune, and her good name to realize, in the United States of America, the ideals on which it was founded.

In 1825 she became the first woman in America to act publicly to oppose slavery. Twenty miles outside the little trading post so presumptuously named Memphis, in Tennessee, she established a commune whose purpose was to discover and then to demonstrate how slaves might be educated and responsibly freed. In 1828 she became the first woman in America to speak in public to a large secular audience of men and women, and the first to argue that women were men's equals and must be granted an equal role in all the business of public life. Along with Robert Owen's eldest son, Robert Dale Owen, she edited a liberal weekly newspaper, the *Free Enquirer*, and from 1828 to 1830 she used its pages, as she used lecture halls throughout the country, to fight for all the victims of the social and political hierarchies of her time.

The pampered daughter of a favored class, Fanny cast her lot with working people and, as speaker and journalist, involved herself in the beginnings of the labor movement in New York. She attacked an economic system that allowed not only slavery in the South but what she called wage slavery in the North, a system that made black women the sexual prey of white men and drove poor women everywhere to the workhouse, to crime, and to prostitution. She came to see what Alexis de Tocqueville did not: that America was by no means a society in which people lived as equals, but one marked by extremes of wealth and poverty which were growing rather than diminishing. She understood that such disparities of wealth made an authentic republic impossible.

Nor did the churches escape her wrath. She showed her skepticism of the religious and sexual pieties of her time when she wrote Mary Wollstonecraft Shelley that men, "like their old progenitor, Father Adam . . . walk about boasting of their wisdom, strength, and sovereignty, while they have not sense so much as to swallow an apple without the aid of an Eve to put it down their throats." She attacked a morality that taught people to spend their money building churches and sending missionaries abroad but that closed their eyes to the destitution and injustice around them. She took on the churches in part because she thought men used religion to keep women foolish, dependent, and at home.[2]

At a time when women's virtue was said to depend on their chastity, she spoke of sexual passion as "the strongest and . . . the noblest of the human passions" and the source of "the best joys of our existence." With the possible exception of Walt Whitman, she wrote more powerfully of sexual experience than any other American in the nineteenth century. In 1827, when propriety forbade women even to mention sexuality, she publicly endorsed miscegenation as a way to solve the race problem in America. She looked to the day when "the olive of peace" would be "embraced by the white man and the black, and their children, approached in feeling and education, [would] gradually blend into one their blood and hue."[3]

In the 1840s she came to believe that governments men had made inclined to war, and was convinced that they did so because they elevated the selfish principle over the generous, in part by restricting women to "the narrowest precincts of the individual family circle . . . by forcibly closing [their] eyes upon the claims of the great human family without that circle." Justice, she argued, could come only when "the two persons in human kind—man and woman—shall exert equal influences in a state of equal independence."[4]

A woman so at odds with the conventions of her time was bound to divide her contemporaries, and Frances Wright was loved and hated with equal extravagance. By the time she was thirty, she had met and dazzled the famous on both sides of the Atlantic. Jeremy Bentham observed that she had "the sweetest and strongest mind that ever was lodged in a female body." The Marquis de Lafayette called her his daughter, his adored Fanny, and paid his attentions so openly that he scandalized not only his social circle but his own family. In old age Walt Whitman remembered that "we all loved her: fell down before her: her very appearance seemed to enthrall us." She was "sweeter, nobler, grander—multiplied by twenty—than all who traduced her."[5]

Because she attacked the churches, however, endorsed miscegenation, and most of all, because she shunned the pedestal prescribed for women, she was labeled "The Red Harlot of Infidelity." In 1829 a New York editor called her "a bold blasphemer, and a voluptuous preacher of licentiousness . . . impervious to the voice of virtue, and case-hardened against shame!" In 1836 Catharine Beecher, exemplar of respectable women, charged that Fanny "stands, with brazen front and brawny arms, attacking the safeguards of all that is venerable and sacred in religion, all that is safe and wise in law, all that is pure and lovely in domestic virtue . . . I cannot conceive any thing in the shape of a woman, more intolerably offensive and disgusting." In 1837, while the press manipulated the opposition to her for partisan political ends, ten thousand people thronged the streets of New York to hear her speak, and the entire police force had to be called out to protect her and her followers.[6]

Some seventy-five years after Fanny Wright was born, a great English novelist mused on the problems of women like her. George Eliot, remembering Saint Theresa of Avila, an ascetic and mystic who founded sixteen convents and fourteen monasteries in Spain, remarked that her "passionate, ideal nature demanded an epic life" rather than the "many-volumed romances of chivalry and the social conquests of a brilliant girl." The latter-day Theresas, Eliot knew, seldom found an "epic life wherein there was a constant unfolding of far-resonant action." Their spiritual grandeur ill-matched with mean opportunities, their lives slipped obscurely by.[7]

Fanny Wright's resemblance to the pragmatic Catholic saint did not escape at least one of her contemporaries. In 1827 the Swiss economist

J. C. L. de Sismondi wrote, "She is a new St. Theresa, in whom the love of principle and usefulness operates as the love of God did in the other." The problem for Fanny was to discover how she might be useful—for any woman in the first half of the nineteenth century who aspired to a spacious, dedicated life faced a formidable set of barriers. She could not matriculate in a university, much less teach in one. Neither in America nor in Great Britain could she vote. The laws that governed her and the creeds by which she lived were all written, interpreted, and enforced by men. A married woman could neither sign a contract, own money she earned, nor hold title to property originally hers by dowry or inheritance. Her children belonged legally to her husband. Her job lay in raising those children, though she was forbidden to know the world for which she shaped them. Modesty and self-sacrifice were the goals held up to her. No one expected her to excel; no one demanded that she be great. No matter how intelligent, ambitious, and dedicated, she was ineligible for a profession and had no natural role to play in any established institution that battled publicly to make the good prevail.[8]

Defying the conventions that would contain her, Fanny Wright chose to live tempestuously and to try for greatness. She traveled farther than perhaps any other woman of her time, and as she ranged, she broke one barrier after another.

For all this, the story of Fanny Wright is hard and disquieting. It tells more about the losses than the gains of America in the nineteenth century. It tells how much people love the rhetoric of equality and how little they are inclined to make equality possible. It tells how self-righteously men fight to hold their power over half the human race. It tells how women crucify the would-be saviors of their sex and how men mock them with that fact. It tells how fragile reason is, and how deadly isolation. It tells of a woman whose strength was tightly bound to her frailty. It is a story of courage, boldness, and waste. Most of all, it is a story not merely of the past: to learn it is to recover a part of our democratic heritage, and to discover that the time for Fanny Wright has not yet come.

The most terrifying thing that ever happened to Fanny Wright happened when she was two and a half: her mother died in February 1798, and her father three months later. Fanny was then torn from her five-year-old brother and baby sister and their home in Dundee, on the coast of Scotland, and taken to be raised in London by her grandfather and her eighteen-year-old aunt. In neither her public nor her private writings would there be a sense of childhood.[9]

A letter from Fanny's mother, Camilla, suggests what might have been. While visiting her sister in the north of England, Camilla wrote her husband on their anniversary: "I need not say how much more rejoiced I should be to have your dear self here, but when I think how tenderly you are employed in caring for our beloved children I less regret your absence, tho it is on the day I regard as the most valued of my life." Camilla's family was among the British lettered aristocracy. She named her son for her uncle, Richard Robinson, who had become Baron Rokeby in 1777. For a quarter of a century he was vice chancellor of the University of Dublin, and he served as Archbishop of Armagh from 1765 until his death in 1794. Camilla's great-aunt and devoted godmother was the gifted bluestocking Elizabeth Robinson Montagu, whom Dr. Samuel Johnson fondly called "Queen of the Blues." Mrs. Montagu defended Shakespeare against Voltaire's attack, and established a salon that attracted people as different as the painter Sir Joshua Reynolds and the author and reformer Hannah More. So brilliantly did she entertain "all the leaders of thought and fashion in the London of the day" that she caught the attention of royalty. Not long before Fanny was born, the papers wrote that the Queen and her six daughters had breakfasted with Mrs. Montagu. And like her aunt, Camilla Wright drew people who admired her and found her charming.[10]

Fanny's father, James Wright, Jr., was a Dundee merchant, related through his mother to Glasgow intellectuals who helped to give the Scottish Enlightenment its name. For more than forty years his uncle, James Mylne, was professor of moral philosophy at the University of Glasgow. James Wright too was a serious student: his special interest was in coins, and his collection was rare and valuable. In his mid-twenties he challenged the authority on the subject on some points of accuracy and insisted that he underrated the excellence of Scottish coinage. James despised aristocracy and those who used "the silly morsels of heraldry" in designing coins, and he argued for representations of "emblems of industry and commerce," such as weavers at their work, mail-coaches, and "whale-fishing."[11]

Like James Mylne, Wright admired Thomas Paine and the principles of the French Revolution, and he was politically suspect for his enthusiasm. According to Fanny, he was the object of government espionage in 1794 for promoting a cheap edition of *The Rights of Man*, and Dundee legend had it that to escape prosecution, he rowed out alone at midnight and dumped his radical coins and literature into the river Tay. When Fanny later discovered some of his papers, she marveled at "a somewhat singular coincidence in views between a father and daughter, separated by death when the first had not reached the age of twenty-nine, and when the latter was in infancy."[12]

James was a poor businessman. He begrudged the time work took away from his family, his coins, and his politics, and the times were hard for trade. But the Wrights lived comfortably in Miln's Buildings at the Nethergate in a new apartment busy with children and the servants on which their class depended. The life there augured well for raising responsible, good-natured young people who would take their places in the community among their peers. Had death not intervened, the world would never have heard of Fanny Wright.[13]

Her brother and sister seemed less deeply scarred than Fanny by the tragedy of their childhood. Richard was raised in James Mylne's home in Glasgow along with his own five children. Camilla, a year and a half younger than Fanny, was left with foster parents in Dundee, of whom she later wrote with the love a child might feel for parents who were especially kind. For the next eight years, however, Fanny had to learn the hard lessons of childhood solitude. In a time and place where children were treated as small adults, she learned to be her own shaping spirit.[14]

She lived in London with her maternal grandfather, Major General Duncan Campbell of the Royal Marines, and his daughter Frances, and it was in rebellion against her Tory guardians that Fanny began to understand the life around her. She later wrote of her "absence of all sympathy with the views and characters of those among whom her childhood was thrown." Her brother's sketch of their grandfather suggests the nature of her rebellion, for Campbell was indolent and convivial, a man who loved the good life as it paraded itself in a great metropolis. In 1809, when Richard passed through London on his way to serve with the East India Company, he wrote home that his grandfather knew nobody but "Lords and Generals" and never dined at home alone. "He is going out today, and we were out yesterday at Mr. Kerr's M.P., who to be sure had a grand dinner, and ten or twelve different sorts of wine . . . we are going to the Opera tonight." By her own account, Fanny came early to distrust the self-indulgence that made that life so sweet.[15]

The beggars of London first inspired Fanny to compassion for the poor. As she walked about the city with Duncan Campbell, she saw thousands begging pennies to buy bread. When she asked her grandfather why these tattered mothers and their children were so poor, he said it was because they were too lazy to work. But once, when he answered a knock at the door to find a gaunt man dressed in rags who said he had eaten nothing for three days and begged to work just for food and clothing, Duncan Campbell turned him away. When Fanny wished aloud that she had money to give the man to keep him from starving, her grandfather called her "a foolish simple girl" who knew "but little of the world." When she asked him why rich people who did not work did not become beggars, he answered that work was shameful: "I could not associate with rich people if I worked ... God intended there should be poor, and there should be rich." And when Fanny wondered if the rich robbed the poor, he replied indignantly that if she indulged such thoughts, she would not be admitted into good society.[16]

Late in 1803, Fanny's uncle Major William Campbell, who was Frances' brother, was killed in action against the Mahrattas at Saswarree in India. Of his property in the provinces of Bengal, Behar, and Orissa, and in the Zemindary of Benares, he willed half to his sister and the other half to his nieces, Frances and Camilla Wright. And William had clearly been a very wealthy man.[17]

The legacy that made the girls heiresses no doubt also made possible Frances Campbell's move, in 1806, to the coastal village of Dawlish, in Devonshire. The nine-year-old Camilla apparently joined her and Fanny then, and soon became the foil for her sister's dazzling presence. The pattern soon was set: Fanny confronted the world while Camilla kept the house. By all accounts gentle and bright, Camilla was also intensely loyal. She looked to Fanny "for guidance, and leaned upon her for support," and life for her became unthinkable apart from her sister.[18]

Death had separated them once before; in 1809 it came again to strengthen their dependence on each other. Late in the spring, en route to India, their brother Richard was killed in a skirmish with the French, and in November of the same year their grandfather died. By the time she was fourteen, Fanny had seen her mother, her father, her brother, and her grandfather die. This was radical deprivation. And she seems to have transformed the turbulent emotions of fear and anger that such deprivation would provoke into lifelong outrage at human suffering.[19]

The two girls probably lived with their aunt in the twenty-room mansion that she called The Cottage, for Richard wrote that Miss Campbell lived in great style, and Fanny remarked that she was "surrounded at all times by rare and extensive libraries, and commanding whatever masters she desired." The Cottage topped a hill and looked down on Lyme Bay, just where the English Channel flows into the Atlantic Ocean. A visitor called it an earthly paradise, with its grand view and terraced walks, its fine magnolia and banks of rhododendron, its kitchen garden with peach trees and apricots.[20]

And for the next seven years, until 1813, Fanny and Camilla Wright lived with Miss Campbell in Dawlish in the gracious style of the British upper middle class. Servants waited on them: they never had to dress themselves or pack a trunk. Governesses and tutors came to their call, and what intellectual nourishment they did not find at home they could get from the group of worldly and experienced men settled nearby. On Sundays they worshiped with their aunt at Dawlish Church in the decorous fashion of the Anglican communion. The seasons came gently as the rolling hills, and the abundant fruits and flowers of Devonshire graced their table. Fanny lived there from the time she was eleven until she was eighteen, as she and Camilla mastered their lessons, learned to swim and ride their horses, paid their calls and took their tea.

For an insight into Fanny's and Camilla's adolescence, we are in debt to another great English novelist. In 1811 Jane Austen published *Sense and Sensibility,* in which a man seems surprised that anybody could live in Devonshire without living near Dawlish. Sharp and conservative, Frances Campbell was a lady from one of Jane Austen's novels, and she brought up her nieces to triumph in the world the author so zestfully describes—a world dominated by manor and parsonage, regulated for those of consequence by the London social season, enlivened by visits for tea. People entertained themselves with hunting, whist, picnics, and balls. Ladies did needlework and on occasion sang for their friends.

In such a world, propriety was a great dictator. It decreed, among other things, that well-bred men like Duncan Campbell should not work. One of Jane Austen's characters, for example, describes himself as having nothing to do: "idleness was pronounced on the whole to be the most advantageous and honourable, and a young man of eighteen is not in general so earnestly bent on being busy as to resist the solicitations of his friends to do nothing. I was therefore entered at Oxford, and have been properly idle ever since."[21]

For women, the possibilities of vocation were a good deal more meager. Jane Austen's heroines concentrate on sorting the worthy suitor from the unworthy—"worthy" invariably having a close, if complicated, relationship to "rich." The first line of *Pride and Prejudice* announces the game played in all her novels: "It is a truth universally acknowledged, that a single man in possession of a good fortune must be in want of a wife." In *Emma* the possibility that a spirited woman will have to become a governess is looked upon as a disaster of sorts—even by those who do not wish her well. It was a world with which Fanny Wright was almost ludicrously at odds.[22]

Had Jane Austen tried to portray the adolescent Fanny, she would have drawn a tall, thin, conspicuous woman, for Fanny was very tall at fourteen and, when full-grown, was at least five feet ten inches. She might have shown Fanny jumping her horse while others trotted, talking of higher mathematics to a suitor who knew nothing but hounds, insisting on the virtues of Byron to people who read only Cowper. In fact, when "a deep and shrewd mathematician and physician" observed that a question of hers was "dangerous," Fanny asked if truth could be dangerous. From his reply, "It is thought so," she concluded "that Truth had still to be found . . . [and] men were afraid of it." Jane Austen obviously could not have put Frances Wright in her frame, for while Fanny learned exquisite manners, she also asked unsettling, radical questions. She asked, "What is justice?" and "Why are so many poor?" She was too hungry to content herself with Jane Austen's high tea.[23]

More important, Fanny did not develop the psychic protection of a sense of humor. She wrote later that "experience taught her, in very childhood, how little was to be learned in drawing-rooms, and inspired her with a disgust for frivolous reading, conversation, and occupation." Jane Austen could have said, with one of her heroines, "Follies and nonsense, whims and inconsistencies, *do* divert me, I own, and I laugh at them whenever I can." Fanny was not amused.[24]

She never learned to be as tough as the comic novelist. She could not use irony or humor to help her live with those for whom she felt contempt. She could not manipulate people, as the novelist did, for her own amusement. She was not subtle enough, or cruel enough, for her own good—if one imagined her good to consist of an accommodation to the small world around her. Fanny, of course, did not so imagine it.

If these were unhappy years, Fanny emerged from them with a strength that people invariably found startling. Her disdain for drawing rooms prompted her to pour her energies into becoming a scholar, and from the small but distinguished group of educated men around Dawlish, she caught the excitement of the life of the mind. She undoubtedly knew John Schank, a gifted naval engineer. She probably knew Sir William Watson, whose many visitors included Sir William Herschel, the astronomer who discovered the planet Uranus. Joseph

Drury, who retired to Dawlish after his tenure as headmaster of Harrow, entertained scientists and scholars from all over England; and the naturalist Thomas Comyns had one of the best private museums in the country there. These men set high standards that governed those of her class, and even by such standards Fanny was well educated. She learned French and Italian. She read classical literature. She spent years confronting the disciplines of history, philosophy, and mathematics.[25]

Her scholarship led her to classical drama as well as to European and English poetry, which she studied in the most fruitful way, by imitation. She found relief through writing: to name her feelings was to understand and to control them. In a poem apparently from this period she wrote of losing a beloved friend:

> Fair star! may every joy be thine!
> May thou ne'er prove the bitter anguish
> Of love so true, so fond as mine,
> Doomed without hope untold to languish.
>
> Oh had I but the Lesbyan's lyre,
> Blue-eyed Sappho's fervid strain;
> Then might I hope thy blood to fire;
> Then should I make thee share my pain.

She learned when she was young that language gives power: if she could be eloquent, she would not suffer alone. She began to perfect that command of language so crucial to the legend she would become.[26]

Dawlish itself deeply influenced her. The Cottage looked down on a coastline that was sinuously beautiful, and at a time when Wordsworth was teaching the English-speaking world to feel the power of nature and the virtue of simple people, Fanny was looking to rural Devonshire for solace. A small village, and remote, Dawlish depended primarily on its own artisans and tradesmen. The most memorable event in its history occurred in Fanny's time: the 1810 flood, which washed away a number of houses. And if Fanny learned in Dawlish the respect for plain people that marked her always, she also learned that life was not the idyll it might seem.

Thomas Hardy began a lifetime of indignant questioning when he saw a boy die of starvation in the fruitful field he had helped to cultivate. By the time she was fifteen Fanny too had discovered that a good deal of human suffering had human causes. She saw how painfully old English peasants labored and how, nevertheless, they were "ejected, under various pretexts, from the estates of the wealthy proprietors of the soil among whom she moved." She saw that wealth had power in the world which age and infirmity did not.[27]

At least three men were building empires for themselves in that part of Devonshire, and Fanny watched these local enclosures as they drove peasants from their ancestral homes and took away the traditional rights to gather food and firewood that had made their lives tolerable. In the 1790s, Drury of Harrow had taken over eight small holdings, consolidated them, and built himself a mansion. What had been a patchwork of small cultivated plots and common lands, he transformed into gardens and parkland, surrounded with a few cultivated fields. A few years later Charles Hoare, who was richer than Drury, bought a number of adjoining farms and made them into the Luscombe Estate. He built a castle and laid out parks, and for years he continued to accumulate the farms nearby. At about the same time, John Inglet Fortescue bought the manor of Dawlish from the dean and chapter of Exeter Cathedral, who had held it since before the Norman Conquest, and sold it piecemeal to the highest bidders.

As Fanny watched these rich men drive the poor from land on which their ancestors had lived as far back as memory and legend could trace, she "pronounced to herself a solemn oath, to wear ever in her heart the cause of the poor and the helpless; and to aid in all that she could in redressing the grievous wrongs which seemed to prevail in society." It was an oath that became the motive force in her life.[28]

Her anger at the cruelty her aunt's gracious world inflicted on the poor led readily into what became her life's obsession: the United States of America. When she was seventeen, she chanced upon Carlo Bocca's *Storia della Guerra dell' Independenza degli Stati Uniti d'America*, a history of the thirteen colonies' struggle to become a young republic. At that moment of discovery, she later recalled, she glimpsed a new life: "There existed a country consecrated to freedom, and in which man might awake to the full knowledge and full exercise of his powers." While those around her were absorbed in the war against Napoleon, Fanny determined secretly to see the nation across the Atlantic against which, in that Tory corner of England, there seemed to be a conspiracy of silence.[29]

Not long after her discovery of America, the anger that had simmered for years between niece and aunt boiled to the surface. Frances Campbell was a woman who reveled in her life of modest grandeur. She was respectable enough, and good enough company, that in later years the Hoares invited her to live with them in nearby

Luscombe Castle. It seems unlikely that she was malicious to her nieces, but she was at least inept. Only eighteen when death forced the two-year-old Fanny upon her, she assumed a premature responsibility that may well have made her rigid. Richard Wright described her as a fussy woman who told him to eat just so much and to wear his gloves constantly. He wished someone would teach her how to give advice: "I would not give one of Mr. Mylne's advices for 10,000 of hers . . . It would make a horse laugh."[30]

But Fanny despised her. She believed her aunt deceitful and cruel, and saw in her "the image of an enemy." Scarred by a bitterness she knew she would carry till death, Fanny felt that she had been victimized since infancy by the "crying wrongs" her aunt had heaped upon her, and whatever the rights and wrongs of each side in their quarrel, it had a profound emotional impact on Frances Wright. The pattern of her relationship with her aunt repeated itself throughout her life: she would feel someone wrong her and turn harshly against him, as though the child whom death had torn from those she loved could never let herself be vulnerable again. She left Dawlish marked with a psychic inflexibility that would never soften. As though freed from a trap and wary of being caught again, she looked suspiciously on permanent commitment and inclined to move restlessly through the world. Rather than put her trust in people who would die or betray, Fanny Wright came to put her trust in ideas.[31]

Fanny's formidable will had its first major triumph in 1813, when she whisked herself and Camilla away from Frances Campbell's home before they were legally of an age to go. They went to Glasgow, to their uncle James Mylne and his wife Agnes, who had nurtured Richard and now welcomed them. They joined the five Mylne children in a college house said to be very cramped, but one that opened onto a university court romantically like the close of an English cathedral. Glasgow, a port on the river Clyde, was a mercantile city where citizens took public affairs and their own responsibilities seriously. The currents of social reform swirled past the sisters' door, and they began to feel the insurgent pulls of modern life.[32]

Glasgow was also the home of one of Scotland's oldest and most distinguished universities, and Fanny and Camilla now lived with a man who had taken the chair of moral philosophy less than thirty-five years after Adam Smith had left it. Oxford and Cambridge for the most part confined their teaching to the learned languages and the transmission of what Edward Gibbon called "the prejudices and infirmities of the age," but Glasgow's intellectual life was both utilitarian and democratic. Although the university excluded women, it took pride in furthering the country's economic and industrial development and even concerned itself with educational reforms: most classes were taught in English rather than Latin, and dedicated and inspiring teachers like James Mylne were objects of respect. Little had changed since Adam Smith had called the Scottish universities "without exception the best seminaries of learning that are to be found anywhere in Europe."[33]

The extended family that Fanny and Camilla joined in Glasgow had been powerfully shaped by its patriarch, John Millar, a friend and disciple of both Smith and David Hume, and professor of civil law and jurisprudence at the university until his death in 1801. Nine of Millar's children survived him, and they and their families offered models of human possibility far more congenial to Fanny than Frances Campbell or her Tory friends had been. Her Aunt Agnes was Millar's daughter. Robina Craig Millar, who would try to replace the mother Fanny had lost so young, had married his eldest son. Another son, James, was professor of mathematics and, with Mylne, showed the family instinct for dissent by regularly voting in the minority on issues of university policy.

The women in the Millar circle cultivated literature and the arts as eagerly as the men did. Frederick Lamb remarked that all the ladies around Millar were "contaminated with an itch for philosophy and learning" and seemed to enjoy themselves wonderfully. "After cheese they hand around the table a bottle of whisky and another of brandy, and the whole company, males and females . . . indulge in a dram. It is very comfortable and exhilarating, and affords an opportunity for many jokes." It seems unlikely that Millar's children would have turned, intellectually or socially, to a frugal table after he died, and Fanny and Camilla boarded richly among them.[34]

The coincidence between Fanny's ideas and those of John Millar can hardly be accidental. A Whig when Scotland was run for the most part by Tories, Millar enthusiastically endorsed the fight against the slave trade. He supported the American Revolution in the interests of "that love of liberty, so congenial to the mind of man, which nothing but imperious necessity is able to subdue." He vigorously upheld the principles on which the French Revolution was fought, and his dismay at the course it took did not lead him, as it did so many others, to support Edmund Burke's crusade and the war against France. A believer in gradual progress and the good effects of manufacture and commerce, he nonetheless wrote that "the pursuit of riches becomes a scramble, in which the hand of every man is against every other." His work is a model of the cool, dispassionate inquiry Fanny later tried to emulate, and his pages explore many of the ideas she later preached to a startled America.[35]

As for James Mylne, he was said to be "probably the most independent thinker of the Scottish philosophical professoriate" of his day. His students called him "Old Sensation," an allusion to the philosophical position which Fanny soon took, that we can know nothing beyond the evidence provided by our senses. A Church of Scotland minister, Mylne exalted reason, self-control, and duty. Like his father-in-law, he opposed the slave trade and endorsed the principle of utility, which looks to the greater happiness of the greater number. And he delighted in Fanny and Camilla: "girls of whom I may be justly vain—well-principled, well-informed, elegantly accomplished, fit to take their places among society of any rank and to be received in it with esteem and respect."[36]

In Scotland, Fanny and Camilla found two sets of sisters, the Millars and the Cullens, who heightened their sense of how accomplished women can become. They often stayed at Milheugh, the Millar family's estate not far from Glasgow, where the Millar sisters so fired one visitor's love of knowledge that she called the days she spent there "the acme of her intellectual existence." The Cullen sisters were equally distinguished, their father, Dr. William Cullen, having been one of the outstanding professors and scientists at the University of Edinburgh. Robina Craig Millar, the youngest of the Cullens, was the bridge between these remarkable people, and she became the most important older woman in Fanny's life. She had married John Millar, Jr., and emigrated with him to the United States, but after he died suddenly in Pennsylvania in 1796, she returned to live with her sister Margaret, whom the Wright sisters called the "Good Spirit." Fanny turned to Robina as to a mother. Talented, charming, and radical in her sympathies, Mrs. Millar lavished her affections on Fanny and Camilla. And one of her letters shows the kind of adulation the elder Miss Wright inspired in those around her: "what an existence you gave and what a world you have carried away! . . . you . . . will soon have all the world at your feet."[37]

At least once, when she was twenty, Fanny flirted briefly with marriage. The man's name was Watson. He formally proposed, and James Mylne thought him "a man of honor and integrity, of generous and affectionate dispositions, of correct habits, of rational and moderate views." Mylne told Watson that if he could accumulate enough money to support a family "of education and habits such as yours and Fanny's," Mylne could approve their eventual marriage. Their engagement, however, enjoyed no very long duration. After Fanny broke it off, Robina Millar observed that she had never thought them suited to each other. Although Watson was amiable and steady and might have saved Fanny "from many rocks on which in your voyage thro' life you might be in danger of being driven . . . a character of his caliber could never have rendered you happy," and she congratulated Fanny on her escape.[38]

About the same time Fanny was doing what was expected of young women—getting engaged—she was doing something altogether presumptuous: she was taking herself seriously as a writer. Mrs. Millar, who became the voice of propriety in relation to her work, assured her that she was a born poet: "You have the imagination, the temperament, the just confidence of genius." Fanny began a long poem, *Thoughts of a Recluse*, and her interest in it lasted a good deal longer than her interest in Watson. She continued for years to write additional passages and tried more than once to have it published. The poem, of which only fragments remain, was apparently Byronic in tone, world-weary and contemptuous when not simply angry. And though Mrs. Millar admired it, she discouraged Fanny's attempts to publish it on the grounds that "no Bookseller would venture upon it because they as well as the author are compelled to suffer for libels." She thought it contained opinions that would seem arrogant in one so young and was afraid it might prejudice readers against Fanny's other work.[39]

Only a few short poems from this period have survived. In some of them Fanny echoed the romanticism of her time and embraced nature, the first of many panaceas she would try and find wanting. More important, she had the stunning self-assurance to talk to Genius as to a familiar, if difficult, friend, and to write of her "fond desire / Of fame immortal." She introduced an idea that, although fashionable, also seems genuine and recurs in her work—the idea that her experience had destroyed some quality vital to life:

> And now, the worst—a heart whose pulse is killed,
> And hath no more to give or to receive,
> Shrunk in itself, all passive, mute and chilled,
> That hopes not, cares not, joys not, nor can grieve.

Fanny thought of this paralysis as a response to the cruelty she had watched and suffered herself, though the sexual suppression that propriety demanded of women of her class might well have been equally to blame. But she also gave a glimpse of the pleasant side of her life, among people who cared for her and for one another:

> Good night! Good night! if we, this day,
>   Have spoke in wrath, be it forgiven
> And may we, on our pillows lay,
>   At peace with Man, at peace with Heaven!
>
> Good night! Good night! Oh, may we greet,
>   In health and joy, tomorrow's light!
> And, as we part, so may we meet
>   In peace and love! Good night! Good night![40]

By Fanny's own account she "passed three years in Scotland, during which period she employed her summers in visiting its Highlands and Lowlands; and her winters in closet study." They were fruitful years for her, and people helped when they could. The university librarian Lockhart Muirhead allowed her free access to everything about the United States, and, no doubt for Fanny's sake, James Mylne took out various books on America. She made one of an informal group that gathered to talk of literature and philosophy, and it was for them she wrote several plays, only one of which, *Altorf*, survives in its published form. It was also for them she wrote a treatise on Epicurean philosophy, later published under the title *A Few Days in Athens*.[41]

Its fable is simple. Theon, a young Greek who has come to Athens to study philosophy, believes a fellow student who slanders Epicurus. On a walk outside town, Theon then tells a stranger how shocked he is that Epicurus has been allowed to corrupt young people, and the stranger turns out to be Epicurus. Ashamed of himself, Theon goes back with him to the garden where he teaches, and there he sheds his biases, learns to weigh evidence, and grows in compassion. The life Fanny imagines as the locus of morality is the life of a school, a self-contained world of talk, and the message it preaches is a generous, high-minded self-sufficiency. Epicurus teaches that a sage must become independent of all he cannot command within himself: "What is poverty, if we have temperance, and can be satisfied with a crust, and a draught from the spring?"[42]

Remarkable for its intellectual vigor, the book is a highly competent representation of certain Greek philosophical schools. Its flaws reflect Fanny's characteristic impatience: the writing is often inflated, and the plot flimsy. But *A Few Days* stands as a moving plea for tolerance, self-

restraint, and loyalty. It is also iconoclastic—and not merely as the work of an eighteen-year-old. Implicitly attacking Christianity as an ethical guide, Fanny describes a moral life in which neither guilt, sacrifice, nor suffering plays a leading role. Her hero dares to honor happiness: a garden is a place of beauty, and in Epicurean philosophy refined pleasure is the supreme guide. Epicurus teaches his students to discipline themselves to avoid both evil passions and uncontrolled appetites: "I think virtue only the highest pleasure, and vice, or ungoverned passions and appetites, the worst misery."[43]

As Fanny sees him, Epicurus, the first Greek philosopher to accept women as students, is a worthy teacher who can "instantly give security to the timid, and draw love from the feeling heart," and he shows life's purpose as the struggle toward wisdom. The book juxtaposes Epicurus and the Stoic Zeno, the former generous and tolerant, the latter autocratic and unbending, and Fanny weights Epicurus' side of the scale. Though he knows the power he has over his students, "he exerts it in no other way," according to one, "than to mend our lives, or to keep them innocent."[44]

Leontium, alleged to be Epicurus' first female disciple, is modeled on Fanny herself, who clearly enjoyed the role of reverent student to a wise, elderly man whom she could then explain to others. Fanny describes Leontium as having "the self-possessed dignity of ripened womanhood, and the noble majesty of mind, that asked respect and promised delight and instruction. The features were not those of Venus, but Minerva. The eye looked deep and steady from beneath two even brows, that sense, not years, had slightly knit in the centre of the forehead, which else was uniformly smooth and polished as marble. The nose was rather Roman than Grecian, yet perfectly regular, and though not masculine, would have been severe in expression, but for a mouth where all that was lovely and graceful habited . . . Her stature was much above the female standard, but every limb and every motion was symmetry and harmony." More learned than the other students, Leontium has "the most acute, elegant, and subtle pen of Athens." Accustomed to receiving adulation as her due, she is called on to silence disputes and give definitive answers, which she does with graceful precision. The attention Fanny attracted suggests that the portrait is not inaccurate, but its self-confidence verges on self-congratulation, a trait that would unnerve and on occasion offend people she met—and one that would in part betray her.[45]

Fanny then, spent this time in Scotland with good people alive to ideas—to literature, to politics, and to art—and yet she was not satisfied. Making a distinction in her journal between the misanthrope and the cynic, she implicitly identified herself with the former, who "will generally be found to have entered life with a warm heart, a lively imagination, and a sanguine temperament; the latter with a cold heart, a shrewd understanding, and a phlegmatic temper. The misanthrope is made by disappointment, the cynic I take to be fashioned by nature." Like the misanthrope, Fanny had a grand conception of what men and women might be and was disgusted when she discovered what they were. The wounds she had suffered so young were the source of her restless anger: they never let her look benignly on the world or rest content with quiet happiness and the fond respect of her peers.[46]

While those long winter months of study, writing, and talk nourished Fanny intellectually, the summers, when she and Camilla traveled in the Highlands, fed her contempt for the social ethics of her time. The year 1814, just after she and Camilla came to Scotland, has gone down in Gaelic history as the Year of the Burnings, when landlords set fire to cottages to force their tenants off the land. In the name of "progress," they cleared people from the Highlands and replaced them with sheep. The Marquess of Stafford, later the Duke of Sutherland, drove five thousand people from their ancestral homes: "He was the product of a class to whom Property was becoming a sacred trust and its improvement an obligation that must take precedence over all others. This class, owning the land, controlling the legislature, officering the Army, dividing mankind into Gentility and Commons, and transporting a child for the stealing of a handkerchief (because it was Property), sincerely believed that its own enrichment must bring a greater good to a greater number." In boats as far south as the river Clyde, Fanny saw uprooted peasants bound for the United States. And in the Highlands, from which her father's people had come in the fifteenth century, she heard grim tales from those who remained.[47]

The Highlanders were an amalgam of Norse and Gael who "raised goats and black cattle, potatoes and inferior oats, brewed a rough beer and distilled a raw whisky for their dreams." The Lowlanders, who for the most part were the agents of the northerners' eviction, looked contemptuously on what seemed their indifference to progress, their satisfaction with poor food and meager huts, their fondness for illicit stills and belief in the Evil Eye. James Loch, a Lowlander who spent forty years helping to move them out, considered himself "at war with indolence, superstition, inefficiency, the obstinacy of a primitive people and the intransigence of the earth itself." One of his critics would say Loch's object was "to drive out that master-piece of sloth and uselessness—man and all his retinue."[48]

The spectacle of the Highland clearances, in addition to the enclosures that Fanny had seen in Dawlish, gave her a suspicion of "progress" that would run as a counterpoint through all her writing. She listened to people assuage their consciences by considering their victims not quite human. She saw the church collaborating with the rich to defraud the poor. With few exceptions, "the churchmen gave God's authority to Improvement, and threatened the more truculent of the evicted with damnation." Or as one spectator described it, the clergy "maintained in their sermons that the whole was a merciful interposition of Providence to bring them to repentance." If Fanny had not doubted the church before, she doubted it now, and her skepticism was unremitting.[49]

Some years later Fanny wrote that Robert Owen would transform the world, and she no doubt first learned about this utopian reformer in Glasgow. He was a friend of James Mylne's, and his industrial experiments at New Lanark, no more than thirty miles from the city, caught the attention of people as far away as Russia. While the government was hanging Luddites for trying to destroy the machines that were taking away their jobs, and while ambitious "improvers" were driving people from the Highlands to make room for sheep, Robert Owen was demonstrating that the successful operation of cotton mills was not incompatible with human welfare.[50]

Owen's was one of the dazzling success stories of early industrialism. Before he was twenty, he ran a factory with five hundred workers; well before he was thirty, he was part owner and manager of the largest mills in Scotland. But fifteen years before Fanny and Camilla came to Glasgow, he had decided he wanted to do something more than make money. He wanted benevolently to interfere with workers' lives. He wanted to practice the theory that the purpose of society was to make people happy, as well as to show that such a purpose was economically feasible. He captured Fanny's imagination in part because he was eager to spend his life for ordinary people, and he seemed to know how to translate idealism into practical terms.

Owen was an odd sort in an age when most mill owners were willing to keep children as young as six breathing cotton fluff and standing fourteen to sixteen hours in temperatures well over 75 degrees. By 1806, he had stopped importing the pauper children who were a standard source of labor for mills in remote places. He had prohibited the hiring of children under ten, shortened the hours of work, and abolished all punishments except fines, or dismissal for the hopelessly intractable. He had added a story to his workers' houses and developed clever inducements to cleanliness in the village and efficiency in the factory. He had replaced the profiteering shopkeepers and brought in good coal and clothes, pure food, and even pure whiskey, which he sold at minimal prices. He succeeded in making his factory and its town a decent, humane place, and he wanted to persuade others to follow his example.

Between 1815 and 1817, while Fanny and Camilla were in Glasgow, Owen published a series of essays about the effect of the manufacturing system on the working class, and especially on children. His arguments altered the thrust of the received wisdom of political economy. It was one thing for John Millar to comment on the demoralizing and dehumanizing tendencies of mechanization. It was quite another for an eminently successful manufacturer to say that though Britain's wealth and power had indeed increased remarkably because of the development of machinery, the accompanying social evils were so great that the loss from them might well be greater than the gain from mechanization. Owen found the laboring classes "infinitely more degraded and miserable than they were before the introduction of these manufactories, upon the success of which their bare subsistence now depends." He inveighed against the profit motive as "destructive of that open, honest sincerity, without which man cannot make others happy, nor enjoy happiness himself." Long before Carlyle, Ruskin, and Marx thundered against the modern system that pitted one person against another and class against class, Owen spoke out against industrialism's legacy of social devastation and argued that it was unnecessary and could be reversed.[51]

Owen insisted to his peers, the British master manufacturers, that the talk about the freedom of the working classes was cant, since the only alternatives they had to working nine to fifteen hours a day were the workhouse, crime, or starvation. His fellow manufacturers tried to discredit him. When he testified before a committee of the House of Commons on a bill to regulate the conditions of work in textile mills, a cotton lord questioned him with such hostility about his religious beliefs that the cross-examination was later expunged from the records. More important, the manufacturers had decisive power in Parliament, and the bill that finally passed in 1819 had been so amended to meet their demands that Owen, disclaiming any responsibility for it, turned to communitarian experiments to find his lever to move the world.

The essence of Owen's philosophy was that people's characters are formed for them, not by them; that all religions and all earlier philosophies had falsely held people responsible for their condition; that society brought them up in circumstances that inevitably made them vicious and criminal, and then punished them for being so; and that it was demonstrably possible to alter society radically, with no violence or loss to anyone, so that people would grow up to cooperate rather than to distrust or despise one another. The state to which he looked forward was governed, quite simply, by the precepts of primitive Christianity.

A man of action, Owen believed that the millennium was just around the corner, and he dedicated his life to bringing it into existence. He created a model that Fanny Wright was to find profoundly congenial. Ultimately he influenced her more, perhaps, than any other person she met in adult life, although it was an influence she came to rue.

In 1816, when she was twenty-one, Fanny began casting about for something to do. She had grown restless; her pleasant, self-contained world of good talk and good feelings had begun to pall. She had read some of the new romantic poets—certainly Byron, Shelley, and Schiller—and had caught their tone. She thrilled, as they did, to the cry of liberty, and with them she despised the tyrants of their time. She envied their moody heroes stalking the world, contemptuous of mediocrity and ready to die for a cause. More pertinent, she felt trapped by the decorum that narrowly bound the women of her class and denied them meaningful work. Among the poor, such decorum was irrelevant, because people worked to survive and women typically drudged longer hours than men did. The same was true in places like the American frontier, where hands were scarce and therefore dear, and where women worked alongside men and at many of the same jobs. Among the aristocracy, girls were often educated with their brothers, and queens and duchesses had proved how capable a gifted woman could be. But for women of the great middle class, from which Fanny came, productive work began to disappear in the last half of the eighteenth century, when the tide of industrialism began to carry work into the factories. The many jobs necessary to maintain a household— spinning, weaving, candle- and soap-making—were now done outside the home, leaving many women with idle hands. Those idle hands became a mark of distinction, a coveted badge that proclaimed the economic security and well-being of a class.

Idleness, however, offended Fanny Wright and made her uneasy, so after three years in Scotland, she and Camilla left the Mylnes and went to London. Fanny said they needed to arrange their financial affairs, perhaps by settling a lawsuit with Frances Campbell over the money held for them in trust. But their finances were also a convenient excuse. Fanny hoped to find something worthy to do, and what she saw and heard in London made her even more skeptical that she could find it in her native land. Looking with a critical eye on the men who governed England, she saw how thoroughly they were the beneficiaries of a society based on class. She began to despair of their ever voluntarily giving up their power and became more convinced that they would use it always against the poor.

The past twenty years had in fact been bad for the poor and politically tempestuous for everyone. The Industrial Revolution had developed machinery that permanently altered the nature of work, bringing a rapidly growing population from the countryside into unplanned cities and destroying ancient structures of community life, but the chances for dealing constructively with these changes had been frustrated by a political counter-revolution in response to the Terror in France. The British manufacturers had joined the aristocracy in making common cause against reforms from below. The land-owners worked to repress any Jacobin "conspiracies" to gain political power; the manufacturers worked to defeat "conspiracies" to increase wages and improve working conditions. Even play and laughter, especially on Sunday, became politically suspect.[52]

By 1815, the men who ran England seemed to be turning the thumbscrews on the poor. A landowners' Parliament passed the protectionist Corn Laws, which, by prohibiting the importation of cheap grain, raised the price of bread and devastated people who depended on it. In 1816, when Fanny reached London, she might well have wondered if the binding strings of British society would hold, as it seemed that the country was on the verge of a class war.

She was introduced to new strains in radical thought and tactics. The period from 1815 to 1820, the years of Fanny's early adulthood, has been called the heroic age of popular radicalism in Great Britain. William Cobbett, its most unrelenting journalist, and Henry Hunt, its most powerful orator, attacked abuses they saw coming from a venal, self-interested group of landowners and politicians. Dissidents pushed to extend the franchise and reform the House of Commons—the radicals arguing for universal manhood suffrage, the moderates for reduced property restrictions on those allowed to vote. They taught Fanny that others shared her disbelief in a Providence that decreed human suffering. With Robert Owen, they taught her to hope that society could be changed.

But by 1816 it was clear that the men who ruled England thought modest change revolutionary. For four years Major John Cartwright had been touring England and Scotland trying to "divert insurrectionary discontent into constitutional forms, and to lay the basis of a nation-wide movement continually petitioning Parliament." But the authorities were frightened and quartered soldiers all over the country. In the fall of 1816 three reform meetings held just outside London were disrupted. In January 1817 a convention Cartwright himself had called in London ended in rioting. The political crisis coincided with extreme economic distress, unemployment in the textile and iron districts, and soaring prices. The Prince Regent was mobbed in the London streets and his carriage window broken. The government suspended habeas corpus and reenacted an arsenal of repressive laws. Later in the year, thirty-five men who had been part of an abortive insurrection were arraigned for high treason, and four were condemned to die. A man executed for high treason was hanged, cut down before he was dead, and his entrails were cut out and burned in front of him. He was then beheaded and his head was brandished on a spike for the crowd's benefit. These outrages were enough for Fanny. In the summer of 1818 she and Camilla decided to go to America.[53]

Fanny wanted to see if life in a republic was as promising as it seemed, but she made her decision for other reasons as well. It was one step further in her rejection of the comfortable role that women of her class were expected to play. She decided apparently at the same time to write Robina Millar a series of letters from America that would serve as the basis for a book. When she and Camilla spent ten weeks that summer with the two Cullen sisters in the north of England, no doubt the four women talked of how Fanny should approach her task.

The act of writing would not itself violate the decorum expected of ladies: Fanny's poems and plays had been her apprentice work and won her a measure of the attention she craved. It was her choice of America that stretched the bounds of propriety. But America offered a subject on which she could try her powers, and a chance to catch the public ear by using a tone quite different from the carping and contempt she found in most British writing on the topic.

To achieve the goal she had set herself, Fanny assumed she would have to take serious risks and work very hard. The Atlantic crossing would be at least a test of endurance, for many ships went down.

Physical conditions in the New World would be harsh beyond anything she had known, and her health in childhood and adolescence had been feeble. Finally, to write the kind of scholarly book she admired would demand months of painstaking research. Fanny determined to do it, and she accepted several letters of introduction from Robina Millar to her American friends.

When Fanny wrote James Mylne that she and Camilla were going, he hurried to Liverpool, hoping to persuade her to change her mind. All her friends were startled, he said, and he was hurt. But when he asked her if a trip to Italy would not be more in keeping with her studies, Fanny replied, "The sight of Italy, dear uncle, prostrated under the leaden sceptre of Austria, would break my heart."[54]

She was able to be firm about going because, by the age of twenty-two, the dominant strains in her character were clear. She guarded her personal freedom jealously and was ready to go to surprising lengths to ensure it. She distrusted authority and was by no means timid in opposing it. Assured in all the forms of social intercourse, she was eager not merely for the respect but for the adulation of her peers. She was restless, energetic, and excitable. She was conspicuous. She was extreme.

In the background of Fanny's story—now and for the next decade—hovers the shadowy figure of Camilla Wright. Like that of so many devoted wives in history, her contribution passed largely unspecified. It is clear, however, that her stunning loyalty to her sister gave Fanny a measure of the psychic strength she needed to act so flamboyant a part on the public stage. When others mocked Fanny or counseled caution, Camilla sanctioned whatever Fanny thought best. She worshiped her sister and gave of herself with a generosity she did not stop to calculate. Fanny took her largely for granted.

On August 3, 1818, the Wright sisters boarded the American packet ship *Amity* bound for New York. During the voyage Fanny wrote a poem in which she compared herself to Byron's Childe Harold, calling her soul "As strange, as proud, as lonely from its birth— / With powers as vast." Much taller than most of the men she met, she must have surprised the American crew as she wandered the deck asking endlessly about how free people lived in a new republic. She wrote in her commonplace book that, "*if* wisdom and virtue are ever to be found more widely spread among a people, it must be among one possessed of Freedom." She thought she was going to a country whose powers and principles were commensurate with her own. She looked on the American republic as on salvation.[55]

Every Farmer
a Cincinnatus

2

Fanny Wright responded to her first ocean voyage with both the stoic spirit and the zest for adventure that marked her life. Too grand to stoop to the complaints that filled other travel journals, she wrote that the trip was dull and uneventful. Still, Camilla developed a horror of the voyage, and Fanny herself later gave advice that is chilling in its matter-of-factness: "take pills regularly while at sea—*and drink plentifully of thin gruel* the first three or four days. Be on deck as soon and as much as possible and above all keep yr bowels open . . . For the first two or three days after every attack of retching drink gruel or water, and when the stomach is cleansed thoroughly up and down take a mouthful of something highly seasoned with salt or pepper. As the appetite comes eat moderately and drink still more moderately . . . Pills of rhubarb and aloes mixed are as good as any." She spent most of her time on deck talking with the sailors when their work allowed and discovered that, unlike their peers in Britain, every one of them could read and write, and most "could converse with you upon the history of [their] country, its laws, its present condition, and its future prospects." She was exhilarated by the prospect of New York harbor and wrote, "I thought it was for the first time in my life that I had drawn a clear breath."[1]

The *Amity* docked on September 2, 1818, four days before Fanny's twenty-third birthday and after a voyage of thirty days. The New York that met the Wright sisters was little more than an overgrown town at the lower end of Manhattan Island. Greenwich Village and the Bouwerie to the north were open country, where New York's elite had farms to engage their leisure. Fanny was startled, in fact, on their first evening ashore by the unfamiliar, and decidedly rural, sound of katydids in song.

They found New York an exuberant, generous city that was small enough to harbor a new republic. Fanny saw neither the extreme wretchedness that marked the English poor nor the fabulous wealth that flaunted the power of British aristocracy. They came during a period of relative tranquillity after the bitter conflicts between the Federalists and Republicans and before the turbulence of industrialization and Jacksonian democracy; and Fanny's angry rebellion against European class society conspired with America's apparent calm to make her idealize what she saw and imagine every farmer to be a Cincinnatus. Years later she wrote that she had first seen America through a "Claude-Lorraine tint."[2]

Because the sisters tried to be frugal, they suffered at first from uncomfortable lodgings, poor servants, and high expenses. But finally they found a high-spirited maid named Mary and a boarding house on Broadway, and they went out determined to find the best in everything. They walked a good deal and took excursions on steamboats and sloops, Fanny taking her chance to quiz travelers from all over the country. She noticed "the polished manners of one or two natives of Carolina" and "the independent air, softened by republican simplicity, of some of the adventurous settlers from the infant West," and she invited them to tell her about "the amazing advance of this country."[3]

Everywhere she looked, Fanny found things to praise. She admired the abundance of comfortable private homes. Every working man seemed honest and industrious, blunt perhaps in his jealously guarded republican rights, but generous to those who came to admire rather than to sneer. She pronounced New York "quite as civil as any city in England, and perhaps a little more honest."[4]

The sisters found good company and good conversation through the letters Mrs. Millar had written to introduce them into New York society. Camilla, Fanny told James Mylne, spent hours insisting that they pay their visits, and when at last she agreed and went, "Oh then I am usually very stupid, though there are some people kind enough to think me so so, and even agreeable, and even sometimes vastly agreeable."[5]

One of the people who welcomed them was the Englishman Charles Wilkes, a conservative nephew of the radical John Wilkes and within a few years president of the Bank of New York. An unofficial host to the city, Wilkes was so taken with the sisters that he offered his services as banker and financial adviser. David Colden, the son of New York's mayor, Cadwallader Colden, was courting Wilkes's daughter Fanny, and the two families were often together. In their company Fanny and Camilla shared the most gracious life the city could offer.

They also sought out people who had come to America for ideological reasons, especially political exiles who had found refuge in America. Martha Wilson, widow of the Irish revolutionist Wolfe Tone, and her son, William Wolfe Tone, became their friends and advocates. Mrs. Wilson found their sisterly love very beautiful, and Camilla painted their Sundays with the Wilsons in tones so engaging that Mrs. Millar replied, "To meet such anywhere is miraculous . . . but in your situation it seems to mark you as favorites of heaven."[6]

Tone was an attractive young man whose impulsiveness would have appealed to Fanny. When he met the British poet George Crabbe, for instance, he rushed toward him, fell down on one knee, took his hand, kissed it, and without saying a word, went back to his chair. The fact that Tone was Irish and therefore a victim of long-standing British imperialism compelled Fanny's sympathy. The fact that his father was a famous rebel against England commanded her attention. There seems to have been something of a romance between them, for Tone later spoke of Fanny ungenerously, in the manner of a rejected suitor, and harshly criticized her book on America. For the moment, however, he did what he could to help her persuade the Park Theatre to produce one of her plays.[7]

Within five months of the sisters' arrival, Fanny realized a dream she must have had since Glasgow: her blank verse tragedy *Altorf* was to be staged in New York. Though she agreed to keep her identity a secret—propriety, it seems, and therefore strategy, required it—she otherwise refused to defer to Charles Wilkes's judgment or follow his advice. He wrote Mrs. Millar that nothing was more degraded than the New York stage, and thus whatever Fanny had to do to convince the theater manager that *Altorf* would fill the house, she did despite Wilkes. But Wolfe Tone was neither disdainful nor indifferent, and he wrote a prologue to the play.[8]

Opening night was February 19, 1819. The Park Theatre seated just under twenty-four hundred people, the privileged in three tiers of box seats that cost one dollar apiece, the average citizen paying seventy-five cents to sit on backless benches in the orchestra pit. Although this was the best theater in New York, the floor of the pit was dirty; its planks were broken; and rats occasionally ran across from under the stage. The cheapest seats were in the top tier, where no self-respecting gentlefolk would sit. The performances began each evening at half past six.[9]

The Wilsons and Tone accompanied the Wright sisters to the theater and watched Fanny's triumph. The next day the *New York Evening Post* described the spectacle: "That the expectations of the audience were highly gratified, was manifested by a greater share of applause than we recollect to have ever witnessed. At every fall of the curtain between the acts, peals of approbation resounded through the house, and at the end of the play loud cries of bravo! author! Altorf! were heard from box, pit, and gallery." The papers were extravagant in their praise, ranking *Altorf* with the best British drama. One critic insisted that the author had "trusted his work . . . to the unprejudiced liberality of an American audience. He trusted a tale of freedom to the feelings of the only nation where the cause of freedom dare be asserted."[10]

It was a heady yet frustrating experience for Fanny. While she listened to the audience call loudly for the author, she had to force herself to keep her seat. She read reviews that flattered her as baldly as she could want, but which assumed that a man had written the play. Her obscurity no doubt galled her as much as the fact that *Altorf* ran only two more nights, and she wanted people to know the play was hers. Although Mrs. Wilson thought Fanny tried harder to preserve her anonymity than most people tried to display their talents, self-effacement went against Fanny's grain. She was no doubt less than peremptory when she said that those who knew should keep her secret. Charles Wilkes apparently told Cadwallader Colden that Fanny had written the play, and the truth was out.[11]

Mrs. Millar took this revelation as a shocking breach of propriety on Fanny's part. The mails took about two months each way, and she knew her letters were likely to come too late to affect what Fanny did. Nevertheless, Fanny's ultimate success, she wrote her urgently, depended on the anonymity of her first works: "Unknown you can take a thousand positions for your advantage and are invulnerable to the shafts of folly or malignity. If not too late I wish you would impress it more strongly on [Wilkes] and your other friends and on *yourself* my dear dear Fanny." Distraught as well that Fanny allowed a female character to say "the burning kisses we have mix'd together," she wrote anxiously several times more, but to no avail.[12]

Altorf provides an introduction to the themes that obsessed the young Fanny Wright, to the lofty tone she took so readily, and to the emotional evasion her culture encouraged in women her age. She had read Schiller and shared his belief in drama as a forum for truth. Like him, she saw the stage as a pulpit, and the poet as one who speaks noble thoughts and shapes high fancies. *Altorf,* like *Wilhelm Tell,* is based on the struggle of the Swiss against Austrian tyranny. Two place names in *Wilhelm Tell,* Rossberg and Altdorf, are used in Fanny's play to name the villain and the hero, respectively. And her play, like Schiller's, gives no hint that truth can ever be hard to know.[13]

The plot turns on a love triangle. Young Altorf, one of the free Swiss leaders, is caught between loyalty to country and wife, on the one hand, and love for Rosina, his first fiancée, on the other. Because Rosina's father, the Count of Rossberg, supported Austria, Altorf's father, Erlach, insisted that he break his engagement to Rosina and marry Giovanna, sister to another leader of the Swiss Republicans. Altorf obeyed his father but remained in love with Rosina. His marriage becomes a mockery—his coldness of course wounding his wife and also offending her brother, who suspects him of disloyalty.

As battle with Austria looms, Rossberg sneaks into the Swiss camp and plays on the brother's suspicions. Thin and wasted by Altorf's desertion, Rosina appears, and the sight of her awakens Altorf's passion and his guilt over abandoning her. When he then escapes with her to Rossberg's castle, his flight is taken as a sign he has deserted the republican cause, and the Swiss mountaineers pursue them. Erlach follows his son, curses him, and dies. Rosina kills herself: "'tis I who broke his father's heart,/'Tis I who shall break his." Altorf then kills himself: "Say, that I have more hapless been than sinning,/More weak than wicked." Rossberg's confession redeems Altorf from the taint of disloyalty, and Giovanna remains to mourn them.

Vigorous and appealing, *Altorf* is nevertheless the work of a young woman afraid of her own emotions. Altorf, Rosina, and Giovanna—all victimized by passion—are called to sacrifice their most powerful feelings on the altar of lofty purpose. Their dilemma is more contrived than convincing, and suppression of self becomes the clarion call of the play. When Altorf seems to choose love over country, his dying father blasts him with a curse.

The flaw in the play lies in its conception. When Fanny made Erlach its moral touchstone, she tried to pass off a patriarchal abuse of power as an instance of self-sacrifice: the moral imperative comes from the father, while the sacrifice is wholly Altorf's. (Shakespeare, dealing with the same theme in *Romeo and Juliet,* saw nothing to admire when Capulet demanded that his daughter marry one of her own kind.) But Fanny was only eighteen or nineteen when she wrote *Altorf,* and her

innocence was more natural than that of older people who also failed
to discover the flaw. Charles Wilkes did report that *Altorf*'s politics and
morals had offended many people, but Thomas Jefferson, complacent
in his rights as a father, wrote Fanny that Erlach was "a model of
patriotism and virtue." *Altorf*'s reception hardly suggested to Fanny
that freedom and self-sacrifice might be more complicated than she
had yet imagined.[14]

Altorf's success on Broadway led Fanny to hope she might see it in
print, and shortly after its New York opening, she asked Martha Wilson
to write her friend the Philadelphia publisher Matthew Carey about it.
A man who shared Fanny's anger at England, he had just completed
his *Vindiciae Hibernicae*, which detailed the barbarous way England
had treated Ireland in 1641, and Fanny counted on him to be a soul-
mate. Mrs. Wilson told him that the London firm of Longworth and
Wiley had sent proposals for publishing *Altorf*, but Fanny, "determined to devote her time and her talents to the cause of Liberty and
truth," believed Carey the more appropriate publisher. The dramatist
herself wrote Carey that she preferred him because of "the sympathy
that it pleases me to think there exists between us in opinion."
Because she expected *Altorf* to be staged again soon in New York, it
was important that the published version appear immediately. If
Carey wanted to take *Altorf* on, she asked him to print from the copy of
the play she had already given to William Burke Wood, actor-manager
of Philadelphia's Chestnut Street Theater. She got the response she
wanted.[15]

Hoping that Fanny did not expect a large profit, Carey agreed to
publish between five and seven hundred copies of *Altorf* and "give it
whatever advertisement an extensive correspondence affords . . . If
they sell, as they probably will, you shall have a fair share of the profits,
which will give you pin money for awhile." His own scribblings, he
added, had not paid him for the time employed at the rate of a good
book clerk: "Were it not for the hope of doing good which has been the
chief object in all my literary efforts and (to an authoress who will
probably sympathize with me I may make the avowal) a little of the
lurking spirit of the ambitious and vanity of authorship, I certainly
never would publish another page." Fanny assured Carey by return
mail that she did not expect ever to be able to turn her writing to
financial advantage. Her life's purpose, she said, was to war against
mankind's prejudices, "a hard and often a thankless task."[16]

When Carey began sending her page proofs, Fanny's enthusiasm reached floodtide. Once she returned a corrected proof sheet to the post office within twenty minutes of its receipt. But late in April her spirits were checked when Carey decided to delay publication until the play was staged in Philadelphia. Fanny responded that *Altorf* would by that time be published in Edinburgh, and as she had come to America in disgust with the London theaters and the Lord Chamberlain's censorship, it would be incongruous for *Altorf* to appear in Great Britain before it did in America. Furthermore, she thought the play would sell well in New York, if not immediately in Philadelphia. Carey, it seems, was unmoved.[17]

Martha Wilson wrote Carey a few days later that the manuscript copy sent to Scotland had been held up in Liverpool, and as the Scotch printing had been delayed, Fanny might acquiesce in Carey's proposal to put off publication. Since Fanny and Camilla were about to leave New York and would arrive any day in Philadelphia, the matter could be decided in person between them. "To grammatical corrections she is docile," Mrs. Wilson added, but "on her verses she is very tenacious; [it] is her principle and her pride to take no poetical help."[18]

The balance in Fanny that Martha Wilson saw—the balance between receptiveness and intransigence, between modesty and aggression—was both necessary psychologically and hard to sustain. In a culture that not only sanctioned but celebrated passivity in women, Fanny had to be defiant to speak out at all. She was daring to become a public person, and a woman who made herself conspicuous not only invited the charge of immodesty but also rejected within herself a set of prohibitions that had been in the air she breathed.

Fanny Wright, after all, was on the edge of cultural blasphemy. She knew that the Bible put women firmly in their place: in Genesis the Lord God tells Eve in the Garden, "in sorrow thou shalt bring forth children; and thy desire *shall be* to thy husband, and he shall rule over thee." Aristotle believed that women were defective men—semen, he thought, contained the essence of human life, while the womb merely provided the nutrients—and Paul, Augustine, Aquinas, and all the Fathers of the Church, followed Aristotle's lead. The tradition that derived from them taught that clearly a woman's place was in the home: she neither talked out of turn nor raised her voice, and most of all, she understood that public matters were properly left to men.[19]

Fanny was leaving sanctioned paths for the hazardous road of the pioneer. The hazards were real. Clearing away the obstacles her culture had erected to bar a woman from becoming a free and public person, Fanny had to use so much psychic energy that she was in danger of having too little left for the intellectual discriminations on which the value of her work depended. She had to steel herself so rigorously to withstand the disapproval she invited that she risked becoming hard. Indeed she risked psychic exhaustion, and she battled obscure depressions that she could not understand. More than a year later, when she thanked Thomas Jefferson for his generous remarks about *Altorf,* she referred to "the chilling disappointments which fall on the ardent spirit in its first intercourse with the world, and . . . those rubs and discouragements which sometimes go nigh, not merely to dispel all its hopes and dreams, but to destroy its energy, and make it forego its efforts after usefulness, and its desire of honor."[20]

Nor did Robina Millar help her assert herself. To insist that attention be paid, Fanny had to defy the woman she had come to call mother. She trusted Mrs. Millar enough to describe her emotional pain, which the older woman assured her was "a morbid state" rather than a permanent condition: "I will hope and trust time, new events, and a thousand circumstances unforeseen may change that deep tone of misery that afflicts my heart. Do not, do not my loved Fanny cease to speak to me for though I feel wretched for your unhappiness your silence would only terrify me . . . How much you are the work of your own mind." Nevertheless, Mrs. Millar continued to tell Fanny to hold herself back: "do not by appearing to demand and court it subject your fair fame to the dirty bespatterings of a world you despise."[21]

But Fanny had now become the woman she remained: a woman who took at least one step more than those who loved her thought wise. As for those who wished her ill, they saw her miles beyond the place where any woman could properly go. And not only was she stubborn: on occasion she was short-sighted. In the middle of March 1819, she wrote a preface for Carey in which she grandly attacked the British stage and looked to America to revive "the sinking honour of the drama . . . England pretends to an unshackled press: but there is not a stage in England from which the dramatist might breathe the sentiments of enlightened patriotism and republican liberty." When she sent a copy to Mrs. Millar, her friend was appalled. People in Edinburgh, she replied, were even more convinced than she of the impropriety of affixing Fanny's name to *Altorf:* "Conceal your name and preface. It would be a small expense and might save you much future uneasiness." The preface could injure Fanny's success because it was written "in a tone of confidence that would excite a feeling of opposition to a young Shakespeare . . . The world will consider your age, your sex, and they will rebel against being taken by storm."[22]

Mrs. Millar's anxious counsels went unheeded. When Carey released *Altorf* sometime that year, it included Fanny's name, the offending preface, Erlach's curse—to which Margaret Cullen had objected—and the line about burning kisses. The preface was indeed tinged with arrogance, and Fanny had rejected advice that was wise along with what was merely timid.

Once she got herself to a place where women of her class did not often go, Fanny pushed on. She asked Thomas Abthorpe Cooper, the actor who was to play *Altorf* in Philadelphia, to read another of her tragedies: "the part of Sforza . . . demands very strong as well as various powers [and] may not be judged by you unworthy of your talents." She hoped to submit all her works to him before offering them to a theater, "that you may have the final refusal of the chief character." None of her other plays was performed, however, and Carey's edition of *Altorf* seems to have gone virtually unnoticed. Although late in September Fanny thanked Carey "for the interest you have uniformly taken in the success of my Altorf," less than two weeks later she lamented that "the fate of my Altorf has been hitherto sufficiently unfortunate." Asking him to let her "discharge the expences and take the risk of loss on my own shoulders," she came uncharacteristically near to acknowledging defeat: "It is the last treaty I shall ever enter into with any theater. If the cult of Thespis be out of fashion, I am not strong enough to change the taste of the age." Carey finally advertised *Altorf* in the *Franklin Gazette* on January 4, 1820, an issue that also announced a performance of the play for the next night in Philadelphia. Neither the play nor the book was advertised again, and for months Fanny apparently suffered from waves of depression that belied the serene command she outwardly assumed.[23]

Despite the rebuffs she met, Fanny persisted in her quest for unlikely experiences and new friends. She left New York in May 1819 with Camilla and did not return until the end of the year. The book Fanny subsequently wrote on America does not give what she airily called "the particulars of our peregrinations," but during the seven months they were gone they went south to Philadelphia and as far north as Montreal and met some of the most influential people in America. In Philadelphia, for example, their circle of acquaintance included not only Carey and Cooper but Correa da Serra, the Portuguese ambassador, and Joseph Bonaparte, brother of Napoleon and former king of Naples and of Spain.

In New Brunswick, New Jersey, Fanny and Camilla made the most important friendships with women that they would ever have. Julia

Camilla Wright

Charles Wilkes

Cadwallader Colden

Julia Garnett

Park Theatre, November 1822

Garnett and her sister Harriet—twenty-six and twenty-five, respectively—were the youngest children of John and Mary Garnett, and like
many of the people Fanny came to know in America, they had recently
emigrated from Great Britain. Disgust with the political situation in
England had prompted John Garnett to bring his family to New Jersey,
and in 1797 they moved into the elegant federal mansion they called
White House, whose rich farmland sloped down to the meandering
Raritan River behind it. The mansion had an impressive and turbulent
history of its own, and saber cuts from the Revolutionary War scarred
its upstairs floors.[24]

The Garnetts welcomed Fanny and Camilla into the life they lived
there with all the worldly grace of the best English squires. Fanny may
have been reminded of her years in Devonshire, but John Garnett,
unlike the cultured men who had first drawn her to the life of the
mind, was politically liberal. She flourished under his eye, reading
history and writing the letters to Mrs. Millar that would evolve into her
book on America. She apparently wrote most of the sections on
Pennsylvania at White House, which means that her conversation
often turned to the beginnings of American independence and to the
Quakers. William Penn, for example, she argued, must have been
"tolerant among bigots, inflexible before tyrants, patient with the
factious, humane towards the criminal, fair and just with the savage as
with the civilized man."[25]

It was at White House that Fanny began intellectually to confront
slavery, "the most atrocious of all the sins that deface the annals of
modern history," and an evil with immense consequence for her own
life. Though she did not absolve America, she argued that colonial
Virginia had fought Britain against its imposition, appealing to the
throne "to release her from the inundation of domestic slavery, which
was forced upon her . . . The history of African slavery is at once the
disgrace and honor of America; the disgrace she shares in common
with the whole civilized world—the honor is all her own."[26]

The fact that John Garnett was not a native may in part explain
Fanny's habit of reading the nation's apologetics so uncritically, for the
realities of American politics could well have escaped a British
gentleman-scholar who lived on the banks of the Raritan. At the same
time, yea-saying was the current fashion, and the Garnetts' circle may
have bemused themselves as well as Fanny with the notion that "the
people" were indivisible and no serious conflict of interest could exist
among them. The representative system, Fanny decided, "has been
carried to perfection in America: by it the body of the people rule in
everything . . . Thus, though the form of government should in some

cases be found deficient, yet as the door is ever left open to improvement, in system it may always be pronounced to be perfect." Those who gathered at the Garnetts most likely hoped to protect at once an English lady's sensibilities and the underside of the national history. Americans were notoriously eager for praise, and anyone who expressed a faith like hers in America's future must have been met with enthusiasm. "There is no calculating the progress of a people in virtue as well as power," she wrote, "whose successive generations shall be bred up under benign laws and liberal institutions."[27]

As the New Jersey spring ripened into summer, the friendship grew between these four women. They would spend the next decade moving in and out of each other's lives, and Fanny was the focus of their attention. She became "the sole object" of Julia Garnett's thoughts—"almost the sole object of my love." And Harriet's devotion was so intense that in 1827 she wanted to follow Fanny and take part in an experiment whose principles she deplored, even at the sure cost of her own reputation. Their love took on sustaining power for Fanny Wright: "The truth of your affection is dearer to me than ought this world cd yield—the beauty of your characters reconciles me with human nature, and sometimes with myself—for it is but too frequently that I am dissatisfied with my own nature and am driven to fear that all the evil I have seen in my short but varied life has done evil unto me, by chilling my affections and rendering me indifferent to the world's good or ill report beyond what is modest or wise. At such times of self accusation your sweet and devoted affection comes like balm upon my heart . . . And I go to sleep at night blessing your names and at peace with myself."[28]

In midsummer, Fanny and Camilla left the Garnetts and set off alone to see America in its wilder forms. They sketched an itinerary that would take them up the Hudson River, north to Niagara Falls, and into Canada. As they got past Albany, they traveled over roads so pitted that the lurching coaches threatened to pitch their passengers onto the road. Among the first to make this journey for what was called pleasure, they arrived at Utica, Fanny wrote, "very tolerably fagged, and bruised as I could not wish an enemy." Nevertheless, it was a great adventure, and the mix of people they found along the way—farmers, mechanics, lawyers, congressmen, country gentlemen—was endlessly interesting to Fanny. All of them, to hear her tell it, were intelligent and good-humored, and they were no doubt drawn by her eager belief in America and happy for the chance to fire her enthusiasm.[29]

In Genesee, for example, the sisters were entertained by James

Wadsworth, a land agent and prominent landholder who had established district school libraries throughout New York State. Wadsworth and his brother had come from New England nineteen years before, purchased land from the Indians, endured years of hardship, and had finally been repaid by success. "Like one of the patriarchs of old," Fanny wrote, "he looks round upon his flocks and herds, luxurious pastures, and rich fields of grain, bounteous heaven ever adding to his store, and feels that, under its blessing, all is the reward of his own industry, the work, as it were, of his creation." His was yet another story to shore up Fanny's romantic conviction that all was possible to anyone determined and hard-working enough to struggle for it. The sight of the wilderness so pleasantly transformed to farmland prompted her to contrast the conditions of the English farmer with those of the American, who had "no tithes, no grinding taxes, no bribes received or offered by the electioneering candidates or their agents, no anxious fears as to the destiny of his children and their future establishment in life. Plenty at the board, good horses in the stable, an open door, a friendly welcome, light spirits, and easy toil—such is what you find with the American farmer."[30]

Niagara Falls engaged Fanny's sense of the New World's grandeur, and the trip across lakes Erie and Ontario to Montreal gave her a chance to compare the English and French invidiously with their republican neighbor. Intermittently ill, however, and uninspired by Canada, Fanny soon turned back to the country that had captured her imagination. As they sailed down Lake Champlain, she thought of the battle of Plattsburgh in the Revolutionary War, where bands of mountaineers and a small, raw American force had joined to defeat an invading army of the best-trained soldiers in the world. She credited their triumph to the simple morals, industry, and, especially, the patriotism of Vermont. American history had become for her a series of lessons in virtue, and America the country where the virtuous life could find its just reward.

Fanny came to so cheerful a conclusion in defiance of the gloom and uncertainty that infected her private life. She got word in Albany that John Garnett was fatally ill, and she and Camilla hurried to New Brunswick to be with him. By the time they arrived in October he had rallied, and they spent a dismal fall with him and his family. Torn as well by the decision about where to live, they filed for United States citizenship; but Mrs. Millar begged them to come home. England, she argued, still had "a vitality of both freedom and virtue . . . because knowledge and education are more widespread." America's maturity was too far distant for them to await it, and the country's fevers too dangerous: "the Old World, Fanny, is still the scene for you. I think if I could have you here, I would never let you go again. Come to England my Fanny, my Camilla and to your mother who loves you." Her wistful hope put the matter plainly to Fanny, and in late December, she and Camilla went back to New York to plan their return to England.[31]

On January 5, 1820, when *Altorf* had its Philadelphia debut, the weather was so bad and Fanny's health so uncertain that she missed the opening. She asked Carey to send copies of whatever the press said about it and hoped he understood "that I shd wish Altorf published immediately upon its representation." The Philadelphia cast was even more dazzling than in New York, and opening night at least as triumphant. In his *Aurora General Advertiser*, William Duane described the applause as thunderous, and both Duane and Carey publicly defended the play against subsequent criticisms that Giovanna was too selfless and Erlach too severe.[32]

But neither good casts, exuberant opening nights, nor able defenders could prevail: *Altorf* did not play again. By late January, Carey's sales had been so slow that Fanny grieved at America's indifference to authors and offered to take fifty copies from his stock. Judged by the frequency with which it was advertised and performed, the play of the season was a little piece called *Where Shall I Dine?*[33]

When the cold weather finally lifted, Fanny and Camilla left Manhattan to see a last bit of America before braving the Atlantic a second time. With Fanny's interest in politics, it was unthinkable to miss Washington. Though no more than the beginnings of a town in 1820—a place of strangers, hotels, boarding houses, foul smells, and muddy streets—Washington pleased Fanny. She liked it for being a mere cluster of villages and dreaded the prospect that it might someday "assume the form and magnificence of an imperial city." The Capitol had been gutted in 1814 by the British army in the second war for American independence, and as she and Camilla explored its two newly restored wings, Fanny worried that the grandeur she saw there would in time produce "a sumptuous metropolis, rich in arts and bankrupt in virtue." In the grandiose master plan for a federal city, she saw reasons for concern about the fate of the republic.[34]

The visit to the capital heightened Fanny's fascination with powerful men, and she began to think that if she could not exercise power directly, she could at least do so vicariously. At the home of Guillaume Hyde de Neuville, the French minister and a friend of the Garnetts, she met Henry Clay, the Speaker of the House of Representatives, who later referred to her from the floor as a "distinguished foreign lady who had honored them by attending their discussions." In the visitors' gallery at the Capitol, a senator introduced her to President James Monroe, whose attention flattered her and who made the possession of great power seem benign.[35]

It was in Washington that she also saw power in its most terrible form, when she encountered slavery at first hand. "The sight of slavery is revolting everywhere," she wrote, "but to inhale the impure breath of its pestilence in the free winds of America is odious beyond all that the imagination can conceive." Her hosts tried to woo her to sympathy. By showing her the squalor in which free blacks lived in Virginia and Maryland, southerners tried to convince her that to free the slaves would be to do the slaves themselves an injustice. She acknowledged the squalor but rejected the argument. The fact that free blacks in the North lived much better gave her evidence enough that the problem was inherent not in black people but in the confusion that freedom brought and in the absence of education and genuine economic opportunity.[36]

She began to look for solutions. "Were the whole race emancipated," she later wrote, "their education would necessarily become a national object," for the whites would have to hire blacks, and the law, rather than a particular man, would be their protector. She sympathized with the slaveholders' dilemma but felt that her hosts had the responsibility of acting to save the republic: "A servile war is the least of the evils which could befall [America]; the ruin of her moral character, the decay of her strength, the loss of her political importance, vice, indolence, degradation—these are the evils that will overtake her."[37]

On their way back to New York, Fanny and Camilla stopped at White House for a painful parting, for they knew they were saying goodbye to John Garnett for the last time; he died, in fact, the day after they left the country. They said calmer goodbyes to the Wilkeses and the Coldens, and on May 10, 1820, sailed from New York on the packet *James Monroe* under Captain Rogers. Fanny suffered on board from a congestion of the lungs that had bothered her since childhood. She was ill enough by the end of the voyage that Rogers ran to a Liverpool chemist's shop to buy her a package of gum arabic, which he had found good for treating the effects of British fogs.[38]

The sisters joined Robina Millar and Margaret Cullen at Allonby, a coastal village in the north of England, where they stayed in an inn that provided "four meals a day and everything but wine and malt and light for one pound four shillings per week, sitting room included."

Mrs. Millar wrote Julia and Harriet Garnett from there that Fanny and Camilla had come back "wholly American in all their sentiments & feelings!" Fanny, who quickly recovered, had "returned in better looks, better health, & better spirits," having found in America a way to focus her powers: "In the natural, moral & political features of your great & growing country, she has found objects to fill & gratify her capacious—her magnificent mind!" And in the Garnetts, she had met "objects of esteem & affection she hardly believed to exist." Fanny at last had work to do and friends to love.[39]

That fall she caught the American public's attention once more when Washington's *National Intelligencer* published on its front page a poem called "The Stranger's Farewell to America," by the "author of Altorf." Willfully ignoring slavery, Fanny exalted America as the home of freedom:

> Shame on the heartless, on the selfish wight,
> Can tread thy shore, and cast abroad his eye
> On thy vast regions, bless'd in freedom's light,
> In active, peaceful, happy industry:
>
> Can walk amid thy race of free-born men,
> Whose fathers broke the stubborn tyrant's rod,
> And taught the truth none will unlearn again,
> That man hath no superior but his God . . .

The poem's tone of eulogy was the tone she strained to keep toward America for at least five years to come.[40]

England, for Fanny, was quite another matter, and her return apparently awakened the sense of oppression she had felt in childhood. Sometime that year her bitterness prompted her to relieve that oppression temporarily by lashing out against Frances Campbell. Responding harshly to an unexpected letter from her aunt, Fanny wondered that Miss Campbell felt no gratitude for the forbearance she herself had shown in the face of "all the crying wrongs that from my first infancy I had received at your hands." She claimed that she had been "very slow to assume the tone of the injured or the accuser and very willing to forget as well as to forgive." But her aunt revealed "as much the absence of feeling as of delicacy." By forgetting "the crying injuries you heaped upon me when my youth, my friendless and orphaned youth, and my feeble health pleaded such unspeakable claims to your tenderness and compassion, by your forgetting these you have forced me (however unwillingly) to remember them. By assuming the tone of the injured, you, Madame, whose cruelties I bore with suffering patience, whose wronging slanders I bore with generous forbearance, or with contempt, with unrecriminating unexpostulating contempt, by your assuming a tone, Madame, which it was mine to assume to you, had not pity as well as pride withheld me, you force me to remind you of all that you have done and all that I have suffered."[41]

Fanny recalled that she was eighteen and Camilla seventeen when her aunt "consented to release us from violence and insult by a removal from your roof." She claimed, however, that Miss Campbell had tried to poison the minds of those who might take them in: "By hints conveyed in words and letters . . . by misrepresentations or absolute falsehoods you accounted for the circumstance of our separation from you . . . and thus shielded your own character by endeavors to blast ours." Fanny closed: "It is beyond your power to irritate me. I had thought it also, until the receipt of your last letter, beyond your power to astonish me." She had no intention, she said, of writing again.

No one knows whether Frances Campbell was one of those women whose respectable façade hides a cruel heart. Child abuse is fairly common, and it is by no means unthinkable that a proper Tory lady would indulge in it. Fanny clearly believed herself its victim, and she built defenses against the chance of being victimized again. Those defenses in turn would cripple her. In 1820 she refused to see that her aunt might not consider herself a villain; in later years she would characteristically fail to understand that decent, well-informed people could legitimately take a position different from her own. Moreover, the haughty rage Fanny unleashed against Frances Campbell she would intermittently direct at others all her life.

She kept her ties with the rest of her family, and early in the fall she and Camilla went to Glasgow to stay with the Mylnes. They spent three weeks in Edinburgh as well; but by late November they were with Mrs. Millar and Margaret Cullen at Whitburn in the north of England, and Fanny settled down to complete her book. Her spirits were high and her company encouraging. She wrote Harriet Garnett: "I wish, my dear Harry this last sentence may not read nonsense, for my good friends have made me talk all the time I was writing it. Positively you must not expect much from my book . . . I grow more doubtful of my fitness for the task every day. 'I must screw my courage to the sticking post,' however, for our dear friends will not let me off."[42]

The book was to be in part Fanny's enduring protest against

*"A Voluptuary under the
horrors of Digestion"* (George IV)

"Manchester Heroes," commemorating the Peterloo Massacre

England, where political oppression, as Mrs. Millar and Miss Cullen described it, had grown more severe. While the Wright sisters were in America, the Tories had moved England even further away from constitutional government. In August 1819, between 60,000 and 100,000 working people had gathered at St. Peter's Field outside Manchester to demonstrate the solidarity of their class, to demand political reform, and to petition for repeal of the Corn Laws that protected British wheat and thereby raised the price of bread. The crowd kept order until mounted horsemen attacked them with sabers, killing many people, and injuring more than a hundred women and girls. Though the Peterloo Massacre provoked immense public anger, the opposition to the prime minister's power was divided, and in December, Parliament pushed through legislation which gave the government authority to undermine any attempts at reform, much less revolution. The police could search houses without warrants. No more than fifty people could gather politically. The stamp duty on periodicals was raised, and it became easier to prosecute for what was called libel or sedition. The government then launched "the most sustained campaign of prosecutions in the courts in British history," and by midsummer 1820, when Fanny and Camilla returned, many prominent reformers were either in prison or dead.[43]

That fall England was in a state of sullen bitterness, and the disaffected were using the unfortunate Queen Caroline as a focal point for opposition to their new king. Fanny followed the profligate George IV's attempts to convict his wife of an "adulterous connection with a foreigner originally in her service in a menial capacity," to strip her of her royal title, and to dissolve their marriage. The sordid business exacerbated Fanny's bias against England, where she found "vice and misery . . . heavier in the scale . . . I cannot see beggary in our towns and villages, and read of injustice in every paper . . . and meet political and religious hypocrisy wherever I turn without feeling pain, indignation or disgust." It was in this context of relentless British political repression and the embarrassment of Queen Caroline's trial that Fanny began to write her paean to the American republic.[44]

Views of Society and Manners in America was the first serious book about the United States written by an Englishwoman. In it Fanny talked about Congress, Indians, southern oratory, mail delivery, women's fashions, the Philadelphia harbor, the Revolutionary War, the pirate Jean Lafitte—matters large and small in a medley that eludes focus and defies summary. Structured as a series of letters to an

English friend, the book's rambling form lent itself to Fanny's concern for the larger meaning behind the daily event. It is an earnest book which here and there erupts in stunning revelation of the command Fanny acquired so young.

It is also a rebellion against her own past, and a partisan statement in the battle for esteem between the Old World and the New. "What country before," she asked, "was ever rid of so many evils?" The book embodies Fanny's need to fancy every American farmer a Cincinnatus, ready for the defense of his country and indifferent to both the lure of rank and the power of office: "Turn where you will, successful industry seems to have fixed her abode. No dark alleys, whose confined and noisome atmosphere marks the presence of a dense and suffering population; no hovels, in whose ruined garrets or dank and gloomy cellars crowd the wretched victims of vice and disease, whom penury drives to despair ere she opens to them the grave." She believed that Americans had been spared the corruptions of soul intrinsic to a society riven with class distinctions and extremes of wealth and poverty. She believed American democracy secure, since people had control over their own public destiny: "the wheel of government, moved by the united impetus of the whole people, turns noiseless and unimpeded, watched by all and suspected by none." Moreover, she confessed what the republic meant to her: "Truly I am grateful to this nation; the study of their history and institutions, and the consideration of the peace and happiness which they enjoy, has thawed my heart and filled it with hopes which I had not thought it could know again."[45]

Nevertheless, she recognized some of its faults. She thought the press abused its freedom. She saw that farmers had to work constantly for mere subsistence. She pointed out the evils of slavery, as well as the problems inherent in the condition of women in America. Along with later travelers, notably Alexis de Tocqueville, she saw a marked discrepancy between the vitality of young women and their withdrawn behavior after they married, for which she blamed their exclusion from education and the duties of citizenship: "Married without knowing anything of life but its amusements, and then quickly immersed in household affairs and the rearing of children, they command but few of those opportunities by which their husbands are daily improving in sound sense and varied information." Good faith and education, however, could solve those problems, she thought, and she wrote with an enthusiast's passion.[46]

She was still too young, however, and her experience as a British lady was too confined, for her to understand two ominous things that happened while she and Camilla were in the United States. During the major part of their visit, the country was suffering from a panic. Cotton prices had dropped in 1818; land values plummeted as much as 75 percent, trade and manufacturing slowed, and unemployment terrorized the poor. Fanny understood the underlying economic causes of the depression no better than most people did, and in her only reference to this prolonged and complex crisis, so apparent wherever she went, she blamed "the imprudent trade which has glutted the market with foreign goods and ended by ruining half the fortunes of the great commercial cities." Plain republicans had been seduced by the luxuries of Europe, she thought, and their home industries suffered accordingly. If only they would be content to dress in their own muslin and stop their ears to the siren call of European decadence, they could solve their problems.[47]

She was also unwilling to believe that many Americans wanted slavery, and she was therefore inclined to dismiss the issues raised by the Missouri Compromise of 1819, which prohibited slavery north of the thirty-sixth parallel while admitting Missouri to the Union as a slave state. She claimed that Congress did not have the power to prohibit slavery in Missouri, but because it could determine the grounds for admission of a new state, she was mistaken. Like the later Compromise of 1850, the Missouri Compromise only postponed the nation's confrontation with slavery, but Fanny chose to see in such political trade-offs the beneficent workings of democracy.[48]

Fanny thus recognized every problem she would later confront directly, but she systematically underestimated how hard each would prove to solve. Because America had no established church, she did not realize the power of official Christianity. She saw how thoroughly women were excluded from public life, but failed to see how profoundly that exclusion crippled them and affected her. A twenty-six-year-old Scotswoman who wondered on paper how Massachusetts could so forget itself as to be reluctant to fight in the War of 1812 was vulnerable to the charge of arrogance. She was also guilty of bookishness, as her discussions lacked the full sense of human experience which her age and sex denied her. Finally, her need to admire America was so intense that James Fenimore Cooper described her book as nauseous flattery.[49]

But the virtues of mind and character behind *Views* were considerable. Fanny showed that human qualities could weigh more heavily in the scale than political bias by dedicating the book to her sometime host, the conservative Charles Wilkes. Though not immune to the lure of stereotypes, she described people's weaknesses, such as those of the slave, as predictable results of the treatment given them. Like John Millar, she looked for the social causes of human failure and the ways they might be corrected. She was deeply ethical and deeply political. She had begun a lifelong quest for justice and for the liberal institutions that would promote it: "The advocates of arbitrary power tell us that men are bad and therefore unfit to govern themselves, but if they are bad, it is clear that they are still more unfit to govern each other." Her book deserved the attention it soon received.[50]

When Fanny finished *Views*, Camilla wrote to their cousin James Mylne at Oxford that they would leave the north of England at "the approach of summer when we shall again be afloat on the wide world." The Garnetts were sailing for France, and Fanny and Camilla resolved to join them there. By April 1821 they were in London, where Fanny corrected page proofs for her publisher, Longman and Rees, and the book was in her hands by the middle of May. Once again she had to remain anonymous: the legend on the title page reads, "By an Englishwoman," but Fanny countered her official anonymity by sending copies to many she thought would find it appealing.[51]

In August the British reviewers took their bludgeons to the book. If the author was political, the reviewers were more so. Although the *London Literary Gazette* gave her a front-page review, it claimed to find internal evidence that *Views* was written by a "red-hot American" and called the book an "encomiastic farrago"—"a tissue of impertinence, and injustice, and falsehood." As for the powerful Tory *Quarterly Review*, more than one person held its nasty review of Keats responsible for his death the same year, and William Hazlitt called it "a receptable for the scum and sediment . . . the prejudice, bigotry, ill-will, ignorance, and rancor afloat in the kingdom." In keeping with its traditions, its reviewer called Fanny's book an "impudent attempt . . . to foist into public notice . . . a most ridiculous and extravagant panegyric on the government and people of the United States."[52]

As a Whig publication, Francis Jeffrey's *Edinburgh Review* was the book's logical defender. Jeffrey was married to Charles Wilkes's daughter, and since *Views* was dedicated to his father-in-law, Fanny might have expected the courtesy of attention. She had met Jeffrey the summer before in Edinburgh, however, and found his manners sickening. When she saw his coterie assembled at his home, she thought them "altogether insufferable—conceit, affectation and vulgarity, all united." Though the *Review* had the power to make if not to break her book, Fanny had obviously refused to sue for Jeffrey's favor. Not only did he not review the book, he did not even list it as a new publication. Its defense was left to *The Scotsman*, published in Edinburgh, which said in a front-page review, "The moral sublime of the American democracy was never so deeply felt, and so eloquently described, as in these 'Letters of an Englishwoman.' "[53]

By the time the reviews were done, however, Fanny had found sturdier props for her self-esteem. Her book was widely read in America, and for the most part gratefully. Furthermore, she had courted the approval of two of the most fascinating and important men of their time—and she had won it.[54]

The Reckless
Disciple

3

Late in July 1821, Jeremy Bentham wrote Richard Rush, America's ambassador to the Court of Saint James: "I want to talk with you about Miss Wright. I am in love with her, and I suspect that you are." Two weeks later Bentham sent her book to the radical tailor Francis Place, along with his own notes on it, and had his secretary call at Longman's to see if the author was in London. The message was returned that she was expected daily, and on August 25 the secretary recorded that Frances Wright came to dinner "sisterless." On the 26th Camilla came as well, and by the next day Bentham had made Fanny give him a written account of her history. By the time she left for Paris two days later, she was his accredited messenger to correspondents in France and Spain.[1]

Fanny had now earned the right to be taken seriously by men like Bentham—not only because she had dared to go to America and to write ambitiously about it, but also because she had been the victim of Tory attack. She had thrust herself dramatically among the dissenters of her time, and it behooved them to welcome her and to take up her defense. The fact that Fanny was a woman, however, and a proper one, presented an awkward problem, for she could neither apprentice herself to their professions nor share in the usual forms of male camaraderie. She could neither practice at their bar nor join their clubs. Men would have to face the question of what to do with a woman who was not looking for a husband and had no intention of merely pouring tea, and she would have to decide what she was to do with them.

Jeremy Bentham was old enough to brush such questions aside, and he did so deliberately. In a letter to one of his disciples, Bentham referred to his "old-established rule, never to see any person but for some specific purpose—public or private." He first took up Fanny Wright because her attitude toward America vindicated the praise with which he had held up the new republic as an alternative to archaic, corrupt European governments. A man who systematically questioned the excellence of established institutions and at the same time contrived to imagine and create institutions that would serve people better, Bentham was known as "the great subversive." John Stuart Mill could call him, along with Samuel Taylor Coleridge, one of the great seminal minds of England in his day.[2]

Bentham became a model to Fanny, as well as an inspiration. His contempt for official wisdom encouraged her own, and so did his readiness to be thought peculiar even in a nation that prided itself on eccentricity. His first meeting with Robert Owen, for example, had to be arranged at some length by mutual friends. Owen wrote that he was to come to Bentham's retreat, the Hermitage, at a particular hour: "I was, upon entering, to proceed up stairs, and we were to meet half way upon the stairs. I pursued these instructions, and he, in great trepidation, met me, and taking my hand, while his whole frame was agitated with the excitement, he hastily said—'Well! well! It is all over. We are introduced. Come into my study!'" When Bentham later met Owen's son Robert Dale Owen, he parted from him with the engaging comment, "God bless you,—if there be such a being; and at all events, my young friend, take care of yourself." He collaborated with his disciple, James Mill, in shaping Mill's eldest son, John Stuart—whose education was surely the most famous and demanding of the nineteenth century.[3]

At times petulant like a boy, and as whimsical, Bentham's sense of humor was often bizarre. He left his body to be publicly dissected because he thought that reverence for mere matter was a superstitious relic of barbarism. At the same time, he willed his skeleton to University College, with the instructions that it be topped with a wax likeness of his head, dressed in his familiar clothes, seated in a characteristic posture, and kept in a box with a glass front: "If it should so happen that my personal friends and other disciples should be disposed to meet together on some day or days of the year for the purpose of commemorating the Founder of the greatest happiness system of morals and legislation my executor will from time to time cause to be conveyed to the room in which they meet the said Box or case with the contents there to be stationed in such part of the room as to the assembled company shall seem meet."[4]

Bentham not only invited Fanny to be his guest at the Hermitage, but took her seriously enough to argue with her. When she told him Socrates was pure as an icicle, he replied that it was his misfortune to read Greek and to know better. What he had read of Socrates seemed insipid, and he saw nothing to distinguish him except his manner of putting questions. Bentham loaded her with his essays, among them ten copies of what he called "Slaps at Slop," no doubt his 1818 essay on the Church of England. His esteem was worth the contempt of half a dozen *Quarterly Reviews*. He had been ridiculed most of his life, yet his iconoclasm had already served England well. He was both an institution and an education in himself, and Fanny now went to school to Bentham.[5]

If she regretted her lack of a university education, Bentham would surely have set her straight. He had gone to Oxford at fifteen and had been required to declare his belief in the Thirty-nine Articles of the Church of England. Although he had reservations about them, he was told it was not for boys to question their elders. He signed, and believed ever after that he had done something immoral, and for the rest of his life he denounced all laws that required such falsehoods and all institutions that rewarded them. Mendacity and insincerity, he was later to say, were the only sure effects of an English university education.

In Joseph Priestley's phrase "the greatest happiness of the greatest number" Bentham had discovered his own maxim. Like John Millar, he saw the "utility" of any act in its tendency to promote the happiness that should be its goal, and the principle of utility became the keystone of his philosophy. He saw British law as a series of contrivances for lawyers' profit, and in a brilliant critique of Blackstone's *Commentaries*, he attacked all theories that exalted ancestral wisdom and authority. His irreverence toward power and the past spurred him to write a tract in defense of his plan for prison reform called the "History of the War between Jeremy Bentham and George the Third, by one of the belligerents." With the help of Francis Place, he wrote an essay "Not Paul but Jesus," arguing that the church established by Paul had distorted the primitive Christianity of Christ. He wrote against oaths. He supported annual elections, a vastly extended suffrage, and the secret ballot. From John Millar, Fanny had learned to cast a critical eye on the institutions of her culture. From

Jeremy Bentham she learned that men can try to change them. For at least three years, though at some distance from one another, they were master and disciple.

For his part, Bentham discovered that Fanny also had practical uses. In a period when no mail sent through public channels was safe from government spies, she became a means of sending letters and parcels to the continent. After she had been in Paris for some time, Bentham wrote of her as "a most trusty, intelligent, and diligent commissionaire," and a means of conveyance "more secure against inspection than the ordinary one." He added, "She is in petticoats (and you will see they are no small ones) *quite* the *man* of business."[6]

It was in Paris, in the autumn of 1821, on Bentham's business as well as on her own, that Fanny met the Marquis de Lafayette, who would more profoundly affect her and her future. She had sent the sixty-four-year-old French hero of the American Revolution a copy of *Views*. He had written her that July to praise it and had asked a compatriot on his way to England to assure her of his "sentiments of kindness and esteem." When she replied, Fanny told him eagerly that meeting him would fulfill "one of the earliest and fondest wishes of my youth." She was about to plunge not only into the vortex of French politics and European conspiracy against established governments, but also into one of the crucial relationships of her life.[7]

Fanny and Camilla had left London for Paris on August 29, 1821. On September 12, just after her twenty-sixth birthday, Fanny wrote Bentham about meeting Lafayette. After only a day in Paris, she had gone off impetuously and alone on a forty-mile trip to the chateau Lafayette called La Grange, only to discover that he had passed her on his way to business in Paris. His family, she said, "received me with every possible demonstration of respect and regard, but were in despair at the absence of the General,—as I was in the same." She returned to Paris the next day, and early the following morning she sent Lafayette a note he soon answered in person. "Our meeting was scarcely without tears, (at least on my side,) and whether it was that this venerable friend of human liberty saw in me what recalled to him some of the most pleasing recollections of his youth, (I mean those connected with America,) or whether it was only that he was touched by the sensibility which appeared at that moment in me, he evidently shared my emotion." He stayed for an hour and came again in the evening to talk earnestly until after midnight. "The main subject of our discourse," Fanny wrote Bentham, "was America."[8]

And well it might have been. In his own youth, of course, Lafayette had dramatically advanced the cause of the thirteen colonies in France, just as Fanny now undertook to defend the young republic against the contempt of European aristocrats. He had succeeded at what he set out to do and was beloved for it, and Fanny no doubt saw him as a model. His heroism during the American Revolution had so moved George Washington that he wept when he told of loving Lafayette as a son. The only child and heir of one of France's oldest families, Lafayette had won the respect of Americans because he was willing to share the ordinary soldiers' deprivations. He had spent a substantial amount of his own fortune providing clothing, shoes, and food for the division Washington gave him to lead, and even met their back pay out of his own pocket. By the time he was twenty-one, he was hailed as "the Hero of Two Worlds," and his passion for liberty was so unremitting that a friend called it his blessed lunacy. When Lafayette told Fanny of Burgoyne and Gates and Franklin, of the camaraderie of the patriot army of the American Revolution—an "army of brothers [who] had all things in common, our pleasures, our pains, our money, and our poverty"—and of "the virtues of that army . . . their fortitude, their disinterested, and sublime patriotism," his drama was no less romantic in its way than Othello's tales to Desdemona "Of moving Accidents by Flood and Field,/Of haire-breadth scapes i' th' imminent deadly breach."[9]

So began a relationship of no ordinary nature—one that would touch Fanny's name with scandal, but whose full dimensions remain obscure. A few years later Stendhal described the general as a man obsessed with young women: "He took each day as it came, a man not overburdened with intelligence . . . dealt with each heroic situation as it arose, and inbetween times was solely occupied, in spite of his age, in fumbling at pretty girls' plackets, not occasionally but constantly, and not much caring who saw." His behavior, and Fanny's, over the next few years would raise the question in the minds of many: was Fanny Lafayette's mistress, or were they devoted like father and daughter, as both of them insisted?[10]

The Garnetts had taken an apartment at 17 rue Saint Maur, a charming old building that had once been a convent, and Fanny and Camilla joined them there. It was a section of Paris where people played out their lives with an insouciance Fanny had never seen. Students from the Sorbonne and the École Polytechnique wandered about the crooked streets and along the quais. Women sold iced lemonade from carts, and masses of flowers from stalls along the boulevards. Not even the stench of a city with few drains and sewers could spoil the Paris of the famous Left Bank, or what Frances Trollope would call its "air of ceaseless jubilee."[11]

The joy of the streets, however, stood sharply in contrast to the grim history of France that they saw figured in the buildings they passed on a short walk from rue Saint Maur. The dome of the Pantheon, the tomb of the revolutionary heroes, towered above the Quarter. Toward the west and nearer the Seine, the eight-hundred-year-old St. Germain des Prés, the oldest church in Paris, stood as a reminder of the enormous power of the medieval Benedictine order, and when she strolled across the glass-roofed bridge onto the Ile de la Cité, she saw the Palais de Justice with its relics of the Terror three decades before, and Notre Dame de Paris, which had survived it all.

Had Fanny been able to learn gaiety and the light touch, she would have learned them now, but instead, she responded to the playfulness around her by working all the more persistently. She responded to the history of France entombed in her part of Paris by beginning to study it under Lafayette's tutelage. Most important, for the moment, she was an author, intent on publishing more of her writing. On September 5, Albert Gallatin, the American ambassador to Louis XVIII's court, sent her a note commending "the correctness" of her picture of America and adding that "the liberality which pervades the whole cannot be but very pleasing to the Americans whom former travellers, to say the least, had not much flattered." By the month's end, Lafayette was not only encouraging Gallatin to help Fanny correct whatever mistakes she had made in *Views*, he was taking her with him to La Grange. "My amiable Companion in the journey," Lafayette wrote Gallatin, is "publishing Her Second English edition, and translating the Book in French, which last object I encourage Heartily as I believe the publication cannot but do good for Both Countries and for the Cause." By mid-October Fanny was so confident of Lafayette's affection that Mrs. Millar was delighting in "the scheme of my sending my letters at present to your loved and venerable Father." In Mrs. Millar Fanny had fashioned herself a mother. Now she began to fashion a father in Lafayette.[12]

For the first time Fanny took it on herself to live vicariously through a man, and the man she chose had a breathtaking range of experience that derived at once from the aristocrat's unquestioned sense of his own right to the world, and the republican's conviction that all people were his fellows. Born Monseigneur Maria Joseph Paul Yves Roch

Gilbert du Motier, Marquis de Lafayette, he had become, during the French Revolution, the man most idolized by the populace. The tricolor, which became the republican symbol, was his idea. On July 11, 1789, when the national assembly was surrounded by troops, and the king was on the point of dissolving it, Lafayette had daringly presented it with the Declaration of the Rights of Man, which he had drawn up with Thomas Jefferson's approval. Four days later, a crowd at the Hôtel de Ville unanimously elected him commander-in-chief of the Paris militia, and he saved many from being literally torn to pieces at the hands of a mob.[13]

He had saved the lives of the royal family at least twice, though Queen Marie Antoinette ridiculed him as a turncoat to his class. (She said she would rather die than owe her life to Lafayette, and so she did.) When the Parisian throng broke into Versailles, killed some of the royal bodyguards, and cut the queen's bed to pieces with pikes and knives, he had led the queen to a balcony overlooking the central court and kissed her hand as a symbol of reconciliation until the crowd cried, "Vive Lafayette!" and "Vive la Reine!" His solicitude for the lives of the royal family had drawn upon him the contempt of the radicals and the threat of the guillotine.

In 1792, after the Jacobins issued a warrant for Lafayette's arrest, he and twenty-two fellow officers had tried to escape abroad but were recognized and captured on the Belgian border. Hated by both the left and the right, he had been kept for five years in Prussian and Austrian prisons. At Olmutz in Austria, he spent at least eleven months in which all communication—reading, writing, speaking—was denied him. He endured a long period when he could see only one other person for an hour each day. His wife and two daughters had joined him for the last two years, living on food so meager and in cells so filthy that the Marquise never fully recovered.[14]

Nor had Napoleon welcomed his release. Jealous of Lafayette's popularity, he reluctantly had made the peace treaty with Austria conditional on their freeing the prisoners of Olmutz, but had refused to allow Lafayette to return to France. In the confusion after Napoleon overthrew the Directory, however, Lafayette had crossed back into France with a false passport and had been allowed to stay, on the condition that he sequester himself at La Grange. He remained one of the few French leaders whom Napoleon neither conquered nor seduced, and after the Bourbon Restoration, he became a rallying point for underground conspiracies not only against the Bourbons but

also against autocratic governments throughout Europe. He became
the "patron saint of all exiles." Charles X would say that only two men
in France had remained true to their principles: Lafayette and
himself.[15]

Lafayette's principles were those Fanny had celebrated in her own
writing. She envied the drama and heroism that had marked his life
and would emulate them if she could only find a way; but as the paths
he had used were walled off to her, for the moment she chose to live
in the grand world through him.

In Glasgow Fanny had studied the theory of parliamentary politics,
and in Washington she had seen something of its practice. In Paris, as
Lafayette's guest and protégée, she immersed herself in the tumultuous life of Restoration politics as she watched from the gallery of the
Chamber of Deputies and learned the language of political dialogue
used by men contending for power. Because of newspaper censorship, the debates in the Chamber were the only forum in which
dissident voices could be raised with impunity. Day after day Fanny
listened to the most polished orators and the most accomplished
politicians in France.

Since 1818, when he was elected to the Chamber, Lafayette had been
the unofficial leader of the parliamentary left, which preached popular
sovereignty and individual liberty and fought the Catholic Church's
political power. He played a conspicuous role in criticizing a government whose task lay in reconciling the old monarchical, feudal,
theocratic institutions with the Napoleonic state—secular, national,
and administrative. This formidable task involved finding jobs and
acceptable places in the social order both for the old aristocracy and
for those who had fought their way to power under the Empire; the
government's failure so far was reflected in serious discontent.[16]

The left had just enough strength to determine the outcome of a
vote by throwing its weight either to the moderates or to the Ultra-
Royalists, who were led by the Count d'Artois, brother to the king and
heir to the throne. By the time Fanny took her privileged seat in the
gallery and in the counsels of the left, Lafayette and his colleagues had
decided to exploit the national discontent by voting with the right in
order to bring down the Duc de Richelieu's moderate coalition
ministry. Fanny described this strategy as "a most amusing union of
votes between the *extrême droite* and *extrême gauche*," and wrote
Bentham that the king, a "cunning old gentleman," had finally turned
the government over to the Count d'Artois. The right then blocked

every moderate, much less progressive, piece of legislation, and a significant part of the left went underground to plot another revolution.[17]

Through a clandestine network called the Charbonnerie, Lafayette contrived a plan to set up a provisional government in Alsace, but he bungled his part. The authorities discovered the plot, and two of his confreres were caught. At the time, Fanny was in Paris, innocently writing Lafayette that the news of the day was of an insurrection in which several military men had apparently been arrested. She ended her letter: "This is a strange world! May the efforts of the good and wise improve it." But those she then considered the "good and wise" had made a mess of things, and others would pay the price. At least six men were executed, among them one General Berton who, just before he died, sent Lafayette the star of the legion of honor that he had worn at the Battle of Waterloo. Fanny wrote a seven-stanza poem in memoriam:

> Eclipsed star! sleep, sleep upon that breast,
> Where Gallia finds her hope amid her sorrow.
> Sleep! like the sun who sinks unto his rest
> That he may rise with freshened beams tomorrow.[18]

She learned to be skeptical of "absurd drawing-room intrigues and fashionable conspirators." Of this period, she recalled that she had "seldom anticipated success to efforts of which the object appeared to her ill-defined, and those who pursued it far from agreed among themselves." The conduct of the conspirators, who were often inexperienced and frivolous, "contrasted strangely and painfully . . . with the serious character of a struggle in which human lives, and those often of the young and the chivalrous, were the stakes of the game." Early in 1822, however, Lafayette had just established his command over Fanny's young imagination, and the wisdom she later claimed required far more emotional distance than she then wanted to put between them. Within the next year she would engage in a minor act of conspiracy herself.[19]

Though Fanny had to stop restively on the fringes of Lafayette's political involvements, when he left Paris for his chateau she often rode in the carriage by his side; and Lafayette's La Grange, which appeared at the end of the drive like a fairy tale castle, captivated her with a new sense of human possibility. Three months after they met, she wrote him that it was a "consecrated dwelling. What sweet hours I

have passed in those walls! I must pass many more there my good
friend and (receive the threat for a prophetic one) *shall* pass many
more there. Hitherto my life has had so little pleasure in it, that I am
sure there must now be a great deal in store for me."[20]

The chateau and the farms together covered more than eight
hundred French acres—equivalent to about a thousand in England.
Fruit trees and chestnut groves bordered the entrance to the park, and
the road to the chateau ran by ponds that served as boating areas for
the guests. The three-sided medieval castle, covered with moss and
tufted ivy, had two main stories above the ground floor and five towers
topped with conical roofs. The moat, thirty feet wide and eight feet
deep, was well-stocked with fish. Cows and sheep kept the park trim,
and scattered benches offered guests a variety of peaceful views. They
could wander through the kitchen garden and into the ice house.
They could inspect the cider press and taste the cider that not only
made Lafayette the envy of his neighbors but brought good prices on
the market. There were even a menagerie and an aviary to amuse
them.[21]

When Lafayette brought Fanny to La Grange, he brought her into the
bosom of the family, and though Adrienne, the Marquise de Lafayette,
had died in 1807, her spirit remained intensely present there. The
chateau and its grounds had belonged to her mother, the Duchess
d'Ayen, a strong and pious woman who had been guillotined along
with her own mother and eldest daughter not long before the Terror
ended. When Adrienne returned to Paris in 1798 after the years of exile
with her husband, she took on herself the tedious and often
humiliating journeys into the world of Paris bureaucracy that were
necessary to regain expropriated land not already legally sold. From
the shambles of the family fortune, she gradually recovered a part and
divided it with her sisters, taking La Grange as her portion and
deciding to make it a fit setting for the man to whom her life was
dedicated. Her integrity, her kindness, and her devotion to her
husband had been shaped into a legend by those she left behind, and
if La Grange was a tribute to Lafayette, it was Adrienne who had
designed it, gilded it, and written the music that would play there in
celebration. Nothing in Fanny Wright's experience allowed her to
understand how powerful Adrienne remained.[22]

More than most aristocratic families, Lafayette's was peculiarly
close. Adrienne had brought up her three children to worship their
father as she did. The horrors they had suffered during the French
Revolution, especially during their years in prison, had tied the

parents and their two daughters tightly together, as did the odium heaped on them by other aristocrats who considered them traitors to their class. The eldest child, Anastasie, married Charles de La Tour-Maubourg; the son, George Washington, married Emilie de Tracy; and Virginie, the youngest, married Louis de Lasteyrie. By 1821 Lafayette had thirteen grandchildren, ranging in age from three to eighteen. Nathalie and Mathilde, George and Emilie's oldest daughters, figure particularly in Fanny's correspondence. All of them had rooms at La Grange and were often there, and they welcomed a multitude of aunts, uncles, and cousins. In a country and a class where exquisite manners were as common as table salt, the family took in Fanny and Camilla, orphans and world wanderers, with their accustomed grace.

La Grange was a world so enchanted it brought out a side of Fanny Wright of which her letters had earlier given no sign. Discarding her wonted caution and reserve, by December she was calling Lafayette her best friend and her father, and speaking of her letters as "the prattle of a child" to a wise man: "You know I am your child—the child of your affection, the child of your adoption. You have given me the title and I will never part with it. To possess this title was the highest of my wishes—to deserve it is my proudest ambition. And in truth my excellent friend I feel that I do deserve it—by the reverence that I bear to your virtues, by my sympathy in all your . . . undertakings, in all your pleasures and all your pains—by the devotedness of my affection, the fulness of my confidence;—by all this and more than this I feel that I merit the friendship and parental fondness of the best and greatest man that lives." She sang with special fervor the hymn to Lafayette that was life at La Grange; for there, he was both patriarch and hero, and his family set the tone of devotion. They decorated the reception-room walls with art that recalled the extraordinary events of his life. Statues and paintings honored the famous men, both French and American, he had known. Flags that had flown on memorable occasions were displayed along with swords and urns that celebrated Lafayette's part in each of his fights for liberty. Whatever his enemies might say, at La Grange he was a great man, and Fanny wanted his attention.[23]

Her competition for it was formidable. There were usually twenty-five to thirty guests at every meal: the ground-floor diningroom, a fine stone hall with a groined roof, seated up to fifty. Apart from his family and their various relations, he welcomed comrades from old wars, both political and military. Americans had a special call on his generosity, and often he seems to have been at home to the entire

Lafayette

La Grange

Jeremy Bentham

Landing of General Lafayette at Castle Garden, New York,
August 16, 1824

American community of Paris. He set a modest table, and he himself practiced the austerity he learned in America by eating only a chicken wing or a piece of fish and drinking only water. As his doctor put it, "his habits of temperance [forbade] him to waste his time and destroy his health in protracted and sumptuous dinners." But Lafayette's good spirits were infectious, and after dinner, in good weather, people scattered about the lawn or surrounded him to hear him talk.[24]

One way Fanny garnered some of the general's time was by proposing to write his life story. It would be the official biography: the life of Lafayette as he would have it. The idea flattered him, and it was a project that required them to spend long hours together. Fanny pleased him so deeply that soon after they met, he had her portrait painted and hung it in his study.

In late January 1822, the two-volume *Voyage aux Etats-Unis D'Amérique* "Par Miss Wright," went to press. Fanny succeeded in putting her name to the book, but otherwise she changed it very little. She had listened patiently to criticism and then for the most part ignored it. She had cut an anecdote about Jefferson to which Gallatin had objected, but replaced it with another just as admiring and had not muted her panegyric to the American Congress. As the French version went to press, Fanny went to England to supervise the further publication of her works there and to see if she could yet persuade the Covent Garden company to produce one of her plays. During the more than two months she was away, Fanny seldom let three days go by without writing Lafayette, and occasionally she wrote twice a day. The tone she took was startling in its intimacy.[25]

On February 4 she wrote from London: "How I shall I greet [your letter] when it comes, salute it with my eyes and lips. My excellent, my paternal friend think of me when you have nothing better to think of. I think of you always." About three trips she made subsequently to the war office, probably on Lafayette's business, she revealed her steadily growing sense of self: "I dare say you marvel sometimes at my independent way of walking through the world just as if nature had made me of your sex instead of poor Eve's. Trust me, my beloved friend, the mind has no sex but what habit and education give it and I who was thrown in infancy upon the world like a wreck upon the waters have learned as well to struggle with the elements as any male child of Adam."[26]

While Fanny was still in Paris, Mrs. Millar had written of the pleasure Bentham would have in seeing her again and added her customary warning about the proprieties: "The Good Spirit says that in case of any awkwardness in the eyes of others it might be as well if he did not ask you to reside with him—but if he does, nothing, if *she* were you, could induce her to refuse him the satisfaction." When Bentham asked Fanny to stay at the Hermitage as his guest, Fanny accepted.[27]

Because he was so careful with his time, she usually saw him only at dinner, but then sat with him until eleven if he had no other company. He had grown more deaf, and she had trouble raising her voice, so she found an hour's conversation with him exhausting. She apparently triumphed over the difficulties, however, because after she left, Bentham wrote his brother that "Miss Wright . . . can and will tell you more about me in one hour than I could tell you in 50, by scribbling under the reproach of conscience." She dined with his colleague James Mill and Mill's wife and talked at their home with Joseph Hume, whom she called "the most able as the most honest member in the infamous London Parliament." Concerned with the relationship between money and power, Hume argued that monopolies of food, trade, and political influence caused the public distress. All of them, Fanny wrote Lafayette, talked chiefly of politics.[28]

She had also struck up a friendship with Frances Trollope, and alternated between visiting her house in Bloomsbury and Bentham's in Westminster. Mrs. Trollope was a respectable matron who counted on sending her sons to Eton and Winchester. Her social position nevertheless allowed her room to express her eccentricity by entertaining unlikely British liberals and European political refugees. According to her youngest son Anthony, she professed "an emotional dislike to tyrants, which sprung from the wrongs of would-be regicides and the poverty of patriot exiles." She was ebullient, sharp-tongued, and garrulous, and because her instincts as a hostess surpassed her husband's modest income, she was able to introduce Fanny to a group of political exiles from the various abortive revolutions throughout Europe. In such a way, Fanny became immersed almost effortlessly in what Lafayette called "The Cause."[29]

One of the men she saw at the Trollopes' was General Guglielmo Pepe, who had helped lead the successful Carbonari uprising in Naples in 1820—only to find it overthrown the following year. Another was Joseph Rey, one of Lafayette's fellow conspirators from Grenoble. Whatever else she might be learning from Lafayette, she was not learning modesty, and about both of them she wrote somewhat condescendingly: though she introduced Pepe as a correspondent to

Lafayette, she called him "a fine warm-hearted patriot but a very crude legislator." His head was not as deep as his heart was warm, and his understanding might be improved if he read her book. Rey, who had "odd notions himself though the best creature in the world," reasoned and systematized "rather tediously."[30]

After only three weeks in London, Fanny was holding court on her own. She wrote Lafayette of having a morning levee at Bentham's "such as might be received in your apartment." Major John Cartwright, the indefatigable founder of the Hampden Clubs, and Pepe had come to call. Among the others were Lafayette's friend Sir Robert Wilson, who had been dismissed from His Majesty's service for alleged sympathy with dissidents and who would soon lead troops in defense of Spanish liberties. "It amuses me a little," Fanny wrote Lafayette, "to find myself sought out by so many grey-headed politicians and philosophers."[31]

A fevered tone marked her correspondence with Lafayette. She worried repeatedly about his well-being when she read of the latest instance of the Bourbons' contempt for popular liberties and wondered if she should be by his side. When he wrote that it pleased him to think she would cheer his declining years and close his eyes in death, she replied with a mixture of pride and sadness: "I am generous enough to feel a melancholy pleasure in the thought that by the common order of Nature the cup of bitterness will be mine, not yours to drink. Yes I will be the ministering spirit to your latter days—But I cannot write of this. My eyes tell me that I am not so generous as I boast myself." A few days later she hedged: "now that existence has many charms for me—that I love and am loved by the wise and the good I can reconcile myself neither to the loss of life nor to its terrors." The first, she said, would take her from her friends; "the latter may condemn me to see them removed from me."[32]

However lavish her language, Fanny clearly was not writing Lafayette as a lover and did not expect him to think she spoke romantically. She was taken with a much younger man, and she cast Lafayette in the role of father-confessor. She confided that she had met a man who moved her "more than is reasonable" and was somehow involved in The Cause. "He has a noble soul and a sweet nature," she wrote, "but I see in him a sanguineness of temper and a contempt of danger which make me apprehensive lest he should some day run upon the enemy's spear too hastily." At the same time she wished more were like him: "The game now cannot be won by long-headed calculators: we want hands of steel and heads of flame." She asked to be forgiven for inspiring a man to passion. She had suffered greatly, she told Lafayette, since she came to London, but her suffering was no matter: she felt more for her friends, for The Cause, and for humanity than for herself.[33]

She gave her young admirer the code name "Eugene" in her letters, and though her references to him were oblique, she saw him a good deal in London and seems to have delayed her return to Paris because of him. Six months later, he may have gone to take part in the liberal uprising in Spain, for he wrote her about "mes frères de Madrid." She drew on her account with the banker Jacques Laffitte to offer him money, which he refused on the grounds that it was not enough to help others and he could manage without it. She worried when his letters did not come and worried sometimes more when they did. A letter from Mrs. Millar suggests that Fanny's interest in him was serious: "Camilla delighted me with her account of Eugene. O may his fate be equal to his deserts—and if so what more could I ask for my Fanny!" But gradually he faded from her life, and nothing she wrote defines what either his coming or his going meant to her.[34]

All the while, Fanny praised Lafayette extravagantly: "It is not every country that is blessed with a Lafayette . . . Oh would to Heaven we could multiply you by 12 and then by the square of 12 and then by the cube of the square and spread you abroad among the nations of the world." She insisted that their relationship had become crucial to her: "I find myself so well when I am near you, so content with life, with myself, with humanity . . . You are my teacher, my conscience, the best of my friends—and life would have no charm for me without your esteem and your approbation." Oblivious to the jealousies she was liable to wake in those around him, she wrote, "I love you dearly, you never had a child that loved you more tenderly, never a friend who felt your interests to be more her own." She would return to Paris bearing gifts: *A Few Days in Athens* and *Altorf* in its London edition were to be her love offerings and her proof that she deserved his esteem.[35]

Longman and Rees undoubtedly took it on themselves to publish the two books, along with a second edition of *Views*, because the latter had sparked some interest in Fanny and perhaps because influential people had interceded on her behalf. The London version of *Altorf*, however, showed that Fanny's self-confidence could slide into an arrogant disdain for fact and for other people's feelings. In the introduction she insisted that she published the book in England because the American edition, which had been "pretty widely circulated in this country," had been "thrown off in haste for the use

of the Philadelphia green-room" and was "exceedingly incorrect." This
was misleading. The American edition was neither thrown off in haste
nor printed for the use of the Philadelphians, and she found no more
than twelve minor changes to make. Certainly Matthew Carey had
been unusually gracious and helpful to her, and now she allowed
herself to be churlish at his expense.[36]

The second edition of *Views* suggests the impatient side of Fanny's
character that would not serve her well. There is some evidence that
Longman and Rees had wanted her to modify the extravagant
admiration to which so many reviewers objected. Rees encouraged
Benjamin Flower to write her before the second edition went to press,
and Flower told Fanny that "in the opinion of many friends to the best
interests of mankind," her praises of America "are carried to an
extreme and are dwelt on with pleasure by the enemies of America as
unnatural and romantic." His brother Richard had helped found
Albion, Illinois, a settlement of English farmers in America, and
Benjamin Flower knew that life had been hard there and mere survival
uncertain. But Fanny brushed aside his suggestions and made only
minor changes. Though she deleted the anecdote about Jefferson to
which Gallatin had objected, she added another that made the same
point. She also wrote a footnote praising the army as extravagantly as
she had praised the Congress. She thereby lost the chance both to
improve her book and to show that she could learn from her mistakes
when she was shown them sympathetically. She had, however, won
the battle to put her name on the title page.[37]

A Few Days in Athens is far more satisfying. Lafayette later told
Thomas Jefferson that Fanny had published it only because he had
asked her to do so: "with her Usual Modest Simplicity the Manuscript
Had Been laid aside when I discovered its existence and insisted on
Her Giving it to the press." Jefferson paid it the compliment of using
seven pages of his commonplace book to copy passages from it, and
he wrote Lafayette that it was a work "equal to the best morsel of
antiquity . . . The matter and manner of the dialogue is strictly
ancient . . . the principles of the sects are beautifully and candidly
explained and contrasted . . . the scenery and portraiture of the
interlocutors are of higher finish than anything in that line left us by
the ancients."[38]

Fanny wrote Lafayette that she would like to dedicate *A Few Days* to
him, as it would be the first of her works to be published since they
met. However, she felt compelled to dedicate *Thoughts of a Recluse* to
him, and naming him both times might be inappropriate. Since

Bentham disliked poetry, *A Few Days* was the only one of her works she might properly dedicate to him. She told Lafayette: "I know he will be sensible to this little tribute of respect—and the more so as he will know that his name will not dispose the general public more favourably to the work."[39]

She adopted the curious fiction in *A Few Days* that she was merely translating part of the Italian version of an ancient manuscript sent her by an "erudite Professor of Greek," and said that the twelve-chapter fragment represented by the present volume gave an idea of the whole. Her readiness to leave it unfinished not only strikes her characteristic note of impatience but also shows an unresolved ambivalence toward the moral life as James Mylne embodied it. She had written the book when she shared his university life of good talk, small groups, and generous feelings. Now she wanted to live in Lafayette's world of action rather than in Mylne's world of reflection, and she begrudged the time and concentration necessary to complete the book. "Well-merited fame," she wrote, "has in itself a pleasure so much above all pleasures, that it may weigh in the balance against all the accumulated evils of mortality."[40]

Fanny's stay in London threw into relief an unsettling side of her character that became more prominent the older she grew. She had written so insultingly of the British theater that it seems odd that she could seriously imagine their giving one of her plays a chance. In her preface to the American edition of *Altorf*, she said that the management of the London theaters presented perhaps insurmountable obstacles to those who would reverse the degenerate course of the drama. Nevertheless, she spent days at Covent Garden and other theaters, offering those same managers at least six of the plays she had written in Glasgow between her eighteenth and twenty-first years. Of her rejections she wrote, "The style of the first refusal was such as to destroy all hopes of attention from the theatrical committee, and that of the second, pretty much all anxiety for their approbation." She seems to have ignored the possibility that her own behavior was in any way responsible for her failure to get her plays staged. Her dogged pursuit of Covent Garden, however, apparently antagonized the tragedian William Charles Macready, who later used every argument he could muster to persuade their mutual friend Frances Trollope that she should not trust her fate to Fanny Wright.[41]

No doubt the highest psychic price that Fanny paid for breaking through so many barriers to women was the price of self-deception. The cruelest revenge her culture took on her for dealing with its rules so cavalierly was to make her lie to herself. Perhaps because she could never fully accept her personal right to the eminence she fought so hard to attain, she told herself she did what she did for the sake of The Cause. Women were supposed to be selfless, and she convinced herself that she was. She convinced herself, further, that her self-sacrifice guaranteed the correctness of the positions she took and the battles she fought. But those she startled or affronted would find it hard to believe she had a purchase on truth and justice. They were taken aback by a woman who seldom entertained the possibility that she might be mistaken, and for her part Fanny never understood how irritating she must often have been. She demanded too much of herself. She demanded, finally, too much of other people. And she never understood that she was doing either.

With something of the same abruptness with which she ended *A Few Days in Athens*, Fanny broke off her stay in England. Before she left, she spent ten days in Whitburn with Mrs. Millar, who wrote that Fanny talked while she wrote and while she ate: "I really believe were we to remain in the same room, she would talk to us in her sleep." But Fanny had grown impatient with inaction. "Men here hug their chains," she wrote Lafayette: "Nothing is talked of . . . but the state of the Treasury." She gave up on Covent Garden. She gathered up her newly published works in copies sufficient to give out to her friends in Paris. She picked up Bentham's commissions to the continent, said her goodbyes, and on April 13 left London to rejoin Lafayette in Paris.[42]

While Fanny had been in England, Camilla had spent most of her time at La Grange, where she was ill and was kindly nursed. She remained there even after Fanny's return, and at the end of 1822 she wrote, "No words can do justice to all the kind and unremitting attentions we have received from [Lafayette] and his amiable family." Harriet Garnett was also with Camilla, leaving only Julia at Fanny's side in Paris to deflect the rumors that were bound to come.[43]

For Fanny spent most of her time among those in Lafayette's circle. She went to the opera with the "kind and dear Lasteyries," most likely M. and Mme. Charles Lasteyrie, Virginie's brother-in-law and his wife. She often saw the Count de Ségur, and her notes to Lafayette more than once proposed that they meet at the Countess de Tracy's, whose weekly gatherings were among the most select and remarkable in Paris. The names of other fashionable republicans crop up in Fanny's correspondence: Benjamin Constant, Lafayette's quarrelsome fellow-deputy, companion in exile of Schiller and Goethe, gifted novelist, and former lover of Mme. de Staël; Augustin Thierry, a promising historian just Fanny's age who was beginning to ponder the connections between British and French history; Ary Scheffer, member of the clandestine Charbonnerie and something of a court painter at La Grange; Garnier Pagès, younger even than Fanny but already a philosopher and a confidante of Lafayette. Their names suggest that she became a familiar in Parisian salons that were demanding schools in wit and elegance.[44]

Most of all, Fanny saw Lafayette. When her uncle James Mylne came to Paris, Lafayette invited the two of them to dine with him and his son George in his apartment on the rue d'Anjou. Fanny's reputation, however, was seldom so well guarded as it could be by her uncle's company, and she did little to protect it. One day, for example, she wrote Lafayette that Julia had an evening engagement she could not break without giving offense. "I shall not break, however, mine to you," Fanny added. "Why should we trouble ourselves about the *on dits?* At all events I shall not think of it today for I must see you and must drive with you." Lafayette seemed as little concerned as Fanny to protect her from scandal. His famous white horses made his carriage conspicuous, and their frequent trips to her convent in the Latin Quarter gave occasion for *on dits*—for rumors—that Fanny cavalierly ignored at her peril.[45]

If the language she used when she wrote Lafayette can be taken to indicate the way she behaved, she was provoking the jealousy not only of his friends but of his family. Her words were extravagant and her possessiveness inappropriate. When in mid-July she went for a long visit to La Grange, she wrote him in Paris that all was well, "except that I find not my paternal friend whom I love better than friend ever loved friend or daughter father . . . La Grange looks very lovely and all its inmates are kindness and goodness personified and my little Cam is sweetly affectionate as is Harriet also but still I am alone without you . . . My friend, my father, if there be a word more expressive of love and reverence and adoration I would fain use it. I am only half alive when away from you." She called him "an angel of goodness" and said he was her God and she fell down and worshiped before him. She seemed oblivious to the likely consequences of the way she acted, and so powerful was Fanny's command over her own circle that even Julia apparently saw nothing untoward in Fanny's peremptory behavior. When Julia herself wrote Lafayette, she alluded to Fanny as "always uppermost in my thoughts and in yours" and said teasingly that she had boasted of his goodness in a vain attempt to make Fanny jealous.

Whether or not Julia succeeded, Fanny left La Grange after only two weeks to return to Paris, where she stayed until the Chamber adjourned and Lafayette could go back with her.[46]

She no doubt believed that in dedicating herself to Lafayette, she was devoting herself to a great set of ideas as they were embodied in one person. She loaned him money when he needed it, and gave him advice whether he needed it or not. She lavished on him the emotional support that anyone must have who succeeds in acting aggressively, much less defiantly, in the world. For the most part through him, she tried to play her part in the fight against tyranny, as she involved herself in various liberal uprisings throughout Europe.

Fanny and her new friends focused their energies on Spain. In 1820 a military mutiny led by Rafael de Riego had forced the Bourbon king Ferdinand VII to swear loyalty to the constitution. The Spanish royalists remained strong, however, and in mid-July 1822 attempted a coup that Riego's forces put down with a great deal of bloodshed. At that point Lafayette decided to send General Pepe as his emissary to the left wing of the Spanish parliament to ask that it declare the independence of Colombia and Mexico in return for money and military support. He expected the latter to be used against the Bourbons in France as well as in Spain.

By late fall or early winter, Fanny was intimately involved in the conspiracy. She and Camilla crossed the Channel carrying seriously incriminating letters from Lafayette to General Pepe. When they met Pepe at Dover, they told him that France might be on the verge of revolution, and he rode back to London full of happy illusions.

Their journey had been daring. Pepe himself was later questioned by customs officials because authorities "had discovered my correspondence with Lafayette, and perhaps the object of my voyage," and two British citizens whom Fanny knew—Sir Robert Wilson and John Bowring, an intimate of Bentham's—were hounded in France that fall by the police. For Louis XVIII had no intention of giving over either France or Spain to middle-class revolutionaries, and in late January 1823, he opened parliament by declaring that French troops were ready to save their southern neighbor for a grandson of Henry IV.[47]

From her privileged seat in the gallery of the Chamber of Deputies, Fanny watched her friends fail once more. When the most accomplished orator on the left, Jacques Antoine Manuel, attacked the Bourbons and their designs on Spain, the Chamber voted to expel him, and the ministry called in the National Guard to take him out.

Lafayette stood and stared down the Guard, and they retreated. But the ministry resorted to the police, and the parliamentary left bolted the Chamber. Though they stayed out for the rest of the session, little came of their defiance, and Fanny learned to distrust "the present energy of the French people whatever it may have been at other times." She concluded eventually that the hereditary power of old world aristocracies made a generous, humane politics virtually impossible, and after her long attendance in the Chamber of Deputies she never again trusted to parliamentary politics to order a society in which she wanted to live.[48]

Events soon proved how fancifully Lafayette had imagined the opposition to Louis XVIII. In April the French army crossed into Spain, and by late August they had broken the back of the resistance. The brutal massacres that followed horrified even the French leader, the Duc d'Angoulême, and Riego was captured and sentenced to die. On the scaffold he took off his cravat and left it for his wife to send, along with a lock of his hair, to Lafayette. With him seemed to die the hopes Fanny and her friends had held out for Spain as well as for European liberalism, and though the old patron of exiles refused to despair, Fanny learned to look on plots such as his as "ill-conducted, and therefore necessarily unsuccessful."[49]

Sometime in 1823 Fanny's devotion to Lafayette began seriously to annoy his family. When she and Camilla left La Grange in early December 1822 for the winter season in Paris, they took an apartment at 8 rue de la Pépinière in the Faubourg St. Honoré—much nearer to Lafayette's than they had been before. Fanny's biography of the general, which was well under way by the following March, must have required that she see him even more frequently. The Garnetts, however, had moved to Le Havre, apparently because they found Paris too costly, and without them, Fanny had only Camilla nearby to provide some bulwark against scandal.[50]

For everything Fanny did was inevitably conspicuous. She was so tall; she took herself so seriously, and she had so little patience with what passed for worldly wisdom. Furthermore, she had preempted a place as close to Lafayette as any outsider could hold, and although many years later she would try to persuade Thomas Carlyle that hero-worship was a mistake, now she wanted a hero of her own. Lafayette was also her conduit into the struggle to make principles work in the real world. He loved her with all the extravagance that an orphan starved for a father's love could want. He gave her a shrine at which to worship, and the eroticism of her devotion matched that of many an early Christian saint or martyr.

The letters they exchanged were heavy with an emotional fervor for which ordinary explanations would not suffice. When he wrote, for example, about the occupation of Cadiz, he began: "I have been far away from you for 24 hours, my beloved Fanny. The time seems to me already quite long . . . But surely tomorrow, at four o'clock at the latest, my beloved Fanny will again be in the arms of her paternal friend, who loves her as she deserves to be loved." She wrote him in turn with a kind of breathless adulation: "I want to see you—but that I do always. I want a chat with you—but that I do always too—I love you dearly, admire you greatly, and honor you more than any among the dead or the living." No doubt they behaved, when they were together, with the same drama that marks their letters, and it is hardly cause for wonder that they provoked the anger of Lafayette's children.[51]

A year later Mme. Charles Lasteyrie, according to Fanny, told her husband, "If I experienced anywhere soever for one hour what I saw [Fanny and Camilla] endure for one week I would have left the house in an instant." The Wright sisters began to suffer the rudeness of a family who resented the elaborate attentions their patriarch paid a Scotswoman almost young enough to be his granddaughter. Fanny's grand illusion about La Grange began to crumble: the "consecrated dwelling" transformed itself for her into a house where little people thwarted the lofty in spirit, and she told herself that they resented her only because they were petty and mean-spirited.[52]

By the spring of 1824 Fanny was ready to leave France altogether. No doubt the election in February and March prompted her decision by adding to her disappointments over the fate of European liberalism and the chilliness of Lafayette's family. The government brazenly manipulated the electoral process to purge the opposition, so that after the election, only nineteen of one hundred and ten liberals remained in the Chamber, and Lafayette was its most prominent victim. He decided to use his newfound leisure to accept President James Monroe's invitation to come to America as the nation's guest, and Fanny hoped to take Camilla and go with him.

The sisters were going first to visit Mrs. Millar and Miss Cullen in the north of England, and Fanny apparently announced that she was leaving France permanently. Lafayette's friend Dupont de Nemours bade her goodbye, "alas, perhaps forever." Imagining her a meteor whose passing would leave them in darkness, he hoped she and Camilla would visit again in the fall. Lafayette arranged for Fanny and Camilla to meet with Vincent Nolte, an agent of Baring's Bank in London, so that they could transfer to him 120,000 francs from their account with the banker Jacques Laffitte. They asked him to invest the money in the Louisiana State Bank, and he readily accommodated them, apparently buying another 20,000 francs worth of stock somewhat later. No doubt they took all their money out of account with Laffitte because Fanny had no definite plans to return to France.[53]

On April 13, two years to the day after she had seen him last, Fanny dined again with Bentham, and she left the Hermitage laden with his essays and several books he loaned her on America. Friends in London beseiged her with the *on dits* about her and Lafayette that had begun to sweep their circle. But she brushed off rumor with the impatience of one who had no idea how deeply it could wound, and she and Camilla went on to Whitburn intending to stay as long as they could.[54]

But suddenly, on May 20, Fanny was back in London, and planning to leave for Dover that evening on her way to France. She shocked Frances Trollope with her single-minded haste, but it was very much in keeping with her sense of her importance to Lafayette, and his to her. Whatever provoked the crisis, Lafayette's family was appalled by the rumors that Fanny was his mistress and exercised undue influence over him. Fanny was going back to Paris to argue that he had only two ways to give the lie to the malicious gossip: he could either marry her, or formally adopt both her and Camilla.[55]

On her first day in Paris, Mme. Charles Lasteyrie, who proved her only ally in the family, told Fanny that the uproar had so upset Lafayette that he had had a seizure, which left him briefly unconscious. She warned Fanny that any repetition of such wrenching emotions could have serious consequences, but when Fanny told her her hopes for ending the crisis happily Mme. Charles instantly dashed them: "Alas," she said, "you know not France or you know not yet that Family."[56]

Fanny tried to rise above it all, but the pain provoked a radical delusion. She looked at Lafayette's daughters, who had spent two years with him in the Austrian prison, and at a son so devoted to his father that he could hardly be said to have a life of his own, and she saw only a "moral desert." She looked at a man surrounded by doting relatives and an impressive circle of friends and saw no "one being with whom he could exchange thoughts." She came to think it possible, albeit remotely, that Lafayette would leave France and his family and remain in the United States with her.[57]

Her refusal to understand how essentially marginal she was in Lafayette's life was a measure of her need both for love and for the usefulness she thought she found by his side. As an orphan who despised the woman who had raised her, Fanny simply could not credit the power of Lafayette's ties to his family. She had never felt—and never would feel—irrevocably bound to a place, a person, or a group of people, and she had no indisputable social place anywhere. People paid attention to her because she made them do it; she was intelligent, articulate, ambitious. But she was a part of Lafayette's world on sufferance; no personal qualities of hers could guarantee her place there. Unlike Mme. de Simiane, rumored to be Lafayette's longtime mistress, she was an outsider, and in the long run, mere principles and brilliance weighed lightly in the scale.

It was in part Lafayette's virtues that obscured a fact so hard. A rebel against his class, a citizen of the world, he wore the mantle of the grand seigneur so casually that an outsider might well fail to notice it. But he was accustomed to the obeisance of others, and he was by no means innocent of having encouraged Fanny's inflated sense of her importance. It was he who first called her his adopted daughter and who wrote no more than six months after they had met that he hoped she could close his eyes in death. It was he who repeatedly invited her to La Grange; who allowed, if not encouraged, her to write his biography; who gave her a pampered place among those who paid their devoirs. She was, after all, a dazzling young woman who would have been shocked that anyone could take his passion for liberty so lightly as to call it his "blessed lunacy." Though she exaggerated her importance in his life, she was indeed a soul-mate.

It is possible, of course, that she was also his mistress and, with a young woman's innocence and desperation, overestimated the sexual power she had over him. Neither too feeble to enjoy a sexual relationship nor too old to be sexually attractive, Lafayette was drawn to young women and unabashed about showing it. Fanny and he were powerfully attracted to each other, and neither was likely to sacrifice a strong desire to win or even to placate the world's good opinion.[58]

It seems more likely, however, that they sublimated their passion, as in effect they said they did. If, on the one hand, Fanny became Lafayette's mistress, she threw away the one weapon her culture insisted was crucial in the battle to hold such esteem as the world offered. If, on the other hand, she implicitly rejected the sexual overtures that he was too kind to make a condition of their relationship, she could have the power over him of the virginal tease and at the same time enjoy the safety of sexual purity. Furthermore, she was too proud to enjoy being only one of the many women in whose plackets, as Stendhal noticed, Lafayette liked to fumble. And if she were his mistress and at the same time proposed that he adopt her, the proposal would be a grotesque invitation to a kind of incest. Although what is grotesque is not necessarily untrue, in this case it seems at odds with Fanny's insistent high-mindedness. The nature of their relationship, however, remains ambiguous, and one of the more tantalizing of the unanswered questions about Fanny Wright.

Lafayette refused her proposal of marriage with the delicacy she so admired in him. According to Fanny, he said that the insurmountable obstacle came from a promise he had made Adrienne. As she was dying, he suspected that her thoughts were wandering to a long-standing affair of his, and he "bound himself by a general vow" never to marry again. He made this promise in the presence of their children and of Adrienne's sisters, and Fanny said it made "its way into the public prints." Lafayette told her that if he alone were concerned, it might be a different matter, but his enemies would attack his family, "who are dearer to me than life." On their account he found Fanny's proposal impossible. Whatever his reasons for refusing to adopt her legally, he continued to use the language they had long since chosen. Late in May he closed a note to her with "your father embraces you with all the tenderness of his heart."[59]

The question that remained unresolved was whether Fanny and Camilla should go with Lafayette to America. The family was opposed. Fanny decided to consult Lafayette's young friend Garnier Pagès, who had ridiculed the rumor that she was his mistress. Referring to "the difference of ages and yet more your known virtues and honor," he had told Lafayette "I am astonished first at its being said, but far more at its being listened to."[60]

On June 1, Fanny went to Le Havre to stay with the Garnetts while awaiting Lafayette's report on the family conclave. The tenth brought her better news in the form of letters from Virginie and Mme. Charles. The family appeared contrite and ready to support Lafayette in wanting Fanny and Camilla with him in America. Fanny believed their contrition sincere, though she thought them probably still hostile to her: "It appears that there have been mischief makers and busy bodies at work . . . Meddling politicians jealous of my supposed influence who had asserted to the son that nothing was done or said without my approbation . . . and that the father was held in leading strings—silly and ill-natured women who supposed intentions of another nature and the Lord knows what—All this operating upon little minds and petty jealousies."[61]

Nevertheless, the family did not want Fanny and Camilla to travel on the same ship with Lafayette, and Fanny had to argue that for them to follow later was to "adopt an underhand mode of doing what we desire." If their union were to continue, she told Lafayette, "it can only do so with honor to you and without prejudice to us by your assuming openly and avowedly the air and character of a protector." If she and Camilla could not travel as his children and boldly face down slander, "late as it is to renounce engagements which my heart will ever acknowledge to be more sacred than any ever made on earth," they would have to part.[62]

She fought hard against arguments she felt were specious. "I would willingly assume the role of a daughter, with the express consent and approval of the family," she wrote to Pagès, "but I do not wish to follow him as an I-don't-know-what and begin again the same life that I have led for too long." She argued that the English sense of honor was so different from the French that she would find it too painful to try to explain the family's point of view to their friends in England. "What is the purpose of being [in America] if we are not with him?" she asked, "and how can we be with him unless it is openly and without embarrassment, without false pretexts—in a word, like two girls with their father?" She continued to believe that she was uniquely important to Lafayette: "I am aware of my obligations to my father, just as I believe that his obligations to me are more sacred than any other, but the more sacred they are, the less they should be wrapped in mystery, and I confess to you that I find it impossible to act in a manner that is contrary to my character and that, in my own eyes, would renounce the dignity of innocence and virtue."[63]

Neither Lafayette nor Pagès found her arguments persuasive. Accepting the inevitable, she decided to sail to America after Lafayette. The family had got what it wanted: short of giving Lafayette up, Fanny had no choice. She had to find virtue in the necessity of overcoming, as she put it, the stupidities of weak-minded people and defying the malevolence of the wicked. In the third week of June, Camilla left Whitburn to join Fanny in Le Havre, and they then went on to Paris to meet with Lafayette and his family before he sailed in mid-July. When they arrived, the family urged them to follow him to America "with such increased earnestness," according to Camilla, that they "consented to hasten our arrangements so as to follow him if possible by the first of next month." They gave in at last so gracefully that Lafayette wrote Mme. Charles that Fanny had not been difficult to persuade, and Camilla had been charming.[64]

From his ship in New York harbor in mid-August, Lafayette wrote the Garnetts that he was preoccupied by thoughts of the packet that had sailed from Le Havre two weeks earlier with Fanny and Camilla aboard. How happily he would fold his two beloved friends in his paternal arms, he said, and how very much he looked forward to showing them New England. To Pagès he wrote that he relished the attention America would pay his dear daughter Fanny.[65]

The Lady Unattended by
a Male Protector

4

Fanny came to America the second time, at twenty-nine, as an authoress of some distinction and a woman of some experience, and she wanted America to pay attention. Not only had she written in high praise of the republic, she had also published two other books of which Thomas Jefferson himself spoke admiringly. All her books celebrated the quest for personal freedom and social justice. She had discovered how inhospitable Britain and France were to the liberal ideals she thought should govern societies, and how intractable the constraints on women there. Now she would test whether America would prove more congenial and more flexible.

Lafayette preceded Fanny and Camilla by several weeks, and by the time they arrived, the tone of his visit had been set: it was a spirited mixture of high-mindedness and hokum, and an extravaganza far beyond anything they could have imagined when they planned in Paris for the trip to come.[1]

On a pleasant August 16, 1824, New Yorkers by the scores of thousands thronged the shores of lower Manhattan to watch the convoy that brought Lafayette from Staten Island. Eight steamboats in full panoply, carrying six thousand citizens and the West Point band, sailed grandly toward anchor just off the Battery at Castle Garden. Finely dressed men and women lined the immense Castle's ramparts and crowded the windows and roofs of houses facing the bay. Hundreds of rowboats and wherries bobbed in the waters below as the lead steamboat, the *Chancellor Livingston*, closed with Lafayette and those chosen to greet him: the grandees of New York, the Knights of Cincinnati, a wealth of military men and citizens ambitious to be touched by history. A wave of cheers overwhelmed the company as Lafayette crossed into Castle Garden. He waved. He shook hands. He took tea. He blushed at the tears and shouts and wild applause. As one of the newspapers would have it, his reception was "expressive of as honest and generous feelings as were ever spontaneously manifested by any people on the face of the earth."[2]

When Fanny and Camilla sailed into New York harbor, Lafayette was well into a daunting succession of the most lavish entertainment the nation could offer. Flanked by his son George and his secretary Auguste Levasseur, he appeared at balls and nibbled his gracious way through one opulent banquet after another. He walked in stately processions and rode along slow ceremonial miles. He met veterans from the Revolutionary War and toasted the past in all its glory. His visit became an entrepreneur's delight, and reputations were made by it. A grape, a steamboat, and a good many babies were named for him; Giles Gardner's son at Hingham was even baptized "Welcome Lafayette." China platters glittered with pictures of La Grange and Lafayette wounded at Brandywine, and Fanny confronted the spectacle of republicans treating a republican as a lord.[3]

Fanny and Camilla's special relationship to Lafayette graced them with an importance they had not had six years earlier, and when they arrived in New York on September 11, no one would hear of their going out to board. Maria Colden, wife of New York's sometime mayor and congressman, invited them to stay in her home, and the newspapers noted that the authoress Miss Wright had come back to America. Immediately they were jolted into fevered last-minute preparations for New York's most spectacular entertainment for Lafayette, a ball at Castle Garden that Fanny said the General delayed until September 14 so that she and Camilla could attend. The Fete, as it was called, became the talk of the nation in an era when the rich and fashionable did not believe in understatement.[4]

Lafayette and his party made their entrance at ten o'clock as the orchestra brought the guests to attention. After he was seated grandly in the blue and white pavilion designed for him, everyone watched a huge painting of "the Genius of the Country" rolled up to reveal underneath what one reporter described as "a very beautiful transparency, representing a faithful view of *La Grange*." As Fanny and Camilla wandered about the floor, they could see Lafayette's picture on gloves and fans, on handkerchiefs and hats, on watchbands, belts, and even military stocks. When they went up the stairs and into the galleries, they looked down through artificial clouds on dancers who seemed to another reporter "like fairies moving in the distance to mellowed music." At two o'clock they left with Lafayette and the rest of his party to board the steamboat *James Kent,* which was to take them on a five-day trip to Albany and back.[5]

Over the next several months Fanny had occasion to meet the most celebrated people in America, her commanding presence drawing many to her and repelling not a few. The party on the *James Kent,* for example, had included Colonel Alexander Hamilton and his mother, Elizabeth Schuyler Hamilton, the son and widow of Lafayette's Revolutionary War companion. And there was one guest on board whose presence by no means boded well for Fanny—a woman who also called Lafayette "Father" and whom the newspapers had noticed by his side at the theater just before Fanny and Camilla arrived.[6]

She was Eleanor Parke Custis Lewis, Martha Washington's grand-daughter, and the first President's "beautiful Nelly." Sixteen years older than Fanny, she was exactly the age of George Washington Lafayette, and in 1795, when Adrienne sent her son to America for safety, Nelly had been at Mount Vernon to greet him. She renewed her childhood friendship with George on this trip, and whether or not he turned her against the Wrights, she took umbrage at Lafayette's patronage of them.

As Washington's pet, she had grown up accustomed to having her way, and was the kind of proper society matron likely to take offense at Fanny Wright. Known for her sharp tongue, she observed the proprieties and wrote witheringly of those who did not. And the hammer blows of personal tragedy had made her bitter. Before she was twenty-one, she had lost her beloved grandfather, and within five more years she had lost her grandmother and two children as well. She got on badly with her husband, and by middle age she had begun to cast her scorn scattershot upon the great of her time. When John Quincy Adams was elected President, she wrote: "I shall not visit Mrs. Adams at all. I do not respect her husband & I despise his Father." Living in a state of almost constant complaint, she not only resented Lafayette's attention to two Scotswomen so much younger than she and less obviously beaten down by tragedy, but also felt her claims to his attention older and more sacred than the Wrights' because of their mutual ties to George Washington. The record suggests, however, that Fanny first met Nelly pleasantly in New York, and nothing seems to have disrupted their trip on the *James Kent* as it made its slow progress upriver and back again.[7]

Lafayette expected Fanny and Camilla to be with him "in Philadelphia, Baltimore, Washington, Yorktown, and during our longer stay in Washington when Congress is in session," and he hoped his friends would welcome them. On the first of October he wrote Jefferson from Philadelphia that Fanny "is very Happy in Your Approbation; for, You and I are the two Men in the World the Esteem of whom she values the Most. I wish much, My dear friend, to present these two adopted daughters of Mine to Mrs. Randolph and to You; they Being orphans from their Youth, and prefering American principles to British Aristocracy, Having an independent, tho not Very large fortune, Have passed the three last Years in Most intimate Connection with My Children and Myself, and Have Readily Yielded to our joint Entreaties to Make a Second Visit to the U.S." Jefferson immediately invited Fanny and Camilla to Monticello: "You mention the return of Miss Wright to America, accompanied by her sister; but do not say what her stay is to be, nor what her course. Should it lead her to a visit of our University, which, in its architecture only, is as yet an object, herself and her companion will nowhere find a welcome more hearty than with Mrs. Randolph, and all the inhabitants of Monticello."[8]

But Lafayette's gentle persuasion could not always protect the Wrights, and something happened in Philadelphia that prompted Nelly Lewis to test her powers of social ostracism. According to Judge Richard Peters, Nicholas Biddle, the financier, "undesignedly" forgot to invite Nelly and her daughter to a reception for Lafayette to which Biddle had invited the Wrights. But something more important probably fueled Nelly's anger. In Philadelphia, Fanny broke the social taboo governing the relations between whites and blacks. She had heard that an agent of the Haitian government, Jonathan Granville, was in the United States arranging to help black families emigrate to Port au Prince, and she asked, through a friend of his, if he would come to Philadelphia to see Lafayette.[9]

As the General's emissary, she met Granville, a dark mulatto, at a private home where he stayed to avoid "any unpleasant mistakes likely to occur in a crowded boarding house." Granville had spent some years in the French army in Europe and had the manners and education of a polished European. At the time, Fanny still hoped that racial prejudice in the North would eventually diminish if people had the chance to meet so fine a man as Granville, but in Nelly Lewis's world, ladies did not make common cause with black men. Neither did they treat them as social equals. Nelly began to speak contemptuously to Lafayette about Fanny Wright and her sister.[10]

By the time Lafayette got to Baltimore, where he was met by Nelly's brother, George Washington Parke Custis, the process of cutting the Wright sisters from the general's entourage had begun. Lafayette wrote his daughters from there that he had seen Fanny and Camilla only in large public gatherings or in the homes of their mutual New York friends. The life he was leading did not lend itself, he said, to private companionship, and his secretary wrote that their manner of traveling made it impossible to include women in their party.[11]

When Lafayette got to Washington on October 12, Fanny and Camilla could see that not only were they outsiders, they were trespassers in Nelly's family compound. Nelly's older sister, Martha Custis Peter, lived in Georgetown, and at the end of his long first day in Washington, Lafayette visited there, as he did again two days later. The following day, he left Washington for the Custis home in Arlington and from there went to Mount Vernon, a few miles away from Nelly's own Woodlawn.[12]

He made some effort to win the family over to Fanny: he wrote Custis's wife Eliza that Fanny was "enthusiastically beloved by some, admired by many, envied by others, as is generally the case with distinguished talents and generous unreserved souls." But despite what Camilla had written her cousin three weeks earlier, she and Fanny did not go to Yorktown with Lafayette in mid-October, nor did they follow him there.[13]

Nelly took the credit, and she wrote a friend as though what she had done were an act of patriotism: "The fair Ws did not go to Mt V-n with the Gen'l, or to York with him, or Alexandria . . . *entre nous* . . . do I not deserve well of my country for this good deed, cost what it may to *myself*, I shall always rejoice that I have *served him so far* . . . I know that but for [me] they would have now be[en] tarnishing his glory by their presence. They were resolved to go, & he could *not say no*, until I taught him how to set his mouth & pen to a *negative* position." Fanny's sex had made her vulnerable to the malicious, and Nelly did not defend propriety alone. The following year Bernhard, Duke of Saxe-Weimar-Eisenach, traveled much the same route Fanny had and repeated stories of her shocking conduct: "I was told that this *lady* with her sister, unattended by a male protector, had roved through the country, in steam-boats and stages, that she constantly tagged about after General La Fayette, and whenever the general arrived at any place, Miss Wright was sure to follow next day."[14]

Fanny was a victim now of the fact that since the days of the Revolution, the scope of acceptable life for American women had begun to shrink. She herself had remarked in *Views of Society and*

Manners in America, "Alas for the morals of a country when female dignity is confounded with helplessness and the guardianship of a woman's virtue transferred from herself to others!" Such a transfer took place noticeably in the first quarter of the nineteenth century, as women were being elevated to the sterile world of the pedestal. Their minds too weak, their bodies too delicate, their emotions too fragile to confront life in forms less attenuated than those found in proper drawing rooms, they were now imagined to require the careful guidance and solicitation of men. Religiosity, delicacy, meekness, and intellectual inferiority had come to be associated with female nature, and the times presented a serious problem to a woman like Fanny Wright who had none of these qualities. A woman who was skeptical of marriage, she could hardly regard the "cult of true womanhood" as anything but a crippling perversion of women's rights to the full range of human experience.[15]

Fanny had begun her second trip to America as one of Lafayette's circle: she held a front-row ticket to one of the grand shows of her time and on occasion even kept the prompter's cards. Now the center of authority in her life began to shift away from Lafayette. Both the general and those who welcomed him to America had lent themselves to a series of extravaganzas out of keeping with her ideas of republican simplicity and inconsistent in their gross adulation of the general with the ideals of equality she prized. Furthermore, Fanny had been right when she argued that Lafayette could still the gossip only by making her legally either his wife or his daughter. But a solution so useful to her cavalierly ignored his family's feelings in the matter as well as the voice of social propriety. George and Nelly Lewis spoke for both, and Lafayette had heeded them. Realizing at last that she could not live her life through him, Fanny finally rejected the vicarious life prescribed for women. As was her custom, she buried the hurt. And as she became disenchanted with the celebration of the Nation's Guest, she cast about for more rewarding ways to live. She focused more intently on slavery and began to move toward a pragmatic attempt to change the thing she hated most in America.

By late October, when Fanny and Camilla left Washington to join Lafayette in Richmond, the enthusiastic receptions no longer charmed her. "Amid all the politeness I see and attention I receive," she said, "my heart is sick." She was troubled by people who owned slaves and believed them unworthy of Lafayette's presence. (The fact that Nelly and all her family held slaves no doubt added a personal bias to her republican convictions.) "I have not yet seen my fellow creatures sold in the market place," she wrote, "and God forbid I shd see it, for I really cannot answer for what I mt say or do." She had, however, seen them manacled and shipped off to New Orleans, and as she forced herself to look full-face at slavery, the elaborate politeness of Southern society seemed merely an attempt to hide its shame.[16]

Despite her disgust with slave owners, she made an exception of Thomas Jefferson. In the first week of November, as she and Camilla rode through the Virginia hills to meet Lafayette at Monticello, she looked forward to sounding Jefferson out on the subject that so troubled his land and his own conscience. Even more than Lafayette, he was her hero and obviously near the end of his momentous life. She told Julia and Harriet that the lamp was on the wane—"nor is it possible to consider the fading of a light so brilliant and fine without a sentiment of deep melancholy." So committed to friendship that his letters have been called a cornucopia of giving, he admired Fanny and allowed no jeering Nelly to spoil her days there.[17]

Jefferson met them at his exquisite home, on what Fanny described as his "little mountain commanding one of the finest prospects I ever remember to have seen." In the days that followed, he showed them over his plantation; they looked at his gadgets—his seven-day clock, the revolving serving door, the dumbwaiters at the ends of the dining room mantel, and his kitchen scales; and he took them to the University of Virginia—the first American university to be free of official church connection. His grandchildren kept each day lively. And best of all, his guests lingered at the long table, or sat in the parlor before the fire, and listened and talked to one of the gifted conversationalists of his day.[18]

In her growing obsession with slavery, Fanny naturally turned for hope to the radical author of the Declaration of Independence. No one knew slavery better than he, or felt its immorality more deeply. His grandfather had been a slavetrader. He himself had owned slaves since he was twenty, and in 1769 he had demanded unsuccessfully that the Virginia assembly allow him to free them. He publicly agitated as early as 1773 for an end to slavery, and as a member of Congress in 1784, he proposed a law that failed by only one crucial vote to prohibit it after 1800 in any newly created state. Nevertheless, as President, he failed to do anything significant to end slavery. And rumor had it that he had had a liaison for more than thirty-five years with one of his slaves, his late wife's half-sister, Sally Hemings.[19]

Whatever the complexities and dark secrets of his own life, however, Fanny discovered that Jefferson did not condone miscegenation. In

1814 he had written that the "amalgamation of whites with blacks produces a degradation to which no lover of his country, no lover of excellence in the human character, can innocently consent." He and Fanny almost certainly discussed the question, for Fanny wrote Julia and Harriet from Monticello that miscegenation had against it a "prejudice whether absurd or the contrary . . . so deeply rooted in the American mind that emancipation without expatriation . . . seems impossible." Fanny believed that black people had as much right to the country as whites, but Jefferson argued persuasively when he wrote: "Deep-rooted prejudices entertained by the whites; ten thousand recollections, by the blacks, of the injuries they have sustained; new provocations; the real distinctions which nature has made; and many other circumstances, will divide us into parties, and produce convulsions, which will probably never end but in the extermination of the one or the other race." Anyone committed to the end of slavery had to face the question of whether blacks and whites could live together as equals, and Fanny was discovering that the question was as troubling as slavery itself.[20]

During their visit to Monticello, Lafayette was more forthright in opposing slavery than Jefferson was. He talked freely against the slave system, insisting that no man could rightfully own his brother and remembering that when he came to America in the Revolutionary War, he spent himself because he thought they were fighting for human freedom. He argued that the slaves should be educated, but Jefferson apparently spoke only of freedom in the indefinite future. Fanny later wrote Jefferson's daughter Martha Randolph that her days at Monticello had been among the most interesting in her life. The rumors about his liaison with a slave woman, and the presence at Monticello of mulattoes who looked very like their master, may have left Fanny skeptical of Jefferson's public position on miscegenation. At any rate, the stand she took differed ultimately from his, although the experience of knowing him matured a sympathy with Southern planters that she would never lose.[21]

Prominent in the circles around Lafayette, Fanny began a busy Washington season—one that Nelly Lewis missed, according to the Wright sisters, because they were there. Fanny held small gatherings to read from *Altorf* and spent a good deal of time carefully studying "extracts from the registers of all the laws of the slave states, bearing directly upon the labor and the government of the negro." She and Camilla created so strong an impression by their frequent attendance on the House debates that the memory lingered until several years later, when Frances Trollope heard that "the most distinguished members were always crowding round them." The main topic of conversation in the salons and galleries that fall was no doubt the presidential election, which far overshadowed any other political question. In mid-December, when Louisiana's tally reached the Capitol, the final popular vote became Andrew Jackson 153,544, John Quincy Adams 108,740, William Crawford 46,618, and Henry Clay 47,136. The electoral total was Jackson 99, Adams 84, Crawford 41, and Clay 37. Because no one had a majority, the election went to the House of Representatives, where each state had one vote. As Fanny later put it, "that office, the noblest that exists upon the globe, was thrown into the midst of an assembly of delegates, as to play at bowls with."[22]

On the ninth of February, Fanny went to the Capitol for the election. From the visitors' gallery, she watched the chamber shift with tense excitement, for people like Jefferson thought Jackson dangerous, and many wanted him defeated. To take the presidency, Adams needed to win on the first ballot, and the New York delegation, which was split 17 to 17, was crucial to him. After a time of nervous indecision, Stephen Van Rensselaer, who had promised not to, cast his vote for Adams, giving him the necessary thirteen states. When Adams then made Henry Clay Secretary of State, he infuriated many who thought he had made a dirty political deal to win the presidency. John Randolph of Roanoke said the deck had been stacked and prompted Clay to demand satisfaction by calling Clay's relationship with Adams an unprecedented alliance between the Blackleg and the Puritan. When Clay's bullet went through Randolph's voluminous great coat, Randolph engagingly said, "You owe me a coat, Mr. Clay," and Clay subsequently commented that trying to hit Randolph was like trying to hit a pair of fire tongs.[23]

Humor, however, was rare as a response to Adams's triumph. Jackson had won a plurality of the popular and the electoral vote, and Adams's victory over him in the House so angered Jackson's supporters that they would spend the next four years destroying everything Adams tried to do. The period that James Monroe had called the Era of Good Feelings essentially died that February 9 as Fanny watched. She later wrote that Adams's election had violated the principle of direct suffrage she thought crucial to democracy, and the next few years would show her repeatedly how far America had come from the beneficent republic she described in her first book.

Wanting now to see the slave system at first hand, Fanny and

Camilla began to plan their own tour of America on the way to meet Lafayette in New Orleans on April 1, 1825. But still another thread was weaving its way into the tapestry of her future. By coincidence, on the day in late November when Lafayette had returned under full escort to Washington, the extraordinary Robert Owen of New Lanark, Scotland, arrived there as well. The former had dominated Fanny's recent past; the latter would radically affect her life to come. Now, in mid-February, a bad chest cold kept her in town for the first of two addresses Owen gave on the new world he hoped to build. Fanny was interested in Owen because, like him, she questioned whether the comforts and leisure of upper-class society were worth the cost the poor paid to maintain them. A man who had told the lords of Parliament and of cotton that better working conditions would be economical, Owen insisted that in any case they were imperative: "I do not hesitate to say, perish the cotton trade, perish even the political superiority of our country, rather than that they should be upheld by the sacrifice of everything valuable in life by those who are the means of supporting them." This was the kind of language Fanny understood.[24]

Owen explained that if people could learn to live communally, they could live far happier, more economical, more productive lives: "If there be one closet doctrine . . . more contrary to truth than another, it is the notion that individual interest, as that term is now understood, is a more advantageous principle on which to found the social system, for the benefit of all, or of any, than the principle of union and mutual co-operation." A system pitting one person against another destroyed elemental decencies, he argued, and was even inefficient.[25]

Owen insisted further that to change human experience fundamentally, one had to begin with the physical surroundings. Because he thought the United States the land of the future, he had just agreed to buy a town in Indiana called Harmonie. It was a new site—not quite what he wanted, but a good start—and he invited people to come to New Harmony with him and begin the new moral world. Washington's *Daily National Journal* said he was either a fool or a sage—nothing in between would do—and wondered how someone who denounced society and its institutions so entirely could believe himself ready to bring in the millennium. Fanny cast him as a sage. Like Owen, she was beginning to think of trying to change her world, and she planned to stop at Harmonie to see the town and the twenty thousand surrounding acres he had bought along with it.[26]

But she had not yet made a connection in her mind between Owen and what she called the "plague spot" of slavery, which preoccupied

her late in February as she got ready to leave Washington. Eastern
Virginia, Fanny had discovered, chiefly exported human beings: "They
are raised to the east as cattle are raised to the west. They are
advertized in the same way, exposed and sold in the same way, driven
in the same way and spoken of and treated in the same way." Slavery
was barbarous, and the solutions proposed to it not only seemed
inadequate, they also fundamentally divided the nation. The American
Colonization Society, for example, which bought slaves and shipped
them out of the country, struck Fanny as an organization that did
"individual benefits at the expense of helping forward the general
evil." Colonization removed black people either too troublesome to be
safely kept or so old and ill they burdened the plantation. Relieving the
individual planter or the community of such people simply eased the
moral and financial pressures that might otherwise force people to
find ways to end slavery. More than this, when colonization societies
paid for slaves, they promoted slavery. "So long as the market exists,"
Fanny believed, "the commodity will be encouraged."[27]

When, as an alternative, Fanny proposed that black people work for
wages, she invariably met with "the most foolish objection imaginable
but not the less obstinantly sustained on that account." Free black
people, the argument ran, would eventually insist they were the
equals of whites, and the amalgamation of the races would, as Fanny
put it, be "induced." She found the bias against this solution short-
sighted: "An impartial spectator opens his eyes in amazement at this
wonderful attachment to pure white skin (the purity of wch the
climate destroys before the age of five and twenty) to wch predilection,
the morals, happiness wealth peace and finally the very lives of a
whole population are to be sacrificed." Amalgamation, in fact, was
"taking place slowly but surely under the present system . . . in the
most degrading and most dangerous manner," and slaves inevitably
resented acquiring "the blood and color of their masters without
acquiring their protection or their privileges." With a European's near
indifference to race, Fanny found nothing to dread in miscegenation,
and for all that she admired Thomas Jefferson, his words had not
made their point with her.

In her preoccupation with this dilemma, Fanny stopped with
Camilla at Montpelier to stay with James and Dolley Madison before
continuing their trip west and south. But though Lafayette put great
store by the Madisons' interest in Fanny, and though she admired
Dolley Madison to the end of her life, the Wright sisters spent only a
day or so with them. Fanny's interest in the great and famous had

begun to wane. Then too, James Madison was a prominent member of the American Colonization Society, and Fanny must have known that one did not offer him a brief for miscegenation. When they left on the mail coach for Staunton, Fanny was searching impatiently for more acceptable solutions than his. Determined to see "slavery in its worst form," she intended to use their trip south to write "an article for our glorious Westminster Review on the subject of American negro slavery."[28]

They headed across the Alleghenies toward the Ohio River. Because mountain weather then was likely to be severe, the trip was daring for someone like Fanny who was prone to develop respiratory infections, and illness plagued her into April and May. Quite apart from the weather, such traveling must have been difficult for a woman. A discreet silence falls over menstruation, but sanitary conditions were minimal at best even in cities, and houses did not have running water. "Linens"—the 1820s equivalent of sanitary napkins—were ordinarily washed and used repeatedly, but this would have been impossible for women going almost 1,000 miles a month by stage, horseback, steamboat, foot, and whatever contrivance proved handy. In the early part of the trip Fanny and Camilla apparently traveled without a maid, and though self-sufficiency of a practical sort was a state for which their Devonshire adolescence had ill-prepared them, whatever they needed done they had to do for themselves or hire along the way. But Fanny courted adventure with the gusto of the early explorers. Quite possibly she traveled farther in her lifetime than any other contemporary woman; certainly few women outdistanced her. The trip she began in March 1825 was one of the most fateful long journeys of her life.

By the second week in March, the Wrights had crossed the Alleghenies and by steamboat followed the western course of the clear, hard-winding, slow-moving Ohio to the tiny port of Mount Vernon, Indiana. Leaving the river there, they pushed their way through thick forest toward Harmonie. Peach and tulip trees were in rich bloom, and massy vines covered trees so tall their lowest limbs were fifty feet from the ground. The land rose to about one hundred feet above the river, and a mile from their goal they saw the forest open onto the three thousand acres the Harmonists had cleared. Before them, in the midst of sheepwalks, orchards, cornfields, and vineyards, lay the town some called the "Wonder of the West," and behind it the lovely Wabash.[29]

They looked down on a village laid out with a craftsman's

Frances Wright, about 1824

Eleanor Parke Custis Lewis

Photograph of a model of New Harmony, Indiana

precision—one that demonstrated what men and women could do if they cared enough and worked together. Big enough for about eight hundred people, it had four parallel streets intersecting at right angles with another six running roughly parallel to the river. Just off the town's center Fanny and Camilla saw two churches, one of them a massive two-story brick building with nave and transept each 120 feet long. From the steeple of the other church rang a bell, a rare touch of Europe for the West, and as the sisters came nearer, they could hear the singing that in part gave the town its name.

Explaining to Robert Owen why they would leave so fine a town, the Harmonist leader, George Rapp, had said that every ten years he and his followers looked for a new place to do good. Owen had bought their village some two months earlier, and Father Rapp had already taken a first contingent of Harmonists to Economy, Pennsylvania, their new tract north of Pittsburgh. When the Wrights first saw Harmonie, however, about five hundred of Rapp's people still worked in the fields and the shops. Jefferson himself may have told Fanny about these German peasants: they were immigrants from Württemberg and primitive Christians, and this was the second town they had completed in only twenty-one years. For the most part they practiced celibacy, obeyed George Rapp, and lived so finely that Robert Owen said of them, "I have not yet met with more kind-hearted, temperate, and industrious citizens, nor found men more sincere, upright, and honest in all dealings, than the Harmonists."[30]

Fanny met Owen's son William here, and his disciple Donald MacDonald, who had come from Scotland in the belief that religion need not be the tie that binds a community, not celibacy the sine qua non for peace. "Though her manners are free and unusual in a female," William wrote of Fanny in his diary, "yet they are pleasing and graceful and she improves upon acquaintance."[31]

For two days Fanny studied the wonders that this disciplined, God- and George Rapp-intoxicated people had wrought in only eleven years. They had built the two churches, one four-story granary and another whose walls were two feet thick, and at least five three-story brick buildings where community members lived. From their distillery and brewery they produced five hundred gallons of beer and seventy-two gallons of whiskey every two days. They kept an inn for travelers and for those who came to buy their famous goods. There was a public store, a movable greenhouse under which they grew lemon and orange trees, and at least four mills for cotton, wool, corn, and flour, some of them run by steam. They had three sheep stables, two sawmills, three large wooden barns, a brickyard, a dye house, and shops for shoemakers, blacksmiths, tanners, wheelwrights, and coopers. They had made themselves a land of plenty: the year before, their peaches had grown so abundant the hogs feasted a month on windfalls.

Fanny carefully watched the deliberate way the Harmonists worked. She watched them plane the trees they had cut, sand their floors, and wash them down. She saw that they forced nothing and rushed nothing. They wore plain homespun and sang throughout the day. Wherever they went, they walked in orderly lines, the men in one line and the women in another. She realized that what they did took neither genius nor special talent but rather persistence, good temper, and the cultivated habit of working cooperatively.

On a Sunday morning the four young Scotspeople climbed to the vineyards and hills with the best view of the town and river. Fanny looked down on Harmonie with a calculating eye, and the calculations were dazzling. When the Harmonists had emigrated from Germany in 1803, the worth of their property averaged no more than $25 apiece. Twenty-one years later, Robert Owen agreed to pay them $125,000 for the town they had built in Indiana and for the equipment they chose to leave behind. At a time when people in Indiana owned property worth an average of $150, and those in Massachusetts something less than $300, a fair estimate gave the Harmonists $2,000 for every man, woman, and child—about ten times the average wealth throughout the United States.[32]

Fanny knew most Harmonists had been poor, uneducated peasants, and now, with slavery in the back of her mind, she wanted to know how to account for what seemed an economic miracle. She had the chance to inquire when she and Camilla had supper with one of the men who had made it possible. He was Frederick Rapp, George Rapp's adopted son and the community's business manager. Impressive in quite a different way from his charismatic stepfather, Frederick Rapp was a "tall, rawboned, sallow complexioned, serious & plain german," and he so impressed Fanny that she began to imagine he might have a place near her in a future whose outlines she was just beginning to see. About this visit to Harmonie she later wrote, "a vague idea crossed me that there was something in the system of united labor as there in operation wch mt be rendered subservient to the emancipation of the south."[33]

The following day Fanny and Camilla set out on horseback for the twenty-five-mile ride to Albion, Illinois, the home of a settlement of

English farmers whom she had discussed in her book on America. Their escort was a remarkable and engaging man named George Flower, and a deafening silence surrounds the close relationship so soon to flourish between him and Fanny Wright. Nine years older than she, he was a square-jawed, clear-eyed gentleman-farmer from Hertfordshire. At ease with the great, as with the humble, he struck Camilla as "one of the most amiable beings I have ever known," a man who had "all the qualifications that go to form an agreeable and intelligent companion."[34]

Short only of Lafayette, George Flower whetted Fanny's appetite for sturdy heroism. He had emigrated less than a decade earlier and knew perils of the frontier that did not turn up in the usual accounts, and certainly not in Fanny's sanguine book on the young republic. He told the sisters, for example, how English Prairie, or Albion, had split asunder at its very beginning. He told about Morris Birkbeck, who in his mid-fifties had left England with his two daughters, a twenty-five-year-old neighbor, Eliza Andrews, and two other young people. Flower had met them in Philadelphia, and they joined together for the journey west. Along the way Birkbeck proposed marriage to Miss Andrews, who rejected him. Flower subsequently proposed and was accepted, and they were married at Vincennes, with Birkbeck standing as father to the bride. Birkbeck could not reconcile himself to the marriage, however, and when the Flowers arrived in Illinois, he refused to speak to them, insisting that any business they had with him be carried on through an intermediary. When the Flowers' party fell desperately ill and spent three weeks near death, Birkbeck and his people offered no help. The boundary separating the Birkbeck from the Flower lands was three miles long, and each man now worked his own side in a silence that had lasted seven years.

He told an even more pertinent story, however—one that could undermine Fanny's sense of the way American politics worked, along with her tenacious hope that most Americans disliked slavery as much as she did. She listened carefully when Flower explained how he and his British compatriots had won an eighteen-month battle against the slavery forces in the free state of Illinois. According to Flower, every office-holder from the constable to the judge favored slavery. Many of the people who had settled southern Illinois had come from the slave states, and as Flower put it, they bribed and electioneered in the streets and the grog-shops with the worst blackguards in the county. They put out word that slavery was ordained by God and that blacks could not take care of themselves. They pressured other whites to vote for a convention to rewrite the state constitution to allow slavery, and they drummed up hatred against the English settlers who opposed them because they had emigrated for freedom. The fight had been so hard, so bitter, and so close that families and friends had split forever.

Those Flower had battled continued to attack both the peaceful blacks settled among the English and the whites who supported their right to live there, and they even captured free blacks to sell into slavery. In desperation, Flower finally sent one Robert Grayham to see if Haiti's President Boyer would welcome the blacks who lived on his land. Grayham came back satisfied, and in March 1823 about thirty people set off for Haiti under his protection. They needed that protection on more than one occasion. In New Orleans the mayor threw most of the men in jail and told Grayham he would sell them for slaves if they were not out of the city in eight days. All their money was demanded in jail fees, and Grayham had to draw on Flower for $360 to carry them out of the country. The blacks wrote back lyrically of their Haitian life, however, and Flower's story reminded Fanny of Jefferson's belief in the imperatives of colonization. It added pieces to the puzzle she was beginning to put together.

George Flower proved a kindred spirit: he had had a good deal of trouble lately among the English settlers, and he and his wife were inclined to leave Albion and join another community themselves. A man who dealt easily with black people, he had often speculated that Harmonie might be a model for a community in which blacks could live and work together, and on their long ride to Albion he and Fanny may have talked about what part of the Harmonists' experience might be useful for slaves.

When the three of them rode into the Flower compound in Albion, Fanny and Camilla found a welcome there, especially from Eliza, George's wife. One of his sisters thought them particularly agreeable and intelligent. Emily Ronalds, an English visitor whose brother was married to another of his sisters, was so taken with them that she decided to join them on their trip to New Orleans. Their eager conversations began to bear fruit in Fanny's mind, and when Flower left them on the Ohio River four days later and returned to what would become New Harmony, he told William Owen that Fanny was very much interested in the community system.[35]

The three women boarded the Ohio steamboat at Shawneetown, below the mouth of the Wabash, and ran into dangers small and large. They dodged sparks that flew from the smokestack and fell on their clothes and on the canvas awnings above them. Their skirts were at hazard from tobacco juice that card-playing, whiskey-drinking men spat at random. Northern snows had begun to melt, and the waters brought great masses of driftwood that could clog the river and splinter the paddle wheels. Huge logs and trees eddied together, and the pilot at the helm would ring a bell to signal the men who stoked the furnaces to stop when he could not steer the boat around them. Snags, "sawyers," and "planters"—tree trunks and branches caught in the riverbed—could rip the bottom out of a boat in minutes. It was an unlikely place for British ladies.

No more than three hundred miles down from Shawneetown, the dark water of the Ohio began changing to lime. The flat land gave way to a smooth expanse of water like an immense marsh, and they came out onto the Mississippi River. Here the perils were greater, and men who played cards and backgammon for high stakes were not the only gamblers. Firing the boilers so hot they sometimes blew their steamboats up, pilots raced each other, and wrecks of rafts and keelboats littered the river. And the closer they came to New Orleans, the more oppressive the moist heat and the thicker the mosquitoes. Fanny said of the latter that they were the size of daddy longlegs and thick as pharaoh's lice, and they prompted her to a rare moment of wit: "If Moses had but thought of Mississippi mosquitoes one plague wd have done the work of seven."[36]

When the boat docked at last in New Orleans, the weather was rainy, and Fanny was ill. Remembering George Flower's story about the mayor and the free blacks, she looked about her with disgust. Slavery, as they had ventured south, had grown more harsh-featured, and in New Orleans she thought she heard the clank of chains and the cries of victims. "Truly this is the Babilon of the Revelations, where reigneth the great Western slavery mud and mosquitoes," she wrote. "Slavery I expected to find here in its horrors, and truly in all its horrors it is found . . . every man's hand is against the hapless slave and every law of man's creation."

Lafayette, however, arrived on April 10 and was eager to be kind. The next day, despite a violent downpour, he called on the governor and the mayor and then went to Madame Herries's Hotel to call on the Wright sisters. Fanny's spirits began to lift, as others paid attention as well. Three days later, apparently at Lafayette's suggestion, the governor went to her hotel with thirty officers in full dress and introduced them to her one by one. The *Courier* complimented her by writing of *Views* that it was "a work no less remarkable by the talents it displays, than by the generous and liberal feelings which pervade it."

The festivities for Lafayette, however, had become so irrelevant to her she scarcely mentioned them in her letters. He was still her "dear General," but her attention was now focused on slavery and fixed on the hope of emancipation.[37]

Steeling herself to look about her, Fanny grew fascinated by the New Orleans mixture of French, Spanish, Creole, African, and mulatto. What intrigued her most were the relationships she saw between whites and blacks. The French, long known as both the best and worst of slaveowners, were more hot-tempered, Fanny thought, than the English or the Americans, and less well-educated than the wealthiest native planters. However, they were more likely to acknowledge their own miscegenation and to provide regularly and decently for their illegal colored families: "The latter have been in many cases educated and provided for as well as emancipated, and where no legitimate wife or progeny existed the whole fortune of the master and father has devolved by testament to the enslaved children. It is in this manner that an independent land holding, and what is more curious *slave possessing* body of mulattoes has been formed and in the streets it is not rare to see some elegant women attired in all the simple elegance of creole taste, and shewing eyes, features and shape far surpassing the grace and expression of creole beauty. The attractions of these dark eyed rich complexioned damsels are such that it has been judged advisable to prevent by law any contract of marriage between them and whites."

Tutored now by her three months' reading in Washington and by George Flower's sobering tales about slavery, she noticed how racial pride and fear had overwhelmed considerations of justice and even good sense. Of a group of free mulattoes who had fought the British under Jackson in 1814 with distinction, she wrote: "They were afterwards deprived of the arms with wch they had cooperated in defense of the country! This indignity has cut more deeply than any other." The jealousy and insolence of the whites had lost them "the good will of the party wch mt have formed a barrier between them and their slaves or have added to their strength against them." The blacks who were themselves planters and slaveholders had had to make common cause "with their oppressed half brethren."

Everything Fanny found out confirmed her sense that slavery was dangerous. She heard of a terrible insurrection some years before that was begun and led by a young mulatto whose legitimate white half-brother had insulted him. She asked why white people, frightened because blacks decisively outnumbered them, should nonetheless continue to bring in more blacks. She was told it was "cheaper and *safer* to *import* and *work out* slaves than to take care of those born in the country." Further, people could buy slaves cheaply in the markets of Virginia, clear new plantations with them, and make a great deal of money. But quite apart from hopes of quick profit, many Southern whites were so ignorant and brutal, Fanny said, that they did not know how to calculate consequences and could "never see danger until it is converted into absolute ruin . . . anxious only to relieve the difficulties of the moment, [they] seek in the slave traffic a support to their sinking fortunes."[38]

Though she found a few people who shared her sense of urgency, the kinds of things Fanny heard in New Orleans made most people despair of seeing slavery end. Relentlessly hopeful, however, Fanny saw its impending doom and the end of white rule in Louisiana. She turned her back on New Orleans convinced that the bias against miscegenation was merely irrational and certainly misguided, and that "at no great distance of time" the state would be peopled entirely with those of mixed blood—the only ones, she thought, who could endure the climate and do the work the soil required.

The Wright sisters, along with Emily Ronalds, left New Orleans with Lafayette, and as their boat steamed upriver, they looked out on the big white porticoed houses that signaled the power of the cotton kingdom. Stunned by the beauty of Mississippi, Fanny wrote, "I cd have wept as I thought that such a garden was wrought by the hands of slaves!"[39]

On April 18 the three women left Lafayette at Natchez, where the *Mississippian* took notice of Fanny's presence at a ball and remarked that her defense of America had "drawn upon her the scurrility of the Quarterly Review, and other hireling presses." The trip upriver, Fanny discovered, was even more dangerous than the trip down. The boat carried five hundred passengers, and the scene on deck was a confusion: "The attendants on board are good for nothing but to stumble against & run over each other . . . Half a hundred french boys jostling and gabbling away morning till night . . . Ladies & gentlemen standing & sitting as thick as leaves on the trees . . . I sit now in my berth in a state room where two can just contrive to turn round, begging [room] for their elbows . . . as is usually the case in this country, the more numerous the perils the less the caution . . . foundered steamboats, lost cargoes & drowned passengers seldom inspire the precaution of tying to in a dark night, or of carefully firing the boilers, so as to present the addition of blowing up to the other perils of the navigation." Fanny and Camilla were on their way to visit New Harmony a second time, and to meet Robert Owen and see the beginning of his great experiment. And all the while, Fanny was trying to piece together a plan that might discover an end to slavery.[40]

In the next six weeks, Fanny Wright made the decisions that led her to be the first woman in America to act publicly to oppose slavery. Exhilarated by a spacious vision of human possibility, she and Camilla seemed to live half a lifetime: "We have traversed such an extent of country, seen such a variety of people made so many valuable friends, and decided on plans of so much importance that a folio volume cd scarcely describe or explain all."[41]

Her dedication to fight slavery was deep and sincere, and at the same time, she knew that the fight was beginning to channel her talents and energies in a way that was good in itself. She knew that women seldom found such a focus, and that she was going against the received wisdom about what a woman's life should be. Some months later Fanny wrote that the "universally marked difference between men and women" sprang from men's "fixed and steady occupation," which kept in "habitual exercise" their physical and mental energies. Work gave men "good health and good nerves" that allowed them "to taste the enjoyments of life without being dependent upon any and to bear or brave its ills with a resisting spirit." Fanny knew that the need for serious work was a human rather than merely a male need, despite the mystifications that had begun to surround "woman's place." And though she had not been educated for work of a practical nature, she was determined to satisfy that need in her own life.[42]

When she and her sister reached New Harmony, Fanny discovered another kindred soul in Robert Owen. Benign and confident that communal forms of living and working had a chance in the nineteenth century and that many of the people who had asked about New Harmony as he toured the East would join them, he embraced a vision even less modest than hers. To a gathering of more than six hundred people, Owen called New Harmony merely a "half-way house between the old and the new" and said his ultimate purpose was to introduce an entirely new state of society, "to change it from an ignorant, selfish system to an enlightened social system which shall gradually unite all interests into one, and remove all causes for contest between individuals."[43]

He found a responsive audience. People who had lived a hard and sometimes brutal life on the frontier hoped to find in Owen's scheme a way to pool their energies and resources, and to gain by doing so both greater profits and good fellowship. Many were taken philosophically and morally by the appeal of community: several families had just arrived from Cincinnati, and they reported many others behind them. A preliminary society adopted the constitution Owen proposed, and when Fanny and Camilla arrived, the newcomers were settling work schedules, job assignments, and the living space each person and each family could expect. Fanny caught the promise: she was soon to write that Owen was working miracles and would revolutionize the North a second time.[44]

It was on her way from New Harmony to George Flower's Albion that Fanny had her first bitter personal encounter with slavery, fighting for the life of "a poor black boy whom I recovered for one moment [only] to lose him again," a boy who had been caught by people who wanted to sell him into slavery. Fanny hired two men to go with her, rode for two days and half a night through the Indiana forests, caught up with the kidnapers, and faced them down. The black boy clung to her skirts, and just as the kidnapers drew their knives, another cadre of men rode in to save the rescuers. They got the boy to a magistrate, who gave him to the sheriff for the night. But the next morning the boy was gone, and the sheriff pleaded ignorance. Fanny blamed herself: she had given in to exhaustion and let others talk her into handing over the responsibility she had taken to protect the boy. The experience steeled her resolve to confront slavery herself. And soon she had developed a scheme for an experimental community that would organize slaves the way George and Frederick Rapp had organized German peasants.[45]

She had begun to work it out in long talks with Frederick Rapp and George Flower on her second visit to New Harmony, and she thought of it as a likely first step in a massive resettlement of blacks and whites in the South. Because it would be impossible to remove the whole black population of the country, she imagined a biracial society in which the two races for the most part lived separately. Virginia, Maryland, Kentucky, and Tennessee—"under a proper system and if set about in time"—could send most of their black people to Texas or to the southern states. Conversely, in Louisiana, Mississippi, Georgia, and Florida, where the whites were outnumbered, they might anticipate massacre by the blacks and mulattoes and would therefore leave. The upper South would become white, the lower South and Texas, black. For this to happen, blacks would have to be educated, trained, and freed. Slave owners would have to be reimbursed for the property they lost, and whites would have to take over the work that blacks had done till then. Fanny was trying to organize a scheme that would solve at least the first two problems—one that was "capable of being rendered *general* and consequently efficient in its effects."[46]

Her plan was based on several assumptions. She assumed that Great Britain had imposed slavery on colonies that did not want it. She believed that the United States had seized upon the first possible chance to act against the slave trade. She continued to believe that most Americans were eager to abolish slavery if only the way could be found, and that there was "as much to admire as to anathematize in the conduct of the master race toward the subject African." She assumed that the people who had been enslaved would be those most damaged by sudden emancipation and that "human enfranchisement—which is but another name for civilization—is, in its beginnings, a slow, gradual, and complex operation." She thought that government could not by fiat abolish "an evil which has its seat in the mind, the habits, and through hereditary influences, in the very physical organization of a race." And she believed that one part of the nation could not ask another to make sacrifices it did not share: slavery must end without forcing slave owners to substantial material loss. Her plan therefore required that slaves, to gain their freedom, work out their purchase price, a process she expected to take about five years. At the same time, they would be given a basic education—"a real moral, intellectual and industrial apprenticeship"—to prepare them to use that freedom well.[47]

She drew large conclusions from Frederick Rapp's experience. She calculated that if slave labor could be organized and motivated as the Harmonists had been, two or three plantations in a state would undersell everything produced by the slave labor in it, and prove that slavery was unprofitable. Nor did she doubt that she could persuade slaves to work like the Harmonists. She would win them to her scheme by kindness and by convincing them "that their labor was for their personal redemption the relief of their race and the practical education of their children."[48]

Her next step was to decide where such an experiment could be fruitfully made. Tennessee appeared the most liberal of the slave states: in 1823 it had twenty antislavery societies, with six hundred members, and Rapp told her she might find available public land there if Andrew Jackson decided to help her. In September, they agreed, George Flower would go with her to see Jackson at the Hermitage in Nashville. Fanny expected Rapp to find a place for the experiment and to join them himself in November.[49]

It was early summer, 1825, when Fanny wrote about her new scheme; but within a few weeks Frederick Rapp's name dropped from her correspondence, and nothing remains to account for her brief connection with him. Rapp had no intention of leaving the Harmonists to join Fanny's community. As a devout Christian, he was deeply committed to the Harmonist Society and spoke of it as the millennium come to pass. For more than twenty years he had subordinated his formidable energies to the mesmerizing power of George Rapp, and he endorsed the absence of personal freedom and self-definition Fanny deplored. Now, as always, she failed to understand religious belief and radically underestimated the hold religion had on many people. Reflecting on this period almost two decades later, she wrote that the Harmonists were "submitted to the spiritual and temporal control of astute leaders" and were oppressed by religion: "Christian fanaticism and subjection were the means employed to stultify the intelligence, and hold the physical man submitted to the will of others." Her eagerness for Frederick Rapp's help led her to ignore his role in this at the time, though her willful ignorance in relation to him was not as costly as it would prove in relation to others.[50]

She now faced the painful step of telling Lafayette her plans, and she persuaded herself that they were contingent on his approval and his consent to her remaining in America with her sister. Heading ultimately for Boston and a ceremony at Bunker Hill, she and Camilla bought three horses, hired a black servant, and made their way across part of Illinois and the whole of Indiana to meet him at Louisville. When they found him, however, late in the second week of May, he had a tale that stilled Fanny for the time: a snag had pierced his steamboat at midnight 125 miles below Louisville, sinking it in about ten minutes. Everyone had managed either to grab a piece of floating wreckage or to swim ashore, and finally all were saved, but Fanny decided not to upset him again so soon with her plan to break away.[51]

They parted with the understanding they would meet in Pittsburgh two weeks later, and Fanny and Camilla rode on, their horses making thirty-five to forty miles a day. In Economy, Pennsylvania, they picked up the formidable patriarch George Rapp and three other Harmonists, and they all got to Pittsburgh on May 30, just twelve hours ahead of Lafayette. Their exhilarating six-hundred-mile ride on horseback had "entirely restored Fanny's health," according to Camilla, "and in a great measure her strength, and the heat wh appears to oppress and overpower everyone else imparts to her new life and energy." The adventure carried her to the peak of confidence she needed to tell

Lafayette she wanted to do something a woman had never done before.[52]

Fanny's need to give her life purpose made her an eloquent advocate. She convinced herself that others were caught up in her own enthusiasm and ready to give all the practical help she could use. Her need to create a home, one that not only Camilla but Julia and Harriet Garnett could share, made her confident she might succeed. Returning to Europe would mean returning to a "life of constraint," she wrote her friends, relieved now and again by a "*visit* to those who cd not in return make *our home* theirs." But if in America they could build what Camilla called their "cabin to shelter us from the storm," they could make of their temporary separation from the Garnetts "a harbinger of future good and happiness to us all." Fanny talked of visiting Europe the next year to bring the Garnetts back: "We have already sketched out a plan of life," she confidently wrote, "and occupations for you all."[53]

During the three days they spent in Pittsburgh, Fanny argued her case well. She explained her plan and told Lafayette that people had encouraged her far beyond her hopes and had assured her she was perhaps the only person, other than Lafayette himself, who could make it work. When he worried about "the ignorant white population of the South who have so long prohibited the instruction and very generally the emancipation of the slaves," she did not discount the danger but thought her sex might guard her project against violence. Fanny also argued that because she was "very generally known and . . . looked upon as a friend by the American people," she would be protected by them. Finally, she thought success certain if Andrew Jackson supported her, and proposed visiting him in Nashville to lay the case before him. Reluctantly, Lafayette gave her his blessing, and Fanny left him to seek others who could help.[54]

Though Fanny was ready now to give up Lafayette, the pattern of his life remained her model. Almost fifty years before, he had risked himself in coming to serve a young people in rebellion. Now Fanny dared to believe that she could do the same: she would put herself at the center of a drama she would write, a drama of sacrifice to high principle. That the slaves had not themselves rebelled like Lafayette's colonists was a fact that Fanny was not inclined to believe crucial.

She and Camilla went on to Philadelphia, where they found the former governor of New York De Witt Clinton, who listened to Fanny for an hour before breakfast one day and went away convinced that she was "the most superior female of his acquaintance." An outspoken critic of slavery, Clinton told Fanny she had given him a "more correct view of the whole surface of Southern slavery than he had previously [received]." They caught Frederick Rapp just leaving for Baltimore, and Fanny commissioned him to ask "an efficient philanthropist" there— no doubt Benjamin Lundy, who edited the antislavery newspaper *The Genius of Universal Emancipation*—to send her the names of sympathetic Tennessee planters. They then made their way through New York to Boston as a last diversion for Lafayette's sake.[55]

By mid-July George Flower had joined Fanny in New York, and soon they were deep into formulating their plans for emancipating the slaves. Fanny called special meetings of philanthropists to explain what they hoped to do, and Lafayette thought she argued so eloquently she converted skeptics into disciples. Because she had loaned Lafayette money before and Congress had now voted $200,000 to replenish his fortune, he offered them $8,000. Fanny, however, refused it. No doubt she wanted to keep herself invulnerable to his family's criticism, but she also wanted to avoid special favors. She and Flower hoped to raise the necessary money through an appeal they planned to circulate and publish. It was in the infinite extension of her plan that Fanny saw the doom of slavery, and so they had to succeed, she insisted, in such a way that other people could follow their example.[56]

If Fanny had been harshly critical before, she tried now, as she and Flower wrote their proposal for the experimental colony, to woo a moderate audience. They calculated the expenses of the colony at a figure higher than might be necessary, and gain at a lower, so that no one could suspect enthusiasm of addling their good sense. Made in a "spirit of equal good will to master and slave," their proposal was a measured statement that took for granted the danger to the planter as well as the damage to the slave. And it acquiesced to Jefferson's fears of a biracial society: Fanny tied her plan to colonization, of which she disapproved, because she thought it politically necessary to do so.[57]

They proposed to buy two sections of public land "within the good southwestern cotton line" and to put fifty to one hundred slaves to work on them, using a system of cooperative labor modeled on that of the Harmonists. They calculated that a slave could work five years under such a system to repay his or her purchase price, as well as whatever expenses had been incurred by sickness. They thought they could begin such an establishment with just over $40,000, and they expected to make about $10,000 each year in cotton. They would hold out "as the great stimulus to exertion, the prospect of liberty, together with the liberty and education of the children." The centerpiece of their proposal was "a school of industry which . . . shall carry order and co-operation from the school-room into the field, the children working, under the direction of their monitors, with such intermission as shall keep their minds cheerful, and their bodies vigorous." For the parents, they planned to hold weekly evening meetings to explain "the necessity of industry, first for the procuring of liberty, and afterwards the value of industry when liberty shall be procured."

Because they believed that slaves would work immeasurably harder when they worked toward their freedom, Fanny and Flower expected the new system to be a boon economically to the South. They believed its success would attract "that floating capital, foreign and domestic, which is now employed in developing the resources of Mexico, Columbia, and Peru." They thought that one successful experiment would lead each slave state to establish another within its borders, and they anticipated that when their plan's economic superiority to the present system became obvious, planters everywhere would contract to have their plantations run accordingly. They expected, as Jefferson did, that white labor from the poorer classes would take the place of slaves who had been colonized.

They were trying to do good by exploiting people's greed. Flower observed that the great obstacle to ending slavery was the amount of capital bound up in the slaves. He and Fanny, therefore, hoped to show capitalists that they could invest in such an association and make money. Secured as it was by land and slaves, the investment itself would be safe. If they could return at least 6 percent profit, he reasoned, "then wealth in the hand of benevolence would become the instrument of removing slavery from the U.S. in the shortest possible time."[58]

What they meant was that America could end slavery if it wanted to. They regarded the details of their plan as provisional, and they expected to improvise as they went. They kept hazy the number of years during which slaves would remain in bondage, because the slaves' readiness for freedom depended on matters no one could anticipate, including the readiness of their children.

Like most people, Fanny and Flower took their ideas where they found them. To the Harmonists their debt was obvious. From the eighteenth century rationalist tradition they took their passion for liberty and education, which they assumed would be a motivating passion for slaves as well. From Robert Owen they took the idea of a school of industry in which children were never pushed beyond their strength but instead blended their time to learn and their time to work. From the evening study meetings where the nineteenth century British working class fought so doggedly for its self-respect, they derived a kind of adult Sunday school, held in the evening after the day's work in the field, where the slaves would be exhorted to prodigies of work and reminded of the virtues of freedom. And they paid obeisance to the American devotion to profit by insisting that no one stood to lose, by assuming that one successful farm would lead to others, and by imagining that neither racial hatred, fear, ignorance, short-sightedness, nor the love of one class for keeping another down could stand against the slave owners' desire to make more money.

They had their proposal printed as an anonymous circular and sent it out for publication to journals they thought sympathetic. Since they did not intend for its authorship to be entirely unknown, Fanny herself sent copies to Jefferson, Madison, and Clay, explaining to the latter that she would be presumptuous to undertake what she proposed without "the countenance & assistance of many distinguished citizens in the South & North." "Cd I add your name to those friendly to the undertaking," she wrote, "I shd embark on it with additional energy & pleasure," and she asked him to send her the names of other Southerners who might sympathize and help. Lafayette did what he could: he sent the proposal to James Monroe and to Chief Justice John Marshall, asking each to judge it candidly and write him or Fanny about it. He wrote Jackson that Fanny meant to consult him on "a delicate But Very Interesting Subject."[59]

Fanny had moved Lafayette from the center to the fringes of her life, and he suffered from his lost importance. Though he thought her plan the best-conceived he had seen, he believed she threw herself into it because she had been hurt through him. Things had not gone as well as he had hoped, he confessed to a friend in Paris, in part because of what he called feminine ill-will. As he saw the matter, he had tried to make up for the spite by abundant affection, but Fanny refused him the implicit trust she had given him before. She scorned criticism and sometimes took advice for reproach. Now, he said, her enthusiastic soul—tired of obstacles to a greater intimacy—had thrown itself into this cause of emancipation. She had turned to it as a way of answering the slanders against her, but it had come to absorb her attention: it had been a means and had become the end. Though oblivious to his own selfishness in the matter, Lafayette gained the insight into Fanny that pain can give. She was a devotee, and she had found a worthier object of devotion than he.[60]

Though Fanny had asked for help, she did not mean to wait in New York for it to come, and she and Camilla got ready to head south to start their new life. Five years earlier they had applied for citizenship, and now they discovered that they had completed their eligibility, even though they had not spent the intervening years in America. The act of becoming citizens was little more decisive, however, than their leaving Lafayette. When they said goodbye in a hot New York July, they all knew it could be their last parting.[61]

Lafayette stayed in the country long enough to celebrate his sixty-eighth birthday on September 6, 1825—the same day Fanny turned thirty—and then boarded the frigate *Brandywine* for his final return to France. Shortly after he left, Nelly Lewis threw a parting dagger at Fanny in a letter to a friend: "Would you believe that *Miss W* asserted in N.Y. that *she* had the *refusal* of Gen'l La Fayette's *hand*. It is *sacrilege*—He said to George, 'People little know the many ties I have, the devotion I feel for your mother's memory, or they would not circulate such reports.'" Fanny's rash devotion to Lafayette had exposed her to ridicule. And though she never admitted the hurt, she salved her feelings later that year with a gentle plague on those around him: "May the evening of his days be smooth; and tho the duty of cheering them rest not with those apparently best fitted to fulfil it well, if he shd not make the discovery it will be as if they were otherwise."[62]

Nashoba
and New Harmony

5

Early in the fall of 1825, Fanny left Camilla in Albion, Illinois, and rode out with George Flower toward Nashville to meet with Andrew Jackson. Because Camilla had been ill when they left New York, and had gone with her sister to what Jefferson called "our medicinal springs," Fanny asked her, as Camilla put it, "to forego the fatigue of exploring with her the state of Tennessee." No doubt, too, Eliza Flower needed help with her three children, and it made sense for Camilla to stay with her in Albion rather than to risk herself again in a grueling ride. She could also look in occasionally on Owen's experiment at New Harmony and learn some useful things about young settlements in the American wilderness. And so Fanny went off with George Flower to make what he called their long "preambulation" with no one to accompany or to assist them.[1]

By his own account, Flower had grown up in an affectionate family that had enjoyed a fair share of refinement and ease. He was much like Fanny: enthusiastic and sensitive, high-principled and proud. At the same time, he was so vulnerable to women that his sexuality had disrupted and marked his life. When Fanny met him, in fact, his marriage to Eliza was bigamous. He had had three children in England by his wife Jane before their relationship foundered in implacable hostility. Unable to get a divorce, he had emigrated to America, in large measure to escape her, and not long after, he met Eliza. By the end of 1825, in seven years, they had had five children, two of whom had died, and it was surely from his own so different experience that he observed of a Shaker settlement that "any society of bachelors and spinsters, without the expense, care, or trouble of childen, and discarding all personal love, may well be orderly, neat, and rich, and generally are so." He added with perhaps a touch of rue, "If they are satisfied under that arrangement, let nobody gainsay them." Years after he rode with Fanny into the Tennessee wilderness, he observed that there was a mysterious antagonism in the order of nature that ran through all life, vegetable and animal. Already he had some inkling of tragedy at the heart of things, which Fanny did not.[2]

When they got to the Hermitage, Jackson received them cordially. He told them he was favorably disposed to their plan and sent them southwest to look over a tract along the Wolf River on the Chickasaw Bluffs. It lay about fifteen miles from the trading post called Memphis and five miles from the Indian line. Early in October, Fanny and Flower rode into Memphis, spent four days exploring, and then saddled up once more for the almost 290-mile ride back to Nashville.[3]

The soil of the tract was second-rate, but Fanny decided on it in part because she thought the land more healthful back from the Mississippi and away from the marshes. "This is a point," she wrote, "but too much neglected by American settlers, who plunge into the fat river bottoms and hunt out sickness from Michigan to the Gulf of Mexico." Flower said they chose it because of "the nearness to Navigation, the health of the situation, & the excellence & length of the season for picking cotton." He also said there was rich land across the river which they could ultimately buy at government prices.[4]

On their return trip to Nashville, Fanny took one of the most difficult steps in her life: she bought ten slaves—six men and four women—for between $400 and $500 each. She had written about seeing slaves manacled and crushed into the boat taking them to the markets of Savannah. She had written about a black boy stolen in the forests of Indiana. Perhaps because it was too troubling, she did not describe what she felt when she bought ten of those she called her fellow-creatures.[5]

In late November, she paid $480 for 320 acres in the tract to which Jackson had directed her. Those who witnessed the transaction included George Flower and James Richardson, a Scotsman from Perth whom Fanny met for the first time there in Memphis. She immediately found workmen to dig a well, to raise two double log cabins, and to clear some of the land, and she also hired a black serving girl and rented a house in town. Using the Chickasaw word for the Wolf River that coursed through her land, she named it Nashoba. She continued to negotiate for another 320 acres and expected within a few months to get an option for 600 more.[6]

She published the plan for her settlement in the local papers and wrote Benjamin Lundy's *Genius of Universal Emancipation* that "the principal people of the state" concurred in it. She announced that Nashoba would soon need carpenters, bricklayers, and other good craftsmen, and she was eager to have free people, white or black, as soon as houses were ready for them. She would open the school "as soon as practicable" and expected to have the various businesses established at least by midsummer 1826.[7]

Meanwhile Flower worked as an equal partner. Concerned as they were about tales of settlers rashly risking their health, and worried that mill dams might be dangerous in that climate, Flower asked Frederick Rapp to inquire in Pittsburgh about a steam engine that would run both a grist mill and a cotton gin. He ordered glass, cotton shirting, linsey for workmen's jackets and trousers, and a variety of nails, hoes, and axes. In mid-November he rode the 370 miles to Albion in eleven winter days to get supplies, and by the first of December he had sent a flatboat laden with meal, corn flour, a yoke of oxen, a wagon, two horses, and "sundry furniture and implements of husbandry" down the Mississippi toward Memphis. Fanny expected him back almost immediately with his family and Camilla.[8]

Lafayette had written Fanny that James Monroe approved the project on the understanding that it be undertaken in the South and that the slaves be colonized. Now Thomas Jefferson, evasive but by no means discouraging, wrote a long and careful letter that was an extraordinary testimony to his respect for Fanny. He told her that the abolition of slavery was not impossible and that "Every plan should be adopted, every experiment tried, which may do something towards the ultimate object." Her proposal had "its aspects of promise." Although he wondered if "moral urgencies" were sufficient to prompt blacks to labor, there was as yet too little evidence to decide that question. He closed on a note as positive as Fanny might have wished: "You are young, dear Madam, and have powers of mind which may do much in exciting others in this arduous task. I am confident they will be so exerted, and I pray to Heaven for their success, and that you may be rewarded with the blessings which such efforts merit."[9]

In James Madison, according to Lafayette, Fanny had "no better friend in the United States." But Madison, ever the more pragmatic statesman, called seriously into question some of Fanny's fundamental assumptions. He took exception to her belief that white labor would come to fill the place left by black and implied that therefore men who owned the land would be loath to let slaves go. He wondered at "the aptitude and adequacy of the process by which the slaves are at the same time to earn the funds . . . required for their emancipation & removal; and to be sufficiently educated for a life of freedom and of social order."[10]

With her proposals for education he saw no insuperable problems but suspected that Fanny knew too little about how and why people worked: "I am not satisfied either that the prospect of emancipation at a future day will sufficiently overcome the natural and habitual repugnance to labour, or that there is such an advantage of united over individual labour as is taken for granted." Spaniards, he said, had offered slaves the chance to work out their freedom, and few had taken it. It seemed to him that fewer still would work hard when they had to share with others the benefits of their work.

To the religious motive and the religious authority that made the Harmonists and Shakers so successful, Madison thought Fanny offered no substitute of remotely equal power. Though she could learn from the Harmonists' "general organization" and the "distribution and details" of the work they did, "the code of rules by which Mr. Rap manages his conscientious & devoted flock, & enriches a common treasury," must be irrelevant to her scheme. He suggested that a smaller establishment would serve the purposes of experiment equally well and be more likely to succeed. Despite his warnings, Fanny should not question "either my admiration of the generous philanthropy which dictated [her plan], or my sense of the special regard it evinces for the honor & welfare of our expanding, & I trust rising Republic."

Madison's bleak viewpoint was both troubling and unanswerable. If he were right about why people worked and what they lived for, Fanny's experiment would fail. She and Flower could not modify their proposal on the basis of what he said without abandoning it, but they could limit its scope. They decided to try a smaller experiment, partly in deference to Madison, but largely because they had not raised the money they hoped for.

They had counted for financial support on an American network similar to the one in Europe that fed The Cause. Accordingly, various papers published Fanny's proposal in October and it circulated in pamphlet form, but by late fall, 1825, no one had sent either slaves or money. Flower thought that avarice and the fear of losing face had kept people from giving up their slaves, though many said they would do so when they saw a flourishing establishment. In early December Fanny began to suspect that no offers of subscription money would come. She wished she had quietly started a small, private experiment and waited to ask publicly for help until she had some practical experience to support the claims she made. Asking for money, she wrote the Quaker Jeremiah Thompson in New York, was a task for which she was "ill fitted . . . There is an awkwardness in suing for assistance, although in a good cause." The world, she suspected, accused her of being presumptuous and vain, as it did most who proposed to reform abuses or to relieve suffering, but she resolved to keep on as ever, though "within the narrow limits prescribed by my own fortune and that of the friends who may voluntarily unite their efforts to mine." If they could raise their food and make their clothing, the money she could commit might do.[11]

She wrote Thompson, however, for practical help. She had discovered that merchants made "exorbitant" profits in the south and west from "a ruinous system of long credits." In order to bypass such merchants, she wanted to open a small store dealing only in cash, investing $1,000 of her own money and putting back into the store whatever profits it made. She commissioned Thompson to send her stout domestic cotton for shirts and sheets, white and red flannels, heavy blankets of different sizes, printed calico, several dozen heavy wool men's socks, and sturdy shoes for men and boys.

Her hopes were plagued with misleading rumors. About the same time she was resolving to cut back on Nashoba, *The Genius of Universal Emancipation* reported that Fanny had "ample funds at command, as several wealthy gentlemen have contributed largely." She hastened to set people straight. Saying Nashoba had a little money and a great deal of good will, she described their funds as "too limited to admit of any thing like a fair experiment of 'the Plan.'" In fact, Benjamin Lundy's editorial comments in the *Genius* made it clear that many people dismissed Fanny's idea, and more than a few seemed hostile. Lundy had sent copies of her proposal to editors he considered friendly to emancipation, but many had declined to publish it. In mid-December he appealed to them again to "comply with so reasonable a request on behalf of a female friend to the 'nation's guest.'"[12]

It was a grueling time for a woman daring to strike out on her own. For almost six months, Fanny lived every day with the precariousness of the financial base on which her freedom to do what she wanted depended. She had asked Lafayette to send her some stock certificates she had left in Paris but learned at the end of the year that he was unable to find them. They represented all of Camilla's property and a third of Fanny's, and Camilla wrote the Garnetts in "amazement and alarm" that "if irretrievably lost as I judge them to be we may be reduced from independence to beggary." Meanwhile the cotton boom in Liverpool turned to bust, and cotton that had been as high as 21¢ plummeted to 9¼¢ by the end of July. Two years earlier, Vincent Nolte, the agent of Baring's Bank, had taken about 140,000 francs from the Wright sisters' estate and put it, at Fanny's request, in Louisiana State Bank stock. At 4.98 francs to the dollar, their investment was roughly equivalent to $28,000. Now the interest rates were sinking, and Nolte, who had taken a major risk speculating in cotton, had gone bankrupt. Fanny thought Nolte's ruin compelled her own, but by late spring in 1826 she was safe: Lafayette had found the stock certificates and Nolte had managed to rescue her investment in the Louisiana State Bank.[13]

Fanny bore her troubles stoically, looked to the future, and found that her commitment gave her peace. She rode out occasionally from Memphis to tell the workers which trees to preserve and which to fell, and to watch the logs and chimneys rise on the cabins that would be their home. New people came into her life: Marcus and Mary Winchester, Anderson B. Carr and his wife, and the Scotsman James Richardson, who loomed ominously over her future.[14]

Marcus Brutus Winchester was a man to win Fanny's loyalty. The eldest son of Andrew Jackson's friend and sometime business partner, General James Winchester, he was an engaging mixture of elegant gentleman and egalitarian who had recently married a free black woman. (They were to have eight children and would call their oldest boy Robert Owen and their second daughter Frances Wright.) In 1819, he and Carr had gone into business together as the first merchants in the Memphis area. In 1824 his father gave him 420 acres in what became downtown Memphis, and he subsequently became a land agent, a county Democratic leader, postmaster, and, when the town was incorporated in late 1826, its first mayor. He built the courthouse and the jail, and his house was the biggest in town. His general store was a place where the townspeople gathered and where Indians and backwoodsmen came to trade, and Fanny learned as much there as an English lady could about American frontier democracy.[15]

About Mary Winchester we know only that Fanny and Camilla came to love her; that she was known for "acts of charity, liberal donations to religious purposes, exemplary and unobtrusive deportment"; and that more than a decade later she would suffer a peculiar form of American cruelty when she was barred by special ordinance from the town of

Memphis as a "free person of color." Carr and his wife remain even deeper in the shadows. Always helpful and neighborly, they were the kind of enterprising people who do best on the frontier.[16]

Richardson, on the other hand, was strangely out of place there. Robert Dale Owen was to call him "upright, impractical, and an acute metaphysician of the Thomas Brown school." Richardson liked to write curtly to the papers on such matters as the nature and relevance of human happiness. When Fanny met him in Memphis, he was slowly recovering from a painful illness that had struck him in New Orleans more than a year before. The prospect of taking part in her experiment gave him the purpose he evidently wanted, and Fanny came to trust him with Nashoba's bookkeeping. She was soon to write of him that he "unites to the invaluable qualities of trust prudence and accurate attention to business a finely cultivated mind with every liberal and generous opinion and sentiment."[17]

These, then, were the people who wove in and out of Fanny's daily life while she waited in Memphis for her partners in the great experiment. The winter was extremely cold. The Mississippi was low and clogged with ice. And nature in its various forms conspired to keep Camilla and the Flowers four hundred miles away in Illinois and for three months delayed their plans. It forced Fanny Wright against her bent to patience.

She was not daunted. The day after Christmas, Fanny wrote a letter to an acquaintance in Paris heightening the romance, underlining the noble purpose, and ignoring the practicalities, slights, and uncertainties of the grand drama that was to be Nashoba. She wrote of forest land still full of bears, wolves, and panthers, and pictured herself galloping her white horse over rough, open country. She slept in log cabins open on all sides, she said, and even in the woods, with a bearskin for a bed and a saddle for her pillow. She endured extremes of heat and cold and had never felt better or stronger in her life. She could now ride forty miles a day without fatigue, and she did so often, going between Memphis and Nashoba, greeting the Indians who were her nearest neighbors as they came to sell their furs. She prayed God for a little rain, drank milk from her cow, ate venison from the Indians, and warmed herself at the great fire in her cabin. She closed by saying, "Je commence à chérir la vie"—I begin to cherish life. It was a letter to spark envious whisperings in the Faubourg St. Honoré.[18]

The frontier realities that Fanny and her colleagues faced were quite another matter, and they culled out all but the very strong. Early that December George Flower almost died. After a few days in Albion, he was unexpectedly called to return to Memphis, but at Flims Ferry, about twenty miles below New Harmony, he was seized with a violent fever. No one would help him except a Tennesseean named Husbands Fewkes, who went to Albion for a doctor and for Eliza, who found her husband "in a Cabin quite alone . . . without food of any kind— covered with dirt—sitting up on a pallet upon the ground—gnawing his fingers ends." For days he lay at the point of death, and it was more than a month before he began to mend. He then got word that ice had stopped the boat he had sent to Memphis the first of December.[19]

Nor did illness and ice seem the only disturbing signs in Nashoba's future. Fanny had learned early on to discount the opinions of well-meaning skeptics like Charles Wilkes, who wrote Lafayette of the Wrights: "They are creatures of a higher stamp than common mortals and with such enthusiasm, there is no reasoning. The experiment they are intent upon must be tried; I much fear it can no further succeed, than to ameliorate the condition of the few fortunate objects which their limited plan enables them to try to the experiment upon. I despair of any extensive or lasting benefits." Despite Wilkes, Camilla had doubted neither their plan's importance nor its ultimate success, but now she discovered that Eliza Flower had been dubious from the first. And Eliza mattered to Nashoba. Already proven in the trials of the wilderness, she jealously guarded her family's interests and sized up her antagonists. "Our domestic felicity their malice cd never inter-rupt," she told Camilla, "and notwithstanding all we have endured I have enjoyed years of happiness that my worst enemy mgt envy me." Now her husband proposed to uproot her and three small childen— one of them a baby at the breast—to take them almost four hundred miles away to strangers, virgin land, and Mississippi mosquitoes even thicker than those in Illinois. She let Camilla know that she had no faith in their colony's success, and Camilla began to read Fanny's letters "full of encouraging and sanguine expectations" with a sense of foreboding. She wrote in fact that if their own experiment failed, Robert Owen's new town would be their "*resource and resting place and one that I cd look to with infinite satisfaction.*"[20]

In assuring Julia and Harriet of their ultimate security, Camilla imagined Owen's experiment as the root of which their own was a branch, and she was correct. Though Nashoba was an attempt to confront slavery, Fanny conceived it as a colony of the same kind as New Harmony. When she heard Owen in Washington, she first heard ideas publicly discussed that she had harbored secretly much of her life, and his conviction allowed her to believe they might have power in the world. Neither Owen nor Fanny, for instance, trusted the commercial instinct to shape a society in which justice and generosity would prevail. Both looked to cooperation rather than competition for the foundation of the decent life. Both were organizing a community without religious sanction and therefore outside mainstream America.

Owen's success in sparking interest in New Harmony, moreover, seemed to prove that he had touched a crucial nerve, that there was a well of discontent in America from which he and Fanny could draw. Despite the universal pursuit of happiness, many apparently had not found it, and Owen's call for people to come to New Harmony to discover how to be happy had proved intoxicating. People attracted to the possibilities of communal life were rejecting the established order, along with claims that incremental reform could lead ultimately to a society in which they could fruitfully live. They were rejecting the rhetoric of individualism as too ready an excuse for selfishness, and against a background of bloody repression in Europe, they were rejecting revolution as a danger that could create a world even more coercive and menacing. Owen's call for people to create New Harmony had come at a time when social experiment was tolerated in the nation; when the pressures of incipient industrialism had not yet made small communities seem a backward-looking answer to economic reality; when, on the contrary, it seemed that an experiment like New Harmony could affect the evolving American economy.[21]

Camilla was also correct when she assumed implicitly that Owen had a greater chance than Fanny to succeed. To push so decidedly against the cultural grain required resources of no common order, and Owen's were abundant. He was beginning New Harmony with a wealth of equipment and machinery. He had a substantial personal fortune and an international reputation. And he had already proved himself as an organizer by turning the demoralized mill town of New Lanark into one of the wonders of the world. Fanny and George Flower, on the other hand, had no more than enthusiasm, intelligence, some money, and 320 acres of land.

But the stories coming out of New Harmony those fall and winter months were troubling to those who had wished the community well. Owen had gone back to England early that summer to close out his affairs, and in his absence the organization had begun to go awry. Over a thousand people now crowded into a town that comfortably held about eight hundred, and disorder was epidemic.

The Harmonists had been famous for their hard work and the excellence of the goods they produced, but people came back from

New Harmony now telling how both land and industries were lying fallow. When Owen had issued his cheerful invitations, he had neglected to say that the town needed mainly skilled craftsmen. By October it had few spinners to turn out wool, few skilled workers to produce cotton yarn, and no one to direct the dyeing house. There were no potters, saddlers, harness makers, leather dressers, coppersmiths, brush makers, comb makers, glaziers, painters, or bookbinders. Nor, apparently, could the town adequately staff the flourmill or the sawmills. As one newcomer, Thomas Pears, remarked, "instead of striving who should do most, the most industry was manifested in accusing others of doing little."[22]

Obviously distraught with the elder Owen's casual disregard for the number of people New Harmony could hold and the kind of people it needed to make it work, William Owen wrote his father in mid-December: "We have *no lime, no rocks* (ready blasted), *no brick, no timber, no boards, no shingles,* nothing requisite for buildings, and as to getting them from others, *they are not to be had in the whole country.* We must ourselves produce the whole of them, before we can build, we must dig and burn the lime, dig and blast the rocks, mould and burn the bricks, fell and saw the boards and split the shingles, and to do all these things, we have no hands to spare, or the branches of business in the Society must stop, and they cannot stop, or the whole Society would stop too." Hogs had destroyed the gardens and eaten the vegetables. By January 1826, they were out of coffee, sugar, thread, paper, and many other necessary things.[23]

As for the spirit of the place, accounts clashed. Richard Flower reported that by December a hundred people had been expelled for idleness or intemperance, while others had left in disgust—"the industrious being no longer willing to work for the Indolent part of the Society." The newcomer William Pelham, on the one hand, insisted that no one brawled or idly delighted to wound another's feelings: "I have not heard an offensive word spoken by a single individual . . . the general tenor of the conversation is of a serious philosophical cast." On the other hand, Thomas Pears, who had begun with something akin to worship for Robert Owen and who had been there three months longer than Pelham, wrote, "we have not yet done with scandal, calumny, nor self-interest, nor the love of power or distinction."[24]

They battled over all the problems of governance. They held at least weekly meetings to discuss community affairs—a seven-member governing committee presenting its rules and the other members petitioning and arguing with the committee. Everyone squabbled about the allowance, which began as a fixed credit of $80 a year for each adult, though according to Thomas Pears, the community decided eventually to provide up to $180 worth of food and clothing annually. Only the laziest, therefore, believed that they were fairly treated. They quibbled about definitions; they disputed procedure. Everyone hoped for Robert Owen's quick return.[25]

Nevertheless, there was an exuberant life to the place that gave heart to people like Camilla and George Flower who wanted it to succeed. Every week there were balls and concerts—New Harmony taking music almost as seriously as Harmonie had, and dancing even more so, as it was one of Robert Owen's passions. They held debates, drills, and parades. Unlike the Rappites, the New Harmonists differed widely on matters of belief, and they disputed religion freely, though it seems without rancor. They listened to itinerant and resident preachers, from Swedenborgians and Universalists to Methodists and Baptists. They gathered on the streets or in front of the tavern to talk of whatever moved them, and they did without the forms and ceremonies so important in the world outside. Young people in particular loved it. But the word from New Harmony to Nashoba would have to be a word of caution.

In mid-January 1826, Camilla learned that the river was rising—the Allegheny snows had begun to melt—and she was soon "on the wing to Memphis." She and the Flowers with their children and their necessaries rode to New Harmony and on to the river to hail a steamboat. None passed ready to risk the trip, and in mid-February they settled for a flatboat winding slowly toward the Gulf. The flatboat got snagged, but by the end of the month they came at last to Memphis.[26]

"After all of our perils disasters and delays," Fanny wrote the Garnetts, they were together at last. Nevertheless, and unaccountably, their sheep and cattle remained in Illinois. The cow Fanny had bought in Memphis would have to do for at least several months. Nor were the supplies Flower had ordered from Economy on their way down the Mississippi. Frederick Rapp had written in December that since the Ohio was solid with ice and nothing could get out until the spring, he assumed they would arrange to get their goods elsewhere.[27].

Flower discovered, further, that Fanny had gotten only one response to her plan—a response that might well have made her wish her appeal had fallen entirely on deaf ears. What he read about Nashoba had elated one Robert Wilson of South Carolina, to whom a relative had left a family of seven slaves whom he was directed to raise and to emancipate as they came of age. Opposed to slavery and unwilling to own slaves, he nevertheless could not afford to pay their way to Haiti or Liberia. When he heard of Frances Wright's proposal, he saw hope for both his slaves and himself, and was ready to go seven hundred miles to reach her.

On February 9, 1826, Fanny had formally agreed to pay Wilson $446.76 for his expenses in buying one of the slaves' unexpired work contract and in bringing them from South Carolina to West Tennessee. In return, she got a "*family of Negroes,* to wit: Lukey, aged between 35 and 40 years, and her six children, named Maria, Harriet, Elvira, Isabel, Viole and Delilah." Fanny agreed to care for them, educate them, and emancipate them within at least fifteen years, as well as to colonize them at her own expense. Lukey was pregnant. Her eldest daughter was about twenty, her youngest under three. According to Wilson, they were lazy, but even had the older ones been tough and eager, no one would have deliberately chosen seven females for the brutal work of clearing forests, building fences, and raising cabins. Still, Fanny could put them to other work that had to be done, and they were the first people she had had a chance to shape for freedom.[28]

On the first of March, just a few days after Camilla and the Flowers landed, the slaves Fanny had bought arrived by steamboat from Nashville. For reasons that remained unexplained, only eight adults came, five men and three women, along with three of their children. The men seemed to be good hands: they were Willis, Jacob, Grandison, Redick, and Henry. The women—Nelly, Peggy, and Kitty—were used to working in the fields but preferred, as Fanny put it, to be idle. She now began her job of gentle persuasion.[29]

They officially broke ground on March 3. The next day Fanny sent Rapp $400, and Richardson made out a long list of the things they needed: three plows and a half-dozen plow molds, hoes and axes, spades and shovels, a dozen small, covered tin pails and pans in assorted sizes, tin coffee pots and cups, flints, tow linen, bed ticking, shirting, a variety of saws, planes, files, hinges, and three dozen thumb latches. When Rapp sent the order off in mid-April—everything except the pewter plates and a slipper bath—he told Fanny that the machinery at Economy, the Rappites' new town, was in full operation and was "much superior to those we formerly had." The contrast was painful. By that time Fanny had realized it would be at least two years before her farm could possibly thrive, and three before they could get a return on their investment.[30]

Still, Nashoba exhilarated Fanny: axes were ringing in the day, and one of the slaves played a fiddle at night while the others sang in chorus. After six weeks, everyone struck her as cheerful and content. Jeremiah Thompson had donated goods worth $580 to begin the store, calling it in his engaging Quaker way "my mite in aid of thy good efforts." She expected a carpenter and blacksmith any day and hoped soon to have a shoemaker. She planned to have two cows brought in the next flatboat of provisions, though she did not think they could bring the rest of their cattle until the fall or the following spring.[31]

She imagined a graceful future. Their cabins were a quarter mile from the Wolf River, and on its banks they would build a washhouse, a bathhouse, and a dairy. They would open some of the wooded land to pasture and make secluded walks along the meadowside. It would be the good life: simple, purposeful, and rich with human kindness.

In every letter, Fanny talked about how busy they were. Despite a great deal of rain, they managed by the beginning of May to raise the buildings they needed immediately and to fence them. They cleared and fenced five acres and started an apple orchard. They put in potatoes, opened fifteen acres for corn, and planted two acres of what Fanny called old ground in cotton. "For this climate we are too late to expect a good crop," she wrote Benjamin Lundy, and "only consider our farm as having made a start for next year." They now had a store to supply the neighborhood and a small tavern to accommodate visitors. They also started regular Sunday evening classes and built a room large enough so the blacks could dance twice a week. The next time Fanny went to New Harmony, she planned to bring back a flute to add to the fiddle. So many people now wrote to inquire about Nashoba that Fanny asked the *Genius* to insert a notice that all such letters should be prepaid. She was amazed at their success: "We were told of difficulties & apprehended many . . . Truly as yet we have found none worthy of the name."[32]

Their letters to Lundy's *Genius* show that Fanny and Flower had thought carefully about how to persuade the slaves to work, and that they were determined to use coercion only as a last resort. With the exception of the oldest girl, Maria, they found the South Carolina slaves lazy. Within three months, however, and without harsh measures, the family was working "cheerfully and steadily," and some had become useful field hands. Lukey, who was six months pregnant, did all their washing, and her daughter Viole began to sew for them. Although the family had the bad habits that slavery typically bred—lying, petty thievery, quarreling, and "among each other . . . the use of abusive language," Fanny saw these habits already diminishing and by no means despaired of curing them altogether, "as we can carry gradually all our views into effect for their employment, comfort and instruction."[33]

Only once did they resort to punishment, Fanny wrote, in "a bad case of theft, malice, and obduracy in one of the Nashville girls." After persuasion had repeatedly failed, they put her in solitary confinement on a diet of bread and water. Within twenty-four hours "her obduracy gave way and we were enabled to release her. As this was the first punishment inflicted, it made considerable impression."

So encouraged by their experience with the South Carolina family that they were willing to accept others, Fanny was nevertheless determined now to select them carefully. She asked Lundy to have those interested send her the number, sexes, and ages of the slaves they proposed to bring. Ready even to buy families of slaves, she and Flower would pay in annual installments but could pay full market value only for healthy black men. They could not pay at all for children or old people, for the expenses of educating the one and maintaining the other were substantial in themselves. They could pay only a reduced price for women because, as Flower put it, they had no value at Nashoba as breeders.[34]

Deliberately holding back the power they had, they treated their slaves as responsible men and women. Instead of wanting to make money from slave labor, they wanted to shape men and women capable of directing their own lives. They did not use the lash, nor did they intimidate the slaves with an overseer's presence. They directed them, according to Flower, "in the usual way that free laborers would be." They fed them three good meals a day and gave them all their necessary clothing. "Their work is conducted by themselves. Advice is given them to refrain from any bad habits they may have contracted." The goal was to inspire "habitual industry voluntarily arising amongst the people themselves, induced by advice and example." Nothing was forced—not even education: "By slackening the hand of authority over them, until it is totally withdrawn, it is believed that they will not only be well disposed and industrious, but prudently managing, and wise."

Such language was not the kind one often heard within the precincts of slavery. The black people at Nashoba had grown up with violence, suspicion, and contempt, and Fanny and Flower knew that the confidence they hoped to build would be a long time in coming. They knew the blacks would tease and test them. They knew that only long after they had proved they meant all the things they said could the blacks afford to trust them and take on the hard job of self-discipline. Fanny and Flower were prepared to wait.

They seem to have had less success with the whites who lived outside Memphis. The neighboring planters apparently did what they could to hinder them. Donald MacDonald, who had left New Harmony in disillusion only a few days behind Camilla and the Flowers, brooded on Nashoba as his steamboat passed the Chickasaw Bluffs: "the surrounding proprietors are said to be very jealous of its interests, & throw obstacles in the way of its progress." Nor were the letters about Nashoba that Benjamin Lundy published wholly encouraging. A South Carolinian wrote the *Genius* attacking Fanny's arrangement with Robert Wilson: "Who would not be a philanthropist, if 460 dollars advanced, would yield 5000 dollars in fifteen years? and who would have the disgrace of being a slave holder, if they could make more out of slaves, than slaveholders?"[35]

Serious problems also arose in the undercurrents that coursed among the whites at Nashoba itself. Fanny later wrote that people brought up in the old world in the old way, as they had been, developed habits that made communal living painfully difficult. The embarrassing truth was that ordinary things could make a hash of high-mindedness. One person's pleasures could savage another's nerves: they mined the field of communal life. The differences between the people at Nashoba shadowed forth inescapable conflicts.

Eliza Flower was nursing a baby and keeping track of two small children. Even had she believed in Nashoba, she could have taken no part in the work that drew the rest of them together. She was bound to resent being peripheral to the central purpose there, and perhaps it was her resentment that prompted the Flowers to settle in Memphis. It provides at least a reason why a man who intended to supervise slaves and manage a farm would choose to live fifteen miles away from where he labored. At the same time, James Richardson's penchant for metaphysics would likely have annoyed George Flower, a gentle but tough-minded pragmatist. Nor could Richardson have found understanding or sympathy for the slow process of self-definition that the blacks had to experience. And there was Fanny herself. Camilla had grown up under the shelter of Fanny's formidable will, but no one else was likely to stand aside and give Fanny the precedence she instinctively demanded. Finally, there were the sexual tensions and rivalries their culture taught them neither to admit nor even to recognize, and these could shred less fragile dreams than theirs.[36]

But by midsummer Fanny felt so good about their progress that she wrote Julia and Harriet twice about their coming to look over Nashoba. Mrs. Garnett was an obvious problem. She could not be "fixed with comfort to any of us" here, Fanny said, but within the year New Harmony should be a pleasant place for her to live. By that time Julia and Harriet could be useful at Nashoba, probably in the schools. Fanny suggested that one of them come as *"avant courier,"* Harriet seeming the more likely. So convinced were Fanny and Camilla that Harriet would soon be on her way they made a list of things for her to bring: sturdy percale, fifty yards of gingham, swiss muslin for neck scarves, two dozen cambric handkerchiefs, two yards of corset material, two boxes of cologne, two dozen toothbrushes, and a syringe. Nor is it clear that the Wright sisters' expectation that Julia and Harriet would come was wholly fanciful. Robina Craig Millar heard that they had "taken a *lease* of a house in Paris, that it might operate as an obstacle" to their going to Nashoba.[37]

By now Fanny's commitment was so complete that she had bought about eighteen hundred acres of land, some of it no doubt the rich tract George Flower had noticed across the river, and she felt confident enough in Nashoba to let it do briefly without her. New Harmony teased her curiosity. Camilla and the Flowers had brought her tales of the tempestuous beginnings of Robert Owen's residence on the Wabash. Each month since then the *New Harmony Gazette* had come spelling out its bewildering mixture of trouble and excitement. And now she wanted to see for herself.

She seems also to have heard the rumblings of the second Great Awakening, the evangelical Protestant revival movement beginning to sweep the country, and she had taken Owen's side in opposition to it. Signing herself "A Friend," she had written the *New Harmony Gazette* defending Owen against the charge of irreligion that newspapers throughout the country delighted in printing. Religion was a belief, she said, while virtue was a practice. Religion was by no means necessary to virtue: "Not only have an infinite number of the purest hearts, and most gifted intellects in ancient and modern times been wholly devoid of religion,—but there exist those who consider religion as decidedly *injurious* to virtue."[38]

Most of those who had come with Owen to New Harmony felt indifferent or even hostile to organized religion, and two were people Fanny had met earlier in Paris. One was William Maclure, a wealthy

Frances Wright in the New Harmony dress

Robert Owen

Robert Dale Owen

George Flower

Frances Trollope

Scotch philanthropist and scientist who felt close enough to Fanny that he once referred to her by her first name—a familiarity unusual for the time. The other was William S. Phiquepal, a French teacher whose schools in Paris and Philadelphia Maclure had subsidized. For some time Maclure had been trying to convince Fanny that her talents would be better employed at New Harmony, where the scale of good, as he put it, was much more extended than at Nashoba. Someone else could run her community, and she could go downriver anytime she had to. As an enticement for her to visit New Harmony, he offered to outfit her school with teachers if she would come to help. It was not an offer she could ignore, and she set off apparently in June.[39]

Maclure was another of the gifted, quirky men whose admiration for Fanny gives an idea how powerful and how promising she was. So shrewd a merchant that he had been able to retire before forty with a substantial fortune, Maclure then came to the United States and devoted himself to science, education, and social reform. He so distinguished himself as a geologist that in 1817 he had been elected president of the Philadelphia Academy of Natural Sciences. He supported schools taught by Phiquepal, Joseph Neef, and his special friend Mme. Marie Fretageot—all of them influenced by the Swiss educator, J. H. Pestalozzi, who would influence Fanny through them. Pestalozzi had convinced Maclure and his disciples that the poor were not in themselves responsible for their poverty but were so devastated by it that they could not, for the most part, rise above it. His students had learned, accordingly, to teach by using concrete objects like blocks and scales, and to emphasize moral and physical education. His influence turned them against the classical languages, which formed the bulk of the curriculum at the time, as well as against coercion and punishment. Maclure and his teachers brought Pestalozzi to the American West, if only in spirit, and his influence was significant on all they reached. Maclure had also become the patron of Charles-Alexandre Lesueur, a naturalist-draftsman; Thomas Say, an entomologist and conchologist; and the Dutch geologist Gerard Troost. He brought all of them with him in January 1826, in a keelboat they called the "Philanthropist," and to which those already at New Harmony referred as "The Boatload of Knowledge."[40]

Maclure joined Owen with some reluctance, suspecting that American audiences felt for Owen "only indifference bordering on contempt." Still, when he visited the school at New Lanark, he remarked on "the vast improvement in society effected by Mr. Robert Owen's courage and perserverance in spite of an inveterate and malignant opposition." After more than a year of Mme. Fretageot's insistent prodding, Maclure finally consented to join forces with him in Indiana.[41]

Now in his early sixties, Maclure was more radical than Owen and more aware of human weakness, including his own. In 1819 a Paris censor had barred publication of some of his essays on the grounds that they were too democratic. Maclure believed that society divided itself into two classes, the productive and the nonproductive. It could also be divided into the governors and the governed, he said, and the divisions tended unhappily to coincide, in that those who governed were also those who did not produce. Most laws, he believed, were unjust, and reform had to begin with the producing class: "None but the millions can benefit the millions."

Nevertheless, Maclure himself was an inveterate benefactor: he devoted much of his wealth and energy to educating those who might lead the way to a future more just. Calling ignorance a truly diabolical evil, he rejected his own classical education, which he said had left him ignorant as a pig of anything useful. He worked instead, as Owen did, to discover how to educate all people to productive lives. He believed that free institutions demanded an almost equal division of knowledge, property, and power, and that schools were "the only mode an individual has to benefit or improve mankind." Such ideas were not uniquely his, but his force of conviction caught Fanny's respect, and he pointed her in directions that she would pursue more boldly than he ultimately thought wise.[42]

While Fanny was in New Harmony then, she saw for herself the extraordinary difficulty of putting together a new community of free men and women. Owen was now reorganizing New Harmony for the third time in five months. Maclure had wanted to stand aside from the tedious if democratic process of making the community run and to spend his time instead organizing the library and the laboratory. But the shifting alliances and uncertain organizational structures had disrupted the calm he needed. He had begun to believe that Owen was dangerously inept, and some of the community anti-intellectual. So he had suggested organizing the community into three smaller units—an Education Society, an Agricultural and Pastoral Society, and a Mechanic and Manufacturing Society—and his proposal had been endorsed by the members. Maclure had paid Owen for the land and buildings he needed for the Education Society, and just before Fanny had arrived there, he had left New Harmony for several months in the belief that his schools would progress in his absence, undisturbed by any of Owen's whims—organizational, philosophical, or financial.[43]

Fanny learned that Maclure would underwrite the expenses of the Education Society and run it as a benevolent despot, for the most part through Mme. Fretageot, but neither Fanny nor anyone else could see clearly what economic relationships were to prevail in Owen's part of town. Was Owen to be employer? Landlord? Philanthropist? Or some combination of the three? Other basic questions remained unanswered. How would New Harmony attract and hold good workmen, who could make a better living in the despised old society? How would social pioneers organize a community of goods? How would they keep the books, much less balance them? Abstractions and high principles aside, it was unclear where they would find the basic ingredients and how they would blend them to fashion the New Moral World.

So much had changed since Fanny's visit the summer before. The wood church had been turned over to shops for craftsmen. They were partitioning the ends of the brick church for school rooms, a library, and a museum, and Troost, Lesueur, and others were busy arranging space for their teaching and research. Owen was working on the houses for married couples so that each would have "a chamber and an alcove," which he expected to be adequate since older children would live in the boarding schools and younger ones would be in the nursery. Because they all would eat in a commons, private kitchens were superfluous.

Fanny also saw an entirely different social life from that of Rapp's Harmonie: it was disorderly, cheerful, and irreverent. The society had adopted a uniform for both men and women that consisted of bloomers, with a dress or jacket over them that came to the knees. However, according to a visitor in April, neither costume nor philosophy had yet been able to transcend certain social differences. One woman told him huffily that "some of the society were too low, and the table was below all criticism." The better educated kept together and ignored the others; "tatterdemalions" lounged on the platform during one of Owen's speeches; and instead of dancing at a ball, many lower-class men sat reading newspapers.[44]

To violations of good form, however, Fanny was indifferent. As a genuine democrat who wanted both to learn and to teach, she felt very much at home in New Harmony. According to her sister, "her talents and influence had no small share in settling many important matters relative to the interests of the School and Society there." She won the trust and admiration of Owen's eldest son, Robert Dale, and of Robert Jennings and Richesson Whitby, and they won hers. She encountered the festering influence of Paul Brown, a dour communist who railed at Owen for refusing to give over his property to all who asked for it. "It is as common for women to be found flocking round a rich man," Brown would write savagely, "as butterflies round a rich slough, more especially if he has anything of a knack at dissimulation."[45]

It was probably in those days at New Harmony that Fanny began to see herself as a public teacher. The Education Society had almost four hundred students, most of them from the community but some from other parts of the country. To get ideas for Nashoba, Fanny studied the practical arrangements Maclure and Mme. Fretageot had made. Because they were determined to prove that students could feed and clothe themselves and learn at the same time, each student worked up to half a day at some kind of necessary labor. In their curriculum the sciences replaced the classics, and each student learned to do intellectually significant work as an apprentice to those who had already distinguished themselves. No doubt Fanny herself was held up as a model. Though not a scientist, she had published two books and a play. She had seriously studied drama, history, political theory, philosophy, and slavery. She talked so well she had held her own with some of the more interesting people of her time, and having a large captive audience thrilled her.

She may have heard Robert Owen give his "Declaration of Mental Independence" in the town square on July 4, or she may have read it later in the *Gazette*. Whatever the mode by which she received it, it had a decisive impact on her. The occasion was auspicious—the fiftieth anniversary of the Declaration of Independence—and Owen argued that in 1776 men had not stood for political liberty alone. They had stood for the right to think freely on "all subjects, secular and religious; and the right to express those thoughts openly." He argued that the greatest men who had signed the Declaration had wanted to go further, but people had not been ready. They were ready now, Owen thought, and he was the man to lead them. They were ready to war against the three evils that had corrupted and confused human history: private property, absurd and irrational systems of religion, and the institution of marriage. He asked, "Are you, indeed, willing to sacrifice your fortunes, lives, and reputations, if such sacrifices should be necessary, to secure for all your fellow beings, the GREATEST GOOD, that, according to our present knowlege, it is possible for them ever to receive?"[46]

Not long after, Fanny wrote that Robert Owen was to "influence the condition of mankind [more] than any individual that has ever existed" and that the principles he advocated "have been mine ever since I learnt to think." Others shared her sense of Owen's importance. The *Gazette* began to date its issues from the day of his speech: "The First Year of Mental Independence," "The Second Year of Mental Independence," and so on. As it turned out, the day was more memorable because two great Americans, John Adams and Thomas Jefferson, died. They had towered over the American past, and one question for Fanny and others like her was whether the future belonged to Robert Owen.[47]

Early in July, Fanny got back home exhausted, and the next months proved disastrous for her and for Nashoba. Just after her return, she planned "to make a ride of 300 miles into the Indian nation" with a Choctaw or Chickasaw guide she hoped to find in Memphis. Her purpose was to see about "some negroes offered me for purchase by the American agent stationed in the nation." Instead, she fell very dangerously ill. She had a severe and painful attack of fever that went to her brain, as her illnesses tended to do.[48]

Camilla believed that Fanny had "exposed herself too much to the midday sun and the nightly dews in attending several of our people who were sick." Because Camilla was busy running their tavern, and Eliza Flower was "slowly recovering from the effects of a milk fever that followed the weaning her child," neither was able to help Fanny in her duties as nurse. Drained by her trip to Indiana, she had worked herself too hard and suffered for it. "But for the skill and yet more the admirable judgment of our friend Mr. Richardson," Camilla wrote, "I am persuaded we cd not have *saved* her invaluable life." Richardson watched alongside Camilla day and night and treated Fanny, Camilla thought, "with a skill and ability that I am persuaded cd not have been surpassed by the first practitioner of the age."[49]

Neither was inclined to take the fever as a cautionary tale. Fanny's illness, Camilla insisted, had nothing to do with the Tennessee climate itself, and Fanny seemed, after ten days' suffering, to be on the mend. They both hoped Harriet would come immediately: one of them could meet her in late November at New Harmony, where she could decide if it was suitable for her mother and sister Fanny. Or if Harriet preferred,

Mrs. Garnett could have her own cabin and garden at Nashoba. But Harriet and Julia both could be "of *invaluable* service" there in supporting "the object that will engross the remainder of our life." Fanny added an optimistic, if shaky postscript: "I have now had since my ten days fever nearly as many of convalescence. I drink wine by the quart. [That] and bark . . . have been my elixir vitae."

Their optimism was premature. Two days later, the fever struck Camilla, and the strain of nursing her brought a recurrence of the fever to Fanny that was far worse than before. For three months Fanny lay in imminent danger, and again her sufferings "were chiefly in the head." Now Camilla thought they both owed their recovery to James Richardson: "without his unremitting care and admirable skill, *Fanny our beloved Fanny* wd have been now quiet in her grave, and I asleep beside her."[50]

In the meantime Nashoba had suffered a crippling loss: George Flower had gone back to Illinois. Although Camilla mourned his going, she wrote harshly of his wife: "she is not in any way suited to fill any station in this establishment nor does she possess a mind calculated to enter into the views connected with it." Flower's abandoning Nashoba is one of the most troubling facts in his life, and in Fanny's.[51]

For Flower was not a man to leave a friend in trouble unless he had no choice. Nashoba had been his idea even before it was Fanny's. He had planned it with her. He had put his life at hazard for it. He had spent himself on it, and a letter he wrote some months later shows how exquisitely at home he had felt there: "Just to hear the sound of your voices and see the lines of your countenances whilst you are talking to me! So one comes to the heart of the matter and really begins to understand those remote, those secret springs of action . . . That is the real pleasure. Then we feel an assurance that we have a glimmering of the truth which words plainly printed and messages conveyed second hand, can never give . . . in silence, in secret and in twilight, in soft suppressed accents [the truth] is sometimes uttered." Even in the fullness of health, Fanny needed Flower at Nashoba. He was an experienced, forceful man who helped her translate her ideas and her good intentions into ways of dealing with slaves. He was a farmer on an infant farm where everyone else could plead ignorance on the score of planting and crops. Nashoba as they had imagined it was doomed without him, and he knew that. Why, then, did he leave?[52]

In 1828 Frances Trollope reported from Cincinnati: "it is said without scruple that [Fanny] has had a connection with George

Flower . . . [which] is said to have taken place *before* she purchased Nashoba. He brought his wife and children to reside there—and they continued to do so till the jealousy of the wife made it impossible to continue together." It seems improbable that in 1825 someone of Flower's bent, who had already asked a woman to suffer ostracism by marrying a man who was already married, would then ask her to move to Tennessee if he was in love with another woman there. It is less improbable, however, than many other things that did happen during this time, and on the evidence it seems likely to be true.[53]

Camilla had said that George and Eliza Flower were very different from each other, but he and Fanny were not. They both were people of rectitude: they were proud and willful—the kind whom a grand passion was likely to humble. They made a long trip into Kentucky and Tennessee alone, in the richest days of manhood and womanhood. They were dedicated at last to a goal commensurate with their powers, each enjoying the discovery of another who had had the same ideas and taken the same risks. Nothing could so call forth the need each had for the other than being in the wilderness together. Nothing could so destroy the barriers that social life puts in the way of passion. They helped each other and worried about each other, and finally—at least, nothing could be more likely—they came to love each other.

And because they were upright people and George Flower was married to a woman they both respected—and because there were three children—they meant to give each other up. When they parted in Memphis after the more than two months they had spent alone together, it would be over, and when Flower returned with his family and Camilla, he and Fanny would dam up their sexual passions and throw their energies into Nashoba. For those who believe that illness provides a relief from great psychic stress, what happened in the next year or so tells a powerful tale.

Flower returned to Albion in late November 1825, but within a few days Fanny called him back to Nashoba. He started toward Memphis but fell so ill that his life was in danger. When he recovered, he delayed his leaving again so long that it seems likely that he subconsciously doubted his powers of repression and denial. Did he leave the cattle behind the following February because he needed a way out? Because he had to make Nashoba fail?

And what about Fanny? By her own account she rode her horse hard and often in the midday sun and slept in the dews at night. She was a clever woman who nevertheless did something foolish. But as the Tennessee spring had come richly on, and the slaves walked before them with a sexual openness she had never seen, all nature conspired to say that passion so strong could not be denied.

The dilemma they faced was insoluble. George Flower was not a man who could leave a second wife and three small children because he loved another woman. So, it seems, Fanny punished her body and made herself ill. Flower had to leave her at Nashoba with Camilla and Richardson. He had no right to nurse her, and a woman as possessive as Eliza Flower could not be fooled.

More than three decades later, when George Flower wrote a book about his life and the English settlement in Edwards County, he did not mention Frances Wright. He did not say he had left Illinois to risk himself in a new venture near Memphis, Tennessee. He said only that just before this time all the hostile feelings in the English settlement had seemed to coalesce to drive him away: "This period was the only exception to an unusually happy life of thirty years duration. And thirty years is a large slice of a man's life." It was one of Fanny's great misfortunes that George Flower was long since married when they met.[54]

One account remains of what they accomplished together. In mid-December 1826, after Flower had gone and Fanny had lain ill for months, William Maclure spent several days at Nashoba and was astonished that everything proceeded so smoothly. Comparing the good order and good conduct of the Nashoba blacks with the disorder and dilapidation he had left at New Harmony, he said the two places contrasted more vividly than the black skins and the white. He even regretted having spent so much money and time on people at New Harmony who did not understand what he was doing and did not much care.[55]

His admiration for Fanny tripled when he saw what she had achieved in so short a time. The slaves worked hard without coercion—even without apparent direction. Though several years later Harriet Martineau would claim to have seen only one clean room in slave country, all the houses he saw were kept in excellent order. Such quiet was maintained that he did not even hear children cry. The blacks worked so well Maclure decided that the prevailing belief in their inferiority was the product of avarice and prejudice, and he predicted they would be vastly superior to whites in any warm climate. He thought Nashoba popular in the vicinity and believed that the next year the community would feed and clothe itself and even make a small profit. A manager like Fanny in a communal system "would save the world an immensity of labor and further civilisation perhaps an age." But the Nashoba Maclure admired had been George Flower's work as much as Fanny's, and his loss the greatest loss Nashoba suffered.

Maclure had visited Nashoba with the hope of persuading Fanny to go to New Harmony more permanently. He had brought along Richesson Whitby, thinking that Whitby could take over for her at Nashoba, though he did not rule out the possibility that she might take her slaves with her to Indiana. Whitby had given up his job as commissary at New Harmony and now began to try to take Flower's place.

Some months earlier Maclure had despaired of Owen's practical sense, writing Mme. Fretageot "that a mine of gold would do nothing towards establishing the community system under his management." He blamed himself for being deceived about Owen: "all the deceptions of my life put together did not amount to the stupidity of the last." He speculated, however, that if Fanny had been in New Harmony to help, "she would most probably have hindered you from exposing yourself and the System to much obliquy and damage."[56]

Mme. Fretageot replied that she would be "extremely pleased" to have such a companion, though Fanny had had a special set of circumstances at Nashoba: she had been "absolutely the Mistress of her slaves" and could direct them without opposition. "They are accustomed to obey, and with her obedience is pleasant." Fanny's talents were unlikely to have "the same effect in so short a time" at New Harmony, however, in part because of "the obstacles attached to her reputation as being without religious principles." This last comment suggests that Fanny had already carried her opposition to the burgeoning revival movement much further than an occasional remark in letters to Europe.[57]

Fanny now told Maclure that she would like to visit New Harmony when she finished several chapters that she wanted to add to *A Few Days in Athens*. She had begun them while waiting out the last long winter in Memphis, when James Richardson was the only person near her who had the leisure for talk and an interest in such matters. She finished them while she was recovering from the fever and Richardson was again beside her. He had written that religion was "wholly subversive of generous virtue" and "absolutely incompatible with independence of thought and feeling," and it is Richardson's spirit, along with Robert Owen's, that broods over this most troubling of Fanny's early writings.[58]

The four chapters represent the kind of broadside attack she had learned from Owen, and for the most part they are on a theme he said was now permissible. Religion, according to Fanny's Epicurus, is the leading error of the human mind, the "poisoner of human felicity," "the perverter of human virtue," "the first link in the chain of evil." It is as foolish to deny the gods' existence as it is to affirm it. But an omnipotent creator cannot be good: "Your deity is the author of evil, and you call him good; the inventor of misery, and you call him happy!" The worship of a creator is, furthermore, absurd: "To fear a being on account of his power, is degrading; to fear him if he be good, ridiculous."[59]

With her matter-of-fact description of how we try to understand ourselves and others, Fanny's Leontium dismisses the inescapable conflict, the brooding doubts, the inevitable loss that are the moral life: "The science of philosophy is simply a science of observation." We must "analyze all these our sensations, thoughts, and emotions . . . examine the qualities of our own internal, sentient matter, with the same, and yet more, closeness of scrutiny, that we have applied to the examination of the matter that is without us: finally to investigate the justness of our moral feelings, and to weigh the merit and demerit of human actions; which is, in other words, to judge of their tendency to produce good or evil,—to excite pleasurable or painful feelings in ourselves or others . . . all is simply a process of investigation." Fanny continued to think of moral experience as of an experiment in chemistry or a problem in long division, and what she now wrote suggests that at some primal level she remained impervious to experience.[60]

Her addendum to *A Few Days* is an angry piece of writing, intellectually flimsy and emotionally brittle. Despite the occasional fine passage, the connection between what Fanny had published five year earlier and what she finished now is tenuous to the point of vanishing, and the weakness of this second part overwhelms its virtues. It is the work of a woman trapped in a personal dilemma and at the same time confronted, in the growing revival movement, by a threat to the freedom of thought she found most hopeful in her adopted country. In this series of preachments, she ridiculed the formal Christianity sinking itself ever more deeply into American public life.

Fanny had built her character on defiance—on her perception that when she was weak, the powers that were strong were hostile to her. Girded for survival, she did not have the psychic luxury of self-knowledge in its deepest forms. When she was in pain, she looked outside herself for the enemies that made her suffer, and armed herself for battle. She could not fight Eliza Flower and win, and so she prepared to take on evangelical religion with heightened fervor. That the enemies she found were often worthy enemies is a measure of her intelligence, her integrity, and her ambition. That she saw the world and her relation to it in terms too simplistic is one measure of what became her personal tragedy.

On December 17, 1826, a few days after William Maclure left for New Orleans, Fanny wrote a trust deed to clarify the legal and economic relationships that would prevail at Nashoba. She had seen and heard enough of the damage done by Owen's confusion on such matters at New Harmony, and she had come so near death she needed to make her purposes clear and do what she could to guarantee that they be honored if she died. She deeded Nashoba to ten trustees: Lafayette, Maclure, Robert Owen, Cadwallader Colden, Richesson Whitby, Robert Jennings, Robert Dale Owen, George Flower, Camilla, and James Richardson, "to be held by them, and their associates, and their successors in perpetual trust for the benefit of the negro race." Reserving to herself the privileges of a trustee, she made two conditions: that a school for black children always be maintained, and that slaves freed by the trustees be colonized outside the United States. She stipulated that the trustees could replace or increase their number, or admit those she called coadjutors, only by unanimous consent and with people who had lived at least six months at Nashoba—"so that by such residence, a thorough knowledge may have been gained of his or her character." Underlining her omission of Eliza Flower as trustee, she wrote that the admission of a husband did not mean the admission of his wife or children over fourteen, nor did the admission of a wife make that of her husband automatic. Once admitted, however, no trustee or coadjutor could be expelled for any reason.[61]

She named ten unrelated people to the trust because she knew of no national institution uncorrupted by the feelings of a majority of Americans against black people. Of the two groups that formally addressed themselves to slavery—the colonization and the emancipation societies—the colonization group, by removing the most troublesome blacks, merely sustained slavery by making it work more easily. The emancipating societies, though "the real friends of the liberty of man," placed their emphasis on religion, and she thought them ineffective because they "tended rather to irritate than convince."

In the schools of Nashoba, no distinctions would be made between white children and black, and no privileges given to either the one or the other. The sons and daughters of slaveowners would be educated to respect and accomplish physical labor, so that they could live independently of the labor of others. The children of slaves would be educated to "fit them for the station of a free people." Consequently, when those children grew up, they would together enjoy "that complete equality of habits and knowledge, alone consistent with the political institutions of the country."

To accomplish such ends, Nashoba needed help, and in the trust deed Fanny asked people to give it, or to come themselves. Though she tried to imagine how people brought up in the world as it was could come together to work toward a more just society, she nevertheless glossed over the inequities of the jobs she described. She expected the blacks to do work "which their habits render easy" and which, for the whites, "their guides and assistants, might be difficult, or unpleasing." She expected the whites to work at what they could do best—teaching, the trades, nursing, farming—and allowed them the option of giving an amount of property equivalent to their labor.

She thus tried to put it beyond the power of malice to suggest that she might use the money sent Nashoba for her own private purposes. She honored her belief that plain speaking was not only a right but a duty. She stated her goals, explained her sentiments, and appealed for help. At the same time, she was even more inflammatory than Robert Owen. Not only did she look skeptically at the marriage tie and cast doubt on the efficacy of religion, but she said that blacks and whites could live freely together if only they were brought up as equals.

Two months later James Richardson went to New Orleans and tried to persuade the newspapers there to print Fanny's Deed of Trust. They all refused, and her appeal apparently gained her nothing more than further notoriety.[62]

Nashoba had remained for the most part a dream on paper. The people there had cleared about one hundred acres of lightly timbered land and fashioned a rough square, each side of which measured about two hundred feet. Their principal buildings included one single and two double log cabins, and another cabin for the slaves' dining room. They had built a storeroom in one corner of the square and several small cabins for the slaves along its outside rim. The carpenter Fanny expected never came—nor the blacksmith, nor the bricklayer.

They had no sawmill, steam engine, washhouse, bathhouse, or dairy. No cattle or oxen were on their way downriver from Illinois. No teachers had joined them, and the school lived only as a distant hope. They had not made it to the good life.[63]

But the work, such as it was, went on. On the first of February 1827, five trustees issued a statement that they had done everything possible to prevent "the leaning of the present generation of men, and perhaps peculiarly of Americans . . . towards speculation, adventure, and commercial gains" from taking root at Nashoba. This meant diminishing their power to borrow on the property in order to buy more slaves and build up a larger institution. They urged slave owners to send black children to be educated: "The formation of the school is what requires the most assistance, and what is considered here as the most interesting and useful object."[64]

No one responded to their appeals for help. No students came to let Fanny try what schools could do. While people told vicious stories about her and Nashoba, Memphis was hit by smallpox and Fanny plagued by recurrences of fever. And so, late in March, Fanny went again to New Harmony, looking no doubt for a boost of spirits.

New Harmony, it turned out, was not the place to get it. For the millennium Robert Owen confidently expected had not come. People instead were angry with Owen and with each other, and he had tried to resolve the tensions by asking them to write out three questions and place them conspicuously in their rooms: "Have we been angry with anyone? Have we spoken ill of anyone? Have we thought ill of anyone?" and he had asked that each person work to replace this "irrational feeling of anger by *genuine and pure Charity for all.*" By March 1827, anger had emerged the decided victor. When Fanny got there, eighty people had just left in despair, and she watched the end of the hope that had been New Harmony. On March 28 Robert Dale and William Owen published a joint editorial acknowledging defeat in the town itself: "The experiment, to ascertain at once whether a mixed and unassorted population could successfully govern their own affairs as a community, was a bold and hazardous attempt, and, we think, a premature one." They called the idea "not as practical as it was benevolent," but said that on the lands outside the town the community system was "in progressive operation."[65]

Robert Dale Owen grasped for new possibilities as eagerly as Fanny did, and in those weeks she fired him with her resilient belief in Nashoba's future. He had always hoped to live communally, but the past year had taught him that he needed to be with people who shared his sentiments and had habits similar to his own. Though the farmers at New Harmony were good people, they were not his kind of people. But Fanny was. He wrote his mother that Fanny had "much good sense, and no little degree of firmness," and speculated that the "community of whites" at Nashoba were "more likely to suit me in ideas and habits than any others that are now associating." Any major decision, however, he would leave to the future, "as there are but very few there at present."[66]

Fanny's overriding concern in the meantime had to be for her health. In an age when a patient was lucky even to survive a doctor's ministering, many avoided medicine altogether and sought health in travel. Fanny decided to go to Europe. The Garnetts' friend J. C. L. de Sismondi had written urging her to abandon Nashoba or, failing that, to travel in Italy and Switzerland, studying "the systems of cultivation that have made the peasants happy, that have given them habits of order and intelligence, that have been the successive and necessary steps for passing from slavery to liberty and happiness." She could go to Italy for her health and at the same time immerse herself in a study that would benefit Nashoba. Though he was six years younger than Fanny, Robert Dale seemed a suitable traveling companion. They talked of forming a congenial party of four or five—the Garnetts and Fanny's cousin James Mylne, they hoped, might join them. They would pass the next winter in Italy, return to Paris in the spring, and then come home to Tennessee.[67]

On May 2 Fanny and Robert Dale boarded a steamboat at Mount Vernon headed downriver, and Fanny soon was feeling so much worse that when they reached Memphis two days later, she had to wait there while Robert Dale went off to Nashoba alone. Camilla and Richesson Whitby came back with him, and the next day they all rode out to Nashoba together, Fanny lying in a hammock slung in a covered wagon.

They decided that Camilla would stay in Tennessee. She dreaded the Atlantic crossing, and neither she nor Fanny believed they should both be gone at the same time. All through a wet Sunday the resident trustees discussed Nashoba, agreed to a number of resolutions, and settled "all matters regarding the negroes." For another week Fanny and Robert Dale lingered, talking of how Nashoba would be managed in their absence, and Whitby took Robert over the grounds, explaining how he hoped to alternate fields, woods, and pasture land. On May 14, heavy with the anxiety of leaving Camilla, Fanny climbed into a wagon, and they lumbered back to Memphis.[68]

That evening they saw Charlotte Larieu, a mulatto whom Richardson had evidently hired in New Orleans to supervise the school at Nashoba. They dined with Marcus and Mary Winchester, and the next morning boarded the *Helen McGregor*, Fanny so exhausted she could scarcely climb the side of the boat. The weather had ranged from an evening at Nashoba that called for a large fire, to a daytime temperature over 80 degrees. The mosquitoes were out in plenty, and fever bedeviled Robert as well as Fanny.

Four days later they docked in New Orleans and went to Mme. Herries's Hotel, where Fanny and Camilla had stayed when they had come to meet Lafayette. Suffering the heat and the heavy moist air while they waited to take ship for Le Havre, Fanny saw many free blacks—one of them Mme. Lolotte's oldest daughter Josephine, who was bound for Nashoba. Most of them were tradesmen, and she talked to them of her own vision of Nashoba: it was a matter of honor with her, as Robert Dale wrote Camilla, to explain "most unreservedly *all* our principles" so that no one might join them blindly. Although Robert remarked on the "wonderful relationships" he saw between white men and mulatto women, he told Camilla "the world as you probably still recollect is a tedious uninteresting world," and his only object in it at the moment was to get out of New Orleans.[69]

On May 30 Fanny was lifted on board the ship *New England*, and a tugboat towed it out into the river. The next day they ran aground on a sandbar, and their only diversion came from a party of six Osage Indians, "their dark solemn-looking faces fantastically ornamented," who lounged on the companionway roof and sang to the Great Spirit for a successful voyage. Fanny tried to endure the heat her illness made almost intolerable by keeping to her cabin. A cheerful Scotswoman with a strong Highland accent whom she had hired to accompany her baked oat cakes, cooked porridge, and cooled her with a large, painted Mexican fan. Robert wrote Camilla that besides the red, white, and black people on board, "we have two goats, two pigs, two sheep, and two alligators, without mentioning a colony of chickens, ducks, and turkeys." On June 9, 1827, their ark finally pushed off the bar into the deeper waters of the Gulf of Mexico and headed for the tip of Florida and the Atlantic Ocean.[70]

Cooperation Has Well Nigh Killed Us All

6

On July 27, 1827, Fanny and Robert Dale landed at Le Havre in the midst of a crowd clamoring to see the Indians. It had been a calm voyage: Fanny had slowly recovered a measure of health, and Robert wrote, "I never was so much at home at sea in my life, nor ever passed a pleasanter time in a vessel." Fanny came back to Europe with a measure of fame, and an image that had caught people's attention. As Mary Shelley put it, "a woman, young rich & independent, quits the civilization of England for a life of hardship in the forests of America, that by so doing she may contribute to the happiness of her species." Within the limits of imagery, this was true, and Fanny no doubt hoped to use it to advantage.[1]

But on July 28 in Baltimore, *The Genius of Universal Emancipation* published an article that changed Fanny and Camilla's lives forever. It had been "politely furnished the editor . . . for publication, by one of the [Nashoba] Trustees," James Richardson. Neither Camilla nor Richesson Whitby had objected when Richardson showed them excerpts from a log he had kept and sent to the *Genius*. The first two entries described meetings that had included Fanny and Robert Dale. After they had left, Whitby had gone into Kentucky to find new recruits for Nashoba, so the most disturbing events recorded had happened while only Camilla and Richardson were there. The important passages, datelined Nashoba, 1827, read as follows:

May 6
It is agreed to continue the plan of work for the slaves, detailed in the published "Communication from the Trustees of Nashoba."

141

Agreed, that if any of the slaves neglect their duty, and thus retard the object of the plan, we will exclude such slaves from the benefit of the plan, and will treat them according to the slave system, until it shall appear that their habits are changed for the better . . .

Agreed, that in case of disobedience on the part of a slave . . . the trustees . . . shall call a meeting . . . and publicly examine and pass sentence on the offender.

May 13

Robert Dale Owen called [the slaves'] attention to the difference between our mode of management, and that to which they had been previously accustomed; and pointed out to them the direct and uniform bearing which our regulations had on their happiness.

May 20

Camilla Wright . . . informed [the slaves] that to-morrow, the children, Delila, Lucy, Julia, and Alfred, wil be taken altogether from under the management of their parents, and will be placed, until our [school] is organized, under the management of Mamselle Lolotte [a free black woman]; that all communication between the parents and children shall, in future, be prevented, except such as may take place by permission, and in the presence, of the manager of the children.

May 26

Agreed, that the slaves shall not be allowed to receive money, clothing, food, or indeed any thing whatever, from any person . . . and, that any article so received, shall be returned to the giver in the presence of the slaves and of the trustees. If the giver be absent, the article shall be destroyed by the receiver, in the presence of the trustees and of the slaves.

Agreed, that the slaves shall not be permitted to eat, elsewhere than at the public meals.

May 27

Dilly having given utterance a day or two ago, to some grumbling at having so many mistresses[,] James Richardson stated . . . that they can get rid of these masters and mistresses in no other way than by working out their freedom . . . that . . . this multiplicity of superiors . . . [renders] the concurrence of at least a majority of the resident trustees, an indispensable preliminary to the infliction of even the slightest possible punishment, for the greatest possible offence.

June 1

Isabel had laid a complaint against Redrick, for coming during the night . . . to her bedroom, uninvited; and endeavoring, without her consent, to take liberties with her person. Our views of the sexual relation had been repeatedly given to the slaves: Camilla Wright again stated it, and informed the slaves that, as the conduct of Redrick, which he did not deny, was a gross infringement of that view, a repetition of such conduct . . . ought . . . to be punished by flogging. She repeated, that we consider the proper basis of the sexual intercourse to be the unconstrained and unrestrained choice of *both* parties. Nelly having requested a lock . . . with the view of preventing the future uninvited entrance of any man; the lock was refused, as being, in its proposed use, inconsistent with . . . a doctrine which we are determined to enforce, and which will give to every woman a much greater security than any lock can possibly do.

June 3

Willis having . . . complained . . . of Mamselle Lolotte's children beating his children: thinking it was allowed because her's are a little the fairest[,] James Richardson . . . told them that . . . all colors are equal in rank, and that whatever distinctions may be established on this place, color shall form the basis of none of them.

June 17

James Richardson informed [the slaves] that, last night, Mamselle Josephine [a quadroon, daughter of Mamselle Lolotte] and he began to live together; and he took this occasion of repeating to them our views on color, and on the sexual relation.

It was the last entry, for the most part, that toppled Fanny's world. Richardson had called attention to the fact that what many white men did in fantasy, and some in secret, he did boldly and now, as it were, in the eyes of the world. The miscegenation horrified Benjamin Lundy's readers, along with the open acknowledgment that Nashoba not only countenanced but preached sexual intercourse without marriage. Lundy himself hoped he had misunderstood the trustees' language: any explanation that could dissociate Nashoba from the "libidinous" practices of Southern slave owners would be both "just and politic." A letter from "one of the most respectable and jealous advocates of universal emancipation," who signed himself "Mentor," marveled that anyone would deliberately reveal practices "indecent," "libidinous," and "repugnant to the safe and honest maxims of christian life . . . who can read without disgust, that an accomplished young English woman . . . apparently concurs . . . in giving a sanction to the formation of illicit sexual connexions, without the obligations of marriage!" He wondered if "the wild and wicked system" of Robert Owen had been surpassed in Nashoba, which was "one great brothel, disgraceful to its institutors, and most reprehensible, as a public example, in the vicinity."[2]

Lundy published only a brief reply from Richardson, saying that his language had not been equivocal and the records could speak for themselves. Richardson had written at length, however, and Lundy's excerpt protected both Fanny's reputation and his readers' sensibilities. Richardson had objected to the epithet "libidinous," writing, "I possess the feeling which it designates in common with every other complete adult animal. But the woman has never lived whom I have wronged in its gratification . . . Does Mentor actually believe that when such a propensity does exist, the legal tie ever prevents its indulgence? Mentor thinks we are instituting a Brothel. I have seen a brothel and I never knew a place so unlike it as Nashoba." He concluded with a tirade against the Christian religion as the chief cause of sexual immorality because of its ridiculous taboos: "For my part, I am an Atheist, and on the diffusion of Atheism rests my only hope of the progress of Universal Emancipation." Lundy thought Fanny would have disapproved, and if not, "the success of the enterprise will be utterly despaired of by her best friends."[3]

Two important entries in the surviving notes from Richardson's Nashoba log did not appear in the *Genius*:

May 24

Two women slaves tied up and flogged by James Richardson in presence of Camilla and all the slaves. Two dozen and one dozen on the bare back with a cowskin.

May 31

Reprimanded Willis for having tried to interfere between Lolotte and one of his own children—and Dilly for having given bread and meat to one of her own children sent to her kitchen by Lolotte.[4]

The picture Richardson had drawn of life at Nashoba was one of black people systematically bereft of the few things they had clung to—in return for righteous lectures on race, sexuality, and what was called freedom. He had described a world that was deeply inhumane. It forced men and women to ask permission to see their children and to talk with them only in the presence of a "manager." It refused parents the right to defend their own. It told a woman who wanted a lock for her door that the establishment philosophy frowned on rape, and philosophy was stronger than a piece of metal. It told people they were lucky because two trustees must agree before they were beaten. It assured them that all those regulations were necessary to their happiness. Had this not happened, it would seem a bad parody.

Even through Richardson's coldly hostile prose, the slaves emerged as vital, resilient human beings. Their managers, on the other hand, were made monsters by theory. The most chilling picture Richardson painted was of Camilla Wright watching in approval while he tied up two women, stripped their backs, and lashed one of them twenty-four times and the other twelve with a leather strap. She also said that a man who tried to force himself sexually on a woman should be flogged.[5]

What they had done was diametrically opposed to the way Frances Wright had tried slowly to build a sense of importance and self-respect in people who had earlier been denied it. Fanny and George Flower knew that preparing slaves for freedom meant allowing them to make choices and, inevitably, mistakes. They had used coercion only once, when they had put a woman in solitary confinement and on bread and water for a day. By precept and example, rather than by force, Fanny and Flower wanted to inspire "habitual industry voluntarily arising amongst the people themselves."[6]

The central question then became: how deeply was Fanny implicated in Richardson's sadism? Did she know Richardson would beat the slaves, and did she give him permission to do it? In the autobiography he wrote in old age, Robert Dale Owen said of Nashoba when he saw it in May 1827: "slaves released from fear of the lash [were] working indolently under the management of Whitby, whose education in an easy-going Shaker village had not at all fitted him for the post of plantation overseer." According to Joseph Davis, Jefferson Davis's older brother, who tried to establish a model plantation in Natchez, Mississippi, and who later agreed to take over Fanny's most troublesome slave, the prevalent philosophy among slave owners decreed that unconditional submission was the only acceptable response from slave to master. Now the resident Nashoba trustees apparently paid obeisance to that philosophy and discussed beating as a viable punishment. Fanny was present when it was agreed that slaves who neglected their duty would be treated "according to the slave system." Robert Dale explained to the slaves how their new treatment would differ from the old, and only eleven days later Richardson flogged the women. Though flogging violated every principle Fanny had ever defended, it seems unlikely that Camilla would endorse something to which she knew her sister irrevocably opposed.[7]

Although Fanny thought Richardson's publication indiscreet, she did not publicly disavow what he did, and if she rebuked him privately for anything other than indiscretion, no evidence survives. Fanny was ill and depressed. She had lost George Flower and, with him, Nashoba as she first imagined it, and she had seen New Harmony fail. No doubt she had been besieged by those who believed she must make some concession at last to Southern mores. Nor did Robert Dale, who had his father's tenderness for the weak, seem to get past the abstraction, "the slave system," to the human reality behind it. In giving in to the prevailing wisdom, they both lost a measure of their own humanity.[8]

As for separating parents and children, Fanny herself had survived the trauma, but with a crippled vision. Because of her peculiar history, she looked on the human ties as well as on the pieties that structured most people's lives with a blinking unreality. This was both her strength and her weakness. It allowed her to look beyond what she saw immediately around her—to entertain bold and generous visions. At the same time, she could not anticipate the costs of realizing them or sense the measure of personal sacrifice they demanded. She had learned from New Harmony's failure that, apart from a few like-minded friends, the "New Moral World" had to begin with children. The task of building was hard enough; the task of rebuilding might well be hopeless. Fanny wrote later that summer that all the Nashoba children had been "separated from the contamination of their parents, [whom] they see only in presence of their directors, and waiting only the arrival of Mr. Jennings from Philadelphia." Hope for a better future had made her cruel.[9]

But why, suddenly, was Nashoba a place where people worried so loudly about sexuality and marriage? A year earlier, on July 4, 1826, Robert Owen had proclaimed that marriage combined with private property and an irrational system of religion to make a trinity of evils: no one, he thought, should be legally forced to remain in a destructive marriage. But shocking as divorce might be to American sensibilities in 1826, it was not nearly so shocking as "free love." Richardson and Camilla carried what Owen said much further than he, and here they obviously followed Fanny's lead. That same midsummer, Owen ran into James Mylne on the streets of Glasgow and told him that, in Mylne's words, Fanny had gone "to much more extravagant lengths than he himself who as I have long known has very little limit to his extravagances."[10]

In the furor that followed, Camilla wrote that when Fanny's health allowed her to finish *A Few Days in Athens*, Fanny would "give at large her views of the sexual relation." Marriage, Camilla said flatly, was "one of the most subtle inventions of priestcraft for poisioning the purest source of human felicity." Both irrational and pernicious, marriage forced people to continue together when their feelings for each other, "as I have known in several instances, have turned to utter aversion." It seems likely that Fanny was using theory to fight for something that mattered to her at the rawest personal level.[11]

If she and George Flower had been lovers, she must have been not only sick but deeply demoralized when he left her at Nashoba. She had lost something and someone invaluable, and her will had not proved as strong as she thought. When Richardson talked about "the slave system," she must have seen it from a theoretical distance. She knew he would do things rather differently than she and Flower had, but could not bear to know exactly what that meant. As for the marriage tie, she had railed against it often, which Richardson and Camilla had heard her do: it had blocked her chance to be happy. She was a proud woman who would have found it hard to believe that something more than the law tied George Flower to his wife. Fanny grasped for adversaries other than evangelical religion, and she found one handily in the institution of marriage. She began to shift the focus of Nashoba from slavery to a preoccupation with how people might live together freely.

Camilla and Richardson had not, it seems, violated the letter of Fanny's law, but they had violated its leavening spirit. Fanny and Richardson had agreed in theory, but he was a petty tyrant, and she was not. Furthermore, in broadcasting what he had done, Richardson had run up a debt that Fanny would have to pay.

In late July 1827, however, Fanny must have thought herself well on the way out of her tunnel of pain. Brooding about Camilla as she came into port, she believed nevertheless that she had left her in a home she loved, among associates she trusted. She was convinced that her own health would not have improved there and that staying would have meant to risk Camilla's health "by continued inquietude and to forfeit my own life." Her first news seemed to justify what she had done. Camilla wrote the Garnetts that she was perfectly recovered, having enjoyed that summer "a degree of vigor that I hardly expected again to experience."[12]

Fanny still tired easily, so she and Robert Dale took a steamboat on the Seine from Le Havre to Rouen, idly enjoying the little villages and cottage clusters, the church spires and old castles they met at the river's every turn. From Rouen they traveled by diligence in slow stages to Paris, where Fanny went immediately to the Garnetts. Their mother welcomed her generously. "How much we must all rejoice at dear

Miss Wright's recovery and safe arrival," she wrote Julia, who was with the Trollopes in England. "She shall have my bedroom and I will take the alcove." Harriet met her with the news that Julia was soon to marry Georg Heinrich Pertz, a German historian.[13]

Some minor gossip had apparently begun, and Robert took time from his visits to the Louvre, and the new giraffe at the Jardin des Plantes, to try to quell it. He wrote his sister Anne of accompanying Fanny to Europe, explaining that he knew "that with the uncharitable and the meddling, such an act of simple friendship admits of invidious explanation." Such an interpretation was a mistake. In Fanny—"a woman of the finest talents and most finished education, of great strength of mind, noble feelings and good dispositions"—he had found someone whose "principles and opinions accorded more completely with my own than those of almost any other person."[14]

Fanny was clearly the more forceful of the two, and the relationship she had with Robert Dale was safely platonic—its nature obvious to both from the first days of their friendship. Few things, he told his sister, would give him greater pain than to forfeit Fanny's good opinion, and he would willingly risk his life for hers. Still, "I am no more likely to fall in love (as it is called) with her than with yourself." Many women were more interesting to him as women—Camilla, "for instance, who without her talents or character has many excellent and amiable qualities." Fanny had been "a little soured perhaps by an unhappy infancy and childhood." He thought her less light-hearted than he and said she took a gloomier view of the world: not habitually sad, she was nevertheless restless and occasionally despondent. He saw much to admire in her, he later wrote, but nothing to love. They would be colleagues, and Nashoba, he told Anne, struck him as the place most likely "for the formation of a community, of which I should wish to become a member."[15]

By the middle of August, however, the news from the *Genius* had undermined Nashoba's future and rocked the little group in Paris. Fanny immediately canceled their trip to Italy, reversed her plans, and vowed to go back that winter. "December or January are fine months," she wrote bravely, "for a southern trip." She did what she could to hide her disappointment and contain her anxiety, but for the next month or so, she behaved so erratically that Julia and Mrs. Trollope thought her brain affected. Her hair started turning white. She had fits of trembling she could not control, and her back began to ache.[16]

She wrote a letter to Richardson that was a model of elegant restraint. What he had done was irrevocable, and partly for this reason,

Fanny dealt gently with him. She believed that when he nursed her through her fever he had literally saved her life. And not only was she grateful for that anxious care, but she had stipulated in her deed that no trustee could be removed for any reason whatever. She wrote him carefully on the impropriety of what he had done: "All principles are liable to misinterpretation but none so much as ours." His manner had been inflammatory and likely to provoke "unnecessary hostility, and misconception." To provoke outrage was to endanger the principles they had embraced: "Were our own happiness our sole object, it might be indifferent in what manner we addressed ourselves to this world we had left . . . But surely Richardson, that is not our only objective—at least it is not mine."[17]

No doubt one of the worst blows came from her uncle, James Mylne, who wondered to Julia if Fanny's "excessive passion for Notoriety has led to an incipient disorder of the mind." He had been stunned when he heard that Fanny was leaving Camilla at Nashoba, "dispirited, and broken-hearted by her absence . . . to encounter all the horrors of a forest solitude." The blacks there, he thought, were debased by ignorance and slavery; the whites, by their adherence to "the absurd principles of her senseless system." Even Robert Owen had the sense to know that Fanny's "folly cannot fail to obstruct the very objects of a philanthropical kind she has in view, and to bring ruin upon her project and disgrace upon herself." He admired what Fanny had initially tried at Nashoba, but now his pride was hurt. He was angry and ashamed. Their kinship embarrassed him, and he had no hope that Fanny could rescue Nashoba. He intended to try to persuade Camilla to come back to "the bosom of her valued and valuable friends."[18]

James Mylne was not a man whose opinion Fanny could cavalierly dismiss. Apart from Camilla, he was the closest thing she had to family and the relative she was proudest to claim. No convincing evidence suggests that the breach between them ever healed.

Charles Wilkes, it turned out, had been equally appalled when he heard that Camilla would stay at Nashoba while Fanny went to Europe: "it may be preparing a torment for both and perhaps much regret." Reluctantly he now wrote Camilla, "I cannot express the pain which this publication has given to your friends here who have seen it . . . I dare not tell you what inferences are drawn from it. I cannot believe they are fairly drawn." He could not imagine her delivering opinions on such subjects as "the propriety of allowing women to have locks on their doors to protect them from insults," much less her concluding that the locks were unnecessary. "I dare not trust myself to say what I fear may be the consequences of these measures if they cannot be explained."[19]

Camilla's answer shattered what hope Wilkes had that Richardson had misrepresented either her ideas or her behavior. He concluded that the two sisters were excellent women who had an overweening confidence in their own judgments, though somewhat inconsistently he blamed the influence of Robert Owen: they were "the dupes and the victims of the wretched sophisms . . . of a madman." He declared that their opinions were "equally absurd and mischievous and equally calculated to shock and offend ninety nine out of every hundred in every decent and civilized society," and wrote Lafayette that he had been "imperiously called upon to express my entire disapproval of such doctrines . . . If I had had any doubt, which I never had, the united opinions of all the females of my own family and of my connections prescribed to me one course—that of breaking off the intercourse between our families."[20]

One man's loyalty held, and that was Lafayette's. "I sometimes think . . . when I look at my old father," Fanny wrote, "that there is an aristocracy in nature herself . . . Lafayette born a noble, bred in a dissolute court, sucking in with his nurse's milk the idle prejudices of his class . . . came out pure from dross and preserves to this hour the artlessness of childhood and the sweetness of a gentlewoman."[21]

Lafayette took Fanny to La Grange and treated Robert Dale with special attention for her sake. She was no longer a threat to his children, and they could ignore the vagaries of her philosophy and treat her now with their wonted grace. She felt the ease of a place she knew so well. She watched the servant girl flitting through the rooms, broom in hand and brush on foot. Several of Lafayette's grandchilden were there, two Lasteyries, a military man or two, the secretary Levasseur with his exceedingly pregnant wife, and so on in the fashion of La Grange. In the peace and tact of French country rhythms, Fanny tried to calm her erratic nerves and plan with Robert Dale the Nashoba of the future.[22]

After a week at La Grange, she and Robert drove with Lafayette back to Paris to see Julia, who left a record of how deeply the change in Fanny and the news from Nashoba had appalled most of her old friends. To her Swiss friend Sismondi, Julia made an extraordinary confession: for nine years, Fanny had been the sole object of her thoughts—"almost the sole object of my love." No one could see Fanny without loving her, but "her very virtues, her sensibility, her humanity, her genuine forgetfulness of self have been her ruin." Fanny's unhappy friends thought her reputation tarnished, indeed her life perhaps sacrificed, "to produce no one advantage—not even to those for whose sake she is giving up her friends, her country, I had almost said her respectability." Like others, Julia blamed Robert Owen for working on Fanny "at a moment when she was incapacitated by fever from judging sanely." Fanny spoke "as one incapable of seeing the consequences of the principles she advocates, principles to which her whole life, all the feelings of her heart, are in direct opposition." Her mind was not sufficiently calm to listen to reason: "She *will* awaken, but what then will be her feelings?" The Garnetts and Frances Trollope worried in fact that Fanny "was not in her right senses." Alive to their dismay but convinced that she and Nashoba were pledged to the search for moral truth and liberty, Fanny had to find new allies.[23]

Deciding to spend the next two months, as Robert Dale put it, rescuing from the old world "a few rational beings who are too good for it and wd be much happier in the woods," Fanny sought out a woman she had never met but one she thought might befriend Nashoba. "If you possess the opinions of your father and the generous feelings of your mother," she wrote Mary Shelley, "I feel that I could travel far to see you." Mrs. Shelley's mother, Mary Wollstonecraft—in Fanny's esteem the most daring Englishwoman of her time—had lived with a man to whom she was not married and had an illegitimate child, and she had written the first powerful polemic in favor of women's rights. Her father was William Godwin, author of *Political Justice* and believer in the overthrow of existing systems of government, religion, family, and private property. She was the widow of the poet Percy Bysshe Shelley, whose defiance of convention resounded through the nineteenth century. She had lived with Shelley when he was married to another woman and had had a child by him before they were married, and Fanny hoped Mary Shelley still had the convictions and the courage of her own history.[24]

Fanny explained that Godwin's principles of moral liberty and equality formed the base and cement of Nashoba. "While we endeavour to undermine the slavery of colour existing in the North American Republic," she wrote, "we essay equally to destroy the slavery of mind now reigning there as in other countries." She imagined Nashoba to be "an establishment where affection shall form the only marriage, kind feeling and kind action the only religion, respect for the feelings and liberties of others the only restraint, and union of interest the bond of peace and security." The political institutions of America allowed free scope for experiment, "and with a practice in view in opposition to all the laws of public opinion, it was necessary to seek the seclusion of a new country, and build up a city of refuge in the wilderness itself." She wished Mary Shelley would join them there.

Though Mrs. Shelley was bound to England because of her son Percy, she was flattered by Fanny's attention and drawn by her reverence to those she herself had loved. "You do honour to our species," she told Fanny, "& what perhaps is dearer to me, to the feminine part of it." She begged Fanny, "public spoiled as you are," not to turn away because she was absorbed in her own private life.[25]

In high romantic fashion, Fanny wrote as though Mary Shelley might rise above the conventions that bound Fanny's older friends and made them doubt her sanity: "I have made the hard earth my bed, the saddle of my horse my pillow, and have staked my life and fortune on an experiment having in view moral liberty and human improvement. Many of course think me mad, and if to be mad mean to be one of a minority, I am so, and very mad indeed, for our minority is very small. Should that few succeed in mastering the first difficulties, weaker spirits, though often not less amiable, may carry forward the good work. But the fewer we are who now think alike, the more we are of value to each other." Early in October, Fanny traveled south from London to spend a week with Mary at Arundel, not far from Brighton. She had wanted "a bosom intimate . . . one of my own sex to commune with, and sometimes to lean upon in all the confidence of equality of friendship." And she awakened Mary's tenderness. Though her son thought their visitor like Minerva, Mary wrote Robert Dale that Fanny was "neither so independent or so fearless as you think," and she rallied him to be Fanny's devoted confidant. But she would not leave England, and Fanny's quest proved disappointing in the end.[26]

Until Fanny left France, she spent most of her time at La Grange, where she stayed in her own room or walked out alone and found the quiet good for her shattered nerves. She tried to win over the Garnetts and those who felt troubled for her. Preparing, for example, to like Julia's fiancé, G. H. Pertz, she wrote that only superior men choose superior women—"only those who are above jealousy and who love the praises of those they love better than their own." She wrote at length to Sismondi, whose opinion bore such weight with Julia and who had been contemptuous of Nashoba. Fanny's letter filled him with remorse for his skepticism. "Not only is she perfectly reasonable," he told Julia, "but even more, so forcibly rational and at the same time so modest." She spoke of the joy of marriage, "and with such contempt of immoral unions between whites and blacks, for which she wishes to substitute unions which honor morality and family sentiment, that I can no longer attribute the meaning I ascribed to her enigmatic words." But he remained confused. "Please lay aside the reserve that restrains us all," he asked Julia, "and tell me clearly what her system is; let me not make some terrible blunder in thinking to guess at it."[27]

But there was no clear answer to his question. When Fanny wrote of Nashoba, her language blurred into vagueness or soared into romantic posturing because she found neither sanction nor model in her culture. Experience had only deepened her early commitment to the principle of equality, but no one had managed yet to discover how free men and women could live together as equals. For all his eloquence in the Declaration, Thomas Jefferson had nevertheless lived as an aristocrat and a slave owner. Her beloved Lafayette was the benevolent despot of La Grange. America, Fanny had discovered, was a society of hierarchies ranked according to color, wealth, and education, and underlying them all was the inescapable fact of patriarchy.

Nowhere in either Europe or America could Fanny or any other woman find a place as an equal. But America was at least free of kings; its institutions were republican; and there equality had, perhaps, a chance. Thinking of Nashoba as a haven and an example, and putting their emphasis on the ideal of community, rather than on a plan to end slavery, Fanny and Robert Dale decided to spend their time in Europe actively recruiting people to join them.

To attract others to her cause, Fanny wrote a letter that she had printed and mailed out to friends and potential colleagues. In it she sketched a radical vision of Nashoba, where everyone would have equal rights, no matter what the color of their skin, no matter what their sex, no matter what their material goods. Moral pleasure would be their only compensation for badly thatched cabins, hard beds, and simple fare. The dirtiest work would have the greatest social value, and together they would discover how human beings ought properly to live. At the same time, she wrote Sismondi that Nashoba's purpose was "to prepare the *two* colors for the coming change. It is to kill prejudices in the white man by raising the black man to his level . . . [to offer] not the mere theory, but the practice of equality beneath the roof of Nashoba . . . a first example of union and brotherhood."[28]

This small community of like-minded souls bore a family resemblance to Epicurus' school as Fanny had described it in *A Few Days in*

Athens. In Nashoba, however, *all* would be teachers and learners, and the common goal would be to create a model for others to follow. If they could get five hundred subscribers, they would launch a newspaper to "agitate . . . the great questions of religion, morality, and politics" and support "extended and radical reform." They then planned to have an agent in Paris and another in London. In the meantime, the job was to find people who wanted to come.[29]

Frances Trollope, of all unlikely people, began to listen to what Fanny had to say. Only recently had she raised her voice in their little circle against Fanny's publishing her Deed of Trust in England: because of her "declared opinions against religion . . . contempt, ridicule, and reprobation would be the result." But because of her family's jumbled finances, she began to imagine that Fanny's Nashoba might offer a haven from impending poverty. At the same time, Fanny's temptation to woo Mrs. Trollope to America must have been nearly irresistible. For all her occasional foolishness, Frances Trollope was a delightful woman. According to her son Anthony, "She could dance with other people's legs, eat and drink with other people's palates, be proud with the lustre of other people's finery." And just after Julia's wedding, when she left Paris with Fanny Wright en route to the coast and then to London, Frances Trollope was so taken with her companion that she thought Fanny "at once all that woman should be—and something more than woman ever was." She was, in fact, "the most interesting woman in Europe," and Mrs. Trollope arranged to spend a good deal of time with her in London and in Harrow, where the Trollopes had recently moved.[30]

Not that Fanny made anything sound easy. She tried to ward off illusion because Nashoba had to have the most determined and even self-effacing help: "Like Pizarro I am tempted to draw a line on the sand & say those who cannot answer for their fortitude let them pass over, & if but three remain let me be sure of them." She warned a young Frenchman she hoped to recruit to weigh what he must abandon and what he must embrace and, more than anything, to weigh his own strength. Very few, even among the young, she said, could survive the challenge.[31]

Her time in London was "necessarily engrossed by a crowd of visitors from morning till night," as she spread her message through such like-minded people as Leigh Hunt and the members of the Cooperative Society. She wrote Robert Dale about promising recruits, among them Harriet and Emily Ronalds, who had gone with her and Camilla two years earlier to meet Lafayette in New Orleans. She counted on a Frenchman named Carnot, who was an excellent printer. Ferdinand du Trone committed himself to come and awakened such interest in Fanny that Mrs. Trollope thought her very much in love with him. But as the hour for leaving England grew nearer, only one person was ready to go, and that was Frances Trollope.[32]

At forty-seven, Mrs. Trollope was neither young nor by any means indifferent to the old world's comforts, but she thought she could pass a quiet year or two at Nashoba while the family fortunes were repaired, and her main hope was apparently to evade her creditors and to escape the embarrassment of being known publicly to have lived far beyond her means. With her husband's approval, she gathered together her two daughters, Emilia and Cecilia; her second son, Henry; a manservant named William Abbott; her maid, Hester Rust; and the emigré artist Auguste Hervieu. Along with Fanny Wright they boarded the ship *Edward* on November 3, 1827, at Tower Stairs and slipped out of England.[33]

Fanny wrote from the ship, "Never was a departure made in greater hurry. It left me no time for seeing or even writing to my friends, or excusing myself from standing engagements." She managed, though, to write hastily to Jeremy Bentham, whom she had not had time to see, asking him to meet Robert Dale, who planned to leave some ten days later from Liverpool. Mary Shelley came to see her off, apparently with sorrow: she asked for a lock of Fanny's hair and kept it by her all her life.[34]

A week after their party left London, they were off soundings in the Atlantic, and three weeks out, they came into the trade winds of the tropics. It was a good time for work, and Fanny used it to write her definitive answer to the criticisms of Nashoba. Eyebrows arched high, Mrs. Trollope watched while Fanny sat on a coiled rope in steerage and read parts to a sailor patching his trousers. She called the article "Explanatory Notes, Respecting the Nature and Objects of the Institution of Nashoba, and of the Principles upon Which It Is Founded. Addressed to the Friends of Human Improvement, in All Countries and of All Nations." It is the most powerful statement Fanny ever made, and the most revealing.[35]

She offered a sweeping challenge to established values and institutions: "Let us correct our views of right and wrong, correct our moral lessons, and so correct the practice of rising generations!" Experience had taught her to doubt that the words people used meant what they professed to mean. "We hear of the wealth of nations, of the powers of production, of the demand and supply of markets, and we forget that these words mean no more . . . than the happiness, and the labor, and the necessities of men." It was a curious truth that necessary work was held in disrepute, while society rewarded jobs "the least useful, nay, frequently the most decidedly mischievous . . . The husbandman who supports us by the fruits of his labor, the artizan to whom we owe all the comforts and conveniences of life, are banished from what is termed intellectual society [and] . . . too often condemned to the most severe physical privations and the grossest mental ignorance; while the soldier who lives by our crimes, the lawyer by our quarrels and our rapacity, and the priest by our credulity or our hypocrisy, are honored with public consideration and applause." Values so skewed, she thought, deserved contempt.

At the psychological center of her treatise she put an affirmation of sexual experience that no one else in nineteenth-century America would approach. Whether or not she had an affair with George Flower, it seems unlikely she could have written as she did without personal experience. Against her culture's insistence that sexuality was shameful, she wrote that sexual passion was "the strongest and . . . the noblest of the human passions," the basis of "the best joys of our existence," and "the best source of human happiness." Self-denial could not lead to goodness. People were virtuous *in proportion as they are happy, and happy in proportion as they are free,"* but institutions and public opinion commanded them to unnatural repression and vicious restraint. Sexual passion could and should be regulated, not by ignorance, laws, or customs, but by a knowledge of its consequences: to create another human being was to take the most important action of all. But the fates would be implacable if people ignored or abused a force so powerful: sexual passion, if distorted, could produce moral and physical disease—could lead to the street, the hospital, or the asylum: "ignorant laws, ignorant prejudices, ignorant codes of morals . . . condemn one portion of the female sex to vicious excess, another to as vicious restraint, and all to defenceless helplessness and slavery, and generally the whole of the male sex to debasing licentiousness, if not to loathsome brutality."

As for the marriage laws, at Nashoba they would have no force: "No woman can forfeit her individual rights or independent existence, and no man assert over her any rights or power whatsoever, beyond what he may exercise over her free and voluntary affections." The school, and the loving community that surrounded it, would provide an alternative to the home itself and to what was often "the forcible union of unsuitable and unsuited parents [which] can little promote the happiness of the offspring." She ridiculed the law that put a stigma on innocent children whom it called "natural," that allowed a man to father any number of children but "exonerated [him] by law and custom from the duties of paternity," and that, when a marriage foundered, gave the legitimate offspring to the father and "bowed to servitude the spirit of a fond mother, and held her, as a galley slave, to the oar." With her insight into cultural bias, Fanny understood clearly that law is too often the work of power rather than justice.

She announced yet another crucial change in her vision, and a challenge as sharp to American sensibilities. The Nashoba she hoped to build would be a biracial community of equals, and the blacks from now on would come only from "the *free citizens of color* who form no inconsiderable, and, frequently, a very respectable body in the American population, more especially in that of the southern cities." Daunted by her experience with adult slaves, Fanny would neither purchase nor accept any more unless the planters who became members wanted to put their own slaves under Nashoba's protection.

Drawing on her personal experience with Marcus and Mary Winchester, who named one of their daughters Frances Wright, Fanny wrote hopefully of miscegenation. She argued that the races were mixing, and "the only question is whether it shall take place in good taste and good feeling . . . or whether it shall proceed, as it now does, viciously and degradingly, mingling hatred and fear with the ties of blood." After black and white children had been educated together, "thus approaching their minds, tastes and occupations," Nashoba would "leave the affections of future generations to the dictates of free choice."

At the same time, Nashoba would repudiate competition as a "vicious" principle "which places the interests of each individual in continual opposition to those of his fellows; which makes of one man's loss, another's gain, and inspires a spirit of accumulation, that crushes every noble sentiment, fosters every degrading one, makes of this globe a scene of strife, and the whole human race, idolaters of gold." Religion would have no place there either. Fanny saw education as the lever that would move the world, and the cooperative system as the principal form that education would take, being "the best means yet discovered for securing the one great end, that of human liberty, and equality."

All Fanny needed was the cooperation of a few like-minded people "now scattered throughout the world." She directed Europeans how and in what seasons to come to Nashoba, asking that they bring the tools of their trade, as well as a mattress, blankets, linens, and the necessities of the table: a good knife, a fork, a spoon, and a cup. In closing, she asked that editors publish the "Explanatory Notes," honoring "the spirit of human inquiry, and disinterested efforts, whether judicious or erroneous, made in the cause of human improvement." She hoped to circulate it all through America.

Fanny had honored her belief that to speak obscurely was to act unjustly. She had carefully explained her assumptions as well as her hopes. She had imposed a poignant trust in the American people.

After seven weeks' sailing, the *Edward* entered the mouth of the Mississippi on Christmas Day, and Fanny and the Trollope clan rejoiced to see the muddy river pouring out to mix with the Gulf of Mexico's deeper blue. Flocks of pelicans bobbed on the waters, and a pilot guided them across the bar, the mast of a ship long since sunk offering dismal testimony that they were nearing port. As they approached New Orleans, Fanny wrote lovingly in Quaker fashion to Julia Pertz to offer Nashoba as a solace and a home if ever she should need it: "if ought ever happen to thee to render a change of place desirable & friendship needful or but soothing to the heart, thou know'st where Nashoba lies & who dwell therein."[36]

But when they docked, Fanny discovered that the Nashoba she had hastened to defend no longer existed. Just two weeks earlier, Camilla had married Richesson Whitby, with whom rumor had it she had lived since summer. In the Nashoba book, Camilla justified "this apparent dereliction from one of the fundamental principles frequently advocated in these records" by the need to bow to the force of public opinion. Although she continued to regard the marriage tie as irrational and "calculated to produce a variety of evils," she had discovered that living "in open violation of the civil institutions of the country" provoked general indignation.[37]

Fanny also learned that three weeks earlier James Richardson had left Nashoba. Having come to the conclusion that he could not live comfortably in the cooperative system, he had decided to go once more into what he called the sordid world of competition. The day after Fanny arrived in New Orleans, Richardson's lover, Josephine Prevot, Mme. Lolotte's quadroon daughter, also left for Memphis.

For the rest of her life Fanny would live with the reputation

Richardson and Camilla had given Nashoba, and her friends hinted that her "Explanatory Notes" might prove as troubling as that scandal. to the American public. William Maclure, who was in New Orleans at the time, passed it along to Mme. Fretageot to publish at New Harmony. He called it a "master piece of Logical reasoning," written in Fanny's usual forthright style, but thought Mme. Fretageot should exercise prudence about including the section on marriage. He suspected it might "injure with some the circulation of your sheet," as people whom marriage had trapped would feel it in their interests "to prevent others obtaining all the benifits on easier terms." Mary Carroll, a friend who ran a millinery shop in New Orleans, felt she could not openly distribute anything dealing with subjects so ticklish but promised to do what she could to promote Fanny's ideas.[38]

Their time in New Orleans was brief, as Fanny was impatient to get to Nashoba. On New Year's Day, 1828, they boarded the *Belvidere*, and on the trip upriver Mrs. Trollope began to suspect that the America she had come with Frances Wright to share was a creation of myth and Fanny's desire. The men in the *Belvidere*'s cabin all called each other "General," "Colonel," "Major," or "Judge." At dinner Mrs. Trollope was taken aback by "the total want of all the usual courtesies of the table," the speed with which they ate, "the loathsome spitting, from the contamination of which it was absolutely impossible to protect our dresses; the frightful manner of feeding with their knives, till the whole blade seemed to enter into the mouth; and the still more frightful manner of cleaning the teeth afterwards with a pocket knife." The conversation, such as it was, was entirely political, "and the respective claims of Adams and Jackson to the presidency were argued with more oaths and more vehemence than it had ever been my lot to hear." A seven-foot Kentucky horse dealer broke up a quarrel between a colonel and a major by calling on the heavens to confound them both and bidding them sit still or be damned.[39]

The *Belvidere* ran aground, and Mrs. Trollope had to endure almost two days more of such companionship. Several steamboats tried and failed to help theirs before it was pulled off the bar with grappling hooks. They got to Memphis at midnight in a pouring rain, and because mud made the new road up the high cliff almost impassable, they lost their shoes and gloves in the exhausting struggle to climb it. But when their messy party at last reached the new hotel that the Andersons had built, word was put out that Fanny Wright had arrived, and everyone hurried to help them into the best rooms in the house. They woke to discover that the heavy rains had made it impossible for a carriage to get through the forests, and they had to stay for at least another day.

Again a public meal fed Frances Trollope's apprehension. The table was laid for fifty, and by the time they arrived, the places were almost all taken. Mrs. Trollope was flattered to be seated next to the hostess, but appalled that her servant William was put just across from her. The company were all shopkeepers, eating in perfect silence, and so quickly that the first few seated had finished almost before the others could begin. "The instant they ceased to eat," said the astonished Mrs. Trollope, "they darted from the table in the same moody silence . . . and a second set took their places, who performed their silent parts in the same manner." The only sounds she heard were of knives and forks and an occasional coughing. She had begun to suspect that she and Fanny Wright might have very different ideas about the basic requirements of civilized life.

The next morning they started for Nashoba in a caravan drawn by two horses and soon came to a bridge made of big tree trunks thrown across a stream, with the trunks of smaller trees laid on top. Although such bridges were picturesque, they trembled when a wagon passed over, and the black driver decided to bypass this one by fording what appeared a shallow space of water. Their pole soon disappeared, however, and their carriage began to sink. They wondered gently to the driver if they should go on, but he only "grinned, and flogged in reply." Soon the front wheels disappeared, and the horses began to plunge and kick, but the driver kept calmly on until the splinter bar gave way. He then said quietly, "I expect you'll best be riding out upon the horses, as we've got into an unhandsome fix here." Fanny, who had sat through it all in apparent calm, said yes, they would have to do that, and eventually they found themselves back around Mrs. Anderson's fire. Fanny, her patience exhausted, left the others at Memphis and set off again on horseback with William Abbott, who later reported that she had easily ridden through places that would have "daunted the boldest hunter."

The following day the Trollope entourage got into a high-slung carriage, and Mrs. Trollope amused herself by watching the cool skill with which the driver wended his way around and over three-foot tree stumps. As they came closer to Nashoba, the forest grew thicker and more dreary, and when, two months out from London, they reached their goal at last, Mrs. Trollope saw that she had made a terrible mistake: "One glance sufficed to convince me that every idea I had formed of the place was as far as possible from the truth." All she could feel was desolation, and she thought that she and Fanny realized at the same moment that they had "erred in thinking that a few months passed together at this spot could be productive of pleasure to either." Fanny seemed utterly indifferent to all the things she herself looked on with dismay: "I never heard or read of any enthusiasm approaching her's, except in some few instances, in ages past, of religious fanaticism." The notion that Fanny had the religious temperament was not original with Mrs. Trollope. Sismondi had earlier remarked on it to Julia Garnett: "After all, your friend, with all her aversion to religion is madly religious . . . like others she has made for herself a mysterious system whose absurdities do not disgust her . . . She is a new Saint Theresa in whom the love of principle and usefulness operates as the love of God did in the other."[40]

It seemed to Mrs. Trollope that Fanny was "perfectly unconscious that her existence was deprived of all that makes life desirable" and was an entirely different person, "in dress, looks, and manner," from the woman she had admired in Paris and in London. When they got to Nashoba, they found no milk, indeed nothing to drink except rainwater. There was a little wheat bread; to the Trollopes the Indian corn bread was inedible. The only vegetables were rice and a few potatoes they had brought from Memphis. The only meat was pork, and they found neither cheese nor butter. Yet Mrs. Trollope thought Fanny unaffectedly surprised that she, as a reasonable woman, found anything wanting in the life there. Fanny ate bits of corn bread and "smiled with the sort of complacency that we may conceive Peter the Hermit felt when eating his acorns in the wilderness."[41]

The bedroom they shared had no ceiling, and the floor was of loosely laid planks. Rain dropped through the roof, and the chimney caught fire a dozen times a day. But Fanny "stood in the midst of all this desolation, with the air of a conqueror," as well she might, according to Mrs. Trollope, since she had apparently triumphed over all merely human weakness.

Each building had two large rooms that were simply furnished but which, Mrs. Trollope discovered, had none of "those minor comforts which ordinary minds class among the necessaries of life." Camilla and Whitby looked like specters and explained their bad health as the fault of the climate. Everyone struck Frances Trollope as miserable. Camilla, she thought, shared her own suspicion that Fanny's "fine mind was not in the healthy state it used to be." Lolotte, whom Mrs.

Trollope called "the New Orleans washer woman," and her three children seemed full of "wretched regret and repining," and the slaves appeared only when they brought logs for the fires.[42]

On entering the Mississippi, Frances Trollope had expected to be "very happy, and very free from care at Nashoba," but it was immeasurably worse than she had imagined possible. Frightened for her children in the "pestilential atmosphere," she borrowed $300 from the community and on January 26 returned to Memphis on her way to Cincinnati, "in all respects the finest situation west of the Alleghanies." She hoped somehow to make a living as she waited for Mr. Trollope to join her there in repairing their fortunes. As for the artist Hervieu, Fanny had decided on the Atlantic that he was fit for nothing but his art and apparently told him so. After looking at the school and seeing that it consisted, as Mrs. Trollope so vividly put it, of "three yellow children running wild in the swamps," he left with her.[43]

Fanny prided herself on mental courage, and she was not one to let it flag in Frances Trollope's presence. She was also probably in a state akin to shock. Although by her own standards her existence was by no means "deprived of all that makes life desirable," Nashoba had clearly deteriorated in her absence, the state of the food being merely the most obvious indication. She had followed Lafayette's example in steeling herself to live frugally, but she could not expect to live in health on a lifetime diet of pork and rice. Camilla and Whitby had been intermittently ill since August. And when Robert Dale arrived from Liverpool a few days after Fanny, he did not bring the recruits both of them had expected.

In the next few months, Fanny learned to live with disappointments that might have swamped a soul less hardy. First, she had to come to terms with Camilla's marriage to Whitby, which remains something of a mystery. Camilla wrote Harriet that the circumstances which decided her on marriage were "of a very peculiar nature and such as it were impossible to explain by letter." To Robert Jennings she said more simply, "various circumstances combined to induce me to conform to the legal ceremony of marriage."

Mrs. Trollope described Whitby as coarse-minded and un-educated—a surly brute who would not let Camilla be a good wife to him—and she said of Camilla that she sweetly accepted her own misery and the disappointment she expected Fanny to suffer in all her schemes. But Frances Trollope was an angry and biased witness. A sensitive, gentle man who felt his lack of social polish might well behave badly under the shock of a British lady's disdain. There is no evidence that Camilla complained of cruelty, and Mrs. Trollope herself admitted that she seemed "greatly attached" to her husband.[44]

Camilla showed little joy, however, in the union and made it clear from the beginning that no bond would keep her from Fanny's side: "wherever she resided there I should be also." Both sisters wrote of the marriage in the most stilted terms, as when Fanny told Lafayette that Whitby had "long been attached" to Camilla "and the intimate knowledge of his excellence and continued interchange of kindness and affection . . . ended by inspiring her with similar feelings." Though Fanny's statements on the matter are all perfectly correct, there can be no doubt that Camilla felt her deep dismay.[45]

Fanny had also to face what Mary Carroll called the "indignation of the multitude" against her. The ocean no longer cut her off from the outrage Richardson had loosed, and since the public by now associated her with Robert Owen, whatever anger he sparked burned her as well. He had come with Robert Dale from Liverpool to New Orleans to preach his own faith, and had issued a challenge there to anyone who would defend Christianity against his onslaught in public debate. Before Fanny sensed what bitter hostility seethed against her, she had also given over her "Explanatory Notes" for publication.

The *Memphis Advocate* apparently published it late that January, and on the thirtieth the *New Harmony Gazette* began to issue it in three parts. In early February, according to Mary Carroll, Fanny's agent pretended ignorance when a man sitting next to her observed that one fine morning Miss Wright might find her throat cut. An enemy circulated the *Advocate* throughout New Orleans, and a former admirer of Fanny's insisted that unless Mary Carroll cut all ties with her, her own character would be destroyed. "The outcry against you for your noble assertion of what you deem the truth," Miss Carroll sadly observed, "is such as to make any one less acquainted with the present state of the human mind totally despair of any liberal or even humane change." The outrage evoked by the Nashoba address eventually prompted Fanny to decide that "the present generation, as a mass, is corrupt past reform." She hoped that future generations would read it "and look back with mingled wonder and compassion on the age when licentious editors and their anonymous correspondents could libel truths so simple, and their readers be won to believe that they, and not Frances Wright, were on the side of common sense and sane morality!"[46]

Nor could even Lafayette deflect the anger against Fanny. Though her new radicalism tried his patience, he believed her sincere and defended her to those whose will to sympathy was more tepid than his. He wrote James and Dolley Madison that Fanny believed total colonization next to impossible and thought the object now was "to soften and finally do away prejudices of colour, by the experiment of common education, for which a seminary should be set up at Nashoba." But though Dolley Madison had very much admired Fanny—"a disposition which I could not prevail upon [Fanny] to cultivate"—her husband wrote him that with Fanny's "rare talents & still rarer disinterestedness" she had created "insuperable obstacles to the good fruits of which they might be productive by her disregard or rather defiance of the most established opinion & vivid feelings."[47]

When Lafayette heard that Cadwallader Colden and Charles Wilkes would no longer receive the Wright sisters, he was afraid that, should Fanny go to New York and find their doors bolted against her, it might unhinge "her fixed enthusiastic mind" and break "her affectionate generous heart." Though the substance of her ideas and Camilla's was probably set, he hoped that the "tender voice of friendship" might restrain them in the manner in which they expressed themselves. But he swayed no one and learned instead that not a single Philadelphia editor would publish the "Explanatory Notes."[48]

The last disappointment was perhaps the most bitter: Fanny had to accept Nashoba's failure both as an experiment to end slavery and as a community based on cooperative labor. About the time that the "Explanatory Notes" reached their readers, they became obsolete, for on January 29 Fanny acknowledged in the Nashoba log that her methods of dealing with the slaves—and the methods of those she had trusted—had failed. The slaves had proved idle unless constantly watched, and so the trustees put them under the management of one John Gilliam for the season to come. The overseer system Fanny and Flower had designed Nashoba to avoid had won out at last.[49]

Two days later, Nashoba's four resident trustees—Fanny, Camilla, Whitby, and Robert Dale Owen—signed yet another communication to the public, this time transforming Nashoba into a society of small capitalists, a plan they called less rational but more practical for them. Ideally, they wrote, a member gave of his or her time and labor as the community needed and was supported by it in return, but this assumed that each member had been trained physically to do the work a community demanded. They had earlier accepted a financial substitute for labor, but in doing so, they had introduced what now seemed an invidious distinction between those who worked and those who did not. Humbled by the fact that "they themselves and the friends they know best and trust most possess not the physical requisites as cooperatives," they decided to abandon the option for work but resolved to educate whatever children they might have to be "physically independent of money." Meanwhile each member of the community would contribute $100 yearly to cover his or her board. When Harriett Garnett heard of the latest change she observed of Nashoba that it had become "merely a boarding house and composed at present of one family."[50]

Behind the polished language lay the facts that not only had they failed in a radical social experiment, but they had also failed abysmally as farmers. In 1827 Nashoba produced only $150 worth of corn, $25 of fodder, $59.28 of cotton—plus 8 dozen eggs, 68 pounds of butter, and 73 chickens. Fanny, who had begun in the belief that land and labor were wealth, insisted, "In principle we were right, but with a view to actual practice in the existing generation we were wrong." She observed ruefully, "cooperation . . . has well nigh killed us all." More than a year later Fanny said of Nashoba that it "savored more of young enthusiasm than mature judgment . . . more of righteous intent than of practical wisdom." She blamed its failure in part on her "then imperfect acquaintance with the character and condition of the American people," as well as the fact that she had assumed "a fairer state of the cotton market than it has sustained."[51]

A casual observer might have thought her untroubled. She bought a lot in Memphis and planned to build a house where Richardson and Josephine could live and welcome them or their guests. She wrote Lafayette that if he sent his notes regularly, within two years she could finish the biography and pay another long visit to La Grange to revise it with his help. As though all Nashoba's future lay happily before them, she told Lafayette that the land was free of debt and whatever money they earned would go "to the one object to wch we stand pledged by my deed—*a school wch shall be especially open to children of color.*" In two years, she thought, they should be ready for it, and she wrote Robert Jennings that they would do everything they could to bring him there as schoolmaster within a year or, at the outside, a year and a half: "We have all had our share of sufferings and exertions. I have had mine, dear Jennings, but they have left me only firmer in my purpose, more inflexible in principle, while they have enriched me with experience, dearly but not too dearly purchased, seeing that it is invaluable."[52]

But Fanny gradually realized that in publishing the "Explanatory Notes" she had destroyed whatever slim chance remained that

Nashoba could survive. Madison wrote Lafayette in February that "her views of amalgamating the white and black population [are] . . . universally obnoxious" and her notions on religion and marriage almost equally so, "the effect of which your knowledge of this Country can readily estimate." Benjamin Lundy wrote that the practices adopted at Nashoba "respecting religion and government are too latitudinarian, and averse to the nature and general opinions of mankind, to promise the usefulness anticipated by the friends of the institution." Although Fanny reported that visitors and sympathetic letters continued to arrive—"Consistent liberty has more secret friends than appears to the eye of the world"—no one offered to join them.[53]

Nor did the reaction in Europe promise more recruits. Harriet believed that Fanny and Camilla had plunged into an abyss: "The gates of the most rigid convent are not so insurmountable [a] barrier betwixt the world and the nun they enclose, as public scorn makes against a woman who has joined such a community as Nashoba." Sismondi wrote what might have been Fanny's obituary: "she is giving her life, her talent, her reputation, not to serve but to injure those negroes and men of color for whom she feels so generous a pity." With such power to effect great things, she had thrown her life away, he decided, and when he heard that she had not yet accepted defeat, he thought her not only mistaken but presumptuous.[54]

Though criticism by now made Fanny only more stubborn, the chain of events had power to move her. First, Robert Dale Owen left Nashoba. An urgent financial crisis called him to New Harmony, but when he got there, he found things less dreadful than he had expected. There was more spirit than when he had left a year earlier; the people who worked hardest were doing well on the individual system, though the informality of the place was little changed. Scientific lectures were given once a week, and the Thespian Society had begun presenting plays. He hoped they might try one of Fanny's tragedies, and he lured her with the idea that she might direct it. He decided to stay. With his father's promise to give him and William the printing office and the lot on which it stood, Robert Dale took over the *Gazette* as editor.[55]

Not long after, another man tried to beguile Fanny away. Apparently a friend of Sir John Bowring and, through him, of Jeremy Bentham, he was Otto Braun, who visited Nashoba and wrote on his return to Memphis that it was a dreary prospect. Will it, he asked Fanny, fatten your stock? Will it provide for your table or produce flowers for the birthdays of your friends? Though Fanny had insisted she would never marry, she had already married herself, he argued, "to a soil which I will not call poor—but I can compare it to a big swollen heavy lubberly lazy scurvy fellow, who can only by physic and training be rendered tolerable in society." Wondering what spirit of revenge united her to it, he proposed to be her banker and steward on a trip to New Harmony. For the moment, Fanny stopped her ears.[56]

In mid-April, Camilla and Whitby left for New Harmony because Camilla believed that a change of climate was "indispensably requisite to renovate my own and my husbands health." She sensed imminent failure at Nashoba, and if it happened, she thought she could happily make her home at New Harmony, "where I could enjoy a greater degree of liberty mental and moral than in any other spot on earth save at my home."[57]

Six weeks of solitude left Fanny ready. In the first week of June she was on a Mississippi steamboat heading upriver to New Harmony. She explained to Harriet Garnett that she was going in order to help unravel the tangled affairs between Owen and Maclure, but they had been settled more than a year earlier. Sixteen years later she gave other reasons for deciding, finally, that she had to move on: "For the first time, she bowed her spirit in humility before the omnipotence of collective Humanity. 'Man Species is alone capable of effecting what I, weak existence of an hour! have thought myself equal to attempt.'" If she continued "an obstinate prosecution of her enterprise," she would endanger her life and lose what chance she had to serve her fellows. At the same time, she had "acquired no ordinary amount of varied experience, and of familiarity with questions upon which hinge the welfare of populations, and the grandeur and duration of empires." She believed that "in her practical efforts at reform, she had begun at the wrong end." She was convinced, however, that "with a view to the accurate comprehension of the vital interests of the country, and of the world at large . . . she had begun at the *right* end." And no one was less discouraged than she.[58]

Fanny concluded that her preparations for Nashoba, and the experiment itself, had given her "the information and the experience . . . to guide the efforts of a really efficient leader of the popular mind." Always eager to find diamonds in dustbins, she believed herself now ready to prepare "the popular mind for the exercise, with knowledge, of popular power." She talked a while longer as though she would go back. But the stage was empty and the drama of Nashoba was done.[59]

The Latter-Day
Saint Theresa

7

On the near side of thirty-three and as a self-styled leader of the popular mind, Fanny Wright began the period that was the most vital in her life. Within two weeks of her arrival in New Harmony in June 1828, she joined Robert Dale Owen as co-editor of his eight-page quarto weekly, the *New Harmony Gazette*. Proposing to buy it in October, when he completed the third year of its current series, she stipulated that she might remove it to Nashoba or anywhere else it might more profitably be published.[1]

As joint editor of the *Gazette*, Fanny became probably the first woman since colonial times to edit an American paper meant for general circulation. Eleven women had run printing presses before 1776, and ten of them published newspapers, but none took the active editorial role Fanny did. In her new position she knocked insistently at the massive door of an exclusive and rowdy men's club. Most newspapers dealt almost wholly with electoral politics, from which women's active participation was excluded by law. And at few times in American history have those papers had such good reason to call their opposition scurrilous and corrupt. By midsummer 1828, they had lined up dramatically for either John Quincy Adams or Andrew Jackson for the presidency, and Fanny found herself in the midst of a newspaper war as vicious as any since Thomas Jefferson's first campaign for the presidency. Nor would the dirt it spattered land only on candidates for public office.[2]

The Jackson people and the Jackson papers, angry still over the general's defeat four years earlier, accused Adams of stealing the 1824 election by making a corrupt bargain with Henry Clay for the presidency in return for the State Department. They claimed Adams betrayed his own friends and the interests of the South and West, though his much-abused alliance with Clay of Kentucky would seem to belie the latter charge. They touted Jackson, who rode grandly in a carriage and four, as a common man, and accused Adams, who walked or rode the public stage, of being a monarchist at heart. Hoping to exploit the new evangelical fervor, they even attacked Adams for being a Unitarian.

The Adams people and the Adams papers accused Jackson of vices ranging from ignorance to murder. They condemned his ruthless campaigns of 1813 and 1814 against the Creek Indians in Florida, his high-handed executions of six militia men and two British subjects there, his fabled duels, and his violations as an army general of both federal laws and official protocol. The most vicious attack, however, they reserved for his wife. As Charles Hammond of the *Cincinnati Daily Gazette* put it that spring, when the American public were "called upon to place [Mrs. Jackson] at the head of the female society of the land," it became necessary to expose her character. As Fanny had publicly repudiated the conventional moral assumptions governing sexuality and marriage, Charles Hammond's treatment of Mrs. Jackson should have told her how vulnerable she would be as a public person.[3]

The facts of the Jackson scandal in skeletal form are these: more than thirty-five years earlier, Rachel Jackson had been the wife of Lewis Robards, a jealous and difficult man whom she had married before she was eighteen. She had lived with him and his mother in Virginia until Robards asked the Donelsons, Rachel's family, to take her back to Nashville. Apparently at his mother's urging, he subsequently went to Tennessee to live with her and her family. Andrew Jackson was boarding with the Donelsons at the time, but because Robards became jealous of him, Jackson left. Some months later Robards returned alone to Virginia, saying he had no intention of living again in Tennessee. Later still, when word came that he wanted his wife to join him, she fled to Natchez with a trading party that Jackson helped to guard against Indian attack. Report flew to Natchez that the 1790 Virginia Assembly had granted Robards a divorce on grounds of desertion, and Jackson asked Rachel to marry him. She did so in 1791. Two years later they discovered that the Virginia legislative act had merely allowed Robards to file for divorce, which he had not done at the time. In September 1793, a jury of twelve men, declaring Mrs. Robards guilty of adultery, granted him the divorce. The Jacksons went through a second marriage ceremony in January 1794 and by all accounts lived together in unusual happiness. Charles Hammond himself acknowledged that "the evidence is full and clear that, as Mrs. Jackson, the lady's conduct had been exemplary and irreproachable." To Hammond, however, that was not the point. In 1828 he published a pamphlet labeling Rachel Jackson a modern Jezebel by whom her real husband had been deceived and disgraced and calling Jackson "her paramour husband." "Everything valuable in human society," Hammond wrote, "depends upon the veneration with which female chastity is regarded . . . were it not for the influence, which that almost angelic quality exercises over the minds of men, the most polished society would . . . degenerate into a despicable state of barbarism."[4]

Rachel Jackson's husband was one of the most powerful men in America, yet the press considered her fair game. For thirty-five years a beloved and eminently respectable wife, she was vilified as an adulteress whose example threatened the foundations of society itself. With so much to protect her, she was shamelessly used by men hungry for power, and if Fanny thought Charles Hammond merely aberrant, she was mistaken. Though many were appalled, many joined his attack. Unable to silence the voices raised against Mrs. Jackson, some of her defenders picked up the rumor that John Quincy Adams and his wife, Louisa, had had premarital intercourse. Such was the level of discussion and such the level of hysteria that sexual questions could inspire in the American republic at the very moment Fanny chose to confront it head-on.

Fanny, of course, had attacked not only conventional sexual morality but also religion. Though Alexis de Tocqueville observed a few years later that Christianity retained "a greater influence over the souls of men" in America than in any other country in the world, Fanny was unsparing in her attacks. What she heard when she got to New Harmony, however, might well have given her pause, for the revival spirit was sweeping the Ohio Valley. George Flower told of seeing a cheerful party of young people at a camp meeting transformed by a preacher who played the stops on the organ of his audience, pitching his own voice in a gathering crescendo to call out their groans and amens. Most of the people he saw were women: charged with a sexual energy their culture said they must ignore, they briefly found release as they gave in to an ecstasy of self-abasement, convulsed by fear—or its pretense—that they would be damned.[5]

Nothing could more deeply repel Fanny Wright, and she described the phenomenon as follows: "by the sudden combination of the clergy of three orthodox sects, a *revival*, as such scenes of distraction are wont to be styled, was opened in houses, churches, and even on the Ohio river. The victims of this odious experiment on human credulity and nervous weakness, were invariably women. Helpless age was made a public spectacle, innocent youth driven to raving insanity, mothers and daughters carried lifeless from the presence of the ghostly expounders of damnation; all ranks shared the contagion, until the despair of Calvin's hell itself seemed to have fallen upon every heart, and discord to have taken possession of every mansion." Instead of muting her attack on Christianity, or diverting it for the period of the hysteria to subjects less fraught with emotion, Fanny, "since all were dumb," took upon herself "the cause of insulted reason and outraged humanity."[6]

But it was not against the circuit riders that Fanny turned her indignation; it was against the pastors and ministers who daily cultivated a soil from which fruit so misshapen grew. When she learned that the pastor of a Philadelphia church had demanded the formation of a Christian Party in Politics to keep all "opponents of Christianity" out of public office, she saw Christianity itself as the villain. In an America where, as Frances Trollope observed, religion was tea-table talk and its strict observance a fashionable mark of distinction, Fanny pitted herself against religion.

For the next two years, in her paper and on the platform, Fanny sounded the themes of equality, rationality, tolerance, and peace. Assuming that habits and beliefs could be changed by rational persuasion, she patiently examined the shortcomings of the society around her. Assuming that Americans wanted to be equals, she showed them how far they were from that goal and set herself to explore the changes the country had to make to achieve it. If she never admitted that she enjoyed her hours upon the stage—if she inclined to believe that only duty to high ideals called her from the quiet, scholarly life she claimed to prefer—she nevertheless thought that men and women could live more nearly in keeping with the ideals of the Revolution than they seemed to do in the second quarter of the American nineteenth century.

On July 4, 1828, at New Harmony, Indiana, Frances Wright became probably the first woman in America to be the main speaker on a public occasion before a large mixed audience. She sounded her conviction that the superiority of the national institutions lay in their capacity for reform, and she demonstrated her instinct for pushing against the cultural grain. In a country ready to vote overwhelmingly to make Andrew Jackson president, she attacked military parade and "all ideas of military glory." To a people inclined to boast of their superiority over any other nation, she attacked patriotism as it was commonly understood: "love of country in an exclusive sense . . . love of our countrymen in contradistinction to the love of our fellow-creatures . . . love of the constitution, instead of love or appreciation of those principles upon which the constitution is, or ought to be, based." In a country most Europeans found peculiarly driven by the acquisitive spirit, she called for Americans "to lay aside luxury, whose wealth is in industry . . . ambitious distinctions, whose principle is equality." She insisted "that Equality means, not the mere equality of political rights . . . but equality of instruction and equality in virtue; and that Liberty means—not the mere voting at elections, but the free and fearless exercise of the mental faculties."[7]

It was a dazzling beginning. But New Harmony was not the place to rout the forces that pulled America from its revolutionary ideals; she had to go where the country's political and economic energies were more vitally engaged. Consequently, she gave her second public lecture on August 10 at the Cincinnati Courthouse, and she spoke there again the two following Sundays. Her lectures were so crowded that she repeated them in one of the theaters, and she was so sensational that Cincinnati crushed in to hear her. Frances Trollope, drawn to the courthouse when she heard a number of other women were going, was stunned by Fanny's commanding presence: "I knew her extraordinary gift of eloquence, her almost unequalled command of words, and the wonderful power of her rich and thrilling voice . . . [but] all my expectations fell far short of the splendour, the brilliance, the overwhelming eloquence of this extraordinary orator . . . Her tall and majestic figure, the deep and almost solemn expression of her eyes, the simple contour of her finely formed head, unadorned, excepting by its own natural ringlets; her garment of plain white muslin, which hung around her in folds that recalled the drapery of a Grecian statue, all contributed to produce an effect, unlike any thing I had ever seen before, or ever expect to see again."[8]

Fanny now knew that what she had earlier mistaken "for the energy of enlightened liberty . . . was, perhaps, rather the restlessness of commercial enterprise," but she refused to believe that Americans would deliberately choose the pursuit of material goods and social distinction over the pleasures of egalitarian society. She believed that the impulse to lord it over one's fellows represented a failure of understanding rather than a permanent human characteristic. No doubt the connections between money and democratic possibilities were not entirely clear in her own mind, and she was not yet so impolitic as to confront the subject directly in public. But she knew that an authentic republic was impossible unless wealth was generally shared. Counting on the civility of the educated heart, she thought that universal free public education could develop the republican spirit that would allow America's republican institutions to work. If Fanny Wright approached her audience with an eighteenth-century commitment to rationality, clarity, and tolerance, she also approached it with a nineteenth-century belief in the saving grace of education. And she approached it as a messiah.[9]

Although she carried a book in which she had written out her lectures, she seldom referred to it, and the breadth of her learning took her audiences by surprise. Her purpose, she said, was to outline "the field of truth" and "to expose such existing errors as must tend to blind the intellectual sight to its perception." At once modest in her personal habits and adept at self-dramatization, she claimed: "I have wedded the cause of human improvement; staked [on it] my reputation, my fortune, and my life; and as, for it, I threw behind me in earliest youth the follies of my age, the luxuries of ease and European aristocracy . . . so will I . . . devote what remains to me of talent, strength, fortune, and existence, to the same sacred cause—the promotion of just knowledge, the establishing of just practice, the increase of human happiness." She had left "the studies and retirement which I love" to do battle in "a world distracted with dissension and profaned with vice." Though she asked merely to reason with her audiences, she inflamed them in ways unprecedented in America.[10]

A century earlier Samuel Johnson had contemptuously compared a female preacher to a dog that walked on its hind legs: it is not done well but one is surprised to find it done at all. And nine years later, when Sarah and Angelina Grimké attacked slavery before large mixed audiences, they were criticized in a pastoral letter that denounced women who "so far forget themselves as to itinerate in the character of public lecturers and teachers" and who thereby "fall in shame and dishonor into the dust." More inflammatory than the Grimkés because she was without religious sanction, Fanny, by her very act of speaking, challenged America's assumption that women, in Mrs. Trollope's phrase, should be "guarded by a sevenfold shield of habitual insignificance." Only in Quaker assemblies had they been allowed, equally with men, the right to speak. The literature of the day glorified what one historian has called True Womanhood, a complex of virtues of which the four most important were piety, purity, submissiveness, and domesticity. And in calling on the nation to educate "the sex which in all ages has ruled the destinies of the world," Fanny Wright threatened every one of those virtues.[11]

Not only did she have the audacity to take the public platform, she also argued that women were men's equals and had to be treated as such in all the business of life. Simply because they were human beings, women needed "the security of well-regulated, self-possessed minds, well-grounded, well-reasoned . . . opinions, and self-approved, consistent practice." Men and women, Fanny insisted further, were mutually dependent, and if women were unenlightened, they would injure and debase the men with whom they lived. Nor could affection prevail between them "until power is annihilated on one side, fear and obedience on the other, and both restored to their birthright—equality."[12]

With equal trenchancy, Fanny scored religion as a divisive and wasteful servant to power. Though she was financially independent and thus a free agent who could speak the truth, the clergy were hired preachers, and "the hired preachers of all sects, creeds, and religions, never do, and never can, teach any thing but what is in conformity with the opinions of those who pay them." Her bias initially shaped by the history of Christianity in Europe and Great Britain, Fanny charged that religion sparked, and "the prolific brain of insatiate priestcraft" encouraged, discord rather than universal charity and tolerance. Twenty million dollars were spent each year in the United States to rear competing churches, publish tracts for the unconvinced, and send missionaries abroad who were ignorant of their native geography and badly spoke their native tongue. Meanwhile, the churches fought serious social reform: "Is any improvement suggested in our social arrangements, calculated to equalize property, labour, instruction, and enjoyment; to destroy crime by removing provocation; vice, by removing ignorance; and to build up virtue in the human breast by exchanging the spirit of self abasement for that of self respect—who are the foremost to treat the suggestions as visionary, the reform as impossible? Even they who live by the fears and the vices of their fellow creatures; and who obtain their subsistence on earth by opening and shutting the door of heaven." She pleaded for her audiences to turn their attention "to your jails, to your penitentiaries, to your houses of refuge, to your hospitals, to your asylums . . . to your haunts of intemperance, to your victims lost in vice and hardened in profligacy, to childhood without protection, to youth without guidance, to the widow without sustenance, to the female destitute and female outcast, sentenced to shame and sold to degradation." Look there, she said, and find a world to reform.[13]

Repeatedly she attacked the corrupting power of wealth, for those with money, she insisted, determined the message people would hear. In the South, for example, she had never once heard a minister "comment on the evil which saps the industry, vitiates the morals, and threatens the tranquility of the country." She found the reason a British radical was likely to find: "The master of the slave is he who pays the preacher, and the preacher must not irritate his paymaster." Nowhere was "the master vice" attacked: "the rich and pampered few are ever spared, or so gently dealt with, as rather agreeably to tickle the ear, than to probe the conscience, while the crimes of the greatly-tempted, greatly-suffering poor, are visited with unrelenting vigour."[14]

She fought against power: the power of the learned over the credulous; the power of the priest over the communicant; the power of the male over female, of slave owner over slave. Persistently she called for the equal distribution of knowledge, which would make liberty and equality possible. If people were not educated as equals, they could not be equal, and if they were not equal, they could not be free: "Do not the rich command instruction, and they who have instruction must they not possess the power? and when they have the power, will they not exert it in their own favour?" She instinctively knew, further, that "While the many are left in ignorance, the few cannot be wise, for they cannot be virtuous."[15]

Fanny ended her lectures by calling for the creation in each community of a Hall of Science, where three thousand to five thousand people could come together to build the institutions of a republican culture. The peaceful revolution that she hoped would bring America back to the ideals of its founders could not be made by people working and living in isolation from each other. They needed a place where they could share ideas and shed prejudices—a community center with museums, libraries, and good instructors. Each center, she hoped, would eventually add a School of Industry where children could get an education befitting citizens of a republic. Before turning back to New Harmony, she lectured in Hamilton, Ohio, and Louisville, Kentucky, encouraging committees to take contributions after each of her appearances toward a Hall of Science.

Over the next year and a half, as she spoke from Boston to New Orleans, she paid her audiences the respect of taking them seriously. She was, as Lafayette said, "quite determined in the pursuit of her

Drawing of Nashoba, April 19, 1828

Cincinnati waterfront (1848)

vocation," and she believed she had found something meaningful to do with her life. Her indifference to the world's opinion—her instinct for defiance—and her desire to be a public teacher, however, were in significant conflict, and this she never fully understood. Overwhelmingly earnest, she awakened hope in thousands of men as well as women. But on the whole, America's response to Fanny Wright exposed the underside of its bright promise.[16]

Public sentiment was harder to change than Fanny yet suspected, and influential Cincinnati was titillated rather than convinced. Socially conservative forces monopolized public discourse, and she and Robert Dale rallied themselves to redress the balance both in print and on the podium. The *New Harmony Gazette* found its purpose in part in reporting what the daily press ignored, such as that Fanny's first Cincinnati lecture was so crowded that the audience spilled out into the hallways, down the steps, and around the courthouse. Despite the sensation she caused, the major Cincinnati papers noticed her lectures only obliquely. The *Evening Chronicle*, for example, rebuffed her by saying there was no such thing as an unhappy marriage, referring to her "celebrated circular upon the amalgamation of the straight and curly haired races," and concluding that "her recent opinions . . . are as inimical to sound morals as they are repugnant to the delicacy and purity of a virtuous female." It printed a letter by "Oliver Oldschool" criticizing her but refused to print her reply.[17]

Charles Hammond, however, published Fanny's response in the *Daily Gazette*, prefacing it with a note regretting that "so much native and so much acquired talent, so much calculated to make her an ornament to society as a wife and a mother, should be thrown away . . . upon associations so much beneath her." Among other things, "Oldschool" had remarked that Fanny would do better taking on the care of a family and had quoted Bonaparte's riposte to Mme. de Staël: the greatest woman is she who has the most children. Fanny replied that Bonaparte's remark was right for a military man who wanted soldiers for his battles and "saw in his fellow creatures only tools of ambition." Educating children justly was superior, however, to merely having them, and taking care of one family was less important than "encouraging the heads of all families to enquire how they may best take care of theirs."[18]

Had Fanny spent her three weeks in Cincinnati looking hard at life there, she might have understood how formidable was the task she had set herself. Cincinnati, in fact, was a fledgling city on the make, "generally considered the most flourishing and best situated town" west of the Alleghenies, and at the time it offered a kind of paradigm of the American heartland.

So far as Frances Trollope could see, for example, Cincinnati offered people nothing to do but work or go to church. The men set themselves in single-minded fashion to garnering money: "neither art, science, learning, nor pleasure can seduce them from its pursuit." Few went to the theater, most women considering the stage an offense against religion. Sundays were especially dreary. It was considered scandalous to write or to read anything except the Bible; "nor do I believe that there is any crime in the decalogue, the perpetration of which would produce so strong an expression of public indignation, as singing a song on Sunday."[19]

Cincinnati was not an ideal city to reform, further, because its mores were old-fashioned and inflexible. Men and women seldom talked together, in part because their lives were so different they had little to share. Women had no place in politics, while men were obsessed with what Mrs. Trollope called "incessant electioneering." In large gatherings, the women invariably went to one side of the room, and the men to the other: "The gentlemen spit, talk of elections and the price of produce, and spit again. The ladies look at each other's dresses till they know every pin by heart; talk of Parson Somebody's last sermon on the day of judgment, or Dr. T'otherbody's new pills for dyspepsia, till the 'tea' is announced." Men dined, played cards, had musical evenings and suppers, "all in large parties, but all without women."[20]

Propriety operated in peculiar ways. To Mrs. Trollope's amazement, women chattered over tea about the Holy Ghost as readily as about ruffles, but were offended if a man used a word like "corset" in their presence. A group of women had recently demanded of a local proprietor, at penalty of losing their business forever, that he lengthen the petticoat of a girl on a sign to cover her ankles. Picnics were frowned upon because it was thought indelicate for ladies and gentlemen to sit together on the grass.

A religious tyranny, she discovered, could be effectively exercised without the government's being in the least involved in the matter. To be thought socially acceptable, for example, one had to belong to one or another of the various sects, though it scarcely mattered which. It seemed that in no other country did religion have "so strong a hold upon the women, or a lighter hold upon the men," and she decided the clergy's power over women came mainly from paying attention to them. Further, religion gave middle-class women something to do:

"were it not for public worship, and private tea-drinking, all the ladies in Cincinnati would be in danger of becoming pefect recluses."[21]

Fanny Wright knew only one way to try to change all this: by clear, rational persuasion. Men and women oppressed by a coercive society or offended by an unjust one rallied to her. She made friends with men like Dr. William Price, an acknowledged atheist, and Josiah Warren, America's first anarchist, who were the kind of tough-spirited eccentrics she particularly moved. Both the angry and the hopeful flocked to hear her too, and a good many who were simply bored came for the show. Depending on the point of view, she was ridiculous, offensive, or grandly heroic.[22]

Not only did the lecture tour make stern demands on Fanny's moral courage, but she had need of her physical courage as well. One evening in Louisville the crowded balcony began to sag. Someone called "Fire!" and the audience began to panic. A member of the audience told later how Fanny stood quietly on stage, calm as a storm's eye, and set an example that broke the stampede and soothed the hysterical.[23]

Fanny and her little band counted the tour a success. They netted more than two-hundred additional subscribers to the *Gazette*. More important, according to Camilla, Fanny succeeded in "the diffusion of liberal principles and the awakening the attention of the public to the necessity of establishing national schools for the rising generation and thus rescuing them from the ignorance and degradation of the larger portion of the present." Impatient with men and women as they were, Fanny set herself the task of slowly creating the people of the future.[24]

Had she known the kind of gossip she inspired, even among her old friends, Fanny might have grown more impatient still with human nature as it appeared in 1828. Mrs. Trollope listened to "the most violent abuse of these unfortunate sisters." Charles Wilkes worried that in order to "gratify a paltry ambition of distinction," Fanny might come to New York: "Nothing can reconcile me to any female . . . giving lectures." Fanny was in irretrievable disgrace among proper people, he added, because she had defied "all that the world respects and values, in either manners or in laws." When the Garnetts wished Fanny would marry Robert Dale, Anna Garnett Stone assured her family that Fanny was living with a Mr. Jennings, one of the editors of her paper. Far more kind but scarcely less troubled, Lafayette wrote that it was "melancholy . . . to be in want of explanations and yet when they come, to find too often causes for fear or sorrow!" Her talents, he thought, tended to evaporate in theories "of the certainty and utility of which she has not a doubt," and he suspected they might have been "more efficaciously employed, even to promote her own humane purposes." Still, he told Jeremy Bentham that "to know, to respect, and to love her, will ever be, in my sense, one and the same thing."[25]

The awkard truth, however, was that America in 1828 offered a woman like Fanny no institutional means by which the energies, talents, and ambitions she had in such abundance could be "efficaciously employed." Not only did Fanny have to find her own forms and make her own way, but she had all the while to fight a fear of women entrenched so deeply in the assumptions and institutions of her adopted culture that no one even understood it was there. They simply knew that a woman had a place, and if she strayed outside it, the walls of the temple would come down. Her peculiar unworldliness allowed her, further, to underestimate what she asked of others, not because she was unfeeling, but because she made such hard demands on herself. Her heroic capacities for self-sacrifice blinded her to ordinary pleasures and pains, and to the terror of change. As she sat in New Harmony plotting her battle with the powers-that-be in America, Fanny had no idea how threatening she seemed.

In August, Fanny and Robert Dale issued a prospectus for what they called the *New-Harmony and Nashoba Gazette* (although by the time the series began in late October, they had decided to call the paper the *Free Enquirer*). Their motive was "to promote the cause of human improvement." Able to do so because they were "unshackled by any sinister interest or personal obligations or responsibility to any individual or to any sect or party of men," they intended to take on every social issue of general importance, sparing neither the powerful nor the pious. Religion, for example, was either true or false, and if the latter, it was not only useless but "mischievous by its idle terrors . . . its false morality . . . its hypocrisy . . . its fanaticism . . . its dogmatism . . . its threats . . . its hopes . . . its promises; and last though not least by its waste of public time and public money." They pledged to conduct themselves with courtesy, moderation, and good taste and to publish any letters written in the same spirit. They chose as their motto, "Just opinions are the result of just knowledge; just practice of just opinions."[26]

Fanny's success on the stage had been so gratifying that she also decided on another lecture tour, this one to the larger cities of the East. She hoped to try more thoroughly the temper of the times and to find a more central place from which to publish the *Gazette*. Robert Jennings, who had tried but failed to start a school at New Harmony, offered to go with her. He had been on the liberal lecture circuit himself from Ohio to New York, and he knew how to make the necessary arrangements. Fanny gratefully accepted his help and his companionship.[27]

But first she had two problems to solve. One was Nashoba, and the other was Camilla. Winchester had written that the Nashoba overseer had betrayed their trust and dissipated both the store goods and the food supplies, and Whitby had gone downriver alone to see what might be rescued from chaos. In mid-October, Camilla, Fanny, and Jennings had the luck to find a small steamboat that could make the trip to Memphis despite low water in the Mississippi, and when they got to Nashoba, Fanny proposed to Whitby that he take charge at least until Christmas a year hence. Won over to William Maclure's belief that staying at Nashoba would be self-indulgent, she judged it "a poor appropriation of her talents to sit down and devote herself to the emancipation of a few slaves." She also thought herself by now "altogether and in every respect incompetent" to do that. She told Whitby that she wanted to spend her time solely on the *Gazette* and on her lectures, and that she would most likely make her home someplace else. Whitby agreed to arrangements that Fanny thought were "not only the best but the only possible and fair under existing circumstances."[28]

The more difficult problem was Camilla, who was six months pregnant. Fanny's new plans forced Camilla finally to choose between her sister and her husband. Whatever had prompted her to marry Whitby, she had done so when she thought her home, and Fanny's, would be either Nashoba or New Harmony. Fanny had now left the one and seemed likely to leave the other, convinced that she could not change America from the backwaters of Indiana. But Whitby was a simple farmer, who none of them apparently thought might survive transplanting to a more urban life. So Camilla told her husband that she would leave him as soon as she could after their child was born to rejoin her sister.

Nothing that either of the sisters wrote suggests how hard that choice had to be. Camilla had been thought finely suited for marriage, and in 1828 marriage was almost universally considered the purpose of a woman's life. Whitby was Camilla's husband and would remain so. To leave him was not only to defy everything her culture had taught her about her natural place, but to commit herself to bringing up a child alone and to living without either sexual pleasure or marital companionship. It was to deprive a man who loved her of his wife and his child. If, as both Mary Carroll and Frances Trollope thought, Whitby was boorish, Camilla's choice was perhaps less than wrenching. But it was a choice that would seem to have imposed on Fanny an extra obligation to her sister.

Fanny apparently saw no such obligation. Though a four-month delay in her plans would not have damaged their chances of success, at the end of October 1828, she left Camilla in the little house they had built in Memphis to face the terrors and dangers of childbirth without her. More than one of their old friends was shocked that Camilla had to endure confinement in a place like Memphis without what Mrs. Trollope called the "sustaining presence of her sister." Camilla wrote bravely to Harriet Garnett about it: "I shall have my good friend Mlle. Lolotte . . . for my next neighbour, and from her I shall receive a mothers care and attention." But Fanny's leaving her at a time so crucial may well have begun a process of deterioration in the relationship that had been central to both their lives since they were children.[29]

What Fanny now proposed was as daring as anything she had ever done, and the journey itself was so difficult that few would have risked it. Defying the dangers of steamboat travel late in the fall, she was heading farther up the Mississippi than she had ever gone, all the way to St. Louis. From there she and Jennings would wrap themselves in buffalo robes and go by stage and wagon across the prairies of Illinois and Indiana to Louisville, Kentucky. Then once again up the Ohio to Cincinnati and Wheeling, West Virginia. And finally across the Alleghenies to Baltimore, Philadelphia, and New York City itself—"the head seat," as Fanny called it, "of popular energy . . . wealth and power, and financial and political corruption."[30]

Their trials began in Memphis, where they waited six days for a steamboat to pick them up. Finally, on November 3, the *Jubilee* arrived from New Orleans, only to stay the night because of a dense fog. They left in the morning, and sometime that afternoon were thrown by a violent shock: they had been snagged, and the boat full of panicky people began to fill with water. The *Oregon*, passing downriver, turned and drew alongside. The captain and crew came on board to help bail water and load the cargo over the side, and they finally stopped the leaks with blankets, carpets, boards, and whatever else they could find. Many passengers spent the night huddled around fires on the shore, and some walked two miles to the nearest settlement. Fanny slept in the berth she had been assigned, in the midst of the debris the accident had left. The next day they gathered to try once more.[31]

Never deserted by her physical courage, Fanny's excitement grew every step of the way, as bands of men and women dissatisfied with conventional politics gathered for her in each major town and wrote ahead to the next that she was coming. They called themselves liberals, or sometimes radicals, and they had a network of communication taut with the encouragement she brought them to fight for a greater measure of control over their own lives. In St. Louis, where the *Missouri Republican* referred to her as "the celebrated Frances Wright," she spoke four times to good crowds and got seventy-five new *Gazette* subscribers.

In both Louisville and Cincinnati she was almost mobbed after her speeches, and constant visitors made it impossible for her to do anything other than necessary work. About fifty Cincinnati liberals, men of wealth and influence, pledged themselves to try to establish a popular institution such as she advocated and hoped she would return to settle there and throw her energies into it. "Were we to do so I have little doubt," she wrote, "that we should gradually unite the great mass of the population." By December, according to Frances Trollope, people there had subscribed $1,300 for what she called a "Temple of Reason."[32]

The excitement Fanny stirred and the numbers she drew, more and more of them women, swelled as she moved east, and a few days in Baltimore convinced her that the West was out of the question. Henry Rogers, a lecturer on natural philosophy at the Maryland Institute who subsequently had a role in founding the Massachusetts Institute of Technology, wrote that all Baltimore had been "wonderstruck" at Fanny's matchless eloquence: "A prodigy in learning, in intellect and in courage, she awes into deference the most refractory bigots." He said that because of "the narrow-minded policy of the proprietors" of sufficiently large halls, Fanny "was compelled to lecture in the Belvidere Theatre." He went to all five of her lectures and wrote that "there were throughout such clearness and reach of thought, sublimity of diction, and often such powerful philippics against the clergy, that every mind seemed spell-bound throughout the term of her lectures." Fanny wrote Camilla in high spirits that she had lectured five times on successive nights "to an audience whose pressure seemed to endanger the building and whose attention and enthusiasm seemed to portend danger to the old system and its servants." At a meeting of liberals to discuss ways to raise money for the Hall of Science and School of Industry, she reported, a committee of "popular and influential citizens" decided to raise the necessary money privately, "as many it is thought will aid the measure secretly who could not publicly."[33]

Although many papers continued to ignore her, the enthusiasm for her in Philadelphia was even more remarkable, and she thought seriously about locating their press there. A schism had recently split the Quakers, and those called Hicksites rallied to her side. Her lectures were announced for the Military Hall, but she had trouble finding a building large enough to hold the throng: "In those we tried the pressure was so excessive that several individuals, men and women, fainted dead away."[34]

Ministers took to calling Fanny the "High Priestess of Infidelity," and a Baltimore preacher said that she was neither man nor woman but someone sent from hell. With their curses sounding in her mind, she faced New York, and the *Free Enquirer* announced it would not respond in kind: "Disgraceful enough have been the political squabbles of our country. Let not the cause of human improvement be sullied with similar stain . . . to abuse and invective we will close both our ears and our pages."[35]

When she got to the city, Fanny wrote Charles Wilkes "leaving it to himself to regulate their future relations," and in a brief note Wilkes accepted what she called "her suggestion of dissolved or suspended intimacy." His rejection was the first of many. As she thought long after about what she had endured in New York, she felt that the public had no right to condemn those who would not serve it or who failed in trying. The consistent reformer "becomes, as it were, excommunicated, after the fashion of the old Catholic mother church; removed even from the protection of law, such as it is, and from the sympathy of society, for whose sake they consent to be crucified."[36]

In early January 1829, Fanny decided to "pitch [her] tent" in New York City because, "all things considered, this is the most central spot both with respect to Europe and this country," the magnet that drew people, letters, and ideas from all over America. And, Fanny knew, the pattern worked in reverse: whatever good they did in New York could "spread far and wide, and invigorate the exertions of good and bold men throughout the land." On January 3, she began a series of six lectures at Masonic Hall to a capacity audience of between fifteen hundred and two thousand people. She called it an elementary course on the nature of all knowledge, physical and moral. Setting a precedent that would continue, several women accompanied her to the stage. Applause interrupted her hour-and-a-half speech, and her harshest critic wrote that "towards the conclusion she received several distinct and thundering rounds of approbation." Some of New York's most distinguished citizens were there, and when she saw Cadwallader Colden, she concluded that she had been right about his secret liberality. She wrote that the beleaguered liberals poured in to see her, happy to find support and breathing room.[37]

She repeated the series in late January and early February at the Park Theatre and later gave it in various places outside the city, attracting people who then became a political organization in embryo. They could count on the New York Free Press Association, which already supported the weekly *Correspondent*, a journal that told what liberals were doing all over the East and as far west as Cincinnati. And there was a small but vigorous network of liberal groups, women among them, in towns up the Hudson River Valley and into the Finger Lakes region, across the Alleghenies, and down along the Atlantic coast, all of them aware of the presence of others and ready to exchange newspapers, correspond, and welcome like-minded people.

Fanny took a room with an impoverished widow in Murray Street, while Jennings rented an office near Broadway to register subscribers and give out information about the *Free Enquirer*. Because of some reputed dishonesty on the part of the *Correspondent*'s editor, George Houston, Fanny and Jennings prepared themselves to restore liberalism's good name. "The many are more likely to come round to us," she wrote, "than to stone us to death."[38]

At the time, she had no reason to use the metaphor of stoning to death as a pun. The same day she used it, however, a series of articles about her began to appear in the *New York Commercial Advertiser* that were as vicious as any aimed at Rachel Jackson. The paper's editor, William Leete Stone, was the proverbial pillar of the community who had championed many of the causes in which Fanny believed: he admired Lafayette, supported Greek independence, and urged Congress to abolish slavery. But he was active in religious groups and spoke sarcastically about broadening the suffrage, and Fanny Wright stirred something so deep and powerful in him that he lost his self-control: repeatedly he returned to the attack, with a rage and hatred so little suppressed that it seemed pathological.

At first he was taken with the way she looked and the way she spoke. Her strong, sweet voice, he wrote, filled the room without apparent effort. Her enunciation was perfect, her delivery excellent, her gestures appropriate and graceful: "So far as these qualifications constitute an orator, we believe she is unrivalled by any of the public speakers, of any description, in this city." Her performance was so fine that "the sensation of the ludicrous, naturally suggested by its novelty . . . was entirely suppressed." He belittled what she said with only a light, gentlemanly touch.[39]

At Fanny's second lecture, two days after the first, she lost for Stone the charm of novelty, and he declared her discourse a rigamarole unworthy of her intellect: "She seemed to want to make the world a universal soup house.—She wanted girls to be instructed as boys are, but did not state who was to attend to plain and ornamental sewing, making pies and nursing children." It was only from a sense of duty, according to Stone, that he went to Fanny's third lecture, where thousands thronged a gothic temple "which, for the occasion, was to be made an Epicurean stye," and from which many thousands were turned away. Fanny paused briefly "to receive the spontaneous burst of applause with which it had wisely been previously determined she should be received." His sarcasm grew even sharper as he described the press and confusion: a window pane was broken; several people were carried out; a child cried loudly.[40]

As Fanny remained "the Lioness of the day," Stone lamented, he had to keep writing about her, and though "our cheeks burn while we record it," at the next lecture "there were ladies there without disguises." The ladies, however, could not get to the seats reserved for them because the crush was so great that no one could move either forward or back. He insisted that this was his last notice of Frances Wright.[41]

He attended her fifth lecture, however, when someone put a barrel full of oil of turpentine at the entrance door and set fire to it, sending billows of suffocating smoke through the lower floor and up the staircase into the hall above. People panicked and jammed the stairs, "all endeavoring to be No. One in the escape." Stone decided finally to leave off sarcasm and games: "it is time we should have done with Miss Wright, her pestilent doctrines, and her deluded followers, who are as much to be pitied, as their priestess is to be despised . . . She comes amongst us in the character of a bold blasphemer, and a voluptuous preacher of licentiousness . . . Casting off all restraint, she would break down all the barriers to virtue, and reduce the world to one grand theatre of vice and sensuality in its most loathsome form. No rebuff can palsy her—no insult can agitate her feelings. It is iron equally in her head and heart; impervious to the voice of virtue, and case-hardened against shame!" He said, once again, that he had done with Fanny Wright.[42]

Then Stone began defending himself against criticism. A fellow editor charged that by taking so much note of Fanny, he had increased people's curiosity and swelled her audiences. Stone countered that it was good that people heard her: "The impression made by hearing her doctrines even *insinuated* publicly . . . has been one of unqualified disgust . . . loathing and abhorrence." To another editor who suggested he was too hard on her, Stone said, "she recommends the encouragement of early prostitution . . . contemns and discards altogether the marriage contract and in effect recommends transforming this glorious world . . . into one vast immeasurable brothel; and concludes by anticipating the blending of the black and white population, as the social millenium."[43]

Nor did he hold back from one last article. At the lecture he professed to describe, someone turned off the gas—"Some wicked wretch, foe to the progress of illumination, had turned the stop-cock of the main pipe"—and the lights went out. When candles were found to take the place of gas, Fanny finished her lecture and was carried into the street by her devotees. She was "discharged with long and loud hurras of applause and triumph, at the head of Murray-street," and Stone was indeed finished for the time with Frances Wright.[44]

Not one editor encouraged or supported her. Some ignored her. Others mentioned her in passing. More than one wrote that people went to hear her because she was an oddity and her lectures were free. The flamboyant Major Mordecai Noah of the *New York Enquirer*—playwright, politician, Zionist—came closest to being fair: "In another age, and with the proper opportunities, she might have been a Semiramide, a Catharine the Second, or an Elizabeth of England, in every thing that regards firmness, decision, and intellectual superiority." But the *Journal of Commerce* decided that her intellect was deranged. Conjuring up "the singular spectacle of a female, publicly and ostentatiously proclaiming doctrines of atheistical fanaticism, and even the most abandoned lewdness," the *Evening Post* raised the specter of riot: "Is there no danger of collecting an unruly mob, which nothing perhaps can restrain short of public force and bloodshed itself?" And the *Post*'s editor, William Cullen Bryant, turned his poetic gifts to satirical ends at her expense:

> Fair priestess of the fragrant rite
> That mingles "spirits black and white";
> Then lady turn thee, yet again,
> To thy own land beyond the main,

> Weeping and stretching o'er the sea
> Her fond imploring arms to thee.
> Yes, go, as is a patron's duty,
> Reform thy native country first.[45]

The presidential campaign of 1828 had brought out the cruelty and mysogyny in America, and in the midst of the newspaper onslaught against her, Fanny worried that she might have been too sanguine in her hopes for what she and her colleagues could do. Nevertheless, she was convinced that the "absolutely degraded" New York press did not speak the voice of the nation.[46]

Fanny fought back in her lectures. Late in January, when she began the series for a second time, she speculated that the circumstances were "unparalleled in the history of the world." Privilege and pretension were trying to "assassinate the liberties of a free state in the person of a single individual, and to outrage public order and public decency, by ribald slanders and incendiary threats, against the reputation and person of a woman." Sympathizing with Socrates and Jesus in their tormentors' hands, she found hope "in my conviction of the destined triumph of the cause I serve" and in a future that "shall write my name and preserve my memory among those of the champions of human liberty and heralds of human improvement."[47]

She fought back in her letters as well. To a friend she wrote that the storm had raged higher than she had thought possible in America, but she had long felt "like some being fallen from a strange planet among a race whose senses faculties and perceptions were all different from my own." Baffled at human cruelty, she wrote Harriet Garnett that her own spirit would "rejoice in another's good fortune—so exult in the talents of a fellow creature so befriend their development and sympathize in their success," but she found a contrary spirit to pervade the world.[48]

The class bias against Fanny was acute, and her old friends remained adamantly opposed to her. Charles Wilkes wrote about the Wright sisters as his "well intentioned but deluded friends" and said that so far as he could judge, Fanny's efforts in New York had completely failed: "The lectures ended in a total neglect and I regret to add that, from the beginning of the winter to the present hour, not only no person of my personal acquaintance, male or female, has visited her or received her, but literally and exactly, I have never met with any person who has . . . Her paper has excited no attention and having met with no opposition is, I believe wholly neglected." By all other accounts Fanny's New York lectures were always crowded, and she had long since given up the social habit of giving and receiving calls. But Wilkes saw no possible recovery for Fanny and Camilla.[49]

She could do nothing but make new friends and colleagues among those who admired her, for she was too proud, and believed too deeply in what she said and did, to acknowledge defeat. Then, too, the persecution swelled the ranks of her followers and strengthened her support. As the *New York Enquirer* noted, "if editors and others will abuse her, she will soon have a party strong enough to sustain her." Not only had some newspapers refused to print her paid advertisements, but they had rejected letters written on her behalf, and those whose letters were refused offered her a sympathy toughened by experience. The Park Theatre once again produced *Altorf* to an enthusiastic audience, and at the end of January, at Thomas Paine birthday celebrations from Albany to Baltimore, Fanny was toasted as an ornament of her sex and a champion of humanity.[50]

It was then that Walt Whitman saw her, and in old age he confessed he had never felt so glowingly toward any other woman. "She was a brilliant woman, of beauty and estate, who was never satisfied unless she was busy doing good—public good, private good." Her morals were always subject to a goody-goody taboo, but "we all loved her: fell down before her: her very appearance seemed to enthrall us." Whitman thought Fanny "the noblest Roman of them all . . . a woman of the noblest make-up whose orbit was a great deal larger than theirs—too large to be tolerated for long by them: a most maligned, lied-about character—one of the best in history though also one of the least understood." If Fanny never knew how extravagantly a gifted poet admired her, she nevertheless flourished as the center of her world.[51]

Camilla's son was born late in January 1829, after a protracted and agonizing labor. The doctor bled her three times and subsequently gave her some castor oil that included a "most noxious ingredient," which provoked a reaction so violent she wrote Fanny that it "went nigh to finish my career." Without Lolotte's careful attention, she admitted, neither she nor her child would have lived. She did not mention Whitby when she wrote her sister, and she called the baby Francis.[52]

Her letter unnerved Fanny. "My own darling, my heart is too full to throw its feelings into words," she wrote. "How sadly I feel the wide distance between us and thee. How I rejoice over thy safety and that of thy new born lamb." Too shaken to write more, she begged Camilla to come as soon as possible. Fanny had earlier had to reassure her that she wanted her to come to New York. Apprehensive, apparently, because she had damaged Nashoba and caused a scandal, Camilla worried that people would use her to hurt Fanny again. But Fanny wrote that in New York "there will never be danger of intrusion from the unsuitable in opinion," and nothing Camilla could do would interfere with her own usefulness.[53]

Weakened by a difficult childbirth and nursing a heavy baby, Camilla could not travel from Memphis alone. "Were I but free I should fly to you, lamb," Fanny wrote on February 21. "But to leave were impossible. The whole country is waking up—invitations pour in from every town and country round about and far off." Robert Dale and two of his brothers were planning to come east from New Harmony, Fanny continued, and one of them might prove a likely escort. William Phiquepal and his three French pupils would leave Indiana and go down the Ohio and then the Mississippi en route by water to New York and could stop in Memphis for her baggage.[54]

Fanny later wrote that when she took over the *New Harmony Gazette*, Phiquepal had "volunteered in a month's time to acquire and to communicate, to his three French pupils, a thorough knowledge of the printing business." He justified the confidence she gave him by publishing a model prospectus and a paper that got to Cincinnati while she first lectured there. He now began the move from New Harmony to New York, so that he and his pupils could replace George Henry Evans as the *Free Enquirer*'s printer.[55]

At the hazard of scandalizing those whose sensibilities had survived the shocks she had already given them, Fanny planned, in fact, to recreate the life of New Harmony's Community House Number One on the outskirts of New York City. Men and women would live as brothers and sisters together, sharing the same house and accepting responsibility for an extended, if improvised family. Apart from Fanny and Robert Dale, they would include Robert Jennings, Phiquepal and his three students, and Robert's brother David Dale Owen. Fanny had cast Camilla in the role of housekeeper for them all.

She had announced her decision to stay in New York without consulting Robert Dale, and by the end of January 1829, she and Jennings were issuing the paper from New York, republishing at the rate of two issues a week the series they had begun at New Harmony at the end of October. With minor editorial friction, they edited and published two different editions of a weekly newspaper for more than three months across formidable distances. But by early March, Robert Dale was ready to leave New Harmony to join their commune in New York. Perhaps because she was not yet well enough to travel, Camilla stayed in Memphis for more than a month longer.[56]

When Robert arrived in New York in mid-April, he discovered how thoroughly Fanny had shaped the world in which they would live and work. She had found a commodious mansion on the banks of the East River about five miles north of the heart of town. It belonged to Richard Riker, the city's recorder, and for $440 a year they also got a poultry yard, a place for two cows, a ten-acre garden, and stables for their horses. A home where they could work in privacy and share the fellowship of those who wanted to turn America in the directions they did, this place seemed to Fanny as tranquil and secluded as their western forests. She expected Phiquepal to set up the printing press there, so that with the exception of their office on Murray Street, the house would hold their entire establishment. With a good servant and frugal tastes, they would live well.[57]

But Fanny was even more ambitious. She paid $7,000 for the old Ebenezer Baptist Church on Broome Street and turned it into a Hall of Science. She wrote Camilla gleefully that "some church speculators had hoped to buy the property for a song," but it was knocked down at auction for three-fourths the value of the land alone. She appointed five trustees to choose competent weekly lecturers—the subjects including arithmetic, anatomy, natural history, reading, writing, and public speaking—and to arrange ticket sales at minimum prices. She stipulated that any qualified speaker "on scientific subjects" could use the hall for a nominal fee if it were otherwise idle.[58]

On Sunday, April 26, 1829, at eleven in the morning, Fanny delivered the opening address, consecrating the Hall to "the sectarian faith" and devoting it to "universal knowledge." As she issued her call for national schools, she wondered if their gathering that day might "mark an era in the moral history of the republic." Mrs. Trollope had reason to tell Lafayette that Fanny "anticipates confidently the regeneration of the whole human race from her present exertions."[59]

The Hall of Science became a central gathering place for New York liberals and a stop for the curious. To the dismay of those who patronized the Bible repository across the street, Fanny and Robert Dale put the business offices and bookstore in the front of the building. Boldly in the window they showed the heroes of heterodoxy—among them Paine, Shelley, Godwin, and Richard Car-

A DOWNRIGHT GABBLER,
or a goose that deserves to be hissed_

The Riker Estate on the East River

The Hall of Science

lile—and the pamphlets and books Fanny and Robert printed themselves. The book store even proved a modest success: according to Robert Dale, their sales reached $2,000 a year.[60]

There were speeches and debates every Sunday and sometimes during the week. The auditorium held about twelve hundred people; the admission fee was usually 10¢, and New Yorkers trooped in to hear Fanny. An itinerant Englishman, who found the audience rapt in her presence, wrote, "the breathless silence that reigned throughout the building made the spectacle the most imposing I ever beheld."[61]

Meanwhile the editors of the *Free Enquirer* carried on their crusade to realize their version of the Founding Fathers' hopes for America. They paid special attention to the problems of women. In attacking the legal disabilities of married women, Fanny ridiculed "that mass of absurdity, injustice, and cruelty, styled the common law of England," which had for the most part become the basis of American law. It allowed robbery and all but murder "against the unhappy female who swears away, at one and the same moment, her person and her property, and, as it but too often is, her peace, her honor, and her life." She criticized the morality that held chastity a woman's one indispensable virtue, and both Fanny and Robert Dale wrote respectfully of Richard Carlile's pioneering British birth-control tract, *Every Woman's Book*. They argued that legislation could not regulate the affections of men and women and that evil was the consequence not of man's fallen state but rather of ignorance and bad institutions.[62]

They analyzed the consequences of unequally distributed wealth, in the course of which they published Matthew Carey's chilling report on the condition of the working classes, especially the seamstresses, in Philadelphia. "Industrious and expert women" who were steadily employed and had no children, Carey discovered, could not average a wage higher than $1.25 a week, so that at most they were left with $26 a year for food and clothing. And this income was only for the rare woman who could find constant work. Many laboring women were widows with small children, and others had husbands who drank or had abandoned them. Because incessant work could not keep them and their children in even minimum comfort, they were faced with begging, stealing, starving, or prostitution. However wasteful and indolent rich women might be, these were not the besetting sins of the poor.[63]

Carey's devastating statistics prompted Fanny to begin shifting the focus of her attention. She understood now that the social and economic facts of American life worked against realizing the principles

Jefferson had framed in the Declaration. She began to speak of the necessities of a democracy, not in terms of its citizens mastering a body of abstract knowledge, but in terms of their creating conditions in which people would live as equals.

On June 2 Fanny returned to Philadelphia and gave a new lecture. Called "Of Existing Evils and Their Remedy," it was the most powerful she had ever delivered, and a Philadelphia Quaker wrote that hundreds would "date their conversion from the eventful second of June." She spoke that day, she said, to people who had seen pauperism grow and watched vice and disorder threaten social peace. She spoke to those "who, by slow degrees, or in moments of desperation, have forsaken honest labour, because without a reward, for fraudulent speculation, because it promised one chance of success to a thousand . . . of ruin." As a response to the suffering around them, some had suggested prayers. Others had suggested fasts. Some had thought to praise God for reminding them the poor would be with us always. Others had wanted to build more jails and poorhouses, or to make laws protecting labor and fixing a minimum wage. Still others had trusted to the benevolent rich.[64]

Fanny now offered a remedy she felt commensurate, unlike the others, with the evil it addressed. State legislatures would mark out school districts and provide within each state for a chain of boarding schools. The schools would be available to children as young as two and would be graduated so that students would move directly from one into another, their parents being allowed to visit but never to interfere with the institutions' rules. The schools would be supported by a graduated property tax and by a moderate tax on parents for each of their children, since Fanny hoped to encourage people to have no more children than they could afford to raise. With no apparent sense of the coercive, much less the impolitic side of her proposal, she called these schools the "nurseries of a free nation," because in them all students would be treated the same. They would eat the same food and wear the same clothes. They would be "raised in the exercise of common duties [and] in the acquirement of the same knowledge and practice of the same industry, varied only according to individual taste and capabilities." The future could be trusted to people so raised: they would "work out the reform of society—perfect the free institutions of America."

Fanny had taken Jefferson's philosophical radicalism and begun to imagine social and economic conditions that would realize its promise. Hers was a genuinely egalitarian vision which, her critics would soon point out, threatened the sanctity of private property and undermined the foundations of the family itself. She was probing dangerously near the nerve centers of American life.

It was more than seven months now since Fanny had seen her sister, whose life had been entwined with hers for more than twenty years. Since they parted, each had gone through experiences more harrowing than either had known before, and without the accustomed presence of the other to share them. Camilla had suffered something like despair: late that summer she wrote that finally life no longer seemed "without its solace, nor its evils unmixed with good." And now she was on her way to Fanny with a child who would be a new and unknown part of their lives together.[65]

It was a hard journey. She left Whitby in April and traveled with Marcus Winchester as far as Cincinnati, where Frances Trollope discovered her very much better than when she had seen her last at Nashoba: "She is again the sweet and elegant Camilla I knew in Europe . . . Her child is one of very uncommon beauty, and appears in all respects just what a mother could wish." Apparently Camilla made the rest of the trip alone. By the end of May she was at Pittsburgh facing the long ride with the baby across the Alleghenies. And whether or not she joined Fanny in Philadelphia in June, she was with her there on July 4, when Fanny addressed another audience at the Walnut Street Theater, and in tones quite different from those she had used only a year earlier.[66]

Fanny was much angrier, and her language more violent. Although her rage had been kindled because she knew far better that decent people were desperate in America, she was angry for personal reasons as well. Camilla had been reluctant to join her sister for fear of making her more vulnerable to attack, and Fanny had hoped to allay her fears. But in mid-June a new kind of attack appeared—this time with the sanction of one who should have been a friend. George Houston's "liberal" press published an anonymous broadside implying that Fanny, and perhaps Camilla, had designs on Robert Jennings.[67]

It had been eighteen months since they had ridden into Memphis with Robert Dale and his father to find Jennings' letter about coming to Nashoba. Writing hastily that they had not yet got Nashoba ready for a school, they urged him to settle his own affairs while they did what they could to prepare the way for him. They sent the letter in care of George Houston at the *Correspondent*, but the letter did not reach Jennings. Now Houston, or someone using his presses, published the letter, italicizing phrases, passages, and sentences to give the impression that Fanny and Camilla wanted Jennings to abandon his family. The cry of "immoral women" sounded once again.

When Fanny and Jennings heard of the insidious broadside, they both demanded the return of the letter of which it pretended to be a copy. Fanny wrote that she had seen Houston only twice, had been "unfavorably impressed" with his character "from his conduct as the former agent of this paper," and was too conscious of her own rectitude to be afraid for anyone to read anything she had written. She said no legal action would be taken. For reasons that are impossible to reconstruct, Fanny had distrusted Houston from the time she got to New York. On January 2, 1829, she wrote Camilla that he had been dishonest. In February she objected in the *Free Enquirer* to his republishing her lectures from the *New Harmony Gazette*. She had not authorized Houston to publish them, and it was against her wishes as the lectures had been hastily written and were very imperfect. She intended to revise them and had allowed their publication in the *Gazette* only because she had pledged herself in Cincinnati "to satisfy the popular request." The *Correspondent* abruptly broke off the speeches in the middle of the second and stopped publication altogether in midsummer.[68]

The new attack was ill timed to reassure Camilla, who recognized her human frailties better than Fanny did, and Camilla wrote Whitby that she was ill most of the time she was in Philadelphia. Fanny, on the contrary, insisted that a dishonest attack from a liberal matured her philosophy: "Violence and misrepresentation I have found neither to disturb my peace of mind, chill my philanthropy, nor relax my exertion." But the anger in her Fourth of July oration belies her forbearance.[69]

She was melodramatic that day, but her challenge to her audience was no less trenchant for that. She entered the theater followed by thirty or more supporters who seated themselves around her on the stage. She first read the Declaration of Independence and then for an hour and a half made a straightforward attack on American public morality. So far, she said, a process based on great principles had produced bad results. A democratic system depended on two conditions: that the people be enlightened judges of their own interests and that their representatives faithfully represent them. Neither condition existed. The unenlightened electorate, "blind to principles" and "occupied with trifles," neglected and even abused their own true interests. Political liberty had for the most part led to the election of men from "a class whose interests are at variance with those of the great body of the nation." It had led, morally, to "a spirit of intrigue and ambition on the one hand—of license, violence, and corruption on the other." Elections had produced electioneering. Newspapers sold to parties were "silent as respects principles, insolently bold as respects men." And their iniquity was the fault of the public, because they catered to a corrupted public taste.[70]

Republican education remained her answer, but she came closer than she had before to confronting the problem of unequally owned wealth. A republic was impossible, she insisted, when wealth was so misunderstood and money so maldistributed: "While . . . enjoyment is calculated by the luxury of the few instead of the ease of the many . . . while human beings count but as an appendage to the machinery they keep in motion . . . think not that canals and railroads are to advance the nation, nor that steamboats and spinning-jennies are to save the world."

Their trip to Philadelphia had yet another important purpose, which was to talk to Benjamin Lundy. Whitby's agreement to supervise Nashoba had only six months to run. Because the slaves had fought everything he had tried to do, and his health was apparently failing again under the strain, Fanny had to decide what to do about them. She had already written the president of Haiti and asked Lafayette to write on her behalf as well. Now Lundy, just back from Haiti, told her he considered it the best place to take blacks freed in America.[71]

With plans for the slaves revolving in their minds, they returned to New York, where Camilla showed off her son to Robert Dale, who seems to have taken the place of the brother they had lost so young. She was relieved to be with friends in the quiet of the East River estate, where people came only if they admired Fanny Wright. Pushing the Wilkeses and their repudiation from her mind, Camilla began to bathe daily in the waters just outside the door and to accustom herself to her new role as housekeeper of the establishment.

She knew she would play a less important part in her sister's life. She had heard Fanny lecture only once before Philadelphia and found her now more eloquent as a public speaker than anyone she had ever heard. Deciding that Fanny could be "the means of effecting a great moral revolution throughout this country," she realized that Fanny's lecturing and her work on the *Free Enquirer* left her little free time. But as she saw Fanny "engaged in pursuits . . . so well suited to her taste and talents," Camilla grasped for some contentment for herself. Grateful for her own beautiful child, she took over the direction of their two female servants and the young hired man who saw to their two horses and the garden.[72]

Their routines were spare. They got milk from two good cows and raised their own vegetables. They had given up both tea and coffee and seldom ate meat. Still, it was a challenge to manage it all: with about one thousand paying subscribers, at $3 annually, the *Free Enquirer* brought in just enough to cover expenses. Reflecting on how hard they struggled to keep solvent, Fanny later wrote of an independent press that thousands read it curiously, while only a few hundred had the integrity to support it: "While it is propping the virtue of the nation and quickening its intelligence, its conductors may find it hard to draw the value of a crust and a draught of water in requital for their labor."[73]

Camilla's place in New York was respectable, and she saw old friends. Late in July, for example, Robert Owen came with tales of having debated a Universalist minister before a Cincinnati audience one thousand strong. Having proposed that all religions were founded on mankind's ignorance, Owen had taken on God and the Reverend for fifteen sittings, and Camilla no doubt listened as he insisted that, the daily press to the contrary, he had almost certainly converted many to unbelief. It was a busy time for Camilla, and it gave promise of being happy enough.

Less than ten days after they came from Philadelphia to New York, Fanny went off to Boston to deliver her lectures on knowledge and the existing evils. As the *Free Enquirer* would have it, Boston was painfully apprehensive at the prospect of her coming. A committee of merchants had signed a circular they sent the newspapers asking that no notice be taken of her. Many clergymen warned their parishioners to shun her, and devoutly proper people tried to keep her out of the theaters. Nevertheless, Fanny spoke on July 30 to a full house, and with equal success on several subsequent evenings. The Reverend Lyman Beecher later wrote that regrettably she won over educated, refined women—"females of respectable standing in society"—and worst of all, women who had been friends to his own children.[74]

Fanny had been the all-engrossing topic of conversation the week before, and the newspapers were too clever either to ignore her or to deal with her viciously. They were mild and playful. One noticed with sly pleasure that a man who had signed the circular against her had been in the audience at her third lecture, "drinking in at his ears the smart saying of Miss W., with all imaginable relish." The *Boston Courier* thought she said nothing the most fastidious moralist and most delicate female might not hear. The *Boston Statesman* wrote that, "in advocating the rights of woman, she did not fail to insure the approbation of every body in the house." Another admired her simple short hair, saying that if it was singular, it was nevertheless more pleasant than the current rage for hair styled with wrought India combs, towers of tortoiseshell, and "tresses newly purchased from the frizeur's." No matter how genuinely Fanny tried to submerge her person in the cause, she no doubt left Boston pleased that she was, as one editor put it, "the subject of conversation in almost every circle, in almost every house in the city of Boston."[75]

Not only the enthusiasm she roused but her own energy of purpose might well have pleased her. Her paper, the *Free Enquirer*, was serious in its criticisms and humane in the ends it sought, and many thought it one of the best publications in the country. In the few months past, her own contributions had been of a high order. She had continued to distrust systems and asked only that people think for themselves. She had written at length about Jesus' amiable character: although Saint Paul's writings condemned him for a bigot, she said, Jesus won her sympathy. She had argued against attempts to prohibit the mails from traveling on Sundays or to enforce any particular mode of Sabbath observance, had called capital punishment legalized murder, and had written, somewhat more obliquely, in praise of birth control. She had offered a rigorous standard of moral behavior: "To judge ourselves in severity, and others in lenity" might "constitute the whole duty of man; and this, because so to judge, is at once so practically useful and so supremely difficult." As she traveled back from Boston, Fanny seemed to look forward to years of fruitful labor in the vineyard.[76]

Four days after she got home, Camilla's little Francis died. Camilla had started a letter to Julia more than two weeks before, and on August 19 she began again in a tremulous hand: "Alas! Alas! how shall I paint my bitter sorrow and anguish my son, my lovely babe, who was playing at my feet while I wrote the above, now sleeps in the cold earth while his wretched and bereaved mother yet lives to bewail her irrecoverable loss." He had had a sudden attack of fever connected with teething. Fanny had come back to find Camilla frantic but still hopeful. "But for her presence and soothing care and tenderness," Camilla wrote, "I shd have been bereft of reason or of life by this stroke so sudden, so severe!" She tried now to calm herself, but at moments grief seized her so painfully she wanted to die: "Can time ever efface from my agonized soul that last moment in which I wiped the death drops from his beautiful brow, and inhaled the parting breath of the precious being that for seven months had sucked the nourishment from my breast! Oh never! never, can I overcome this loss—Oh could you have seen him—his brilliant eye beaming with sweetness and intelligence beyond what is usual at so early an age." Fanny added in helpless postscript: "It is sad to centre the affections too strongly and closely in beings so fragile yet how to help it!"[77]

It was an age when many children died, and women often sat by the bed of death. They embroidered their pain into elaborate tapestries of mourning and solaced themselves with Mrs. Felicia Heman's popular poems about tragic death and inconsolable grief. There is no way to know how many women sank into despair or went mad because they lost what they loved and could find no other purpose. Most had other children to bind them hard to life. But Camilla began to slip into blankness.

A month later she wrote her husband that she was weary of existence: "While reason tells me the folly of indulging in regrets as vain as they are useless, the source of my sorrow is still the same. My lovely babe is torn from my bosom, my soul's best treasure is departed and there is now nought on earth that can yield me satisfaction. My days pass in bewildering thoughts and withering recollections of past comfort and fondly cherished hopes now forever blighted." She found herself useless, and the depth of her affliction was "beyond the reach of sympathy or of alleviation."[78]

She tried to submerge her grief in running their large establishment and helping as her sister's amanuensis. But Fanny's exuberant sense of purpose was doomed to rub Camilla's wounds with salt. Mary Carroll, who saw the sisters late in August, observed that Fanny was buoyant with hope: "She is in her proper element . . . Her susceptibility to much enjoyment and highly excitable temperament unite in supporting her under the utmost fatigue both mental and physical." Fanny had even become "quite fleshy," but Camilla was the very image of despair.[79]

More cruelly even than Fanny's sense of purpose, her emotional distance may well have chilled her sister. At the very time Camilla felt bewildered with grief, Fanny, to hear her tell it, approached what she called the tranquillity of wisdom. Only those enjoyed it who felt benevolent toward the whole human race, she said in the *Free Enquirer*, who gave each thing its just due and were "neither betrayed by sensibility into weakness, by disappointment to misanthropy, nor by injury to anger." Her object, she grandly wrote, was the improvement of the people of America, which "tends to nerve and to soothe my mind."[80]

The three years past seemed to Camilla a wretched tangle of loss, mistake, and failure, and the anguish of the baby's death would not leave her. She could not go back to Whitby, though he remained her husband. Robert Dale could be no more than a brother. Fanny was lost to her causes. And just at the time when Camilla felt irreparably bereft, Fanny decided to leave New York with William Phiquepal to take her slaves to Haiti.

Some time after she left in mid-October, Camilla confided to Harriet a painful truth: "the sister—the friend with whom from my earliest childhood I have felt my being identified—for whom I have suffered much and with whom I have sympathized still more is no longer the sharer of my thoughts and feelings and only ceased to be so from my discovering that *I shared not hers.*" Fanny had withheld something from her, or so Camilla thought. And Camilla in turn had withdrawn into her own solitude. She thought of herself as a minor object of interest that had, among others, once filled Fanny's heart but was now less important, "if not altogether lost in the midst of the wide sea whereon she is now embarked." Her own regret, however, she called merely selfish and said it had in great measure given way to her satisfaction in seeing Fanny "engaged in a cause worthy of her talents and . . . all important to the welfare of generations yet unborn." Always before, even when surrounded by an adoring circle of friends, Fanny had not been happy: "there was ever a yearning after something wch was wanting to fill her mind and give full exercise to her uncommon powers and energies." Now she had found what she wanted, and she was more tranquil and in better health than ever before. And Camilla was alone.[81]

Guiltily toying with the hope that other places and other companions might bring her back to life, Camilla wrote Julia, who lived in Hanover, Germany, asking if she would care to see an old friend: "Often in my souls desolation have my thoughts turned to thee sweet Julia, as one who could sympathize with my affliction and pour the balm of comfort into my wounded spirit." But propriety triumphed, and Julia denied her. Harriet read Camilla's letter, as it came first to Paris, and wrote, as she passed it along, that she herself would write Camilla and talk of the difficulties of the German language, of the cold, of Mr. Pertz's situation—"all as objections to *our* living at Hanover." Camilla's going there, Harriet felt, would not do. Perhaps Lafayette could persuade James Mylne to ask her to come keep house for him. The Millars, she thought, might "receive her without danger to themselves—you could not . . . How deeply must we deplore this . . . My heart bleeds for her."[82]

One person held out her hand. Mrs. Miller wrote to say her home and her arms were always open to Fanny and Camilla. But Camilla turned her down.[83]

Fanny, for her part, was looking for the apocalypse. Like many very different people in the 1820s and 1830s, she sensed a looming crisis, and she spent her last six weeks in the East before she left for Haiti talking about the form it might take and trying to shape that form to her own design. In late August 1829, she delivered a new lecture she called "The State of the Public Mind and the Measures Which It Calls For." A moral excitement was loose in the world, "new in its nature, and rapid in its progress," a rampant commercial spirit, and a brutal competition that ruined small capitalists and oppressed the working class. The banking system gave unfair advantage to speculators and capitalists and in turn depressed the wages of industry. The professional classes monopolized power and prestige, and everyone suffered from "a false system of education stolen from aristocratic Europe."[84]

Come the crisis, she saw three alternatives. They could allow such a state of things to continue and watch it finally destroy American liberties. They could see the nation torn apart by violent revolution. Or they could legislate a gradual but radical reform. For Fanny, education offered the only hope that reform might come in time to relieve the present generation and improve the next. National boarding schools would lift from parents the burden and responsibility of their children while educating the generations to come. To bring about such schools, she proposed the creation of popular assemblies like those the colonies had convened to deal with England. A standing committee in Philadelphia, she suggested, could begin a correspondence with similar committees in cities spread through the states.

Fanny gave the surplus proceeds of subsequent lectures to a model assembly just formed in New York City, the National Association for the Protection of Industry and for the Promotion of Republican Education. Essentially a working-class organization, it promised to gather information on the conditions in which working-class people lived and on the wages they were paid. It would analyze the forces that kept them poor and powerless and evaluate the existing public schools. As if to give point to Fanny's critique, its first revelation would be that twelve thousand children in New York between the ages of five and fifteen were "entirely destitute of the means of instruction."[85]

Fanny and her colleagues now had speakers, a newspaper, an organization, a network of correspondence, and a cause. Their press was issuing ten of her lectures in a two-hundred-page edition. Societies of free enquirers and associations of working people were springing up in towns and cities all over the East. Philadelphia's Association of Working Men was even discovering its political muscle by asking each candidate for the state legislature his views on equal education, the banking system, and lotteries. It remained to be seen how much popular interest they could arouse, and how much they could sustain.

In mid-September, Fanny went to Philadelphia and faced apocalypse in miniature. Her group had paid $75 to rent the Walnut Street Theater for a Sunday night, but the notion that the "High Priestess of Infidelity" might defile the Sabbath by speaking on it had caused an uproar. The theater's stockholders repudiated the managers' orders and canceled the agreement. The liberals then rented Washington Hall, but when Fanny got to Philadelphia on Saturday, she discovered that the wife of the proprietor was being subjected to "threats of arrest, prophesies of riot and disturbance, and forewarnings of persecution and loss of patronage to her husband." Fanny released her from the agreement and issued a notice asking people to assemble at a given time. By seven o'clock Sunday evening a crowd had gathered in the streets near Military Hall and was packed so tightly no one could get through. Speaking briefly from a carriage, Fanny harangued her listeners to take home the lesson that they needed a hall of their own, and she promised to return.[86]

Two weeks later she was back to offer herself as a test case for the constitutional guarantees of the right to assembly. She prefaced her lecture by describing the earlier episode as "a league against the liberties of the majority, the rights of individuals and the free and fair interpretation of the institutions of the land." One Philadelphia newspaper had printed a letter citing the laws about Sunday observances that she had purportedly broken. In turn, she cited the Declaration of Independence, the Constitution of the United States, and the Constitution of Pennsylvania, the latter to the effect that "the citizens have a right, in a peaceable manner, to assemble together" and "every citizen may freely *speak*, write and print on any subject." If the newspaper letter were correct and a statute existed preventing "worldly employment" on Sunday, "I, for one, whenever the people may request my services, shall be found ready to meet the penalties attached to its violation." She had meddled as little with Christianity, she said, as with Judaism or Islam: "neither I nor the peaceable thousands of worthy citizens, designated by this journal as a 'tumultuous mob,' attempted to disturb their congregations, or to bar the door of their churches against ingress and egress." If people wanted to come together on their day of leisure, no one could presume for any reason to prevent them. Again she left the surplus proceeds from her lectures in the hands of a local group, this one organized to collect money for a hall open to the public.[87]

She spoke almost frantically during those last weeks before she left for Haiti—in Wilmington, Delaware, in Providence, Rhode Island, and several times on Broome Street in New York. In her farewell address at the Hall of Science she turned even more sharply on the established churches. The attacks made on her in the name of Christianity, her ugly experiences in Philadelphia, and the agitations for a Christian Party in Politics and against the transportation of the mails on Sunday—all these had convinced her anew that the main enemy of republican values and institutions in America was the organized church. Hers was not only a battle over who controlled America but also a holy war. She announced that her primary object was the destruction of "priestcraft": "with their faith I meddle not, and would counsel them not to meddle with the faith of each other."[88]

In early October Fanny wrote a preface for her collected speeches that shows her keen sense of her own power. She had challenged the victimization of the neglected female mind by "a priesthood, whose very subsistence depends, of necessity, upon the mental and moral degradation of their fellow creatures." Rallying to the cause of "insulted reason and outraged humanity," she had consequently inspired "a kindling of wrath among the clergy, a reaction in favour of common sense on the part of their followers, an explosion of the public sentiment in favour of liberty, liberality, and instructional reform, and a complete exposure of the nothingness of the press." Some months earlier, Lafayette had gently mocked Fanny's inflated notion of her new prominence. Judging by her last letters, he wrote, she expected to trigger a revolution in the American hemisphere, or at least among the states of the union.[89]

It was perhaps inevitable that Fanny should have an exaggerated sense of her own influence. A woman less sure than she of her invincibility would never have taken on so many powers in American society. At the same time, she could legitimately discount the attitudes taken to her by the press, because the newspapers reflected only a portion of the public mind. The people whose causes she championed, furthermore, had flocked to her with an exuberance that obscured their political insignificance, and she so much wanted a better world that she convinced herself that it was near.

Her confidence was reflected in the letter she wrote the British radical Richard Carlile, who had defied the laws limiting freedom of the press and endured six years in Dorchester gaol on conviction of blasphemy: "Great things are in preperation here. We have succeeded in starting the public mind in the great northern cities Boston, New York and Philadelphia on a plan of national education, equal, protective, republican . . . If the public mind advance in the ratio it is now advancing a few years will effect a moral revolution in this country." She divided the world into two classes, "those who wish the good of mankind at large, and those who only wish their own." How the generous in spirit might save the republic from the greedy until the enlightened next generation could take over was a question Fanny left for the future. Armed with the unshakable belief that her cause was just and her motives pure, and convinced that her future was clear before her, she headed for upper New York State to see how near the provinces might be to peaceful revolution.[90]

Her Wisdom
and Her Folly

8

In October 1829 Frances Wright set out with William S. Phiquepal on a journey that would take them eventually to the black republic of Haiti, where she would fulfill the pledge she had publicly made to free her slaves. The Haitian secretary-general, Joseph Balthasar Inginac, had offered them asylum and liberty: four months earlier he had written to promise that they would be placed on farms under proprietors known to be just and to assure her that they would be entitled to half of what they produced. He said that as soon as they reached Haiti, all her expenses would end.[1]

Four years' experience had convinced Fanny that the Nashoba slaves could not support themselves, much less produce enough to defray the costs incurred in buying, freeing, and colonizing them, and they had proved a constant source of anxiety and financial loss. Fanny did not believe that colonization would spell the end of slavery: the numbers involved were much too small to affect a social and economic evil so immense. She did believe that blacks had as much right as whites to live in the United States and even to govern it. But her experience with the problems of free blacks, even in the North, convinced her that their lot in America was too hard. Hatred for blacks was so entrenched that she felt obligated to give her former slaves liberty in "a country free at least from the ascendance of color." So in mid-1829 she wrote Whitby to bring them at the year's end to New Orleans, promising that his obligation to them as well as to her would end there.[2]

With the idea of lecturing as she went, Fanny planned to take the western route to New Orleans, going first to Albany, next across New

York to Buffalo, over to Pittsburgh, and down the Ohio and Mississippi rivers. She thought of herself as preparing "the popular mind in our minor towns to follow the lead of the cities," where she knew her cause was strongest.[3]

Until that fall, when Phiquepal left New York with Fanny to go to the Caribbean, his role in her life was insignificant. He was not among the New Harmony people she made trustees of Nashoba. She had not mentioned him to Julia and Harriet Garnett, or to Mary Shelley, or to Lafayette. When she and Robert Dale wrote hopefully about a community at Nashoba, neither of them spoke of William S. Phiquepal. His name first appeared in Fanny's correspondence in February 1829, when she told Camilla that he might stop off in Memphis for her luggage on his way to New York to print the *Free Enquirer*.[4]

He was useful to Fanny now, apparently, because he had once lived in the French West Indies and could be expected to negotiate more easily than others she knew the arcane passages of Caribbean ports. Furthermore, he had taught his students how to be self-sufficient in all the needs of daily life—how to make their clothes, even their shoes, and how to raise and prepare their food—and that kind of practical cleverness could be helpful to a woman taking thirty-one freed slaves from New Orleans to Haiti, especially since George Flower's experience had shown that it could be a hazardous business. Robert Dale and Jennings had to stay with the *Free Enquirer*. And Camilla was too nearly destroyed by her baby's death and her distancing relationship with her sister to go with Fanny on a long and grueling journey that also meant watching her in public triumph.[5]

However convenient Phiquepal seemed to Fanny as a substitute for those closer to her, in choosing him as a traveling companion, she had to brush aside the general contempt in which he was held by those who had known him longest and worked most closely with him. Mme. Fretageot, who had taught with him in Paris, Philadelphia, and New Harmony, refused even to speak to him. William Maclure, who had supported him for years, now complained that all he had ever done was dissipate Maclure's money and destroy his property. He thought Phiquepal ignorant, impossibly vain, and a complete failure as a teacher "by being of such an irritable bad temper and worse habits." In Paris, Maclure said, Phiquepal had treated half his students so harshly that they left him, "and the other half are unfit for any serious employment, full of caprices and whims like him self." Maclure wished that someone would tell him what good Phiquepal had done him, as it would relieve his mortification at being "the dupe of such a madman."[6]

It was in the winter of 1826, when he stopped off at Nashoba, that Maclure was writing most contemptuously of Phiquepal, and it seems unlikely that he would have held his tongue in Fanny's presence. She had lived in the midst of the warring factions at New Harmony, and she must have known how little respect or fondness Phiquepal inspired among his peers. But the self-confidence so crucial to Fanny had begun insidiously to harden into arrogance. She could not believe a man of parts so meager would do her irreparable harm.

The first weeks after they left New York City in mid-October were cold and nasty: it rained incessantly, and the mud was often ankle deep. Fanny lectured almost every evening she was not traveling, and often in unlikely places. In Utica she had to speak in an old circus—"black, dirty, forsaken and in exceeding disrepute and disrepair"—and at Syracuse in a cold and ugly theater. But people confronted Fanny all along the way—in stages, on steamboats, along canals—asking her to explain her views and meet their neighbors. She began to boast that superstition's reign was drawing to a close.[7]

Ten years earlier, when she had first traced the Mohawk Valley route, Fanny had been eager to see the best in Americans and their institutions. Now, in the heart of the "Burnt-Over District," that breeding ground for the evangelical revival that had drawn her to the lecture platform a year and a half before, she wanted to rouse people to the menace of "priestcraft" and ignorance in their midst. She told the people of Utica that by pouring the wealth of the Erie Canal into churches, missionary and tract societies, and Sunday schools, they had forfeited their "common sense, social happiness and all liberty whatsoever." She found unparalleled clerical oppression there: "Each man fears a spy in his wife, an enemy in his neighbor, and loss of bread as well as a good name, should he breathe a doubt respecting the saving efficacy of all the jugglery, grimace and absurdity" that stood for institutional religion.[8]

In Auburn, the clergy and their partisans used means that Fanny thought scandalous to keep her from speaking, and still the court-house was crowded every evening. She made a conquest of Orestes Brownson, who resigned as Universalist minister and editor of the *Gospel Advocate* to become a contributing editor to the *Free Enquirer*. Brownson described Fanny as "a woman of rare original powers, and extensive and varied information," and he particularly admired her grace under attack. When the evangelicals "did all in their power . . . to render her personally odious" and she heard the hard things people were saying, she quietly remarked at the end of a lecture that she had noticed the spires of six meeting-houses in their beautiful village and had heard that several other denominations planned to build churches: "It is evident that religion must have been well-discussed among you, and that you are eminently a religious people." She had not missed her cue: "I have travelled much and visited many countries, and in no place have I been so uncourteously received, or been the subject of so much personal insult, as in your most religious village. Perhaps it will not be inappropriate for us to spend one evening in discussing the subject of morals!"[9]

In mid-November Fanny and Phiquepal went from Rochester to Buffalo, where a snowstorm kept them long enough for her to speak four nights to packed houses. By the end of the month they were in Pittsburgh, where she delivered all but one in her series of lectures. A few hours before she was scheduled to give her final speech, the commissioners revoked their permission for her to use the courthouse. Their excuses were feeble, but again she had surplus receipts to leave in the hands of a committee pledged to do something about education.[10]

Her ebullience seems never to have deserted her. She sent Robert Dale a four-part parable in biblical style called "The New Book of Chronicles." Telling how the people had roused themselves against the soothsayers and merchant princes, she gave a thinly veiled account of the last year's events and her role in them: of the battles from press and pulpit to discredit her, of the nascent political party of journeymen workers that she and Robert Dale supported, of the dismay of the influential editor Major Mordecai Noah and Tammany Hall in the unwonted power of those whom they could not control.[11]

As Fanny headed down the Ohio to Cincinnati she had good reason to be pleased. She heard from Syracuse that influential citizens had been taken by what she said, and one of her correspondents wrote that they understood her better than he had expected, "as many of the remarks and positions laid down by you were necessarily of an abstract and metaphysical nature." Instead of the monster the priests had led them to expect, "they saw only a plain republican woman, and some who almost expected contamination in your very touch are now your advocates."[12]

She gave three lectures in Cincinnati, where Mrs. Trollope remarked on "that dry, cold, masculine, dictatorial manner that has been growing . . . since she commenced her public lectures." When they got near New Harmony, Phiquepal left her for a visit there, and Fanny went on down the Mississippi alone. On January 3, 1830, she wrote

Maclure from New Orleans that she found herself with no leisure whatever: "I have now work chalked out for the whole of this winter and following summer, and cd wish, when revolving it in my mind, that I cd be in twenty places at the same time."[13]

After looking over a number of ships, Fanny decided to charter a 163-ton brig called the *John Quincy Adams*. Whitby turned the slaves over to her, though she kept them on the steamboat in which they had come from Memphis until January 6, when they moved directly onto the brig. It was an anxious time for Fanny, Flower's experience, among others, making her afraid that traders might get hold of the blacks. Phiquepal apparently did not arrive in New Orleans until after she had made all the necessary practical decisions. For example, she joined with James Breadlove and her friend Marcus Winchester in a business venture that she hoped would help cover her expenses. She would take a cargo of pork and lard for sale in Haiti and return with a shipful of coffee.[14]

If Fanny hoped that Phiquepal would take on the burden of the trip's last stage, she was disappointed, and Robert Dale said she was "*compelled* to accompany her slaves to Haiti, finding no one to whom she cld safely confide them." But she expected the trip to be brief. On January 18, the day before she was to leave, she wrote that she would be back in New Orleans before the close of March and would then visit some of the Mississippi and Ohio towns she had missed on the way down. She wrote happily of the liberals' sure progress and her part in it.[15]

After a thirty-day voyage with Phiquepal and her former slaves, Fanny was received into the circles of the military men who governed Haiti and was celebrated as the friend and advocate of the African race. She wrote Lafayette that President Jean Pierre Boyer, the members of his government, and the Haitians in general showed her every flattering attention. Secretary-general Inginac gave a banquet for her and proposed a toast so effusive that Fanny was embarrassed. She was the first white woman so honored on an island where, fewer than thirty years before, whites had been mutilated and massacred by their rebellious slaves.[16]

Better still, Boyer was even more generous than she expected in receiving the people she had brought. Four years earlier he had stopped giving routine allowances and travel grants to American blacks because so many settlers had taken adavantage of them and then left Haiti disenchanted. Now he took Fanny's former slaves onto his own land on one of the best cultivated parts of the island. They had cabins, gardens, water, and everything else they needed, including tools and provisions to last several months. Waiving rent or any other fees, he promised that when they had given evidence of good conduct and shown they were ready to start their own farms, he would see that they got a grant of government land in fee simple. On top of this, Fanny reported, "the president generously assists me in covering the expenses of their removal hither."

For all that she tried to deny it even to herself, Fanny was emotionally exhausted. For more than a year she had been subjected to cruel and bewildering attacks. She had lost touch with her sister and watched helplessly as Camilla began to give in to despair. Letting herself rest now, Fanny lingered longer than she had intended. Mingling in the easy social life of Haiti's mulatto aristocracy, she and Phiquepal spent a month together on the island. There were garden parties and dinners, rides on horseback, strolls through Port-au-Prince. Four years earlier she had apparently had a transforming experience with George Flower when they went to buy the slaves whom she had just given their freedom, and she was not a woman to believe it could never happen again. By the time Phiquepal left Haiti on March 17, he and Fanny were lovers.

He took the *John Quincy Adams* and its cargo back to New Orleans to close "the very troublesome commercial affair" in which Fanny had entangled herself. He planned then to take ship for Le Havre, but Fanny expected him soon after in New York. On the day he left, she watched his ship sail by Inginac's gardens along the shore. Though she was one of a cheerful party, she had to keep rousing herself from reverie. In the days that followed she kept up her visiting, but she wrote Phiquepal of being preoccupied in crowds, of finding the place where he had recently stayed as forlorn as she felt herself, of feeling the hours heavy and tedious in his absence. She also had been "oppressed with lassitude and passed the day reading on the sofa, feeling my solitude and often speculating respecting the progress of the John Quincy Adams."[17]

She decided to return home by way of Philadelphia rather than New Orleans.Though she felt some qualms for the promises she would break, she was anxious for Camilla and wanted to learn how their cause progressed in the eastern cities, so on March 25, 1830, she sailed from Port-au-Prince on the *Enterprise*. She complained later of exhaustion from rough weather and the shock of suddenly passing from the genial tropics into a cold gale that swept the east coast as she neared it. But Fanny had rarely suffered from seasickness before.

Alone, on a ship sailing north from the Caribbean, she began to face the fact that she was pregnant.[18]

Fanny now confronted her ultimate vulnerability as a woman, and she confronted it at a time when she had triumphed over every other restraint on women's lives. She was hated and feared, to be sure, for her insistence on speaking out with a voice women had not found before. But she was revered too, and many were inclined to follow her and to share her risks. For the first time in her restless life, she had found ways to be happy. She had found work she believed in and could do well. And she had found colleagues in a task commensurate with her powers and her ideals.

She had promised never to marry, and perhaps she considered having her child alone. But she had also written more than once of the terrible burden society put on children it called illegitimate. A man and a woman, she argued, bore an ultimate responsibility to the child they conceived. She knew, from the vicious attacks against her, that any child she bore out of wedlock would be granted no quarter in the world. She knew that this time she had no choice.

She had no choice, despite the fact that Phiquepal bore little resemblance to those who had attracted her before. Fanny was indeed drawn to older men, and he was sixteen years her senior. He was handsome, too, and no doubt he had his charm. But he was a person of no genuine distinction of either intellect or spirit. Something of a black sheep in his family, he had rambled about in Europe, the Caribbean, and America with no evident purpose and to no apparent end. He called himself a doctor, a scientist, a teacher—but Maclure had come to think him a fraud. Years later, Robert Dale Owen described Phiquepal as suspicious and headstrong—"a man well informed on many points, full of original ideas, some of practical value, but, withal, a wrong-headed genius, whose extravagance and wil-fulness and inordinate self-conceit destroyed his usefulness." He said that Fanny had found in Phiquepal "an unwise, hasty, fanciful counselor." And a Quaker friend who wrote that he was "visionary, nervous, and irritable" speculated that Fanny, who was not in the ordinary sense a man's woman, would never have married and become a mother had she not been "under the influence of a species of hallucination." Heavy with the shards of the life she had so proudly crafted, Fanny landed on April 23 in Philadelphia.[19]

On reaching New York after a six-month absence, Fanny suffered another terrible blow: Camilla was visibly sinking. She had discovered that Julia would not have her in Hanover. Robert Dale, whom she loved at least as a brother and who was probably in love with her, had responded to the impossibility of their situation by burying his emotions in work. By his own account naturally indolent, he nevertheless rode his horse the five miles to and from the city and worked twelve hours every day. He wrote articles for the *Free Enquirer,* did most of the editing, and read proof himself. He lectured at the Hall of Science and as far afield as Boston, took on official responsibilities in the struggle for control of the Working Men's party, and surreptitiously edited the fledgling *Daily Sentinel,* a newspaper for the working class. Camilla's isolation was complete, and by the time Fanny returned, Robert Dale had despaired of her recovery.[20]

On May 1 Fanny wrote cryptically in the *Free Enquirer* that private business demanded her immediate attention, and she set feverishly to work. She had quietly decided to go to Europe and wanted to order her affairs in New York to give the impression that she might return within a few months. Much of what she did suggests that she was very angry. She discovered that a Quaker, Dr. William Gibbons, had written a scabrous pamphlet he called "An Exposition of Modern Scepticism." Published first in mid-December 1829, it quoted letters to the *Free Enquirer* to prove that Fanny's followers advocated promiscuous, if licensed, concubinage, and said their principles offered no remedy for the evils of life other than a pistol or a hangman's noose. By February 1830 the pamphlet had gone into a third edition, to which was appended an endorsement signed by six other Friends, and it circulated in meetinghouses throughout the Union.

Robert Dale attacked the pamphlet, pointing out that Gibbons had quoted passages from letters to the *Free Enquirer* as though they expressed the editors' views, even when the editors had explicitly taken issue with them. Now Fanny abandoned her policy of ignoring slander and published a two-page response to Gibbons. Her character "grossly assaulted," and her writings and principles "wantonly misrepresented," she defended herself by pointing to "a life exhibiting one active scene of exertion in the discovery of truth . . . in the aid and advocacy of human liberty . . . in breaking the chains of the African, and pleading the cause of the poor and the neglected at the bar of humankind." She asked those who had read Gibbons's pamphlet to read her writings and Robert Dale's, predicting that they would find there a set of views "rational, constitutional, peaceable and desirable . . . promising to ameliorate the human condition, to cement human hearts, and gradually to banish crime, want, misery, riches and poverty from the earth."[21]

On May 9 at the Hall of Science, Fanny gave a lecture called "A Review of the Times," which she was to give repeatedly in the weeks to come. After her visit to Boston the preceding summer, Lyman Beecher referred to her as part of "a conspiracy in our land against the being of God, and our civil, and social, and religious institutions" and threw his own formidable energies into a "countervailing movement" against her. Fanny intended her new lecture to be an answer to such evangelical attack and to the tiresome cry of "infidelity," which stood then for religious skepticism. Insisting that the great intellects of every generation had discarded the prevailing superstition, she saw in history the equation of the word "infidelity" with political honesty and common sense and said "if doubters in miraculous revelations and biblical theology, are to be styled infidels, they can only wear the name in common with all the wisest and boldest patriots of America's revolution." She cited Jefferson to prove that George Washington was not a Christian: "he believed not in the priest's God, nor in the divine authority of the priest's book." John Adams had distinguished between sectarian dogmas, about which everyone argued, and the moral imperative to behave justly to one's fellows. Jefferson and Franklin, Ethan Allen and Horatio Gates, were what the clergy would call infidels: "all disbelieved the compound Jewish and Christian system, and looked upon its mysteries and its miracles as upon nursery tales."[22]

Fanny understood that her battle with the evangelicals was fundamentally political. Her greatest sin in their eyes was "to suggest the means by which consistent republicanism might be developed in practice, human happiness secured, and the equal rights of all established." It was one of the many she was fated to lose. If the last quarter of the eighteenth century had seen the flowering of Deism in America, the nineteenth century saw the inexorable progress of Protestant sects. For every Baptist in 1800, there would be three in 1840; for every Presbyterian, there would be four forty years later; for every Methodist, there would be seven. In 1800 there was one church organization for every 1,740 people; in 1850, one for every 895. But in 1830 Fanny was not ready to concede the fight.[23]

She was in the grip of a vision—that of men and women living equally in a society devoted to the good of all, of masses organized to exert significant control over their own lives. Nobody knew how to create such a society, but in the spring of 1829 Fanny had put her ultimate faith in education, and her immediate faith in the first efforts of New York working people to come together politically. As Robert

Dale wrote, he and Fanny were "virtually and indirectly, but not immediately, the first movers" of the New York Working Men's party.[24]

The original Working Men's party had appeared in 1828, when Philadelphia's Mechanics' Union of Trade Associations decided to enter politics to promote "the interests and enlightenment of the working classes." Similar parties quickly sprang up in cities and towns throughout the northeastern United States, often in support of the ten-hour day and usually siding with journeymen striking against their masters. Made up for the most part of such skilled workers as carpenters, glaziers, bricklayers, and printers, they proved "the closest thing to a classic ideological party in the entire antebellum period."[25]

Their sympathies engaged from the party's early days in New York City, Fanny and Robert Dale guided the Working Men persuasively in the direction of educational reform. In the fall of 1829, however, just as Fanny was leaving New York for Haiti, they had discovered a rival in the Working Men's counsels. At an important meeting ten resolutions were passed unanimously, one of them supporting "any peaceful and effectual measure which shall tend permanently to equalize the possession of landed and of all other property." A report called for a revolution "such as shall leave behind it no trace of that government which has denied to every human being *an equal amount of property on arriving at the age of maturity*, and *previous* thereto, *equal food, clothing, and instruction at the public expense*." The author of the report and the resolutions was Thomas Skidmore, a machinist and an able, persistent radical.[26]

Though Robert Dale had gone to the meeting simply to observe, he was elected secretary, and so a statement about the report and the resolutions went out over his signature. In the next issue of the *Free Enquirer* on October 31 he hastily dissociated himself from Skidmore's brand of radicalism. He wrote privately that "he who expects wisdom from Mechanics, trained as they are, will be disappointed," and from upstate New York Fanny urged the Working Men's party to caution.[27]

It was crucial, she insisted, that they begin reform at the right end. They could not accomplish everything at once, and they could not afford more than one major issue. Republican education "alone, as it seems to me, can set the vessel of the republic fairly and safely afloat." People were not yet ready for an equal division of property: "Equalize fortunes at this hour, and knavery in one year would have beggared honesty . . . credulous simplicity would have yielded all to the crafty hypocrite."[28]

In the November elections, despite a rabid press campaign against them, the New York City Working Men's party ticket polled 6,090 votes out of 21,000, elected one of its own to the New York State Assembly, and brought six other candidates close to office. Though Fanny had had nothing directly to do with the party platform or its candidates, the papers tagged them "Fanny Wrightists" and "Wright Reasoners," and they survived those labels, as well as diatribes like Stone's in the *Commercial Advertiser*. He called the Working Men "poor and deluded followers of a crazy atheistical woman . . . lost to society, to earth and to heaven, godless and hopeless, clothed and fed by stealing and blasphemy." After the election the daily papers continued to quarrel about it and to give Fanny more credit for political skill and management than she could justly claim. But when George Henry Evans, the twenty-three-year-old British printer who had first put out the *Free Enquirer*, began publishing the *Workingman's Advocate* that fall in New York, Fanny took it to be proof that she was right in trusting to the energy and ability of the working class itself.[29]

Shortly after the party had proved its political appeal, the *New York Evening Journal* began openly to support it. At the same time it editorialized against the Skidmore faction for what came to be called "agrarianism," the proposal to solve the nation's problems by dividing the wealth equally among its citizens. Robert Dale and George Henry Evans sided with the *Evening Journal* against Skidmore, and by the year's end they had driven him out of the party. The *Journal* faction then coalesced in opposition to Fanny's idea about state boarding schools.

Robert Dale had absorbed Fanny's confidence in her ability to persuade the Working Men that everything depended on changing the environment in which children lived. "If the children from these State schools are to go every evening, the one to his wealthy parent's soft carpetted drawing room," he asked, "and the other to its poor father's or widowed mother's comfortless cabin, will they return the next day as friends and equals? He knows little of human nature who thinks they will." In December he had published Fanny's speech proposing state boarding schools, and the Association for the Protection of Industry and for the Promotion of National Education, which they had started, memorialized the legislature to appropriate $100,000 to establish a model school somewhere in the middle of the state. Each town and county was to send a proportion of its children to the school, which would then maintain and educate them at a minimal charge to the parents. But after purging Skidmore, the Working Men's party voted simply for an educational system open equally to all.[30]

In mid-February 1830, the *Daily Sentinel* appeared with Robert Dale's secret editorial help, and in the spring he wrote a series of essays in it supporting state guardianship. The first violent reaction came from the New York Typographical Society, which accused the plan of being dangerously visionary and potentially destructive of elemental social ties. Mechanics' and Working Men's Associations that had sprung up all over New York State were uncertain in their support for it, and the farmers seemed ready to reject the idea that their children should live away from home.

Neither Fanny nor anyone else, however, had yet learned the listening and compromising processes necessary to democratic insurgency, and she was convinced that the new world had to be made with new people whom only a radically different educational process could create. Education without state boarding schools, Robert Dale argued, was a "paltry palliative" that would continue aristocracy in America. But just after Fanny returned, they discovered that the *Evening Journal* had called the idea of national schools "one of the wildest fancies that ever entered into the brain of the most visionary fanatics"—a system designed "to sever those strong ties of affection that keep families together." The Working Men's party was about to splinter again, and Fanny bore some responsibility for its second schism.[31]

On May 21, with forty-seven of its seventy members present, the party's General Executive Committee repudiated a report made up largely of excerpts from Robert Dale's *Sentinel* essays as "a specious attempt insidiously to palm upon the Committee and the great body of the working classes the doctrines of *infidelity*." Over furious opposition, and by a vote of twenty-five to twenty-two, they adopted a report endorsed by the *Evening Journal* faction. Of this meeting the *Courier and Enquirer* reported that there was "a hot battle for full two hours and one half. One party abused the other, and they reciprocally charged each other with being ten times—nay a hundred times worse than 'Regency' or 'Tammany' men." At a protest meeting on May 26, which the *Courier and Enquirer* described as "one of the wildest, most singular scenes—short of personal violence and bloodshed—which ever took place in this country," the two factions battled for the right to speak for the Working Men's party, and each claimed victory.[32]

Fanny shouted treason to the people's interests. In early June she wrote in the *Free Enquirer* on "Plots and Plotters" and raged at the "open treachery of the TWENTY FIVE . . . as contrived by Tammany and the combined agency of all the corruptionists of the city." As the plot thickened, so did Fanny's prose. Her opponents continued to call her followers "agrarians" and "infidels," and as rational explanations failed of their effect, Fanny became more inflammatory.[33]

The bitter struggle they fought out in the weeks and months to come ended not with two factions of a single organization, but with two separate organizations. Thomas Skidmore and his followers had left the party in December 1829, so within eight months of the promising November 1829 election, the party was irrevocably split into three. Most of the working-class organizations and journals outside New York City opposed state guardianship, and even Owen backed down from his insistent support of it. At the Working Men's first state convention in late August, the *Journal* rather than the *Sentinel* delegation was seated, and the idea of state-supported boarding schools for all American children became a relic of history.

Fanny and Robert Dale were no doubt right in believing that the *Evening Journal* faction wanted to use the Working Men's party for its own political purposes, though its sin may have been no more heinous than wanting to shape it to a different vision of the American future. But if they were arguably right in believing that the kind of education they proposed was the only education that could make America truly republican, they nevertheless allowed themselves to be seduced by their own eloquence. The idea of state boarding schools, at least in this context, was Fanny's: it did not arise from among the people themselves, who for the most part wanted to hold on to their children. It had no widespread support and therefore no political future. The campaign Fanny and Robert Dale conducted for state boarding schools dissipated the party's meager political strength and in November 1830 Tammany swept the elections.

To blame Fanny and Robert Dale for the failure of the Working Men's party, however, would be to misread political reality. They were repeatedly subjected to unprincipled attack by the Democratic press and Democratic politicians, who did what they could to discredit them personally and to destroy them as a political force. Journeymen workers had little money to spare, no experience in politics, and only fitful interest in the battles fought in their behalf. Poor and working people had not learned how to organize: they had neither the time, the power, nor the votes to play significantly in the game of coalition politics. And the Democrats were sufficiently shrewd and adaptable to show some interest in their demands and thereby win their allegiance. Perhaps more important, the lower middle class for the most part bought the ideology of Jacksonian America: they believed that if they were smart, lucky, and hard-working, they too could get rich, and as historian Edward Pessen has said, that kind of optimism kills off ideological politics.

The hostile forces Fanny had awakened continued to goad her. On May 28, in the midst of her battle for the Working Men's allegiance, editor William Leete Stone published his most vicious attack in the *New York Commercial Advertiser.* Under the title "Fanny the Philanthropist," Stone claimed to have documents proving that Fanny could drive the fabled Yankee trader to tears. Twenty-seven of the thirty blacks she had taken to Haiti were said to be free already, according to Stone, "and were only coaxed to go along with her, to assist in the comedy of 'raising the wind.'" Furthermore, she had figured out how to make a handy profit. She had reportedly paid Captain Lawrenson of the *John Quincy Adams* $1,600 for the brig but allowed him to carry two hundred barrels of his own cargo. He was to register his freight in her name at customs in Port-au-Prince, according to a contract clause which Stone printed in capital letters: "THE SAID LAWRENSON TO ALLOW THE SAID WRIGHT THE REGULAR DUTIES ON THE SAID ARTICLES, AS ARE CHARGED IN THE TARIFF OF DUTIES OF THAT ISLAND." Fanny could then charm the customs officials and the chief of state himself into remitting the cargo duties, and she would pocket the money the captain had paid her: "Magnanimous Boyer!—Fortunate Fanny Wright!! . . . The goods were entered in the name of the philanthropist, and the courteous Ebony remitted the duties to the lady Topaz, amounting, we are told, to NINE THOUSAND DOLLARS, which sum the Captain paid over to his fair constituent . . . The President was lavish of his presents to his fair visitant, and among other things put into her hands a purse of ONE HUNDRED DOUBLOONS—enough to pay for the whole concern, and leaving the duties, over and above the value of the three slaves actually emancipated, as a clear profit on the speculation!"[34]

For the second time in a month, Fanny fought against a personal attack. On June 2 Stone printed her itemized denial, prefaced by the sentence, "No person living—not even Miss Frances Wright, shall be intentionally treated with injustice in this paper." A model of restraint, her rebuttal declared Stone's statement untrue in both its details and its implications. She gathered up the bills of sale for the people she had taken to Haiti, along with the account of the customs duties paid at Port-au-Prince, and made them available for inspection in the *Free Enquirer* office. The total of the duties in American currency "amounted to about one-third of the sum falsely stated to have been paid to me by the Captain of the vessel." The president of Haiti had in fact given her somewhat more than the equivalent of one hundred doubloons, she said, to cover her immediate expenses in bringing her people to the island. His gift would have served the purpose he intended had others not taken advantage of her "ignorance of commercial affairs, as well as of my peculiar and anxious situation in the port of a Slave State, charged with the responsibility of emancipated people of colour." She pointed out that the expenses of taking her former slaves to Haiti were only a fraction of what the Nashoba experiment had cost her: it had involved four years of her life and, calculated merely in financial terms, "reduced me from comparative affluence to a moderate competency." According to Robert Dale, Fanny had spent $16,000 on Nashoba and the slaves, which was more than half her fortune.[35]

The fragmentary notes that remain make it impossible to disentangle Fanny's finances in the matter of her Haitian trip. The *John Quincy Adams* apparently left Haiti with 11,000 barrels of coffee and nine tons of logwood, but when the business in New Orleans was finally done, Fanny, Winchester, and James Breadlove appear to have lost $431.48 each. Fanny took a consignment of 422 sacks of coffee on board the *Enterprise*. Another 150 were to follow three days later, and her agent in Haiti was to reclaim the remainder from a merchant who was delaying delivery. Of her cargo to Philadelphia her expenses, in Haitian currency, totaled $4,612.50, just over $4,000 of which was the cost of the coffee. The value of the *Enterprise* cargo in American money was somewhat more than $2,000.[36]

Stone was not a man to admit that he was wrong, certainly not where Fanny Wright was concerned. He did say he was disposed to believe the rumor incorrect that had accused her of taking people to Haiti whom she had not freed herself, but the other information had come from "a source of the first respectability," an official at Port-au-Prince. Without acknowledging his juggling of either amounts or currencies, he now said that the exact amount of the customs duties had been $7,607 in Haitian money. Though the purpose of the contract clause at issue was obviously that the captain should pay the tariff on his own merchandise, Stone implied that Fanny had not repaid the captain for his portion of the duties which Boyer allegedly remitted. "The Captain . . . had no idea of the performances which were to be exhibited on board of his vessel," he added, "when he shipped the fair lady, with a gentleman in green spectacles, the adult colored persons and the pickaninnies, black and yellow, with the cargo which went to so happy a market. As to the nature of these performances, decency compels us to be silent."[37]

The only real charge that remained was that Fanny had gotten favored treatment. A woman bringing thirty-one new citizens, so far as she knew at her own expense, was preferred commercially over those whose purpose in Haiti was merely trade. That, however, was not the way Stone put it.

Nor was he the only journalist who attacked Fanny personally. Until the November elections of the year before, Major Mordecai Noah had been a friendly, even jocular enemy. Noah, however, was serious about electoral politics and passionate about Tammany Hall. Jackson had just appointed him Surveyor of the Port of New York, and he thought he knew where his political advantage lay. To frighten New Yorkers anxious about holding onto what they had, he continued to call the Working Men's party "agrarians" long after they had purged Skidmore and his disciples. He wrote a parody in which he said the "robbing of mails, picking pockets, shoplifting, housebreaking, and other natural modes of restoring this equilibrium of property, are in strict accordance with the rule of *Wright* and the eternal fitness of things." He called Fanny "Miss Epicene Wright." And on June 19 he published, with a running commentary, the two-year-old letter Fanny had written Jennings from Memphis.[38]

He prefaced the whole with Shakespeare's lines: "She never told her love, / But let concealment, like a worm i' th' bud, / Feed on her damask cheek." The craving Fanny had shown after strange and unnatural excitement, he said, suggested some morbid passion that prompted her to madness: "She is a female Rousseau and revenges the neglect of men to her indescribable charms, by throwing society in confusion." Jennings himself was a poor creature, "but Frances Wright [has] a mind of a masculine character, nerves that cannot be shaken, arrogance and vanity equal to any mad enthusiast that ever breathed." Her career, however, was drawing to a close, and American virtue was safe at last from "the mad attempts of a sorceress." It was another day's work in yellow journalism, and no doubt many wealthy New Yorkers smiled over their morning tea, satisfied that even the Democratic press was putting Fanny Wright in her place.[39]

Announcing in mid-June that she would go to Europe until after the fall elections, Fanny neither betrayed her pain nor renounced her vision. To "the young mechanics" at the Hall of Science she gave as eloquent a plea for human fellowship as she would ever make: "Occupants of the same earth, citizens of the same country, creatures of the same form and nature, we are partitioned off into classes, and arrayed against each other, in despite even of our own will, by the habits of our youth, and the contrasted and conflicting interests of our after years." The working class was the only large group among the many fragments into which society was splintered; the best feelings and the soundest sense appeared among them; and their interests "more nearly approached to the great natural interests of man." In a parting address at the Bowery Theatre she insisted that the great ideal of a republic was still attainable through education: something like economic equality would come when knowledge spread, privileges were abolished, and people grew contemptuous of mere wealth.[40]

Despite the splintering of the Working Men's party and the heightened press attacks, Fanny did not spend her last days in the United States in public retreat. She spoke often before she left, and always to packed houses. When Mrs. Trollope heard her in Philadelphia, she saw more women in the audience than she had ever seen in an American theater: "Miss Wright came on the stage surrounded by a body guard of Quaker ladies, in the full costume of their sect. She was, as she always is, startling in her theories, but powerfully eloquent, and, on the whole, was much applauded." Her last speech in New York was crowded with three thousand people, half of them women, and Major Noah wrote that Fanny's "doctrines and opinions and philosophy appear to have made much greater progress in the city, than we ever dreamt of."[41]

Fanny's faith in her cause was still so strong that she rewrote her will, leaving Robert Dale all her property, including her interest in the *Free Enquirer*. She wanted the remains of her fortune devoted to the cause to which she had given her life and trusted Robert Dale to carry on as she would have done. She announced that she was leaving because she did not want her name "to be made a scarecrow to the timid, or a stumbling-block to the innocently prejudiced" and said she would "take the present season for attention to some more private interests of my own."[42]

On July 1, 1830, missing the annual independence celebration that had played so prominent a part in her recent life, Fanny and Camilla sailed for England on the *Hannibal*. Robert Dale wept. But among the many New Yorkers happy to be rid of Fanny Wright was Philip Hone, the erstwhile mayor. He confided to his diary that Fanny had apparently hoped to marry Lafayette, who, however, had been "saved from the disgrace of such a connection." A female Tom Paine, she had given lectures "the object of which has been to break down the moral and religious ties which bind mankind together, and to bring into disrepute the institutions which have been revered by all good men."[43]

The *Courier and Enquirer* published "a doleful Ditty made upon the departure of that 'mother of the Gracchii' Frances Wright, the 'petticoated politician,' " to be sung to the tune of "Oh! Put the Onion to Your Eye":

> For she had gold within her purse,
> And brass upon her face;
> And talent indescribable,
> To give old thoughts new grace.
> And if you want to raise the wind,
> Or breed a moral storm
> You must have one bold lady-man
> To prate about reform.

Less than a year later, according to Frances Trollope, Americans had fallen silent on the subject of Fanny Wright: "How easily do the wonders of a day pass away! Last year I hardly ever looked at a paper without seeing long and repeated mention of Miss Wright. Her eloquence and her mischief, her wisdom and her folly, her strange principles and her no principles were discussed without ceasing. Now her name appears utterly forgotten."[44]

Mixing with None but
French Society

9

Some three weeks after leaving New York the *Hannibal* reached England, and Frances and Camilla Wright disappeared. Six weeks later a baffled Richard Carlile wrote Fanny to say that people in London asked about her often. Robert Owen, he reported, who had gotten a letter via Paris from Robert Dale in New York and assumed Fanny had brought it, knew no more. Carlile speculated that Fanny, "on reaching the Downs . . . must have heard something of the new French Revolution" and flown to Paris to watch it at Lafayette's side. "But, pray . . . drop a line to some one in London, to say, that you live, for you have formed high expectations of a continued and important public life in many bosoms in this town and country."[1]

It was a dismal contrast—those high expectations on the one side, and on the other the furtiveness her pregnancy forced upon her. Fanny no doubt felt that contrast bitterly: she now had to hide, and hiding was foreign to her nature. But she did it so well that for all the labels yet to be hurled, no one called her sexually immoral or tagged her baby illegitimate. For once, she got what she wanted.

But the price she paid was very high. She cut herself off from everyone who had loved her. She retreated into a tight-lipped privacy from which, for twenty years, she emerged only fitfully, and she became, for those who wanted to know her, very nearly opaque. From 1830 until shortly before she died, no one knows much about what really happened to Frances Wright, and in a different way, neither did she.

Early in October 1830, Fanny wrote Lafayette elliptically that she and Camilla had come to France and intended to settle there: "I have done what I could to make myself forgotten at this moment in America, and the public motives which decided me to this have made me less regret that private ones should have led me just now into retirement." Those private motives had been connected "with the health and spirits of our dear Camilla. These are . . . reviving and will authorize me, I trust, ere long to embrace you."[2]

She was yet more devious with Robert Dale, who wrote despondently in August that he was now fighting the battle alone. Fanny and Camilla had left "a terrible blank" in his domestic circle, "just such a blank—the worst of all—which the loss of intelligent female society always leaves, and which nothing else can effectively replace." He bore his loneliness by reminding himself that their absence would be of no very long duration, as he expected them back in several months. Sometime that fall, however, Fanny told him she had accepted a pressing invitation to lecture in London and would delay her return until the spring. In November she wrote enigmatically from Paris that she wished she "might shrink somewhat less from personal contact and individual communion with my fellows than I find the case at the time present." By now she was at least eight months pregnant.[3]

So brilliantly did Fanny wrap the mantle of secrecy about her that for many months no record of her private life exists. All that remain are the letters and essays she wrote to analyze what was happening in France—and to try to influence the course of its history. Just after she and Camilla landed in England, the people of Paris threw up barricades against their king, so that Fanny confronted the first major revolution of her lifetime. And right at its center was her beloved Lafayette.[4]

Late in July violence erupted at the Palais Royal, when Charles X imposed new ordinances tightening the vise on the press, dissolving the newly elected Chamber of Deputies, and narrowing the electorate to those who were his natural allies. When the opposition papers defied the government, the police broke into their offices and destroyed their presses. But the workingmen and women of Paris tore paving stones from the streets and threw up barricades almost every thirty feet against the king's soldiers, and by July 28 the tricolor flew again over the Hôtel de Ville and Notre Dame. The next day, as whole regiments began to defect and crowds sacked the Archbishop's Palace, Talleyrand reportedly looked at his watch and said, "At five minutes after noon, the elder branch of the Bourbons ceased to reign." Lafayette then accepted command of the Paris National Guard and announced that he would immediately reorganize it to keep peace in the city.[5]

For almost a decade Lafayette had been Fanny's political mentor, and together they had plotted revolution when France invaded Spain six years before. The revolution they had talked of then had finally come, and Fanny's hopes that France would move toward republican government centered necessarily on Lafayette. Soon after she crossed the Channel, she began sending him long cautionary letters of political advice.

As Fanny anxiously waited in the provinces for news from Paris, Lafayette played out his last important role on the stage of history. Credited with the power to make himself the constitutional monarch, he chose instead to support the Duc d'Orléans, head of the younger branch of the Bourbons. In a gesture reminiscent of Versailles years before, Lafayette took Orléans through a menacing crowd, up the stairs and onto a balcony at the Hôtel de Ville, the headquarters of republican Paris, and embraced him in the folds of a tricolor. The crowd below was won over by Lafayette's endorsement, and long afterward, Alphonse de Lamartine wrote that the republican kiss of Lafayette had made a king.[6]

Reluctant at first to condemn Lafayette's support for the Duc d'Orléans, Fanny nevertheless wondered if he had been duped. Orléans had professed to agree completely when Lafayette told him that the French people needed "a popular throne surrounded by republican institutions." When the old general then gave his blessing, Orléans received the throne as King Louis-Philippe from the deputies and peers met in royal session. As the weeks and months passed, however, Fanny saw that Louis-Philippe had no intention of granting the republican institutions he had led Lafayette to expect. Convinced that the old general's position was crucial to France, Fanny was ready by the end of October to tell Lafayette that he was being used.

She had no faith, she wrote, in a constitutional monarchy: "its *constitutional pledges* are *oaths* and *paper* while its *monarchical force* is *plenty of money and plenty of patronage.*" She thought the government made a fatal error in believing that the discontent throughout France was not real, "that it is *provoked* and not *inbred* in the popular mind, and that the better informed and better disposed part of the population are averse to all more radical changes." The National Guard was the key to future progress: "Keep it bound to yourself and all is safe, but—be sure of this—*there are no means left unemployed to loosen it from your hold.*"[7]

At about this time Fanny wrote the *Free Enquirer* in a more radical vein. The struggle in France was different from any that had preceded it in that it was "openly and acknowledgedly a *war of class*" and that "this war is universal." Further, she recognized what she most deplored, "that the people will win no redress but what they carry by force."[8]

She was persuaded now that Lafayette had made a fatal mistake. It would have been more prudent and dignified, Fanny wrote in the *Free Enquirer*, had a republic been proclaimed at the beginning. "While privileged legislators sat down to decree that they had *saved the nation from the Republic*, the nation have had time to discover that it is saddled with all the old burdens under new masters." The liberal leader Casimir Périer himself said there had been no revolution; the person of the king had merely been changed.[9]

Fanny's skepticism of the government proved correct. Once the regime had survived its first five months intact, it found Lafayette an embarrassment. The ministry hastened to make clear that the new government had made no promises in return for his support. The Chamber of Deputies moved to reduce his power by changing the Guard from a national force under a single command to a collection of municipal forces for maintaining order locally, thus removing the power base that had made Lafayette a potential threat to the king. Taking his principal staff officers with him, Lafayette resigned, as did his close friend Dupont de l'Eure, the Minister of Justice. But Fanny proved wrong when she anticipated that Louis-Philippe would hurt himself if he dismissed Lafayette. Although some eight hundred students demonstrated in front of the old general's house, they created no serious disorder. On December 27, 1830, Lafayette issued his last order to the National Guard, and on December 30, the *Journal des debats* declared the revolution over. Twenty-five years later, the Quaker Amos Gilbert, who followed Fanny as editor of the *Free Enquirer*, wrote that she had never finished her biography of Lafayette because "the hero of her work committed what she deemed an irretrievable error . . . the elevation of Louis-Philippe to the throne of France."[10]

Sometime that December, or perhaps early in January 1831, Fanny's child, a daughter, was born. Fanny called her Sylva, after one of Phiquepal's names, and told no one. Camilla seems to have been in the south with friends.

Soon after, Fanny showed herself in Paris at a reception at Lafayette's. James Fenimore Cooper wrote Charles Wilkes, "She looked haggard and much changed for the worse." Her appearance "excited much attention," and she was treated as a pariah. Cooper, who had never been introduced to her, thought it would show disrespect to his wife to ask to meet her now, as the women avoided her: "I do not think she repeated her visit, though I doubt not Lafayette sees her in private."[11]

Harriet Garnett was baffled. In January she had heard that Fanny was in Paris, but Fanny did not write her. Camilla was apparently in Bordeaux at the time "and much out of spirits." A month later Harriet finally heard from Fanny but, she wrote Julia, her letter was "so cold, so changed . . . that I have not had courage to reply to it." Fanny had said she would return to America in the spring but would come back to Europe "to prosecute studies she can only continue in France." She was staying with a friend "and does not appear . . . at the general's soirées."[12]

In February Robert Dale wrote his friends that Fanny would not lecture in Great Britain after all and would leave Le Havre for America about March 10. "*Camilla* talks of passing the summer in Paris," he reported, because the climate agreed with her and had already, so Fanny had told him, "restored her to that health and cheerfulness which she lost at the death of her boy; and which I was beginning to fear she wd never recover."[13]

But Camilla died on February 8 in a little flat on the rue Montaigne. A month later Fanny wrote Robert Owen: "A few words and those painful I know to you and to all my friends will suffice to explain my silence. *Camilla died in my arms* . . . of a sudden attack of hemorrage, after having flattered me with perfect recovery from the weak state of health and spirits wch had decided me on a voyage to Europe. Wm Phiquepal and Genl Lafayette have rendered me all the aid and sympathy wch circumstances have demanded and my heart cd receive." According to Harriet, Camilla had come to Paris from the south and got an apartment by herself—"not with Fanny, who remains with Mr. Phiquepal"—and had died the fourth day after she arrived.[14]

Camilla had been essential to her sister for almost twenty-five years: Robert Dale called her Fanny's good angel. In the pair they made, Camilla played the role of the traditional wife: she kept the scrapbook of Fanny's triumphs and crowed to friends and family over them. She was both sounding board and echo chamber, and now she was gone.[15]

Only a few people had proved important to Fanny's self-esteem. The Garnetts, for example, were among those few, and of them Fanny had written: "The truth of your affection is dearer to me than ought this world cd yield—the beauty of your characters reconciles me with

Frances Wright d'Arusmont and Phiquepal d'Arusmont, 1835

Frances Sylva d'Arusmont

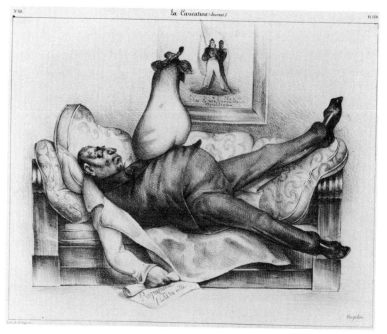

"Le Cauchemar," *Lafayette's nightmare of Louis-Philippe*

"Enfoncé, Lafayette!"
Louis-Philippe exulting over the funeral of Lafayette

human nature, and sometimes with myself . . . your sweet and devoted affection comes like balm upon my heart . . . I go to sleep at night blessing your names and at peace with myself." But Julia and Harriet had been merely important; Camilla had been crucial.[16]

The circumstances of their last year and a half together made Fanny's loss all the more irreparable. Whatever had happened between them—whatever harsh words were said, whatever the wounds given and received—Fanny had failed Camilla, and she knew that. Camilla's death left her with a burden of guilt mixed with an irretrievable loss. It left her with a formidable psychic struggle for survival.

For the next few years, everyone who wrote about Fanny wrote of a woman who carried bravely on, but who was at the same time remote and demoralized. She withdrew into a thorny isolation: within five years she lost or repudiated every important friendship she had known when Camilla was alive.

Fanny did not return to America in the spring of 1831, and Phiquepal went in her stead to see to her financial affairs. Robert Dale wrote that she could not face "the life of publicity which awaits her here . . . the rougher and more public advocacy," and in April, after Phiquepal sailed for New York, she went into seclusion at the country home of his friend, Dr. François Magendie, a prominent French scientist. She wrote Harriet that she intended to make France her home and to live a private life.[17]

Fanny then took on the job of making the best of what she had to do. For years Phiquepal had been out of touch with his family in Agen. His mother's consent was legally necessary to his marriage, and now Fanny wrote the family in almost defensive praise of Phiquepal. She seemed apprehensive that her American notoriety might bias them against her. But the mother consented, and the marriage took place on July 22, 1831, in the mayor's office of Paris' tenth arrondisement. Lafayette, Dr. Magendie, and the naturalist Pierre Jean Turpin were among the witnesses. Fanny had discovered that Phiquepal's family name was d'Arusmont, and she took it for her own. Though she had written more than once on the subject, she made no legal provision to keep her property in her own hands.[18]

Sometime that fall she made her marriage generally known. She told Harriet she had been married for some time and wrote Robert Owen that she had kept it secret from all but "the few old french friends who were its witnesses." She had done so, "because I was little desirous to have the public mind in America, wch I had succeeded in awakening to matters of real import, diverted from these even temporarily to gossip of my private affairs." She wanted complete privacy now, and "under my new name, and mixing with none but french society," she had found it.[19]

Despite her courage, when two old friends saw her later that fall, what they saw was bleak. In November Harriet wrote Julia that she had found Fanny in the midst of a very great muddle: "I found her with a child a twelve-month old, a little girl, like her, and naked, for she wears no garment except when she goes out." Harriet was nervous and upset. Fanny was kind but cold: "Old friendships I think she has forgotten, old scenes have vanished from her mind. She did not speak of poor Cam, who certainly felt the same things with her sister." Fanny seemed no older, except that her forehead was deeply furrowed. She apparently doted on her child and was attached to her husband. But the sweet playfulness of her manner was gone: it was Fanny, and at the same time it was not Fanny at all. Harriet's spirits failed her: "A bedroom, a dirty girl, a naked child, Fanny en robe de chambre, a stove and child's victuals cooking—how different from the elegant boudoir in which we used to find our loved Fanny writing. I thought of the past, of you and poor Cam, and I felt I own very unhappy. I have not had the courage to return, and shall probably seldom see her I have loved so well—too well, alas!"[20]

Late in December Mme. Fretageot discovered Fanny unannounced. Knowing nothing of her marriage, she had asked Lafayette's secretary for Fanny's address and made her way up a dark staircase to a fourth floor apartment, where she was shocked to find Phiquepal and then to recognize his adopted son, Alexis. "You may imagine what exclamations, Mr. Phiquepal! Madame! Both at once," she wrote William Maclure. When she asked where Fanny was, she got no answer. In her amazement she saw a door at the other end of the room and pushed through it to discover Fanny staring speechless at her. She had been undressing a little girl and almost let her fall. When Mme. Fretageot lunged to catch the child, Fanny broke her trance and asked who had given out her address. Instead of answering, Mme. Fretageot said she had hoped that Fanny would see her with some pleasure. Fanny answered only that she received no visits. When Mme. Fretageot said she must be absorbed in writing, Fanny replied no, she was totally occupied with her family. "I made no question about that family," Mme. Fretageot told Maclure, "because I perceived she was much disturbed." She asked instead if Fanny visited Lafayette, and Fanny replied that she had stopped going several months before. When Mme. Fretageot observed that people in America thought Fanny was busy writing Lafayette's biography, Fanny said, "Ah!" When she asked if Fanny would come to see her, Fanny replied that she would not; she never went anywhere. And when asked if Mme. Fretageot might visit her again, Fanny did not answer.[21]

The room consisted of a bed, a few chairs, and a marble-topped stove, and as the older woman reported it, "the whole together has not the appearance of comfort." Fanny did not move when her guest got up to leave, nor did she come to help when she heard her stumbling against chairs and tables in the dark. Some months later, when Mme. Fretageot heard that Fanny and Phiquepal were married, she wrote Maclure: "I really pity her with all my heart, is it possible she would have ended in such a manner? better if she had drowned herself."[22]

It was only a year since Mary Shelley had written Fanny apologetically for intruding herself on one "whose noble mind is filled with such vast interests—and whose time is occupied by such important plans." As for herself, Mrs. Shelley found her youth wasted, and "all the incentives to existence" failing within her. "Yours is a brighter lot, a nobler career . . . I am made of frailer clay—and should have sunk before difficulties which serve to edge your heroic spirit." Yet the challenges to Fanny's heroic spirit had all but crushed her. Late in 1830 she had written, with a candor she would not show again: "To live in the world as though not of the world, may be very scriptural, but it is little agreeable; and, to judge from my own experience, they who most follow the precept most regret the necessity which compels its observance."[23]

Fanny's apparent indifference hurt her old friends. Once, in mid-January 1832, she seemed to Harriet more like her old self. Her iconoclasm was now exercised on child rearing. Trying apparently to bring up her daughter in a more natural fashion than current styles dictated, Fanny dressed Sylva in a loose shift or nothing at all. "Her child is beautiful, even with a scald head and every disadvantage of dress," Harriet told Julia. "I often think you wd not like to dress yr little ones in this manner." But at the end of March Harriet wrote that she saw Fanny seldom, "for I feel my society gives her no pleasure, and she has not written to you! I own this silence weighs upon my mind." A month later she heard that Fanny had given birth to a second daughter on April 14, and had suffered not at all during the delivery, but Fanny was not the one who told her.[24]

When Lafayette learned from Harriet that Fanny would be confined a second time, he went to see her. He had complained the previous summer that Fanny neither wrote nor visited him, and now he admitted she would not have sent for him on her own. He too was hurt. "I have not written to her," Harriet told Julia in May, "and why should I write? She will only think it a trouble to answer my letter. She does not think of any of her friends, of those who have been so much attached to her." Harriet discovered later that Fanny did not write Julia "because doing so awoke too many painful ideas of the past. She said she had twice written long letters to you, and then tore them." When Harriet saw Fanny after the second child was born, Phiquepal was the one who took charge of the children. "She has written in reply to my *third letter* to tell me that she is recovered and the children [are] well," Harriet said, "and she will not write again."[25]

Paris was then in the grip of a cholera epidemic. Every day a great black cart passed along the streets taking the dead from almost every house, and the streets were thick with litters carrying the dying to hospitals. According to Harriet, eighteen hundred people were buried on one day, and as many as fifteen hundred for several days running. The stench and sounds of death in almost medieval form transformed Paris into a waking nightmare.[26]

Perhaps it was cholera that killed Fanny's baby daughter early that summer. Julia Garnett's mother wrote her own daughter on June 29: "Miss Wright that was, has lost her little girl. Harriet has written to her but has not received an answer. Perhaps she is in the country with her eldest child." Nothing remains to tell how Fanny survived her baby's death.[27]

Fanny gave the birth date of her second daughter, who died before she was three months old, to the older child. Officially, Frances Sylva d'Arusmont was born on April 14, 1832. The lie was maintained all Fanny's life, and all of Sylva's.

Fanny had made her isolation even worse than it had to be. Lafayette had disappointed her politically, to be sure, and she had been snubbed in the bosom of his family. Julia and Harriet, she must have known, had rejected Camilla's pleas for help, and now Harriet could not invite Fanny to visit her at home because her mother would not allow it. Fanny had reason, therefore, to moderate, but not to destroy the love she had felt for them. They had loved her extravagantly, and they found her now unwilling or unable to give them more than formal politeness in return. Whatever hopes she had for human fellowship she rested in her small family.

In the fall of 1832, Robert Dale came to Paris with his nineteen-year-old bride, Mary Jane Robinson, and his sister Jane. The daughter of one of the *Daily Sentinel's* supporters, Mary Jane had heard Fanny's first lectures at the Park Theatre in 1829 and had become a familiar at the Hall of Science. She had married Robert Dale that April in New York, and in keeping with the principles of the *Free Enquirer*, he signed a statement objecting to the law giving a husband control of his wife's person and her property. Jane Owen met Fanny now for the first time and saw the clear-minded enthusiasm that had captured so much attention. Robert Dale, however, sensed that Fanny's nerves had received a shock at her sister's death from which he thought she would never recover. Some years earlier Fanny had written that at a French fireside one found "much more evidence of domestic peace, social cheerfulness, and mental and moral congeniality" than in America. Yet Mary Jane discovered in 1832 how little Fanny and Phiquepal enjoyed those blessings in their life together.[28]

They had taken a home in Passy, and there on the quiet edge of Paris, Fanny and Robert Dale looked back on the two years they had collaborated to raise the standards of American journalism and the political consciousness of the American people. When they took over the *Free Enquirer*, Robert Dale would write, no one in America had a public forum in which to exercise fully his or her freedom of speech, and to doubt the received wisdom in either religion or morals. Now it was possible, they thought, to express unreserved skepticism without inspiring half so much criticism as Unitarianism had done twenty years earlier, or Universalism as recently as a decade before. They had, furthermore, presented what they considered "certain great, leading principles in morals and in politics, which we consider the base of just reasoning and of correct practice." They looked back with pride.[29]

Fanny, however, had found herself frustrated in trying to discuss elementary truths coherently "through the medium of disjointed articles and paragraphs." She now wanted to do a major analytic work, showing how all her ideas existed in relation to each other and to the whole, and she intended to devote herself to the scholar's life in the relative seclusion it demanded. She and Robert Dale formally resigned as editors of the *Free Enquirer* to go about their personal lives.[30]

Robert Dale and Mary Jane planned eventually to go to New Harmony to share in the development of the town and the lands around it, but in the meantime Robert, who had taken a somewhat patronizing view of his bride as a diamond in the rough, thought a winter spent outside the great city of Paris in Fanny's company a fine chance to polish her to a more brilliant luster. He told Mary Jane that reading aloud was the most useful of all accomplishments and that she might search the world without finding a teacher more competent than Fanny. He therefore left her in Passy in early September 1832 and went to join his father in England. Fanny and Phiquepal had talked of moving to New Harmony as well, so Robert Dale intended to go on to America to settle their business in New York and get houses ready for both families in New Harmony the following spring.[31]

Mary Jane was miserable at being left behind, although she admired Fanny and more than once told Robert Dale that Fanny and Phiquepal were kind to her. Still, she was a candid woman who tried to be fair, and in the long letters she wrote her husband, a picture emerges of Phiquepal as neurasthenic and taciturn, and of Fanny as sometimes querulous and insensitive, but most of all very remote.

Mary Jane soon came to realize that the household had little shared life. Within two weeks after Robert Dale's departure, the three adults had become strangers who seldom saw each other except at table. "Fanny tells me that I must take care of myself, for that she and Phiquepal will be much engaged all winter, so the understanding is that we are all free to follow our own 'desires.'" At times Mary Jane spoke of them as a loving couple whom she plagued with her company—"Frances, Phiquepal and the child are all to each other as you are to me"—but they seemed more often to go their separate ways, and she envied them only fitfully. Robert assured her that for all their excellent qualities, Fanny and Phiquepal were both fidgety people.[32]

Phiquepal was often ill. Lafayette had got him appointed director of a model agricultural school, but he could not keep the job, apparently because he had serious trouble with his eyes. They often became so inflamed he could not see to write. "He seems to me very much dejected," Mary Jane wrote, and he "talks and eats very little." When he went to Paris, he came back exhausted and had to go to bed. They dined at two because Phiquepal slept better when they did; but he and Fanny were seldom well the same day, and when they were both ill, "they eat nothing and say nothing." Little Sylva became the center of the family, and Phiquepal her jealous guardian. Fanny and he had agreed that her education would be primarily his responsibility, and he frowned on Mary Jane until she proved to him that she would not spoil the child.[33]

Fanny often changed her mind. Only a few days after Robert Dale had left, she began to doubt their plans abut going to New Harmony to live. She told Mary Jane "she could not bear the idea of subjecting Sylva to that climate." Because she had money invested there, however, someone had to look after it: "She seemed to feel that she must part with her husband or her child, poor creature." Mary Jane soon realized that Fanny's indecision had been at the expense of her own happiness, for if Fanny had decided earlier that she was not serious about wanting a house in New Harmony, "Mr. P might have gone to attend to her business and you could have staid here and let the house alone."[34]

Mary Jane tried to do her share by becoming what she called "the lady manager of all things." Phiquepal gave her 150 francs and a book to keep accounts, so that she could "relieve Fanny of cares to which she is not equal." But soon she discovered that instead of being a help to Fanny, she was a burden. Had Mary Jane not been there, Fanny told her, she would have taken her family to board in Paris. Mary Jane simply could not satisfy them: "After two or three conversations in which Fanny insisted that I was tired of keeping house, Fanny and Phiquepal took the reins in partnership ... Mr. P., you know, likes everything done in the best possible manner ... Fanny and Phiquepal ... for a day or two looked rather gloomily upon me." Lafayette and his daughter-in-law once came to call, but no one else seemed to break into their isolation except a woman they brought in to cook their meals. Mary Jane decided finally that her failure as their housekeeper had been inevitable: "Dear Robert, I do not wonder that I did not please, inasmuch as it is my belief that an angel from Heaven could not." She wondered only that her husband, who knew the people involved, had not seen how it would end. Fanny said that though Mary Jane did not know how to keep house, she herself could have made her into a good cook in three months had she liked. "This latter remark made me smile," the younger woman wrote. "Sorry should I be, if I could not do both better than herself."[35]

At the end of six weeks, when Mary Jane heard that Robert Dale had missed the season's last ship to New York, she burst from the prison that Passy had become and crossed the Channel to him in grateful relief. She left Fanny and Phiquepal in the mutual solitude that was to be their life.

Not long after, they moved back from Passy and took an apartment between the Palais du Luxembourg and the Jardin des Plantes. It was the part of Paris where Fanny had first lived twelve years before, and unlike her own life, it had changed very little. To be sure, instead of Louis XVIII or Charles X riding with his entourage in brocade and rubies, she could occasionally see Louis-Philippe walking the streets with a friend or two, dressed more like a banker than a king. But Catholicism seemed to be regaining the influence it had lost, and most believed that people were more interested than ever in making money and in enjoying their tranquillity undisturbed.[36]

It was, indeed, the Paris of *La Comédie humaine*. Nearly an exact contemporary of Honoré de Balzac, Fanny spent almost fifteen of the last years of her life in the places and among the people about whom he wrote. And Balzac's pages make clear that Fanny was even more out of place there than in the Jane Austen world of her adolescence. Chronicling the massive social change that the Revolution had begun and the Empire continued, Balzac described people obsessed with money and hungry for power. Most of his characters believed that money provided the tools—the fine rooms, the elegant clothes, the splendid table—with which one built the interesting life. It bought, as one character told another, the equivalent of the sword and buckler and armor of an earlier day.

As a woman and a foreigner, Fanny took no natural part in social Paris. As an egalitarian, she was contemptuous of the scramble for gold and power, and she simply withdrew. She avoided even the obvious battles. When Frances Trollope's book on America became a *cause célèbre* and supporters of Louis-Philippe used it to denigrate democracy, Lafayette asked Fanny in effect to tell the public that Mrs. Trollope had gone to America to avoid her creditors, thereby discounting her judgment of it. But Fanny ignored him. Although the feminist movement in France grew steadily after 1830—dominated by women who shared Fanny's ideals and organized within the working class— Fanny apparently had nothing to do with it. Instead of making common cause, she pushed still deeper into her cosmos of abstractions. Amos Gilbert later wrote that Fanny had neither the taste nor the talent for anything but the elevation of her fellow human beings, whom she thought of in the abstract: "she could pass unnoticed all the wretchedness in the streets of the French Metropolis, at the same time that the struggle for liberty in Poland convulsed her. She overlooked the Paris paupers in the intensity of her gaze at the Polish patriots."[37]

She would find the essence of her life, then, in the world of ideas, and during this period the idea that came to dominate her thoughts was that only moral development could effect social progress: neither violence, nor the arbitrary redistribution of wealth, nor political action could bring about the millennium. Like Phiquepal's friend Auguste Comte, she spent the next years elaborating a theory of history that imagined reform taking place without loss to anyone, without disorder and without pain, at the expense of neither principle, prejudice, nor interest. But however consoling as a vision of the future, this theory of historical process would not serve her well. It was so radically at odds with her own experience that it may have tempted her precisely because it allowed her to ignore or even to deny her failure. It also let her slight the reformer's central question, which asks how to get from here to there. Its intellectual inadequacy for the burden it had to carry was no doubt responsible for the vagueness that began creeping into her thoughts and the increasing puffiness of her prose.

In the spring of 1833, for example, at Robert Dale's request, Fanny wrote the Owenite John Minter Morgan in England and told him that wise reform was having its way and "All efforts now work for good." Although three years earlier she had said that people would win no redress but what they carried by force, and even more recently she had written "the reign of money . . . promises to close in convulsions," now she insisted that no one would be injured and everyone would benefit. Violence and wrangling belonged to mere faction and party: "The public mind looks and waits for something better—for practical truth presented with cleanness and simplicity . . . speaking at once to the comprehension and conviction of all . . . satisfying the wants and calming the anxieties of each and every individual; assailing no class, disputing with no prejudices, forcing no habits, sacrifising no interests but fencing with new securities the peace of society and the independence and enjoyments of individuals." What this wonderful truth might be Fanny did not say, nor did she suggest why it had hitherto proved elusive. She did say that both she and her husband had been preoccupied for years with its discovery, and "the similarity of our researches, wch induced our union, has aided our researches to a result." If circumstances interfered, however, "with the devel-opement of the truths present to our minds," she was sure that others would take their places. She concluded: "Enquiry once started rests not until it has obtained a satisfactory answer, and my faith is firm, and my mind at peace in the conviction that the day is not distant when the civilized world will see practically to read such an answer."[38]

Such were the strands of thought that Fanny was weaving in those years in Paris when she kept so nearly her own counsel. Her writing suggests a woman out of touch with deep human feelings, a woman living on the frozen surface of genuine emotion. Her estrangement from her own past grew deeper, and the course of her thought more remote, from the suffering humanity that was its intended focus and beneficiary.

The gulf between mundane reality and the terms in which Fanny had come to think of it became apparent in the spring of 1834 when she went to London and hired the Freemason's Hall to give a series of lectures. Publications like *Isis* had kept her reputation alive since 1830, and the radical press turned out to hear her. But the crowd fell off sharply after her first lecture, and the newspapers confessed disappointment. The *Pioneer* reported: "She rather seemed to affect the oracle . . . We could not carry any thought away; her figures seemed like shadows, which we could not grasp." The *Poor Man's Guardian* thought Fanny too abstract for English people, who wanted to know how to exchange their "present state of poverty and servitude for one of competence and liberty." What people wanted to be told, the *Guardian* wrote, was *"How are we to get out of our present troubles?"* This was the first time Fanny had been subjected publicly to the criticism of sophisticated radicals, much less to a thinning audience, and she was told, in effect, that she had nothing to say.[39]

Her experience in London came hard after another that, however she tried to ignore or deny it, left her all the more alone. Lafayette had become ill that winter, and according to his doctor, the Princess Christine de Belgiojoso attended him whenever his health allowed him to receive her. "The general had, in a manner, adopted her among the number of his children and entertained for her that pure attachment which superior mental qualities always inspire in those who can feel and appreciate them." The princess, it seems, had taken the place that Fanny had fought so hard to keep ten years before. And it was not Fanny who closed Lafayette's eyes when death came on May 20, 1834. She left no record of how she felt or what she thought when this man whose imprint on her life had been so deep passed irrevocably out of it. One thing, however, was certain: that in trying to conquer her own pain and disappointment, Fanny had crushed too much of the life-giving force.[40]

The Woman
Everybody Abuses

10

For almost a quarter of a century, the sustaining myth in the life of Frances Wright was the one that issued from Thomas Jefferson's Declaration of Independence. She still thought of the United States as of a country consecrated to freedom. She felt that she had come closest there to realizing her own full humanity. And in the fall of 1835, when she was forty years old, she decided to return to America.

There was some talk of looking into her investments. But in fact Andrew Jackson's war against the Second Bank of the United States had caught her imagination: she saw in it the chance to go back to the public platform, fighting this time on a side that had powerful popular support and in a cause she believed central to republican government. She launched into an experience that she would later call the most extraordinary struggle of her life. In terms of her public career, it was also the most full of pain.[1]

She felt too that America was in trouble, and she wanted to help. The nation, it seemed, had caught the temper of its chief executive: it had begun to erupt in periodic violence, some of it carried out by men of property and social standing. Lynch law seemed to be spreading; arsonists attacked a convent outside Boston; gamblers were hanged in Vicksburg; the mails were burned in Charleston. A black man called McIntosh was roasted alive over a slow fire of green wood for killing a white man in St. Louis, and the judge, whose name was Lawless, blamed the abolitionists for setting McIntosh on. In Baltimore, troops fired into a crowd, killing twenty people and wounding one hundred. In New York, an anti-abolitionist mob rioted three days, ruining sixty houses and six churches, and leaving Manhattan shaken in its wake.[2]

The crisis engaged Fanny's ambitions and focused her vision of the republic. No doubt she hoped to recreate in America the time that Camilla had said was the happiest of her life, when she and those around the *Free Enquirer* fought to bring America closer to its ideals. Remembering her own dangerous fever and therefore worrying about the climate's effect on small children, Fanny left Sylva in Paris with their neighbors, Pierre Turpin and his wife, and in November 1835 she and Phiquepal sailed from Le Havre, bound on the southern route to New Orleans. Their goal was Cincinnati, where Phiquepal's adopted son Alexis was setting up in the brewery business, apparently with Fanny's money.[3]

When they came to port around the turn of the year, the most troubling stories they heard had to do with slavery, and Fanny discovered that Americans could no longer stay neutral on the subject. Since 1831, the thumbscrews had tightened on the public consciousness. In January of that year, William Lloyd Garrison began to publish the *Liberator* out of Boston, advocating immediate and uncompensated emancipation. In August, the slave Nat Turner led a small group of men in Tidewater Virginia to massacre more than sixty white men, women, and children. Positions on slavery began to harden. Emancipation societies disappeared all over the South, rhetorical defences of slavery became more shrill, and churches split.[4]

Abolition was cast in the language of Christianity and was led by people like the wealthy New York merchants Arthur and Lewis Tappan, who supported all the Christian causes Fanny opposed. They fought for strict Sabbath observances. They participated actively in the Sunday School Union, the Bible Society, the Tract Society, and the Home Missionary Society, all of which Fanny had attacked in the *Free Enquirer*. As patrons of the evangelist Charles Grandison Finney, they had leased New York's Chatham Street Theatre and subsequently built the Broadway Tabernacle for the revivals Fanny so deplored. Arthur Tappan had founded the *New York Journal of Commerce* to give the city a daily newspaper free from "immoral advertisements," and in 1829 this pious sheet had done what it could to foul her name. And though many of the abolitionists were poor, others had grown wealthy from what Fanny considered the exploitation of white labor in the North. Their posture of Christian moral superiority inevitably made her skeptical.[5]

In mid-January 1836, while Fanny and Phiquepal made their way by steamboat up the wintry loneliness of the Mississippi, Cincinnati's mayor presided at a courthouse meeting about James Birney's decision to establish his abolition newspaper, the *Philanthropist,* just outside the city. As a major port, Cincinnati's economy was intimately tied to that of the South, and its merchants were anxious about anything affecting their ordinary trade. The issue of abolition aroused feelings as turbulent in Cincinnati as in Charleston, South Carolina.

Birney tried several times that evening to speak at the courthouse, but no one was prepared to listen. The meeting adopted a report deeply hostile to antislavery and resolved, among other things, that those present would "exert every lawful effort to suppress the publication of any abolition paper in this city or *neighborhood.*" When Fanny docked in Cincinnati, she heard not only that Cincinnati was hostile to abolition, but also that the House of Representatives had just passed a gag rule that now automatically tabled all antislavery petitions.[6]

The anger over abolition simmered that winter, and in April, riots erupted that ravaged the city. Fanny, who had declined to address her fellow passengers on the Mississippi steamboat on the ground that she spoke only when she felt the "deep and grave conviction of a public service to be rendered," had found that conviction again by May. She proposed to address the public in the same courthouse where she had begun lecturing seven years before.[7]

What she did not realize was that by now she was an infamous woman. The fear of female deviance was reaching deep into the culture, and Fanny had become the symbol of most things women should not be. Earlier that year in Concord, Massachusetts, the British abolitionist George Thompson had been ridiculed as a Fanny Wright-ist and had barely escaped being killed. Her name was used repeatedly to discredit liberal causes: a writer defending workers and their organizations had to say that summer, "If this is Fanny Wrightism, let them make the most of it." With the possible exception of Peggy Eaton, the maligned wife of Jackson's first secretary of war, Fanny was the most controversial woman in Jacksonian America. Blind to her own dark image and to the uproar that followed wherever she went, Fanny spoke of herself as the harbinger of calm. But once more she showed that her vision of America and of human dignity was at odds with mainstream America.[8]

Fanny gave two lectures at the Cincinnati courthouse on successive Sundays, the first, on May 15, to present "a general view of the civil history of the United States." The situation of the country was "critical beyond what is generally imagined," and so she described its "political institutions in their true character of simple beauty and saving power" to discredit its enemies by showing how they worked against the public good. In her second lecture, on Southern slavery, she hoped to unite and tranquillize the public mind at a critical moment by converting a subject of discord into a subject of union. But one man spoke for the many who held to their old image of Fanny when he described her as "this *petticoat* advocate of agrarianism, this antagonist of the marriage contract and villifier of the scriptures." She herself was proving a fertile source of discord.[9]

Yet Fanny was not elaborating the positions that had brought her such notoriety. Startling the few people who actually listened to her, she spoke in a style grown elliptical and obscure and took stands in some cases diametrically opposed to those she had argued before. Furthermore, the allies she sought now would have been unthinkable eight years earlier. In 1829 and 1830, for example, the *Free Enquirer* had regarded both national parties as engines of the well-to-do and the politically corrupt. Robert Dale had written of Tammany Hall that "a more profligate set of politicians does not exist." No one, in fact, had ever accused the Democratic presidential candidate Martin Van Buren of putting principle first: so adroit was he at political manipulation that he was called "The Little Magician." Furthermore, he had taken stands quite at odds with Fanny's. Before he became Jackson's hand-picked successor, Van Buren had led the faction in New York that bitterly opposed De Witt Clinton, whom Fanny in 1825 had called "the first statesman probably in the country, and one the whole country seems to look to as a future President." At the 1821 New York State convention, he had led the conservative opposition to universal male suffrage. He did, however, endorse economic policies that appealed to Fanny, supporting, for instance, a constitutional amendment to prohibit federally sponsored public works. And Fanny now championed his candidacy for president.[10]

In becoming Van Buren's advocate, Fanny blurred, if not reversed, her position on the issue of free speech. Repeatedly she had attacked John Adams for the Alien and Sedition Acts of 1798, and in 1829 she had even offered herself as a test case for free speech in Philadelphia. Martin Van Buren, however, as vice-president, cast the deciding vote in the Senate for a bill forbidding postmasters to deliver abolitionist literature in states that barred it. By speaking for him, Fanny countenanced the Jacksonian suppression of dissent.

More than that, Jackson's party, with its southwestern axis, helped protect the South's peculiar institution. Jackson himself was one of the small number of men who owned many slaves: he had property in various places in the South and more than a hundred slaves at the Hermitage in Nashville alone. At a time of increasing Southern intransigence on the subject of slavery, very few, if any, Jacksonians dared openly to oppose it.[11]

For Fanny actively to support a party that would protect the institution she had given four years of her life and almost half of her fortune to end seemed an aberration that called for explanation by her friends. The simplest was given later by the Quaker Amos Gilbert, who argued that since the greatest opposition to the spread of liberal views came from the Whigs, Fanny "became a partizan on the other side, and for a season was politically insane. What she wrote during the paroxism would not have been recognized as her work, either in sentiment or style." The Democrats, he continued, later "restored her to sanity by pulling from under her the platform from which she was proclaiming the right of the colored man to self-ownership," and after that she was "free from party predilections."[12]

What Gilbert did not know, however, was how isolated Fanny had been for more than five years, and how scarred by the harsh demands she had made on herself. She wanted to be happy again, and as she had found her greatest satisfaction in public advocacy, she now too quickly seized a popular cause to champion. She mistook the Democratic party—a pragmatic political machine embracing diverse interests and sometimes conflicting views—for an ideological party. Accepting perforce a president's need to preserve the Union first and supporting Jackson's stand against the Second Bank of the United States, she assumed the Democrats would come around to her agenda for the nation. She took it for granted that they intended to go on to abolish concentrations of wealth and finally to allow slavery to disappear. She was mistaken.

On May 28, Charles Hammond commented in the *Gazette* that abolition was a topic at present so interdicted "that even Madame Frances Wright Darusmont forgetting all her ancient amalgamation notions, has more prudence than to discuss it." His gibe gave Fanny an opportunity to make some disclaimers and to underline her lawful intent. In a letter to the *Gazette* on June 4, she dissociated herself explicitly from abolition and philanthropy, and implicitly from Birney and his abolition paper: "Whatever epithets the anger of misguided party, or misconceiving prejudice may have coupled with my name . . . that of *philanthropist* cannot be one of them; a title which, however good in its etymological and dictionary meanings, has ever been . . . as foreign to my ambition as to my regard." The word "abolitionist," she said, now referred to one who espoused violence and opposed constitutional processes, whereas she had always seen "all human reform as a work not *governmental or controlling*, but educational, administrative, and industrial [and] I could never propose to myself or others any measures that should run counter to public opinion or national sentiment."[13]

Her letter, however, was troubling and paradoxical. She defended the character of the Southern planter, from whom she said she had never experienced "aught but respectful treatment, and confiding, open-hearted hospitality." She nevertheless assured her readers that racial blending in America had for the most part "violated decency, and brutalized character," and Fanny knew the Southern planter was responsible for much of what she deplored. Insisting that she represented "a tone of thought and a mode of proceeding" that disarmed prejudice and calmed passions, she courted a kind of acceptance and respect America now would never give her.[14]

In Philadelphia, where she went in mid-June, Fanny attacked "*the insurgents against equal rights*" and took the Jacksonian party line on slavery: "I now *fully know*, what I formerly surmised, that the question of slavery is . . . a pretext for the fomenting of disorder and the breeding of disunion." But however peaceful her intentions, the owners of large buildings in which she might speak did not associate Fanny Wright with calm. She was refused the use of all the theaters and most of the public auditoriums. Her committee finally arranged for her to rent the Military Hall, and early in July she gave her first lecture there, advertising subsequently that she would speak the following Thursday on Southern slavery.[15]

On Wednesday of the next week, however, the mayor's office circulated an official proclamation forbidding her speech, "apprehensive that the subject is one calculated to create an unpleasant excitement, and perhaps lead to a breach of the peace." Fanny then wrote the mayor that her course was peaceable. She would happily explain to him what she intended to say, so he would understand that her position could provoke no disturbance. Meanwhile, she would change the topic to chartered monopolies. The mayor replied, in Fanny's words, "that the objection was the same to any and every discourse which might be proposed by the same individual."[16]

Fanny thought of herself as "a public teacher known and popularly respected from Maine to Mexico," and her ire was aroused. Over the three weeks that followed, she carried the battle for her right to speak to places both likely and unlikely outside the city, where the mayor's edict could not follow her. People heard her speak in heavy rain and traveled out to a fairgrounds, by one account some five thousand strong. On one occasion her speech was canceled when a group of rowdies destroyed the speaker's stand. Some papers carried her ads and indignant letters, but when they wrote about her, they attacked her. Nor did they shrink from making threats. The *Pennsylvania Sentinel,* for example, saw her as a "foreign female stroller," insolently determined to denounce American institutions: "when accompanied by a flagrant violation of the Sabbath, and the exhibition of a disposition to excite riot and violence—[her conduct] merits not merely public reprehension, but legal punishment." The *National Gazette,* implying that Fanny had been chased from Paris "on account of her disorganizing principles and precepts," warned: "Fears are entertained that she may not escape personal injury if she persists in her degrading career. Her friends, if she has any, should forcibly detain her in town."[17]

Whether or not her friends tried to keep her away, Fanny met one of her last audiences in an abandoned factory on the falls of the Schuylkill River near Laurel Hill Cemetery. The building was old and rickety: none of the doors hung on their hinges, and all the windows were gone. The interior was gloomy and the speaker's platform rough. When Fanny came in with two other women, she was met with cheers and hisses. The crowd outside picked up stones from the cemetery quarry and began to throw them through the windows. "The outer door was barricaded inside," reported the *Gazette,* "but terror predominated both in the bosom of the lecturer and the lectured, the latter enduring the two-fold pain of being assailed by Fanny within and the stones without." A paper less hostile wrote that about a thousand people heard her despite the disturbance outside the building. Urged on by men dressed like gentlemen, boys threw stones, and though some people were slightly injured, the police did nothing to stop them.[18]

On this occasion Fanny explained that the North had to uproot its own white slavery before it could counsel the South on the slavery of blacks. She thought that Northerners tried to prevent her speeches because they did not want to hear about their own responsibility. American institutions, however, would triumph; circumstances would change; and the North would set a righteous example: "then the evil of the south may be transformed into a good, the source of its poverty into a source of wealth, and the rapid improvement of its lands and development of all its resources may be effected, at one and the same time, with the civilization, enfranchisement and colonization without the North American continent, of the now slave population, conjointly with the introduction of enlightened white labor." How this might be accomplished she left for future explanation, except to say that it would come about "without loss or injury to any existing individual," and the process would be completed "judiciously, constitutionally, beneficially, and yet radically."[19]

Fanny had lost none of her flair for holding center stage, and she left Philadelphia with a tart rebuke for her enemies: "insinuations I answer not, nonsense I heed not, slanders I despise. A life of integrity is my answer alike to the malignity of party and the vituperations of individuals." In Lancaster County, Pennsylvania, she added a new lecture on the history of the Federalists "With a General View of the Hamilton Financial Scheme," and she spoke several times around the state before she returned to Philadelphia just after her forty-first birthday.[20]

As if to show how serious the crisis over slavery was and how thin the edge of civility that summer, Cincinnati erupted just as Fanny left Philadelphia. A mob of the town's most respectable citizens broke into the offices of James Birney's printer and destroyed his presses, which they dragged down the street and threw into the river. The mayor, Charles Hammond wrote, was, "to say the least, a quiet spectator of the violence" and spoke up long after the presses were broken. The mob went to the black section of town and destroyed several buildings, and during the next two nights they rioted again. Rumors coursed the city that Birney would be tarred and feathered.[21]

Cincinnati had yet another lesson to teach Fanny. About the same time she published her three addresses, one of its most aggressively respectable citizens attacked her. Catharine Beecher had devoted her life to educating women to be good mothers and homemakers, or to be the teachers of women who would in their turn become good mothers and homemakers. Her attack on Fanny Wright became the prototype of the attacks that conservative American women launch on women who differ: "who can look without disgust and abhorrence upon such an one as Fanny Wright, with her great masculine person, her loud voice, her untasteful attire, going about unprotected, and feeling no need of protection, mingling with men in stormy debate, and standing up with bare-faced impudence, to lecture to a public assembly . . . There she stands, with brazen front and brawny arms, attacking the safeguards of all that is venerable and sacred in religion, all that is safe and wise in law, all that is pure and lovely in domestic virtue. Her talents only make her the more conspicuous and offensive, her amiable disposition and sincerity, only make her folly and want of common sense the more pitiable, her freedom from private vices, if she is free, only indicates, that without delicacy, and without principles, she has so thrown off all feminine attractions, that freedom from temptation is her only, and shameful palladium. I cannot conceive any thing in the shape of a woman, more intolerably offensive and disgusting." If Fanny thought her new position had won people's confidence, had inclined America as a whole to listen to her, Catharine Beecher could tell her she was badly mistaken.[22]

In mid-September Fanny wrote the preface for the volume of three speeches she had just delivered, and she published it now at her own expense. She dedicated the volume to the people of the United States, for whose "mental instruction" she had composed it. She wrote in "a spirit of active, untiring, and all-devoted love to this nation and to humankind" and referred to herself as "the individual who, nine years ago, had arrested in [Cincinnati] the flood of superstition." Despite what she knew of the Quakers and Benjamin Lundy, or of James Birney's long experience with slavery, she claimed "a more intimate acquaintance with the bearings of the slave question than any other individual."[23]

The self-confidence she had needed to break from her past—to dare things that women had not dared before—had hardened into a blinding self-importance. In fighting for her own right to address the public, for example, she insisted she was not an abolitionist. But the main free speech issue in America in 1836 was indeed the question of whether abolitionists could take their turn in print and on the podium. The preceding October the New Yorker Gerrit Smith had argued that the gag rule in the House of Representatives and the attempts to keep abolitionist literature out of the mails raised the question "whether the whites at the north shall become slaves also . . . The demand which slaveholders now make on us to surrender the right of free discussion . . . involves their own full concession, that free discussion is incompatible with slavery." In dissociating herself from people like James Birney and Gerrit Smith and claiming that abolition was a pretext for disrupting the Union, Fanny played into the hands of apologists for the South's peculiar institution.[24]

In the essay on slavery that Fanny published in 1836, she seemed far more cautious than Lafayette had been a decade earlier, though he had written Julia Garnett that his caution "in some instances displeased Fanny." When she asked "How can we end slavery?" she seemed to answer, "We cannot end it now or in the foreseeable future." She took a position, in fact, that shifted the focus of moral indignation from slavery: "the evil which corrodes and convulses human society is the degradation of human labor; its enslavement in some countries, its subjection in all." Sympathizing with the planter who cited the vicious conditions under which people lived and worked in New England factories, she told the North to reform wage slavery there in order to set an example the South could follow. Furthermore, she was afraid of what would happen to the slaves after emancipation, believing that in the event of immediate abolition nothing could "save from more than Russian brutality and stone-heartedness, a master population suddenly absolved from all the responsibilities of ownership, and yet left in close contact with a race to which, however despised, they once owed and yielded food, shelter, care in sickness and sustenance in old age, but which they would then be not only free to neglect, but ever tempted systematically to defraud, oppress, and positively to destroy by the slow torture of over-work, under-food and, their consequent, chronic disease." Certainly, she now decided, miscegenation was not the answer, being "in this country repulsive, and, therefore, impossible." To argue, however, that the black people in America could all be colonized outside the continental limits of the United States was to indulge a fantasy unlike the position she had taken ten years earlier, when she imagined that blacks and mulattoes would take over the Southern states and Texas. Furthermore, she dismissed the practical problems involved by saying it would be premature to discuss the details of her "gigantic plan of colonization," although that plan would be "necessarily very different from all that now exists."[25]

But more than anything, Fanny evaded the topic of slavery. She wanted America to understand that one problem had to be solved before any other, one to which she had turned her attention six years earlier when she began to ask fundamental questions about money and wealth. Why, she had asked, when science and technology could make the earth a paradise, were people starving? Why were workers still getting only a pittance in return for their wealth, which lay in their time and energy and skill? The answer seemed to rest in the nature of money itself, for money and wealth, Fanny concluded, bore an inverse relationship to each other. To produce wealth was by no means to make money. "The two operations indeed are so distinct that the object of all is to shun labor, and to embrace what is called a *lucrative profession.*" With few exceptions, money was made by those who had it already, and money—a contrivance of man rather than a phenomenon of nature—created both poverty and luxury. Banks issued money and for the most part controlled who got it. Banks, therefore, were the enemy. Andrew Jackson seemed to agree when he determined to destroy the U.S. Bank by refusing to renew its charter.[26]

As she followed the Bank War, which began in earnest 1832, Fanny discovered that not only the president but a powerful wing of his party shared her animus to banks and her suspicion of paper money. Missouri Senator Thomas Hart Benton, for example, said in the Senate, "I look upon the [Second Bank of the United States] as an institution too great and powerful to be tolerated in a Government of free and equal laws . . . its tendencies are dangerous and pernicious to the Government and the people." The Bank made the rich richer and the poor poorer: it was a monopoly, exclusive and antirepublican. Phiquepal thought that the resistance to Jackson's veto of the Bank's charter sounded like a conspiracy of the kind that had destroyed the French Revolution of 1830 after the three glorious days in June. Many other people agreed with Benton, Phiquepal, and Fanny, and so the Bank War had given her the chance to speak in public for the first time in defense of a popular idea.[27]

Fanny's exaggerated claims for the Democratic position on the Second Bank had their roots in her tenacious faith in the United States: although European countries were beyond hope, America was not. Determined to believe that the exploitation of the many by the few derived from a set of financial arrangements and institutions rather than from human nature, she argued that the United States had to disentangle its finances from those of the bankrupt European nations, particularly from those of Great Britain. Furthermore, it had to repudiate the strong central government Hamilton had promoted in funding the national debt. She explained that Europe had provided two distinctly different kinds of immigrants to America, "those who came for liberty and those who came for plunder." The former supported the Jeffersonian vision of a weak central government and direct and frequent elections, as she did. The latter had insinuated themselves into the American fabric through the Second Bank of the United States and its tributary institutions, and if not routed, they would bankrupt "the whole material force, and moral and industrial energy of the American nation." Unlike the Democratic position, Fanny's attack was essentially an attack on capitalism: she castigated Northern manufacturers for exploiting the poor and called their system wage slavery. In return for paper money and "*promises to pay . . .* they will appropriate American lands, mortgages on American real estate, shares in American internal improvements," and by such means "the privileged orders of Europe, having drained their own people's life-blood, may now gorge themselves . . . with the heart's blood of America." The Second Bank of the United States was "the most convenient saddle in which the monarchies of Europe may ride the American democracy," and Andrew Jackson was the efficient agent of its destruction. A year later Fanny called Jackson "the true saviour of the species."[28]

Fanny's deification of Jackson remains something of a puzzle, though he inspired equally unlikely people to heights of similar extravagance. Another British radical, William Cobbett, called him "the bravest and greatest man now living in this world, or that ever has lived," and many Democrats talked of him with awe. But Thomas Jefferson had thought him dangerous, and Jackson was not the kind of man Fanny ordinarily admired. He did little, either by precept or example, to encourage learning or respect for education. He was a bully whose temper was notorious and whose hero was Napoleon Bonaparte. He was a speculator whose land deals had made him rich. He often disdained the law and, in the case of Georgia and the Cherokees, even the Constitution when it presumed to defy him. To exalt Jackson, Fanny had to ignore many things and to forget that, unlike Jefferson, he showed no sign of being troubled by chattel slavery.[29]

No doubt she liked Jackson because he had humiliated the British at New Orleans in 1815, and she felt an affinity for his fabled determination and courage. It is tempting to imagine that she identified with him because he was popularly identified with common people. Her faith in her own role depended on her belief that ordinary men and women were on her side. They listened to Jackson, as they would listen to her. They trusted him, as they would trust her. But most of all, Jackson spoke the language Fanny thought crucial to republican government, and he used his power to help make that language law. She was convinced that the central tyranny that destroyed all hope of democracy was the tyranny of money, and she believed that Jackson had acted decisively against it when, in mid-July 1832, he vetoed the recharter of the Second Bank of the United States. She was also convinced that the republic must remain intact, and Jackson had faced down John C. Calhoun and his threat to take South Carolina out of the Union.

Caught in the turbulent emotions of the time and in her own settled abstractions, Fanny understood neither the uses of demagogy nor the actual practice of American politics. Like most of her contemporaries, she did not see the Bank War as more complicated than the rhetoric that made it a war between good and evil, or between democracy and aristocracy, or even between a sound currency and a weak one. Among other things, it was a duel between two irascible men, Andrew Jackson and the Bank's president, Nicholas Biddle, each bent on the other's political destruction. It was a battle between the rhetoric of Jacksonianism and the rhetoric of business, and it was also a war between a federal bank and a plethora of state banks. It was not, after all, a war between America's haves and have-nots, between the big people and the little, but a war between two powerful groups differently aligned for control of America's economic expansion.[30]

This is not the way Fanny would have it. Parties, by her definition, were evil: therefore, there could be only one party now in America, and it was the anti-Jacksonian, or the Whig. The Jacksonians, or Democrats, on the contrary, were the nation. She then jumped to the conclusion that to support Jackson and his heir-apparent was to rid America of the pervasive influence of the Bank of England, embodied as it was in the Second Bank of the United States: "a sort of hydra, with many heads but one brain, and that brain ever working for the feeding of its own heads alone, at expense of the whole mass of the nation on whom it preys."[31]

Fanny did not, however, stop where many Jacksonians did. She insisted that those who stood for chartered monopolies, or for concentrated, exclusive wealth of any kind, violated American principles and stole American wealth just as thoroughly as those who supported the Second Bank of the United States. Imagining the intimate financial connection between Europe and America as a marriage between an old rake and a young heiress, she envisioned a world controlled by financial powers not unlike those of England's central bank: a "monstrous creation which, either by force or by fraud, by coercion or by corruption, by force of arms, by treasonous practices, secret tamperings, bribery, hush-money, diplomacy, palaver and mystification, has strangled or is strangling the national independence and popular liberty of every state upon the globe." Its purpose would be "the subjugation of the whole industry and credit of the civilized earth to one monstrous monopoly-monarchy." The Rothschilds would become the prime ministers of this supranational government, and they would be assisted by the presidents of banks and boards of trade who dictated policy to governments throughout the world. To prevent this, she insisted on a kind of Fortress America: "Peace with all the world is the axiom of America; but *peace at arms' length*—peace without the involvements and the hazards of financial consolidation."[32]

Fanny had perceived the central danger of concentrated wealth, but verging on self-parody, she dissipated the power of her insight in overstatement and distortion. She could be brilliant and ridiculous, insightful and obtuse—all in the same paragraph. Her sense of human complexity, which was fragile at best, appeared to vanish altogether. There had never been much of what Henry James called "felt life" in Fanny's writing, and now there was none at all. Her inclination to abstraction mushroomed to the point of overwhelming any sense that she was looking at real people in a real world. She seemed to have grown hard.

The emptiness of her private life, along with the facade she had built to hide it, constantly worked against her. She had married Phiquepal to ensure her child's legitimacy, and they were not yet estranged in a conscious, much less a public way. Three years later, Fanny would defend her husband to William Maclure as her "fellow laborer in the good cause of human reform ... Often have I regretted the false influences wch were the means of separating you from his labors in the only real field of effective human improvement—juvenile education." Nevertheless, by 1836 they no longer counted on each other's company.[33]

In early July of that year, Fanny wrote Sylva from Philadelphia that her father was on his way to New York. In August she wrote that he had left her on the Susquehanna to return to Cincinnati. They seem then to have gone quite different ways—Fanny to argue for Van Buren in New York and to consult with Abner Kneeland in Boston about joining him as contributing editor to the *Boston Weekly Investigator*. By December Fanny was back in Philadelphia, Phiquepal was in Paris with Sylva, and they were not together again until midsummer 1837. During this separation she did something that stunned many of the people who cared for her.[34]

The problem that surfaced now had begun six years earlier, when Fanny had loaned Robert Dale Owen and his brother William $11,000. In 1833 Phiquepal had gone to New Harmony to draw up mortgages on their property there, and according to Alexander Maclure, threatened to hire a Cincinnati lawyer to press his claims against the Owens. He seems to have carried back to Paris a burden of complaint that began to estrange Fanny from the man she had thought of as a brother. In the spring of 1836, Robert Dale asked his brother Richard in Cincinnati to pass along a friendly message to Phiquepal. He and William might be able to pay all they owed that summer, but barring accident, they would at least advance the $1,000 due sixteen months hence: "And tell Frances, that if business or inclination call her to our part of the country, we can shew her some improvement on the Harmony she formerly knew . . . she will find here many old friends who will be delighted to see her once more." Robert Dale also asked "whether she received, in France, a series of 3 or 4 letters from me, containing a condensed view of our former [New York] business." Fanny did not respond.[35]

In March 1837, however, Fanny published an editorial in the *Boston Weekly Investigator* that is inexplicable in its claims and devastating in its cruelty. She charged that "Mr. Robert Dale Owen, formerly my friend and assisting editor in the Free Enquirer," had told others that her silence toward and about him "originated in no individual convictions of my own but in a business misunderstanding between himself and my husband." She claimed that because he wrote to that effect "in a letter addressed to the office of a public journal," she was obliged to contradict him. Robert Dale knew that his behavior "forced upon me the conviction that his principles were not my principles." Consistent with a rule of conduct she had adopted in early youth, "and which he knows me to have followed in cases somewhat similar to his own, I interrupted at once and for ever, all intercourse with him." Since then, business between them had been conducted solely by her husband. Robert Dale, she insisted, could not possibly misconstrue the circumstances.[36]

Robert Dale had no idea what had brought down Fanny's wrath upon him. A man of normal human frailties to which he frankly admitted, he wrote the *Investigator* "with much regret and more surprise." Alluding to the holiness of friendship and the pain at its breaking, he apologized for bringing the public into what should have been a private matter. But he expressed bewilderment, as he had spoken rarely of the differences between him and Fanny, and had written no more than three people even briefly on the subject: "These were old friends of mine, in whose honor I have confidence." He had assumed they would be surprised at his ignorance of what she was doing, and he mentioned simply that he thought the misunderstanding that apparently existed between them had originated with others. He could not imagine "a remark more charitable, less calculated to offend . . . expressed in a private letter . . . never published, and never, of course, intended for publication." Fanny, to be sure, had the right to disagree, but "she *publishes* her dissent. Reflection cannot, I think, fail to produce in her naturally strong and discriminating mind the conviction, that this was an error; an error both in judgment and in feeling." He hoped that Fanny would "live to recognize and regret the deep injustice she has done me."[37]

Nothing suggests that Fanny either recognized the injustice she had done him or regretted the pain she had given to someone once so dear and trusted that she had willed her fortune to him. She later misrepresented her professional relationship to Robert Dale, who had been joint editor of the *Free Enquirer,* by saying she had bought the paper and then appointed him "as her assistant editor." She battled nastily over the mortgages she held and dismissed him from her life.[38]

Robert Dale's was the last of the old friendships Fanny had cherished—friendships that had sustained her and in some measure tied her to ordinary human experience. Camilla was gone, and so was Lafayette. She had turned from Mrs. Millar, and from Julia and Harriet Garnett. She had alienated James Mylne and Charles Wilkes and his family. She had some friends still, and many admirers. For example, after hearing her in Philadelphia, a dazzled correspondent wrote Robert Owen's *New Moral World* that his high expectations had been more than gratified. But no one took the place of those she once had loved.[39]

Her family seemed little more than a formality. Nine years earlier Fanny had burst through the most tenacious nineteenth-century conventions to write against beliefs that crippled or diminished human sexuality. Now that she was married, and bound by the institution she had then attacked, there is no sign that sexuality played any further part in her life. A Cincinnati carpenter, Joel Brown, wrote that Fanny and Phiquepal did not even sleep in the same bed because they thought it unhealthy.[40]

Her relationship to her daughter was distant, and she left Sylva for long periods with no crippling regrets. In giving her over to others, Fanny followed the cultural patterns of the British upper middle class from which she came: parents counted on nannies and governesses to raise their children and sent them off to boarding schools when they were very young. To give Sylva up to her father's tutelage was to show more concern for her emotional health than most parents who habitually trusted their children to strangers. But the fact remains that Sylva was no reservoir of emotional strength for her mother. She was

the reason Fanny had given up her freedom. She was more a duty than
a delight.

Just before the 1836 elections Fanny went to New York and spoke to
full houses for Martin Van Buren. Insisting that she had no party
affiliation, she nevertheless spent her public energies supporting
Democratic candidates for national office and attacking everyone who
presumed to do otherwise. Neither the *New York Times* nor the
Evening Post, both of which backed Van Buren, acknowledged her
support. The only editorial attention she got came from her old
antagonists, the *Courier and Enquirer* and the *Commercial Advertiser*.
The *Courier* had turned Whig, a conversion Nicholas Biddle had
apparently made attractive, and it came at Fanny with a sour,
misogynist vengeance: "this disgusting exhibition of female impudence, has no redeeming excuses. One could very well afford to hear
his own opinions of propriety abused by a woman, if the traduction
came from between a pair of pretty lips." The newspaper called Fanny
"a great awkward *bungle* of womanhood, somewhere about six feet in
longitude, with a face like a Fury, and her hair cropped like a convict,"
and pitied the husband who had to endure her.[41]

The papers in Boston, where she went next, for the most part
ignored her, and a month after the election she was again shut out of
the courthouse in Philadelphia, this time by order of the county
commissioners. In early January 1837, she spoke in Wilmington,
Delaware, where the *State Journal* wrote: "Her reception . . . was
anything but flattering to her principles or person . . . She and her
lecture were turned into ridicule by the audience . . . she abandoned
her intention of making a second appearance." Though she lived in
Philadelphia for most of 1837, Fanny apparently gave up trying to
speak there.[42]

She spent her time in that city publishing a sixteen-page monthly
journal she called the *Manual of American Principles*. When she had
gone to Boston, her primary reason for the trip was to see her old
colleague from New York days, Abner Kneeland, who now published
the *Boston Weekly Investigator*. He had a subscription list that pleased
her, and he agreed to let her contribute editorially to the paper. (To
join Kneeland was by no means to calm the fears of those who thought
her dangerously radical, because he had been tried four times for
blasphemy and had been convicted at last, two of the trials having
ended in a hung jury, and he was conducting his own appeal before

the state supreme court.) They agreed she would then put out a "revised and amended edition of the political division of the Boston weekly Investigator . . . intended to furnish a Text Book of American principles, together with such political, historical and philosophical knowledge, as is more immediately indispensable for the correct popular understanding of those principles." For the first seven months of 1837, Fanny sat doggedly in Philadelphia explaining in the pages of the *Manual* what British history had to teach Americans about Whigs and political reality.[43]

She did this apparently to set right some of her old friends and colleagues, among them the printers George Henry Evans, G. W. Matsell, and John Windt, who had split from Tammany in late October 1835. Calling themselves the Friends of Equal Rights, this group, like the Working Men's party before them, accused the Democrats of acting despotically and supporting state monopolies. They thwarted a Tammany meeting by blocking the election of the party slate, and the bosses, leaving in disgust, turned out the hall lights. Those who remained pulled Locofoco matches from their pockets, lined the platform and the room with two hundred candles, and went about their political business. This group, first called Locofocos in derision, stood for the hostility to all monopoly that Fanny now preached, taking it as an axiom that law rules the poor and money rules the law. As Fanny later put it, government became "an engine of Juggernaut. Contrived, not to frighten the wicked, but to run down the helpless. To feed the knave. To gull the simple. To rob industry. To crush, or to delude and to demoralize, the masses."[44]

The Locofocos were both her old friends and, so long as she spoke on immediate reforms, her natural allies. Slavery aside, they were the radicals of their day, yet they had broken with Van Buren and bolted the Democratic party, ridiculing Fanny's candidate as the puppet of monopoly and supporting three Whig candidates against Tammany Hall. Demonstrating that American political parties were neither so ideological nor so single-minded as Fanny thought, they had adopted the familiar strategy of trying to purify Tammany by opposing it. Their tactic was not unlike that of the French leftists in 1822 when Lafayette led his fellow deputies to vote with the Ultras to bring down Richelieu's moderate government. In 1822 Fanny had thought the strategy "most amusing." Now she treated a political maneuver as a philosophical conversion that must be reversed: "My old and still dear friends!" she wrote, "you are no more Whigs than you are Hottentots."

Convinced that a Whig was the same wherever he lived, Fanny spent more than half the next year laboriously analyzing British history in the *Manual* to expose Whiggery for what it was.[45]

The year 1837 was a dark one in the life of America. At one point fifty thousand New Yorkers, by Horace Greeley's count, wanted for life's necessities—food, shelter, and work. Since 1834, prices had risen by 50 percent, but by April they were plummeting. Philip Hone wrote in his diary that lots in New York which had cost $480 the previous September now sold for $50. In Britain the third year of a poor harvest caused wheat prices to rise, cutting the money British workers had to buy cotton goods. American cotton, which had sold the previous December for 19¢, brought only 9½¢. Mills in Boston and Lowell were idle. Debts for which cotton had been given as collateral became uncollectible, and merchants holding such debts declared bankruptcy. On May 10, banks in New York, Philadelphia, and Baltimore suspended payments. Twenty thousand people gathered in Philadelphia's Independence Square to protest the suspension and denounce the banking system. Robert Dale Owen wrote that the bankruptcies in New York had reached $250 million, and that two-thirds, perhaps three-fourths, of the wholesale merchants were gone.[46]

Van Buren, who became president on March 4, had to sustain the public wrath against the economic disorder without the shield of Jackson's popularity. Benefiting from public anger over the state of the economy, the Whigs triumphed in New York City in April, winning not only the mayor's seat but also the Common Council with all its patronage, and they began to topple Democratic incumbents throughout the nation. The panic of 1837 destroyed the incipient labor movement.

Fanny's response to these crises was to analyze the ways the powerful had defrauded the common people throughout British history in order to persuade Americans not to be gulled in the same way, and to make them understand that until the United States secured its financial independence from Europe, no genuine reform was possible. She assumed that as soon as Americans realized that the Bank of England was founded on thievery and make-believe, they would cut themselves off from England and reform their financial operations. Her obsession with money and financial power was central to all she wrote, as well as to all she evaded. It might have put her in the mainstream of political debate at that time, had it not been for America's phobia against women who differed. She was crippled as well by the profound limitations placed on her participation in public life, which had given her so little chance to understand how political change actually took place.

She chose to issue the *Manual* from Philadelphia in part because the "conspiracy against the national liberties and independence holds here its central court," and she wanted to convince the citizens of Pennsylvania to destroy the Second Bank, chartered now as the United States Bank of the State of Pennsylvania, "root and branch. No bargaining, no compromise." Aiming to give her readers no less than a "test of philosophical and political truth," Fanny intended to provide the knowledge "immediately indispensable" to solving American problems. She explained in the *Manual* how the nations of Europe had bankrupted themselves, and then coerced and swindled the rest of the world of its wealth. She believed that what the Bank of England called "money" was mere forgery, and that "foreign capitalists" were nothing other than insolvent debtors. Unlike the British Tory, who lived by the sword, the British Whig lived by fraud. The former was the highway robber, the latter, the city thief: "The one assaults you and leaves you dead on the road side. The other cuts his way neatly through your kitchen window, and subtracts all that you have in the house." Fraud was an improvement over force, but much better was to be hoped for the world.[47]

In trying to persuade Americans that Whigs had always betrayed the common man and woman, Fanny argued that the Glorious Revolution of 1688 had been neither glorious nor a revolution. It had been a "Transaction," the work of privileged men who substituted the controlling power of wealth for that of birth and divine right. The nation's working people, those who had crafts and skills and might be usefully employed, had simply got a different master.

Nor was "Whig" merely the name of the party that had come to power in England in 1688. Like "Tory" before it, "Whig" stood for "the power claimed and exercised by some, to live at expense of others." On a world scale, that power had been exercised largely by Great Britain, which could find any pretext for "violating Law in the name of Religion, Justice in the name of Law, and everything in the name of Order, Morality, or Necessity."[48]

Jefferson had first defied Great Britain when he wrote his Declaration. Jackson faced that nation down a second time when he "cleaved in twain the yoke of [America's] financial bondage, and thus prepared for the regeneration of the Republic and the true advent of Humanity."[49]

Both optimistic and paranoid—a veritable handbook of political demonology—the *Manual* spoke a tongue even more extreme than the overcharged political language of the day. Much of what Fanny said was true: Great Britain was the most powerful nation in the world, on a scale grander than any other before it; the empire it built was a way of exploiting others for its own satisfactions; and the common people had always lost in the convulsions of British and European history. But the *Manual* remains deeply disturbing. Fanny's emotional need to believe in "the regeneration of the Republic and the true advent of Humanity" distorted her judgment. She wrote her paean to Jackson in the face of evidence that his policies did not correspond with his rhetoric. On April 13, 1837, for example, Poulson's *American Daily Advertiser* reported that Jackson had created 357 new banks, in addition to 156 branch banks, had increased banking capital by $179 million, had put $123.5 million more paper money into circulation, and had increased loans and discounts by $389 million. Fanny had failed to understand that Jackson favored state banks and opposed only a central bank. Furthermore, she exaggerated her power, believing that if she could make everyone understand what had happened in England in 1688 and how England's central bank worked, she could help turn America around. But the machinations of British politicians in the late seventeenth century were of little interest to the ordinary American voter on whose wisdom Fanny was certain the republic's future depended. With the exception of the revolutionary period, intellectual concerns had not played a weighty role in American politics. And her message was unlikely to reach even the voters interested in her topic and able to penetrate her prose.

In 1829 and 1830 Fanny had been part of a larger network of speakers, journals, and organizations—fragile in relation to the dominant powers in American society, but nonetheless significant. Now she was virtually ostracized, and her name was a derisive label: no more than a handful were likely to take her seriously. Then, too, what she deplored in Great Britain seemed to be happening in America. If power could corrupt, America was building powerful parties and economic interests. The solutions that the Democrats or indeed the Locofocos offered were inadequate to the problem they were meant to address, and they had no chance of ushering in the millennium.

The *Manual's* organization was desultory (Fanny was much given to "by the way"). It also bore the marks of someone talking to herself. Fanny referred in it to the American public's indifference, and she said later that the American people were not yet a reading people. Perhaps because she realized at last that no one was listening, she broke it off abruptly after July 1837, giving no explanation for its end. Her last words, in fact, were "much more remains to be said."

She stopped writing it apparently when Phiquepal and Sylva arrived in Philadelphia from Paris. Almost two years had passed since Fanny had seen her young daughter, who was by all accounts promising and very like her mother. But within two months her husband and child were in Ohio, and by October 1837 Fanny was in New York to speak in favor of candidates for state and federal office who supported Van Buren's new bill providing for an independent treasury. Sylva and her father would be together in America for two years, living for the most part in Cincinnati, but only occasionally were the three of them in the same city. Fanny's family was not in New York to support her when she sustained as brutal an onslaught as any yet hurled against her.[50]

The Independent Treasury Bill established government depositories for government monies and required legal tender for payment. The Jacksonian answer to the Bank of the United States, it indirectly gave state banks the resources to back the paper money they issued. Mistaking a set of financial arrangements for political salvation, Fanny and the radicals took the bill to embody the people's control over the people's money: the country's wealth would be safe from the abuse of banks and private entrepreneurs. Many Democrats as well as Whigs were also deluded as to its power to affect the economy. They charged Van Buren with turning Locofoco and called the scheme a conspiracy against private property. Conservatives on both sides thought the nation on the verge of revolution.[51]

The quality of Fanny's arguments for the independent treasury, however, were irrelevant to the response she evoked. The opposition press used her notoriety as a political weapon. Despite disclaimers from all sides, the Whig *Daily Express* did everything it could to link the administration, the Locofocos, and Fanny Wright, hoping to discredit the first two by slandering the third. "She now opens her lectures flushed with new hope of a realization of her ideal equality of men, women, children, colors, races, and breeds,—with her eye already upon that Infidel Utopia that she has dreamed of and dwelt in for years . . . the Globe is her Bible,—(she knows no Christian Bible,)—and [Senator Thomas Hart] Benton is her God,—(she knows no Christian God.)" As the *Express* would have it, Fanny had come to New York to lead by her petticoat strings the party that had just thrown the respectable Democrats out of Tammany Hall. "The battle of principle we are waging," roared the *Express*, "is the old one between society, order, morals and religion, and infidelity, anarchy, the riot, butchery, and blood of the French revolution."[52]

The *Evening Post* observed that the Whig strategy was to deceive the public and prejudice it against the Locofocos. Using its boldest headlines short of those to announce national disaster, the *Express* nevertheless continued to describe Fanny, cradled in the Jacobinism of the French Revolution, as the beginner of Locofocoism. "This new phrase, *divorce* of the Government from the people," it wrote, "is but taken from the *divorce* vocabulary of Fanny Wright." Under yet another headline, "Attacks upon Property,—Fanny Wright," the paper insisted that as soon as the Locofocos succeeded in abolishing associated property, they would abolish individual property, and one man's wife would belong to everybody else.[53]

The election that began on November 6 was over by the evening of the 8th, and a packed Masonic Hall cheered repeatedly as large Whig majorities came in from almost every ward in the city. Hundreds of people at the foot of Fulton Street burned tar barrels that lighted the harbor side of Manhattan, and the Whigs taunted Tammany with their stunning victory. The year before, Van Buren had won New York City by 1,069 votes. Now the Whig candidate for the state senate won by a final count of 2,861. A week later, under the title "From What We Have Been Saved," the *Express* wrote, "From the moment that bird of ill omen, Fanny Wright . . . made her appearance as a haranguer on politics in the city . . . the contest became one of antagonistic principles, as fierce as was ever waged in any part of the earth."[54]

Fanny had spoken twice that fall at Tammany and on six successive Sunday evenings at the Masonic Hall. In mid-December she tried to speak at an education meeting at the Broadway Tabernacle, but the audience shouted her down and told her to go hold forth at Tammany. She apparently began another lecture series but abruptly canceled it, for after so exhausting a schedule and such unrelenting abuse she fell ill and went to Cincinnati. By late January 1838, however, Sylva and her father had left Fanny there and gone to live in Philadelphia. Whoever nursed Fanny back to health over the next nine months, it was not her husband and her seven-year-old daughter. Nor did Phiquepal's chatty letters hide the burgeoning closeness between father and daughter that threatened eventually to cut Fanny out.[55]

Nothing compelled Fanny and Phiquepal to live in different cities; neither had to be in one place rather than another, but invariably they went their separate ways. By September 1838, Fanny was in New York, and Phiquepal and Sylva were back in Cincinnati. The family remained apart until late in the spring of 1839, and two months later Fanny sailed with Sylva for France, while Phiquepal returned to Cincinnati for yet another year and a half. The letters they occasionally wrote, though fond enough, struck a note of fussy propriety. The parents were yoked, and resigned.

Fanny was plain now—some even called her ugly. She had deep furrows in her forehead, and the dresses she wore were dowdy. In late 1837 a woman who had known her in New Harmony wrote that Fanny was "more obnoxious now than ever—her best friends regret her course and are unwilling to support her." She had forced herself to live a shriveled life. Her best friends might well regret her course, for propriety had exacted a deadly toll.[56]

In mid-January 1838, the Cincinnati *Chronicle* published an article titled "What a Woman Has Done." Its subject was Fanny Wright, and it suggests why her public appearances had come to cause such havoc: "The *mobs* which have disgraced this nation before the civilized world, may be traced directly to the influence of Fanny Wright's sentiments, as propagated by herself and *her followers.* Her spirit of misrule now so alarmingly prevalent, had its origin in the attempted subversion of the *domestic constitution,* by this high priestess of infidelity. Her influence on the morals of a city and indeed of the nation at large, has been generally underrated in making an estimate of crime and its probable consequences.—With a brain from Heaven and a heart from Hell, she has employed all the powers of her intellect, in removing the ancient land-marks of morality and social order, and in diffusing the worst principles of the French revolution through this land of the Puritan Fathers . . . She has set in motion a train of causes, which will never cease to operate, until that day when God shall come to make inquisition for blood, and to destroy the wicked with the breath of his mouth. Many a happy home has been rendered a moral desert by the trace of her footsteps, many a parent worse than childless, and many a wife more desolate than a widow . . . the streams of guilt and misery . . . will flow, from this one fountain of infidelity . . . until the broad river of death empties its turbid flood into the lake that burneth."[57]

A woman who had left her sanctioned niche, Fanny seemed to have pulled society's linch-pin as she stepped down. At a time when many doubted the social fabric would hold, she had become the focus for fears and hatreds so intense they transformed her into a scapegoat: she was Pandora, a witch, a crazed prophetess, a high priestess, a Power. Two years later Orestes Brownson, who had never thrown off

Fanny's influence, proposed a variety of anticapitalist reforms, including the abolition of inheritance. He was pilloried, as Fanny had been, for preaching the overthrow of the church and the destruction of property, but he remained in constant demand as a speaker for the Democratic party. Fanny and her enthusiasm, in contrast, had become an albatross to the Democrats, and they were not long in casting her off.[58]

On September 23, 1838, just after her forty-third birthday, Fanny gave the initial lecture of a series of five in Masonic Hall, at the podium from which she had first addressed the people of New York nine years earlier. She wondered if they were nearing "the last war this Earth shall know—that between its Kings and its Peoples." She argued that the political quarrels that made up so much of history were only so many skirmishes between wings of the same army. The battle in England between the Whigs and the Tories, for instance, was a mock battle between those who equally lived off working people. The real struggle everywhere was between those who ruled and those who were ruled, between property and industry. The great enemy was the British banking and funding scheme, and the first mortal blow to be struck against that enemy would be the passage of the Independent Treasury Bill: "on your ballot boxes now hangs suspended the fate of the old world and the new . . . Go for the Independent Treasury Bill and . . . Bankruptcy yawns beneath the thrones of Europe."[59]

The only major newspaper that paid consistent attention to Fanny was the *Daily Express*, which despised and feared her. In the midst of the uproar that followed her appearance, the paper wrote, "What a shame and a disgrace is such a woman to her sex or to any party!" It hoped to do what it had done the year before: to discredit the policy of Van Buren's administration by linking it with Fanny. It mocked her wrath: "The poor Bank of England was pushed about like a feather in a thunder storm, and the United States Bank, unpitied in its retirement under the weaker stroke of Andrew Jackson, received a blow from her long arm, which a boxer might have called a finisher." But the main purpose of the paper was to make the identification: "Locofocoism . . . Is Fanny Wrightism."[60]

The second lecture was more tumultuous. About thirty women appeared on the platform with Fanny, but midway through her speech the audience exploded. They hissed and applauded. Hundreds of canes pounded the floor. People shouted and hecklers hooted street cries. The applause and howling grew deafening until, as the *Express* would have it, "Fanny at last put forth her bony finger, and with all the power of one of the Witches in Macbeth, stopt the boiling of the popular cauldron."[61]

The next Sunday a mob broke up Fanny's lecture. The *Evening Post* cut into its silence to comment briefly on what is called "a disgraceful scene." Fanny was in the midst of her lecture when an uproar swelled, once again of canes pounding the floorboards, of shouts, thumpings, hisses, and "a volley of expressions of the most vulgar and indecent kind." The *Post* told those who did not want to hear Fanny to stay at home. The *Express* thundered, "Riot and Revolution is the element she creates and breathes in."[62]

A week later the crowds were outside as well as inside Masonic Hall. The mayor had stationed police officers around the building, many of them in ordinary dress. Fanny announced that she would give the lecture she had intended for the week before, when she had been interrupted by a mob of loafing Whigs. At this, the catcalls and obscenities started again, but the police officers in the crowd put down the turmoil, and Fanny was able to finish the lecture. According to the *Courier and Enquirer,* she and her friends were rushed as they left the hall, but the marshals and watchmen formed a hollow square and kept them from the mob. A bodyguard of admirers surrounded her as she made her way up Broadway, taunted by clusters of young men and idlers.

The worst Sunday was the next, October 21. As many as five thousand people heard her speak, and by the time she finished, ten thousand were in the streets outside the hall. It took an hour for the men in the audience to get out of the building. And as the large number of women began leaving, the hoodlums in the mob that lined the passage flipped up their bonnet brims, called them whores and harlots, and yelled obscenities at them.

The crowd was on the thin edge of riot, and her enemies were bellowing for Fanny. As she came down the stairs, the mob surged toward her, yelling and screaming, and came up hard against a double cordon of police, who lined a passageway leading past the door and to the corner of Anthony Street. The mob lunged against the police as Fanny hurried along to a waiting carriage. The police rushed her into the coach as the mob screamed behind her, some of the men running after it as the frightened horses quickened their trot. She left behind what the *Post* and the *Express* called a horrible din of oaths and shouts, and some of the mob followed her all the way to the door of her lodgings in Canal Street. Every quarter then seemed to erupt in violence. The police arrested several people, and it was late at night before the mobs scattered and quiet once more descended on the city. The *Express* scowled that Fanny was costing New York about $400 in extra police.

Fanny insisted that the newspaper accounts were exaggerated. Her committee inside the hall had made sure no noise interrupted her hour-and-a-half speech; she had not, as the *Star* suggested, climbed out a window to escape the mob; and one Justice Taylor assured her that the ladies leaving the building had not been molested. She chastised the *Evening Post* for its "singularly sustained silence . . . during the whole of last week" and its refusal to censure or even to comment on the outrageous scene it had described. Three-fourths of the city's press was either a farce or a nuisance whose daily business was to provoke riot and then to mistake its causes. The police had been two hundred strong, and that should have been sufficient to protect her and her audience from the "vulgar, insolent and brutal aggressions of some of the leading organs of the whig press, and of their organized rioters in this city."[63]

The following Sunday, October 28, Fanny spoke for the last time at Masonic Hall. Calling her lecture "What Is the Matter?," she insisted that her series of talks had been merely a pretext for the hubbub of the month just past. By Fanny's account, "the matter" was that the American Whigs, who were truly loyal, had caught on to the Federal Tory Whigs, who were traitors to republican principles. The loyal Whigs had begun to repudiate the Tory Whigs, who had then made "of my person a last battle ground." Nothing, to be sure, could be gained by doing this: "Say that they should succeed in tearing me to pieces, or stoning me to death, as they have at different times attempted—what then?" Doing so would not prevent passage of the Independent Treasury Bill, which would mean "the first emancipation of a government at once from the odious enthralment, and from the corrupting influences and overwhelming tyranny of the money power." To pass the bill would be to snatch the American eagle from the bloody clutches of the "Leopard of England" and to allow it to soar aloft on the wings of freedom. Thus high on metaphor, she ended her tenure at Masonic Hall.[64]

By November 7 it was clear that whatever Fanny's role, the Whigs had once more triumphed in the elections, and the Democratic press began to talk about purging Tammany to get the Democrats back into political fighting form. To add to the party's humiliations, stories leaked to the press of massive peculations by Jackson's appointee to New York Customs, Samuel Swartwout.

Fanny was meanwhile looking for a hall to rent and trying to make suitable arrangements "for re-opening and following out to its close, the series of discourses commenced, and so strangely interrupted some weeks since in Masonic Hall." Though she had spoken at Tammany Hall four or five times over the course of the years, she had never hired the hall for her own use and in her own name. Now Tammany made it clear she was not wanted: she was too great a liability for a party that no longer had a political margin. One writer said she had been driven from Tammany by a popular movement. Fanny herself described it as the sachems shutting the door of the wigwam in her face and shortly completed her break from the "so-called democratic Party" by saying, "*Let Party perish but let society live!*" She finally rented Clinton Hall, in a disreputable neighborhood somewhere near the old Park Theatre, where she had first watched *Altorf* performed almost twenty years before.[65]

The contrast was painful. When *Altorf* had opened in the city's finest house, she had been surrounded by the most discriminating New York society. Her devoted sister had sat by her side, and all around them had been friends who thought of Fanny with a touch of awe. But the public had not then known her name. Now she was the most easily recognized woman in America, but she lectured alone before a suddenly indifferent public, on what she hoped would be a "temporary footing in this saloon." As she looked around her at the first meeting, the setting seemed far too meager for the occasion: "Most assuredly this place is not such as I should choose nor as the People should occupy. In fact the People cannot occupy it. The People are the *mighty many.* And when I look round this narrow space I feel that both they whom I address and I who speak want that inspiration which the presence of thousands alone can impart." She had with difficulty secured the hall for twelve Sunday nights, however. She hoped for a faithful assembly of a thousand—not a "mere haphazard audience curious to see the woman whom everybody abuses," but people who would come through wind and rain to ask, with her "how and in what way the world may be made happy."[66]

Only one woman left an account of Fanny's meetings there. She was Elizabeth Oakes Smith, who had just arrived in New York, and had found Fanny Wright the great topic of conversation. Flaunting her relatives' disapproval, Mrs. Smith determined to hear Fanny and persuaded her husband, on a wintry Sunday, to go out in heavy fog to a hall they discovered was unutterably dreary: "We went upstairs and turned into a very dirty, dimly lighted hall, filled with straight wooden benches, and only three persons in them. The appointed hour had already arrived, and slowly, men, one after another, sauntered in—several women also, some with babes in their arms, and all bringing an atrocious odor of tobacco, whiskey, and damp clothing. At length there might have been fifty persons, not more, present, and these began to shuffle and call for the speaker. It was all so much more gross and noisy than anything I had ever encountered where a woman was concerned, that I grew quite distressed, and the bad atmosphere nearly made me faint." When Fanny opened the door at the back of the platform and stepped out, Mrs. Smith saw a woman whose smile had a touch of sadness, but who had "an earnestness and wholesomeness . . . that made their way to the mind and heart." Fanny seemed so superior to her audience that Mrs. Smith at once sympathized with those who had come and regretted the prejudice that kept intelligent people away. Indifferent to the smatterings of applause, Fanny said not one word "which any sound-minded man might not have said with approval."[67]

And so Fanny had to endure the humiliation of finding herself inconsequential not long after people had risked their limbs and their reputations to hear her. Little she had suffered could have been more terrible. Standing up to authority had been exhilarating. People who treated her shabbily had shored up her belief in her own superiority. But now she spoke to empty benches and blank walls, and being forgotten was quite another matter.

The burden of Fanny's message could hardly account for the hysteria she inspired in New York. With a woman's insight into cultural deprivation, she had simply opposed a system, which later generations would call "The Establishment," that seemed to work "for the enriching of the rich, the empoverishing of the poor, the feeding of the idle, the starving of the industrious, the corrupting of the honest and the rapid multiplication of our privileged, professional and idle or genteel classes." She shared with other radicals an instinct for opposition, as she did a sense that "the haves" involved themselves in a vast conspiracy to bar the gates against "the others."[68]

Though each person had a body, a mind, and a moral sense, Fanny argued that society kept people from developing them equally. In white America, the laboring classes developed their bodies; women developed their moral sensibilities; men of the professional and intellectual classes developed their minds. Society allowed these men to rule by exploiting the women and working people. They garnered to themselves too large a proportion of the nation's wealth, too many of the things that made life easy and pleasant. The women they married, smothered by propriety in their homes, became extraneous to the real life of their times. Though the work this class did was increasingly irrelevant and burdensome to the truly productive forces in the economy, they persuaded the rest of the nation to envy them and covet their lives. As monopoly, or business, absorbed the wealth of a state, so it usurped the power. It ruled the press, subsidized political parties, influenced votes, decided elections, and corrupted public officials. It governed the government and made a mockery of freedom.

Feminism aside, Fanny held this perspective on American society along with a handful of radicals, mainly in the cities of the East. What she considered unique in her contribution to the American public were her lectures about "the nature and history of human civilization from its first rise in Asia to the final development it is destined constitutionally to attain in these United States of America." Using an approach she called scientific, she elaborated a theoretical structure to explain how all history necessarily led up to the republicanism she held so dear.

By going to the root of the word *religion,* meaning "that which binds," Fanny discovered four "binding and regulating *political principles* or *Religions*" in the course of human history: the religions of priests, of country, of kings, and of the people. (Though most of her audiences no doubt called themselves Protestants, Fanny told them that Protestantism, far from being a religion, was a mere bundle of theologies and had never been anything but a "divisio," or rending asunder of human societies: "a more complete cutting and slashing of Society than Protestant Christianity with its adjunct and agent the Banking system has effected wd be difficult to conceive of.") The first religion bound the earliest civilizations of Asia; the second characterized the city-states of Greece and the Roman Republic; the third started with Augustus Caesar, flourished with Constantine, and continued through modern Europe; and the last opened on July 4, 1776, in the United States of America.

In each epoch the religion had made the community possible; it was the informing belief that united people and motivated their actions. At the same time, the national economy or political framework provided the machinery of that community. Over that machinery two great principles had struggled for mastery: the enslavement of human labor for the advantage of a few, and the enfranchisement of human labor for the good of the many. Fanny described how well or badly the religion in each era corresponded with its principle of political economy. When she discussed America, for example, she noted the discrepancy between its religion of the people and its political economy, which exploited them. Jefferson's Declaration spoke the young nation's religion; Jay's commercial treaty and Hamilton's financial scheme established institutions that undermined justice for the sake of the privileged few. The dynamic of history led inevitably, she insisted, to a final religion, the religion of humanity: "a real worship of the species, and devotion to the public good, on the part of the individual." Civilization, she argued, now approached the goal so long sought and so invariably missed because, "having tried every possible wrong road we have now nothing left to try but the right one."[69]

The change to a better world would come, Fanny thought, as people decided they wanted to change, and it would begin in the places where they lived and would work up the scale of organized society. Because speculation would be abolished, greed and envy would no longer debase the world. The body politic would take over all the state's real property—its mines, lands, quarries, buildings, and every kind of capital—and would adequately compensate its present owners to the second generation. Each nation would be organized from the ground up, from small to large, and the public wealth would be administered in the public interest. Money could be abolished, and people would find useful work and help in time of need. They would find equal rights to equal chances and reward in proportion to what they contributed. Perhaps it was this last vision of a communal rather than a competitive society that brought ten thousand people into the streets of New York and called out the police in double force.

What Fanny said was dubious as history, as strategy, and as prophecy. And her audiences eventually drifted away because she bored them. She bored them because her vision was feminist and egalitarian, and Jacksonian America was inclined to neither. She bored them because her elaborate historical construct was willed and flimsy; they could not find in all her talk of Asian priests and Roman emperors a compelling reason to believe in the near advent of the religion of humanity. She bored them because her idea of historical process and her notions of the future were fantastic, and fantasy has little power to nourish. She bored them because her tone was magisterial, and this they could not accept from a woman.

Still there remained something grand about her. Despite the crippling attacks against her, despite the shriveling of her personal affections, despite the hardening of her character and the recurrent illnesses that plagued her, she relentlessly kept in sight an exalted vision of human possibility. Guileless to the extreme of self-destruction, she saw that America betrayed its promise and missed its chance by allowing a few people to monopolize the good things it offered. Alexis de Tocqueville to the contrary, Fanny saw that American society was marked by inequalities that were growing instead of diminishing. She saw inequality as the root of injustice and recognized that an unjust society doomed everyone in it to be less by far than what they promised.

Sometime in March 1839, Fanny conceded defeat. She said that either the time was unpropitious or the people who came to hear her had no other reason than curiosity: "If this last should have been the only motive, it is certainly more than time for me to desist, not only from the present but from all other labors in the public service." She announced that she expected her husband and daughter after a separation of many months and would retreat to private life.[70]

When Phiquepal brought Sylva from Cincinnati, Fanny decided to take her and go back to Paris. Phiquepal advised her to leave public life until some special occasion demanded her return. "The whole living world is topsy turvy," she wrote William Maclure in mid-June, "and the few honest and clear sighted lovers of its weal have a hard matter to render it service with any certainty of not seeing their efforts counteracted or, worse, not turned into positive sources of evil."[71]

With her thoughts still stubbornly fixed on human improvement, Fanny sailed from America once more on June 20, 1839, and Philip Hone yet again noted her going: "In the list of passengers in the packet ship *Quebec* which sailed to-day for London is Mme. Frances Wright D'Arusmont, better known as Fanny Wright, the quondam friend of Lafayette, who was thought to make desperate love to him, the apostle of infidelity, the idol of the Locofocos, and the oracle of sub-treasury politicians. Let her go home or go to the Devil, so that she never visits us again."[72]

The Last Drops
of Bitterness

11

Fanny left New York in 1839 intending to watch the political storms in France and England from a quiet window in Paris, and she said that she lived thereafter in all but seclusion from a world with which she had no sympathy. For a period spanning ten years Fanny had keyed herself to the excitement of the thousands who came to hear her, but now, apart from an abortive lecture series in London, she had to find what purpose she could in solitary writing. A woman who had been extravagantly admired and sometimes loved, she now lived for the most part alone. For seven years her marriage steadily deteriorated, until in 1846 she and Phiquepal began a bitter legal fight over property that lasted until she died. As she felt the pride that sustained her ceaselessly buffeted, the restlessness that marked her life grew more extreme, and she glanced from one rented room to another, fighting with all who seemed to cross her. At least twice more she suffered from prolonged nervous collapse, so that her last years are both a study in loneliness and a lesson in the perils of isolation.[1]

As though in echo of her life, Fanny's writing during these years is more abstract and hermetic than her early work, and except for the portion that is decidedly feminist, it rises less frequently to the heights of rhetorical power she had so easily captured. In 1844, for example, in response to what she called several trifling mistakes in a newspaper article about her, she wrote a sketch of her past up to her first lecture in New York. To this account she appended seven "Political Letters," and the two were published together that year, both in London and New York. She called the sketch a biography and wrote it in the third person, and though this convention was common to the age, her little book's impersonality suggested a dangerous psychic remoteness. She even gave a political reason for its thin human texture, explaining that she had always done her best to remember that "they who feel conscious that their motives of action are different from those of the world they live in, should keep themselves, as far as possible, aloof from all ties likely either to embarrass their own proceedings or the feelings of others." Although she later told Thomas Carlyle that he was mistaken in celebrating heroes, she wrote about herself in a form of hagiography, as in the statement: "Clearly distinguishing the nature of the move, Frances Wright determined to arouse the whole American people to meet it, at whatever cost to herself."[2]

Engaged in her own revisionist history, Fanny ignored, magnified, or changed facts as it suited her purposes. Forgetting that a female slave at Nashoba had proved so dangerous Fanny was forced to take her to a neighboring plantation, she claimed that "all her serious difficulties proceeded from her white assistants, and not from the blacks." Having once written that Robert Owen would change the world, she now barely mentioned him other than to explain in a footnote that he made no real experiment at New Harmony.[3]

She used the autobiography as a vehicle for theory. Instead of describing what happened at Nashoba, she discussed the process by which blacks "must be made to go through a real moral, intellectual, and industrial apprenticeship" that would prepare them for freedom. White Americans, peculiarly fitted to command, would direct the blacks in clearing the forests, breaking up the soil, draining the swamps, opening roads—in short, taming the South. At the same time the blacks would learn all the practical arts, including the use of machinery. They would then leave a country "prepared for facile cultivation by the white race" and would go to tropical climates they were "fitted by organization no less than experience" to conquer. Indians and Africans would create wealthy empires "where now stretches . . . the deleterious swamp, peopled by the savage, the reptile, and the beast of prey." Fanny called this process "civilizing" rather than "exploiting" the blacks.[4]

This shapeless monograph—lofty, remote, defensive—is the work of a woman long out of touch with the best impulses of her past and the sources of her power, though she managed to admit to one mistake. In the "Political Letters" appended to the autobiography, she acknowledged what she called a socially and politically disorganizing error in her published work. Religion, as she now understood it, was crucial to any society: it bound people together. She was still unwilling, however, to accept other people's definitions of religion, and she did not include Protestant Christianity in that category, or indeed much of what historically had passed for religion.

She made one significant addition to the ideas she had preached in New York in 1838. The subjugation of women both in body and soul, she argued, was the first and most important tool in the species' enslavement. Women were the intellect and soul of society—that which looked to the conservation and happiness of the species— while men represented "that which looks to individual conservation and selfish gratification." The base element had suppressed the finer: force had quelled the instinct of the mind. The possibility that this insight arose from her own experience in marriage was a possibility to which she made no reference.[5]

Three years later Fanny spoke once more in public, only to discover that her line of thought had become so obscure she could no longer hold her audience. In the spring of 1847, she agreed to give a series of lectures at the Unitarian South Place Chapel in London, a gathering spot for British radicals. She announced that she would speak on "The Mission of England Considered with Reference to the Civilizational History of Modern Europe." George Jacob Holyoake, the editor of *The Reasoner* and the most experienced journalist in the socialist movement, was delighted that Fanny had come, and gleefully arranged to report the lectures for her admirers who could not get to London.

The series began well. After Fanny's first lecture on May 11, Holyoake quoted a poet who said she would make a magnificent Lady Macbeth. "Free from that painful air often observed in women who advocate the rights of women, Madame D'Arusmont's air is that of a woman who *has them*." Her lecture was nevertheless "in advance of many of the auditory," and Holyoake suggested that people prepare themselves by reading her "Political Letters."[6]

At the end of her fourth lecture, Fanny canceled the series, saying her health made it impossible for her to go on. Holyoake could barely contain his disappointment, as he thought she had used her health for an excuse to cover her anger at the dwindling numbers who came to hear her. Though her London audiences were meager compared to the ones she had drawn in America, he said, they included "as many persons of known practical intelligence as, with so profound a subject, any one, of whatever celebrity, could have gathered together in England." The prestige of South Place had guaranteed the diffusion of Fanny's ideas, and many had come on excursion trains from as far away as two hundred miles to hear her.[7]

Fanny insisted that a nervous attack soon after she began the fourth lecture had made her stop. Although she denied that she was mortified by the scanty numbers in the hall, she admitted that a larger audience might have lifted her out of herself. As it was, she had to face the public's "general indifference to that cause" to which she had pledged her life.[8]

She announced, however, that she would give Holyoake "The Mission of England" for *The Reasoner*, "the cheapest, and all but the only press open to the popular use, and removed from the influences of some one or other political party." To publish the lectures was to perform "the important service now demanded by suffering Europe, and suffering Humanity." Several days later, however, she abruptly changed her mind and withdrew the lectures, apparently on the grounds that *The Reasoner* was atheistic and thus "an impossible organ for the work at hand." In exasperation, Holyoake replied that as her promise had involved him in serious expense, he had no alternative but to publish the first lecture: "I cannot conceive you guilty of such a break of faith and honour both to me and my readers as this countermand involves & it will damage us irreparably to confess it."[9]

Since Holyoake had gone to prison for his support of a free press, he was qualified to judge when he said it had taken courage to support Fanny. His was the only newspaper that would print her work, and he and his friends were the only people who paid her any attention: "No other party care anything about her, and precisely for the reason that she is heterodox." Furthermore, she had known what she was doing when she gave him the lectures, because she had withdrawn them once before. She had then stipulated that there be no controversy about deity in any issue in which her "Mission" was to appear, and he had agreed.[10]

Holyoake was poor, and so was his paper. When Fanny withdrew the lectures, she recognized neither the trouble nor the expense he had taken on, and he wrote the Sheffield radical Isaac Ironside, "Greatly have I mistaken your character if you are more in love than I am, with Philanthropy which plumes itself upon a public virtue too exalted to estimate the sacrifice it makes of others."[11]

The issue between them turned on their different uses of the term *religion*. Holyoake believed that Fanny withdrew the lectures because she heard the paper was atheistic. "Madame D'Arusmont is not exactly the person whom I should have expected to find bowing to this miserable prejudice, and practically asking the pulpit permission to speak . . . Her 'Few Days in Athens' . . . is atheistic to an extravagance . . . And for all the argument she has ever published since, in favour of religion, she is an Atheist now." Fanny said she refused, as always, to lend herself to "doctrinal antagonism . . . or opinionative discussion . . . My object is to bring men out of disputation into study, &. out of theology and antitheology (one and the same things) into Religion." Insisting implicitly on her right to define *religion* idiosyncratically and in defiance of historical religions, she was convinced now that men and women needed a binding emotional commitment at the core of the societies in which they lived. But her peculiar position cut her off both from those who were Christians and those who were not, and her behavior had been erratic and unfeeling. Ironside, who spent hours with her, wrote, "I do not think she is mad, but she seems to me to attach far too much importance to her 'mission' than it warrants."[12]

During the middle years of the 1840s—years of intermittent illness for Fanny and growing estrangement from her family—she accomplished her major work, *England the Civilizer.* A handful of young men paid her homage—men like Ironside, Holyoake, and Thomas Finlay, who ran the Free-Thinkers Tract and Bookshop in Edinburgh. But she had to cling to the scraps of esteem she got from these few strangers, and her intellectual and emotional isolation showed in her new work.

In 1846 a fire mysteriously destroyed many of Fanny's papers, but she worked quickly to reconstruct what she had lost, and by March 1848, *England the Civilizer* was out in Britain, its title page bearing the legend "By a Woman." Whatever led Fanny to publish it anonymously, its authorship was not a well-kept secret. As usual, she distributed it to people with access to power, sending eleven copies to Richard Rush, the American ambassador to France, and asking him to pass them along to Alexis de Tocqueville and each member of the provisional government in Paris.[13]

A handful admired it. Holyoake wrote, "It ought to find its way into all libraries, and become a class-book with students of English History." But the major journals and papers ignored it, and Fanny soon faced daunting competition. At the beginning of 1849, a friend wrote that the London sales were slow. Macaulay's *History of England* was so popular that she was dubious about Fanny's success: "Your book may one day tho' not now, be read with profound interest."[14]

Very few books have had less of the popular touch about them, and its central intellectual perception about the historic abuse of male power would not be seriously considered again for almost a century.

Like all of Fanny's writing, it tells inadvertently a great deal about its author.

The work of a rebel and scholar, *England the Civilizer* reveals the breadth of Fanny's knowledge and the great energy of her intellect. Among her American female contemporaries, even Margaret Fuller pales in comparison. Looking out over history with the radical conviction that "no human being can be, or ought to count for, more than a unit in the great collective sum of civilized society," and refusing to see things merely as others saw them, she gave an account of British and European history that serves as a rejoinder to the smug, boastful Victorian and his counterpart across the Channel or the Atlantic. She labeled the Reformation, for example, the "Dispute." She wrote that for all its horrors, the French Revolution was the most wonderful political drama ever enacted and one of the great steps toward human emancipation in mind and body. And she extended her iconoclasm now to heroes, exalting Arnold of Brescia, one of Abelard's students and otherwise obscure—a man "who first astonished Europe with the cry of freedom" and died a "malefactor, a rebel, and a heretic."[15]

She gave special attention to the national revolutions in England, America, and France, sifting through a mass of material to find evidence for her theory that polarity was a universal phenomenon of nature and society—that attraction and repulsion, for instance, were not in conflict but were the opposite ends of a graduated scale. Each had to work harmoniously, she argued, in any whole system. Male and female, analysis and synthesis, individual and species, union and liberty—each was equally necessary to truth and life. Governments, however, were incapable of preserving the necessary polarity: though they were established to protect a legitimate interest, inevitably each began to tyrannize as it grew preoccupied with perpetuating itself.

The problem with governments was largely that they elevated the male principle, which recognized no motive power but force—either directly, as violence, or indirectly, as corruption—and worked for "the propagation, the conservation, and the enjoyment of the individual." The female instinct, on the other hand, worked toward "the conservation, care, and happiness of the species." Driven by the generous rather than the selfish impulse, "the female instinct assumes a character commensurate with the wider range of the human faculties, and originates, sustains, and promotes the whole scheme of progressive civilization." Governments accomplished the triumph of the selfish principle by stifling or perverting the generous—"by forcibly circumscribing all the holy influences and lofty aspirations of woman within the narrowest precincts of the individual family circle . . . by forcibly closing her eyes upon the claims of the great human family without that circle." Justice would come only when "the two persons in human kind—man and woman—shall exert equal influences in a state of equal independence."[16]

Her theories were shapeless enough, and sufficiently impervious to proof, to impose no fast limits on narrative description. Though her insights have the gift of illumination almost a century and a half later, she could not illustrate them adequately, much less prove them. The disciplines of psychology and anthropology did not yet exist to provide her with data that might develop her perceptions about the misuse of male power. Given that men had for the most part ruled and run society, blaming "the male principle" was safe, if inexplicit. But she gave too spacious a role to deliberate intention in the behavior of governments, believing that they act more coherently than they can. She said nonsensically, for instance, that the feudal system was established to protect labor.

In *England the Civilizer* Fanny's willed cultural optimism triumphed over her sense of the horrors and injustices of the past. Although America, for example, was governed for and by its adult white males, and women's interests, liberties, and independence were sacrificed there, women's exclusion ensured that they, unscarred and uncontaminated, could work for society's ultimate salvation. No losses had been in vain; no torture lacked its ultimate vindication. Those who awaited the Second Coming, however, were more likely to be gratified than Fanny, who put her hopes in the way frankly man-made governments might behave in the future. The last fifth of the book describes a kind of millennial fantasy. England would give Scotland and Ireland back to their native people and would divide itself into five provinces. And so it would go throughout the globe. Every country would break down and reorganize itself into smaller units, and a federation of essentially self-sufficient communities would give the peoples of the world unity without restraint and independence with security. The "three bright-eyed sisters"—production, distribution, and education—would replace the "four violent brothers"—law, trade, superstition, and government—and the thirteen principles of justice would reign.

Fanny's thesis was that the present was untenable, and therefore everything must and would become different from what it ever had been. She called on England to listen to Frances Wright: "Come! in this last extremity let woman's voice obtain a hearing. Woman! who never asked, nor asks for self . . . Who never felt, nor feels, saving for others and for collective human kind." She called on the Pope to dissolve the Jesuits and protect civilization against barbarism. She called on England, together with Rome, to command strife and disputation to cease, and sects, rivalries, and parties to vanish from the earth. Governments and money would disappear, along with commercial trade, and "man, relieved of all sordid motives by the disappearance of the governing tool—money, will recover the soul that he has lost."[17]

As for herself, Fanny was prepared for the change. All her property stood in the names of her family, and if what she set forth in these pages should be realized, she would forego her claims to her share and enlist in the future. In closing the book, she noted that she had solved "the great problems . . . which have held the world in warfare through all time."[18]

Idiosyncracy is hard to measure almost 150 years in the past, and the twentieth-century eye looks back astonished at the millennialist delusions rampant then. Robert Owen and Robert Dale, for example, amazed their friends by turning to spiritualism in their later years. And Charles Fourier, whose ideas coursed through Paris when Fanny lived there, believed that as the world worked its way to utter harmony, people would discover a sea of lemonade and a whole new set of beasts: an anti-lion, an anti-whale, an anti-bear, anti-rats, and so on.

But there is a disturbing strain in Fanny's life and work for which terms like eccentric or idiosyncratic seem inadequate. She was always inclined to overestimate her influence and to discount the human feelings on which her efforts at persuasion would seem to depend, so that she repeatedly undercut herself. Now, in *England the Civilizer*, she indulged a fantasy of overweening personal power, to the neglect of any commonsensical understanding of how historical change actually comes about. As she was finishing her book, Isaac Ironside warned her: "rest assured, my dear Madame, that even if your 'Mission' should never appear at all, the world will still go round with its average degree of velocity."[19]

Such a strain should not obscure the freshness of her major insights, however, as it would be ninety years before another woman rediscovered those important ideas that gained credence only as the twentieth century neared its end. In *Three Guineas*, Virginia Woolf found, as Fanny had, that the world men had made was inclined to war, and she understood that the instinct to battle was sex-related. Like Fanny, she saw that the education men shaped and the professions they followed—the rules of the games by which they played—all sparked and sanctioned the love of invidious distinctions that led ultimately to war. Together they saw that men had claimed the world and the intellect for themselves and had relegated the hearth and the heart to women. Both of them believed that such a parceling out of wholeness was corrupt, corrupting, and, in the end, destructive. Both of them argued that only when women were let out of the private house and allowed to bring their different instincts and perceptions to bear on the larger problems of making a decent world could there be a chance of realizing what Fanny called "the destined triumph of the cause I serve."[20]

There is no evidence that Virginia Woolf read Fanny's writing, but a handful of distinguished American feminists did. Elizabeth Cady Stanton kept her works, along with Thomas Paine's, on her library table; Susan B. Anthony owned her *Biography, Notes and Political Letters* in the New York and Boston editions; and the two of them, along with Matilda Joslyn Gage, used her portrait as the frontispiece for their *History of Woman Suffrage*. In 1860 Ernestine Rose, who had followed Fanny to the platform at Tammany Hall, saluted her as the first woman in America to speak for sexual equality. Some two decades after Fanny's death, Paulina Davis spoke of her at the twentieth anniversary of the National Woman Suffrage Association: "Looking down from the serene heights of her philosophy she pitied and endured the scoffs and jeers of the multitude, and fearlessly continued to utter her rebukes against oppression, ignorance and bigotry. Women joined in the hue and cry against her, little thinking that men were building the gallows and making them the executioners. Women have crucified in all ages the redeemers of their own sex, and men mock them with the fact. It is time now that we trample beneath our feet this ignoble public sentiment which men have made for us; and if others are to be crucified before we can be redeemed, let men do the cruel, cowardly act; but let us learn to hedge womanhood round with generous, protecting care and love."[21]

But Fanny's radicalism made her a problem to most of her contemporaries because the feminism that began to develop in her lifetime did so largely in the benevolent organizations that women formed in cities throughout the nation. Most of these women were reformers rather than radicals, and while they questioned women's traditional role, they never endorsed anything like the thoroughgoing transformations Fanny insisted were essential to social decency, if not survival. They neither protested the factory system nor believed that society itself had the obligation to care generously for those who could not care for themselves. They founded the first daycare centers but shied away from communal forms of living. Like their sisters in the abolition movement, most were at least nominally Christian, and Fanny's skepticism, as well as her notoriety, frightened them away.[22]

For seventy years the energies of the women's rights movement in America focused increasingly on the right to vote, and Fanny, like Emma Goldman after her, thought the efficacy of the ballot exaggerated. Individual women like Goldman, Charlotte Perkins Gilman, and Crystal Eastman shared Fanny's belief that the economic structures of society must be transformed. But not until late in the 1960s would a new generation of feminists resurrect the possibility that men and women, as Fanny hoped, would write her name and preserve her memory "among those of the champions of human liberty and heralds of human improvement."[23]

Not only was Fanny denied followers among her contemporaries, along with the influence she hoped for during her lifetime, but she was denied domestic happiness as well. During the 1840s it became increasingly clear that her husband was a man she could neither love, like, nor respect. Separated from him more often than not, she put Sylva in boarding school and lived alone in Paris for more than a year after she left New York. In early 1841 Phiquepal came again to Paris but told Fanny she must go to America on business. In May 1843, she was again in the United States, apparently alone.

She gave up her vision of America as a better world, but she still preferred to live there—possibly because she expected Phiquepal to stay in Paris. Though a few years later she criticized the American government as "the most decidedly anarchal and supremely corrupt of any on the face of the globe," in 1843 she nevertheless began fashioning a home in America. She took over the Nashoba estate from Richesson Whitby, and it was probably on this trip, when she went on to Cincinnati, that she engaged Joel Brown to build her a two-story brick house.[24]

She was there in Cincinnati in early 1844, when the British Embassy notified her that she had inherited property in Dundee, Scotland, on the death of her second cousin, Margaret Wright. With a maid named Barbara, whose father was the Nashoba overseer, Fanny sailed to meet Phiquepal and Sylva in Dundee and to see how substantial the inheritance might be. She found it to include a piece of land somewhat larger than twenty-three acres along the King's Highway and another in the city with several houses, at least one warehouse, and a large garden. The inheritance made her wealthy once again, and the greed that her wealth inspired finally destroyed her family.[25]

Her legal arrangements for the Dundee property suggest that she had grown wary of Phiquepal. Having secured his necessary consent to do so, she created a trust—one of the only devices in Great Britain at the time that allowed a married woman some control over her own property. According to the stipulations, Fanny had sole benefit of it during her lifetime. The annual proceeds would pass to Phiquepal if he survived her, and then to Sylva and her heirs. Fanny stipulated that Sylva's husband could have no part of it.

In mid-August 1844 Fanny and Barbara sailed from Liverpool on their way back to Cincinnati. Fanny had hoped—or so she said—that Phiquepal's scientific work could be wound up at the same time as her business affairs in Scotland so that they could all go home together. Home for her now meant Cincinnati and the house Joel Brown had built. Home for Phiquepal, however, meant France. He and Sylva left Dundee for Paris, and they stayed there.

In 1845, the year Fanny turned 50, she had what was probably another nervous breakdown. Phiquepal later said that her hard work on a new set of lectures and her disappointment in being unable to give them caused a relapse of the brain fever she had first contracted at Nashoba. Fanny herself described it as the onset of "violent palpitations of the heart and throbbings of the arteries." The fragments of correspondence that remain show her living on the hard edge of her emotions, even more cut off from that rich ebullience of manner that captivated so many people when she was young.[26]

The latent hostility between Fanny and Phiquepal was also beginning to surface. While she was in America suffering from this latest nervous collapse, he took Sylva to London to see Fanny's aunt and erstwhile guardian Frances Campbell. Fanny apparently discovered this, and for her husband to court the enemy of her childhood must have seemed the ultimate betrayal. Miss Campbell, however, knew as well as Fanny did that they came about her money. She had no intention of leaving her estate to Fanny's daughter, and after more than a month of desultory correspondence, Phiquepal and Sylva went back to Paris without seeing her.

In April of the next year Fanny sailed for England, expecting them to join her in London. Instead, she found a letter saying that Sylva was seriously ill and asking that she come at once to Paris. When she got there, she found her fifteen-year-old daughter, as she later described it, languishing from the effects of a sudden growth spurt but already improving. However, she made the staggering discovery that her own papers had somehow been destroyed by fire, "the immediate result of the observation and labour of years being thus annihilated."[27]

It was then that the hostility between Fanny and Phiquepal burst its bounds. He later claimed that her character and sentiments had completely changed and that she announced in violent and insulting language that the three of them were incompatible. That autumn they began their bitter property fight, Fanny looking to the law to return some of her estate to her own ultimate discretion. She got her trustees to issue a deed of retrocession whereby she could sell the Dundee property after Phiquepal's death and without Sylva's consent, and Phiquepal began to cut off that portion of her estate that he controlled absolutely to prevent her from ever using her money again for any of the purposes for which she had used it before she married. The next summer he took Sylva to Cincinnati, where he drew up a deed for property to the value of almost $30,000 and named his adopted son Alexis trustee. One-third of the estate's annual proceeds would be paid out to Phiquepal and one-third to Sylva. Fanny would get her third only if she signed trust deeds guaranteeing that the Dundee and Nashoba estates would pass intact on her death to Sylva. In less than a year, Fanny was reduced to writing from London for a pittance of her own inheritance to live on.[28]

Their Cincinnati lawyer sided with Phiquepal, and Alexis, whose brewery business had undoubtedly been started with Fanny's money, treated his former patroness with studied contempt, refusing to send her money until she agreed to sign the trust documents. Some months later Phiquepal sent her a hundred pounds, though he worried about spoiling her by giving her money before she signed over the property.[29]

In early 1848, Fanny capitulated, signing trust deeds in Paris, Dundee, and London guaranteeing her various properties to Sylva as Phiquepal had demanded—deeds she soon repudiated on the grounds that she had been coerced. According to Fanny, after she signed the final document, Phiquepal threw off the mask, "saying that he had got what he wanted: that he and Sylva were independent of her, and could do without her." She went to Nashoba to live, and by the end of 1849, Phiquepal and Alexis were again talking about cutting her allowance. She claimed that because she refused to register and thereby validate the Nashoba Trust Deed in Shelby County, they stopped her support altogether.[30]

She got a new Cincinnati lawyer, W. Y. Gholson. Though she was "afraid of men, as I have some reason to be," she trusted him and thought "the whole of the paper scaffolding built up against me must fall to the ground if the first step in the ladder be taken away." She spent her second winter at Nashoba in a small cabin she said was so carelessly built that a gust of wind could burst open the door, and the outside dampness crept pitilessly in. The furnishings were spare, her sight was bad, and her memory, she wrote Gholson, was as bad as her sight whenever she thought of Sylva. She wanted to break through the barrier that was rising between them: if she could recover control over her estate, she thought she would also regain her daughter.[31]

In the fall of 1850 she filed a divorce suit in Shelby County and a chancery suit in Cincinnati for the recovery of her estate. She no doubt hoped that her case would set the precedent in Ohio for giving married women control over their own property.[32]

In her account of their marriage, Fanny argued that Phiquepal had been poor, and she had married him mainly out of compassion. The catalogue of his cruelties and her complaints stretched on to almost forty separate items. She had an estate worth $150,000; Phiquepal, on the other hand, had brought nothing into the marriage and had earned nothing during it. Nevertheless, he forced her to live so poorly that she had to borrow. And after 1844, he had begun to alienate their daughter's affections.

Phiquepal retaliated. He wrote Fanny a letter and sent a duplicate to the American consul in Paris, whose support he enlisted against her. In it he struck the pose of compassionate friend. When he read the bill Fanny had drawn up against him, he wrote, what grieved him most was the sight of "that moral malady, that quasi destruction into which I then saw Frances Wright falling." He offered pity for "that disorder of mind whose first dawnings I had perceived many years since . . . I even sympathize with and forgive you, for having again thus failed."[33]

All the rage of a man so long dwarfed by a powerful woman poured onto his page: "Your life was essentially an external life. You loved virtue deeply, but you loved also, and, perhaps even more, grandeur and glory; and in your estimation, unknown, I am sure, to your inmost soul, your husband and child ranked only as mere appendages to your personal existence." He had imposed on himself the sacrifice of attending her lectures but could not impose it on their child. Sylva's education had been the main object of his life, while Fanny had often interrupted that education by her caprice and by the life she led traveling from one land to another, from one hemisphere to another. He called attention to the pain of defending his daughter against her

Phiquepal d'Arusmont and Sylva d'Arusmont

Frances Wright in her last years

own mother, and said the letter was a last, friendly warning. If there had been a hope of placating Fanny, he destroyed it now.

With the familiar bias against a woman who had dared to assert herself, the consul, Robert Walsh, wrote that Fanny would be wisest to abandon her legal proceedings: "Miss d'Arusmont's future welfare and peace of mind depend, in a degree, upon the sensibility, moderation, and discretion of her mother." Both Phiquepal and Walsh's letters were printed and apparently circulated to discredit Fanny.[34]

On January 21, 1851, the circuit court of Shelby County nevertheless found for Fanny on the grounds that her husband had abandoned her despite her unexceptionable conduct. And when Fanny subsequently heard that Sylva had arrived in Cincinnati, her anxiety lifted. There her friends could watch over her, "and her deranged father cannot carry her off, as was my fear, beyond reach even of my enquiries." Five weeks later, though she had heard nothing from Sylva, Fanny still believed she could influence her daughter: "Nothing but the conviction that this [legal] course is calculated to open her eyes to the real character of the tortuous path of intrigue and vain ambition in which she has been involved, by a mad and a bad man, would have moved me to engage in it, or sustained me in pursuing it."[35]

She had yet to suffer her bitterest humiliation. In the middle of March, Sylva came with Phiquepal to Memphis and refused to see her mother alone. A month later, the sheriff's deputy served Fanny a writ in a legal proceeding by which Sylva was trying to take Nashoba. Fanny wrote the sheriff of Shelby County, "My own child (in the hands of wicked men) is the party claiming to oust her mother from her house and lands." Nevertheless she persisted in believing she might yet win Sylva back.[36]

She steamed once more to Cincinnati, and in late July the judge heard arguments preliminary to her chancery suit against her former husband. Judge Robert Warden declared the case a singular one, in which he was called upon "to review the history of two lives . . . that are closing in suffering and sorrow . . . a fearful picture . . . of broken ambition, disappointed hope, and lost happiness." He wondered "what demon it was that turned all this love to hate, and their home into hell." Concluding that Fanny was "aged and infirm," he granted her the allowance she sought, pending completion of her suit to regain her property.[37]

In mid-September Fanny tried once more to win her daughter. She wrote Sylva that her heart was always open to her and asked her to arrange a time and place where they could meet. According to Sylva, the interview lasted five hours, and Sylva told her mother that further meetings were useless. Fanny wrote Gholson in near despair: "The last time we met I fear I was ungracious to you . . . But the past week brought to me, as you know, yet a new anguish, & I had foolishly failed to foresee that such was or could be in store for me. I had hugged the belief that I had previously emptied the last drop of bitterness. I conceived that your unmatched professional ingenuity wd compass for me the recovery of my child by rendering palpable to her intelligence the base trickery & falsehood of the Jesuit who holds her in his toils as an insect in the net of the spider. But this had not to be . . . For me she is lost."[38]

Fanny had just passed her fifty-sixth birthday, and she should have been at the height of her powers. But when Joel Brown, the Cincinnati carpenter, saw her on the street, he thought she looked nearly worn out.

Fanny's hopes for her daughter would never be realized. Though she was in Cincinnati at the time, Sylva did not see her mother in her last illness, and after Phiquepal died on March 23, 1855, Sylva and Alexis turned against each other in yet another fight over property. She became an ardent Christian and referred in her old age to the "infidel trash" in the *Free Enquirer.* She found the moral of Fanny's life in her belief that "the present woman's movement is tempting my sex to man's province to the neglect of its home duties & joys [and] of the rising generation." And in 1874 she testified before a Congressional committee against female suffrage. "As the daughter of Frances Wright, whom the Female Suffragists are pleased to consider as having *opened* the door to their pretensions," Sylva begged the Speaker and the members of the House committee "to *shut* it forever, from the strongest convictions that they can only bring misery and degradation upon the whole sex, and thereby wreck human happiness in America!"[39]

If Fanny's last years were full of pain, she remained a brave and considerable woman, and Joel Brown painted an engaging picture of her as she struck him in the mid-1840s, the least engaging period of her life. She moved into the unfinished house he and his brother were building for her, and Brown worried that she had done so in order to make them work harder. But he soon discovered that she actually slowed them down: she cared less that they finish the job than that they listen to her talk about how to improve the lot of working people. She also insisted that they eat at her table, where Brown said he learned as from a walking encyclopedia.

He was taken aback by how plainly Fanny lived. She moved a charcoal furnace into the house, along with a cot, a few chairs, a table, and a writing desk. She ate crackers and boiled food—a potato or two, an egg, a piece of beef—and drank tea or coffee. Brown's wife thought her the most ignorant housekeeper she had ever seen: she "could not sweep a room and do it correctly, could not pack a trunk properly" when about to start on a journey. Fanny regretted, Brown said, that she had not been taught general housework instead of the "aristocratical noncence" of her childhood. Even the things she did well she seemed to do peculiarly. When she was working on a speech, she would write a few sentences and then walk around whispering to herself to memorize the lines. Whenever Brown saw her on the street, she was whispering to herself.[40]

He thought Fanny the most entertaining "controversalist" he had ever met: she spoke precisely and never repeated herself, and she had decided opinions. No woman should give up her natural rights when she married, Fanny insisted, "not even her person without her consent." The woman should determine how many childen she had, and they should bear her name instead of her husband's. Brown later found that she had been clairvoyant. Within fifty years the United States would be covered with railroads, she predicted, for which farmers and poor workers would ultimately pay. Railroad traffic would center in New York and other large cities and would create scores of millionaires eager to control government at every level.[41]

But Fanny paid a high price psychologically to maintain the apparent self-sufficiency Brown admired, and her restlessness grew. She crossed the Atlantic seven times in her last thirteen years. She went back and forth between London, Manchester, Sheffield, and Dundee. More frequently even than in her thirties, she steamed up and down the Mississippi between Cincinnati and Memphis, and she visited Haiti, according to Brown, at least twice. This restlessness, along with the breakdowns that periodically afflicted her and the delusions of power that infect her late writing, suggest the possibility of manic-depressive illness. At so great a distance in time, and with mere scraps of letters for evidence, one can do no more than speculate on the nature of her problem. But she had always had recurrent bouts of "fever" and depression, and Camilla said that her suffering tended to go to her head. Robert Dale Owen wrote of the "restless and desponding moods to which, though not habitually sad, she was subject." And Fanny herself spoke of wide mood-swings, though she put it philosophically when she wrote that Robert Owen "reconciled me with life, and gave me hopes for the human race as high as my former despair had been deep." After Camilla died, Fanny endured at least three long periods of collapse. The episode in 1847 with G. J. Holyoake was patently an instance of psychosomatic illness, and though he was a biased witness, Phiquepal's testimony to her "disorder of mind" cannot be wholly discounted. Her passionate intensity and her arrogance, the extremes to which she drove herself, and the treasured friendships she destroyed all suggest a woman plagued with what might now be diagnosed as manic-depressive illness. Like many who suffer from that disease she was highly creative, energetic, and stubborn. At the same time, she was abrupt and narcissistic, and found it hard to listen to anyone else. Her low periods were more prolonged and far more severe than those of most people.[42]

Of course in the first half of the nineteenth century, Fanny was not even likely to find intelligent medical attention, much less access to psychiatric help. The standard doctors' remedies were bleeding and cupping, from which many patients died. She was at least spared the peculiar horror of the period that began in the 1850s, when women's nervous illnesses were sometimes treated surgically by removing the uterus, the ovaries, or the clitoris. But the social stigma against mental illness and the ignorance that surrounded it were so intense that it seems likely Fanny simply denied the problem. Given the suffering that periodically afflicted her, her courage and her accomplishments, as well as the insights she wrested from pain, deserved a tribute her generation denied her.[43]

It is also possible that her suffering was primarily the result of social deprivation, its periodic nature corresponding to the rejections she endured. For the world she was born into repeatedly denied the full range of its resources as well as its gratitude to Fanny Wright. She had been blessed with great natural gifts of intelligence, energy, and courage. Her very stature made it seem she was born to command. To these she joined disciplined work, frugal habits, and bounding ambition. Though her claims to selflessness were exaggerated and misleading, she did not look for the ordinary kinds of reward, such as wealth or social standing. She wanted to matter in the life of her times. She wanted to help people improve their lives. She wanted them to look up to her because she deserved their esteem. She wanted, simply, to be great.

But to the world she lived in such ambitions were inappropriate. Her neighbors thought her perverse and ungrateful when she did not give thanks for the comfort to which she was born and the easy, gracious life that was hers for the asking. She could not go to school in any serious fashion with her peers. She could not prepare herself for any profession by means of which people rendered service to their fellows. She could not find a job to test her powers, her perceptions, and her ideas, nor was she welcome among those who aspired to lead society and improve the world.

The guardians of society convinced her that an illegitimate child bore an ineffaceable stigma. She believed they would listen to her only on condition that she live, in apparent harmony and for all her life, with the man who fathered her child. For too long she believed that if that man deserved neither her love nor her respect, self-deception was nevertheless preferable to social disgrace.

And when she violated many of their taboos, these same guardians unleashed their vengeance against her. Their mildest weapon was ostracism. The press called her a whore who threatened the very foundations of society. They teased, ridiculed, gawked in curiosity and amazement. They mobbed her, after a fashion, and when they tired of her, they simply let her drop.

She had, in turn, her share of human weaknesses. In her relentless high-mindedness she must have been a trying companion, and her arrogance became insufferable. She laughed too seldom and talked too much. She lived, for the last twenty years of her life, in something like emotional and intellectual isolation. She tried, it seems, to exorcise the ghosts of the past, and she ended up talking to herself.

But if she had the wound, she also had the bow. She scorned the obvious targets and ranged far beyond most people of her generation to ask how to make life worth the having. Again and again she attacked the hard questions—about money, privilege, and power—and scoffed at those who contented themselves with the old excuses for misery and injustice. She was right in saying that later generations would know that she, and not those who attacked her, spoke for a sane and healthy morality. The issues she raised are vital issues still, while those who mocked her rank among the curiosities of history.

The end was agony and anticlimax. In January 1852, Fanny fell on the ice in Cincinnati and broke her thigh. She went to the Hotel for Invalids and spent two months there in almost constant pain with only a maid to give her a measure of personal attention. Though the trouble of her last years had made her more sensitive to other people and more grateful for their friendship, she had always counted on her self-sufficiency. During the next tortured months, however, she allowed herself to depend on others. Gholson was the most important to her, and he thought she made some progress. At the end of April he wrote her friends at Nashoba that though she would always be a little lame, she was beginning to think again about what ought to be done in Tennessee.[44]

She had a series of young women to help her. Barbara had long since been replaced by Louisa: then came Ann Murray, and then Marie Barrot, and Margaret, whose last name is lost, and Mary Chancy, and finally Anna Spenser. The rhythms of kindly life reached her from Nashoba. Her neighbor Mrs. Howze wrote that the brindle cow had died from a fall on the ice, and that she would have finished Fanny's comfort if it had not been for staying with Burchet, who was ill: "The boys . . . are striving diligently and faithfully to abide by all your good advice to them . . . I do miss your encouraging smiles and advice so much." As if to prove herself impervious to pain, Fanny had a dentist make some twenty-odd visits to fashion her a new set of teeth, and she paid him in old gold.[45]

But the agony persisted. Always a woman of physical courage, Fanny now was tested in the cruelest ways. She asked Gholson to send the first volume of *Uncle Tom's Cabin* because "I am in great anguish and require something to draw me out of my suffering." When the weather changed, it heightened her pain. Sometimes she was brave, and sometimes she was not. In early June she wrote Gholson, "You wd distinguish this morning how completely I am changed in soul yet more than in body. The overtension of the nervous system induced by every species of moral suffering followed by much physical agony seems at times to have made a child of me." She thought if only she could get some sleep, she would feel life return. "A little steady summer, fresh air and the pleasant sound of friendly voices" might yet restore her.[46]

She continued to plan. In September she bought a set of books on Ferdinand and Isabella and ordered Prescott's *History of Mexico*. In late November she took out a year's subscription to the weekly *New York Tribune* and laid in twenty-five bushels of coal. She began, if uncertainly, to think of the holidays.

But on the thirteenth of December, 1852, Fanny faced her death and wrote her will, abandoning what Phiquepal called her "visionary schemes" and leaving the bulk of her property to Sylva, "who has been alienated from me but to whom with said property I give my blessing and forgiveness for the sorrows she has caused her mother." She gave her last kiss to a Cincinnati acquaintance to pass on to her daughter. And so she died, it seems, with dignity.[47]

Fanny's death passed largely unnoticed. Sylva came from New York for the funeral and persuaded Gholson to give her the papers Fanny had willed to him, including work yet unpublished. Complaining that she had hated to hear her mother speak in public, Sylva kept that work to herself and passed it along to her own children with an ambivalence about Fanny that ended in its disappearance. By cutting her official birth date on it, Sylva used her mother's gravestone in Spring Grove Cemetery to perpetuate the myth of legitimacy that Fanny had given so much of her life to maintain. And another monument outside Memphis, Tennessee, was as cavalier with fact and as dubious about its subject. A misplaced road marker for Nashoba has the dates wrong and fails even to mention slavery: "To the south lay this plantation. Here, in 1827, a Scottish spinster heiress named Frances Wright set up a colony whose aims were the enforcement of cooperative living and other advanced sociological experiments. It failed in 1830." Strangers and later generations would have to pay the honor properly due Frances Wright, who had spent herself recklessly in pleading the urgent and commanding justice of the people's cause.

Abbreviations

Notes

Index

———————

Abbreviations

CW	Camilla Wright
CWW	Camilla Wright Whitby
FT	Frances Trollope
FW	Frances (Fanny) Wright D'Arusmont
G Letters	Garnett Letters, Houghton Library, Harvard University
GK Papers	Gholson-Kittredge Papers, Cincinnati Historical Society
HG	Harriet Garnett
JG	Julia Garnett
JGP	Julia Garnett Pertz
RCM	Robina Craig Millar
MJO	Mary Jane Owen
RDO	Robert Dale Owen
W Papers	Theresa Wolfson Papers, Martin P. Catherwood Library, Cornell University

Notes

1. Jane Austen and the Rebel

1. George Jacob Holyoake, *The History of Co-operation* (London: T. F. Unwin, 1908), I, 240–241.

2. FW to Mary Wollstonecraft Shelley, 20 March 1828, *The Life and Letters of Mary Wollstonecraft Shelley*, ed. Mrs. Julian Marshall (1889; reprint New York: Haskell House, 1970), II, 180.

3. FW, "Explanatory Notes on Nashoba," *New Harmony Gazette*, 30 Jan., 6 and 13 Feb. 1828.

4. FW, *England the Civilizer: Her History Developed in Its Principles* (London, 1848), pp. 13, 22.

5. Lafayette to Jeremy Bentham, 10 Nov. 1828, *Works of Jeremy Bentham*, ed. John Bowring (Edinburgh, 1843), XI, 4–5; Horace Traubel, *With Walt Whitman in Camden* (New York: Appleton, 1908), II, 205, 499.

6. *New York Commercial Advertiser*, 12 Jan. 1829; Catharine E. Beecher, *Letters on the Difficulties of Religion* (Hartford, 1836), p. 23.

7. George Eliot, *Middlemarch* (London: J. M. Dent, 1959), I, xiii.

8. J. C. L. de Sismondi to JG, 9 Sept. 1827, G Letters.

9. *Gentleman's Magazine* 68 (March 1798): 259; *Scots Magazine* 60 (May 1798): 364. See also *Biography, Notes, and Political Letters of Frances Wright D'Arusmont* (1844), reprinted in FW, *Life, Letters and Lectures, 1834–1844* (New York: Arno Press, 1972).

10. Camilla Campbell Wright to James Wright, Jr., 11 April 1796, W Papers; George Edward Cokayne, *The Complete Peerage* (London: St. Catherine Press, 1949), XI, 70–71; John Busse, *Mrs. Montagu: Queen of the Blues* (1928; reprint Folcroft, Pa.: Folcroft Library Editions, 1977), p. 4; Elizabeth Montagu, "An Essay on the Writings and Genius of Shakespear, Compared with the Greek and French Dramatic Poets" (New York: Augustus M. Kelley, 1970); Elizabeth Robinson Montagu to unknown addressee, 1791 (#11 MS. 392S), National Library of Scotland. The Theresa Wolfson Papers at Cornell include voluminous notes made by Alice Perkins early in the twentieth century from diaries, letters, and manuscripts in a trunk then owned by Fanny's grandson, the

Reverend William Norman Guthrie. The trunk has since disappeared. Letters cited here in the Theresa Wolfson Papers rarely refer to original manuscript material, but rather to Perkins' notes.

11. James Wright, Jr., to John Pinkerton, 14 Aug. 1795, Pinkerton Papers, National Library of Scotland.

12. *The Reasoner* 7 (Nov. 1849): 325; FW, *Biography,* p. 6.

13. The property James Wright, Jr., inherited from his father, Alexander Wright, was eventually transferred to his uncle, James Wright, Sr., to satisfy his creditors. General Register of Sasines, #RS 3/2286/12–23, Scottish Record Office.

14. In her autobiography Fanny wrote: "Her brother passed his boyhood under the charge of his grand-uncle, Professor Mylne," adding that her "infant sister remained some years at nurse in the neighborhood of her native town." FW, *Biography,* pp. 8–9; Alice Perkins and Theresa Wolfson, however, wrote: "The boy Richard . . . was placed with the family of Watson cousins, children of Duncan Campbell's elder sister . . . The two little girls, however, were taken at once to England." *Frances Wright Free Enquirer: The Study of a Temperament* (New York: Harper Bros., 1939), p. 7. Because of discrepancies or mistakes such as these, I have depended on Perkins and Wolfson only when I have been unable to find other sources. Because Alice Perkins was the last to have access to Fanny Wright's trunk, however, her notes are a crucial source of information. I do not always follow her spelling, her abbreviations, or her punctuation, and in other quotations I sometimes substitute "and" for "&." Translations are not indicated.

15. FW, *Biography,* p. 9; Richard Wright to Miss Watson, 3 June 1809, W Papers.

16. Joel Brown, unpub. memoir of FW, Public Library of Cincinnati and Hamilton County, pp. 19–21. The memoir is written on the backs of stationery with a letterhead dated September 1893. According to a note signed, "Alexis Brown, son of Joel Brown," the memoir was written about 1889. It therefore represents the memory of a very old man, as Joel Brown had first worked for Fanny in 1843, and he is often mistaken.

17. See Sir Duncan Campbell, *Records of Clan Campbell in the Honourable East India Company, 1600–1858* (London: Longmans and Green, 1925), pp. 268–269; William Campbell's will, dated 30 Aug. 1803 and probated 27 May 1805, Public Record Office (PROB 11/1425), London.

18. FW, *Biography,* p. 9.

19. Ibid., p. 8; *Gentleman's Magazine* 79 (Nov. 1809): 1176.

20. Richard Wright to Betsy Watson, 12 June 1809, W Papers; FW, *Biography,* p. 9; Beatrix F. Cresswell, *Dawlish—The Estuary of the Exe and Notes on Chudleigh* (Dawlish and London, 1902), p. 18.

21. Jane Austen, *Sense and Sensibility* (London: Macmillan, 1951), p. 90.

22. Jane Austen, *Pride and Prejudice* (London: J. M. Dent, 1954), p. 1.

23. FW, *Biography,* p. 10.

24. Ibid., p. 15; Austen, *Pride and Prejudice,* p. 49.

25. Henry G. Morgan to the author, 5 Aug. 1977. I am indebted to the late

Mr. Morgan, chairman of the Dawlish Museum Society, for information about Miss Campbell and her neighbors and about Dawlish during this period.

26. W Papers.

27. FW, *Biography*, p. 11.

28. Ibid.

29. Ibid.

30. Richard Wright to Betsy Watson, 25 July 1809, W Papers.

31. FW to Frances Campbell, 1820(?), W Papers.

32. See James Coutts, *A History of the University of Glasgow, 1451–1909* (Glasgow: J. Maclehose, 1909); David Murray, *Memories of the Old College of Glasgow* (Glasgow: Jackson and Wylie, 1927); Douglas Sloan, *The Scottish Enlightenment and the American College Ideal* (New York: Teachers College Press, 1971).

33. Adam Smith to Dr. William Cullen, 20 Sept. 1774, quoted in Sloan, *The Scottish Enlightenment*, p. 32.

34. Frederick Lamb to Lady Melbourne, n.d., quoted in William C. Lehmann, *John Millar of Glasgow, 1735–1801* (Cambridge: Cambridge University Press, 1960), p. 82.

35. Ibid., pp. 376, 387.

36. Quoted in Murray, *Memories of Glasgow*, p. 103; James Mylne to Mr. Watson, 15 July 1815, W Papers.

37. Elizabeth Dawson Fletcher, *The Autobiography of Mrs. Fletcher* (Boston, 1876), p. 344; RCM to FW and CW, 26 July 1818, W Papers.

38. James Mylne to Mr. Watson, 15 July 1815; RCM to FW, 4 Sept. 1816, W Papers.

39. RCM to FW, 28 July 1817, 9 Oct. 1818, W Papers.

40. W Papers.

41. FW, *Biography*, p. 13.

42. FW, *A Few Days in Athens* (Boston, 1850), p. 122.

43. Ibid., p. 40.

44. Ibid., pp. 12, 112.

45. Ibid., pp. 24–25.

46. FW, 23 July 1818, "Commonplace Book," W Papers.

47. John Prebble, *The Highland Clearances* (London: Secker and Warburg, 1963), p. 58.

48. Ibid., pp. 63, 78, 117.

49. Ibid., pp. 71, 109.

50. See *The Life of Robert Owen Written by Himself* (1857; reprint London: Frank Cass, 1967); Frank Podmore, *Robert Owen: A Biography* (London: Hutchinson, 1906); G. D. H. Cole, *The Life of Robert Owen* (London: Ernest Benn, 1925); Margaret Cole, *Robert Owen of New Lanark* (London: Batchworth Press, 1953); J. F. C. Harrison, *Quest for the New Moral World: Robert Owen and the Owenites in Britain and America* (London: Routledge and Kegan Paul, 1969). For the influence of Owen on women and the feminist movement, see Barbara Taylor, *Eve and the New Jerusalem: Socialism and Feminism in the Nineteenth Century* (New York: Pantheon, 1983).

51. Robert Owen, "Observations on the Effect of the Manufacturing System," in his *A New View of Society* (London: Everyman's Library, 1963), pp. 121–122.

52. See Asa Briggs, *The Age of Improvement* (London: Longmans and Green, 1959); Elie Halévy, *The Liberal Awakening, 1815–1830* (London: Ernest Benn, 1949); E. P. Thompson, *The Making of the English Working Class* (London: Penguin Books, 1976).

53. Thompson, *The Making of the English Working Class*, p. 666.

54. FW, *Biography*, p. 14.

55. FW, "Commonplace Book," W Papers.

2. Every Farmer a Cincinnatus

1. FW to HG, 7 July 1826, G Letters; FW, *Views of Society and Manners in America* (1821; reprint Cambridge, Mass.: Harvard University Press, 1963), pp. 7, 8.

2. See George Dangerfield, *The Awakening of American Nationalism, 1815–1828* (New York: Harper and Row, 1965).

3. RCM to FW and CW, 9 Oct. 1818, W Papers; FW, *Views*, p. 12.

4. Ibid., pp. 17–18.

5. FW to James Mylne, n.d., W Papers.

6. RCM to FW, 19 Nov. 1818, W Papers.

7. Elizabeth Dawson Fletcher, *The Autobiography of Mrs. Fletcher* (Boston, 1876), p. 154; RCM to FW, 2 Sept. 1822, W Papers.

8. RCM to FW, 9 Oct. 1818, W Papers.

9. "The Post Goes to the Theater in Old N.Y.," *New York Post*, 1 July 1982.

10. *New York Evening Post*, 20, 22 Feb. 1819.

11. Martha Wilson to Matthew Carey, 1 April 1819, Edward Carey Gardiner Collection, Pennsylvania Historical Society.

12. RCM to FW, 17 April 1819, W Papers.

13. FW, *Altorf* (Philadelphia, 1819).

14. Jefferson to FW, 22 May 1820, *Thomas Jefferson Correspondence*, ed. Worthington C. Ford (Boston, 1916), p. 254.

15. Martha Wilson to Matthew Carey, 1 April 1819; FW to Carey, 1 April 1819, Gardiner Collection.

16. Matthew Carey to FW, 4(?) April 1819, W Papers; FW to Carey, 4 April 1819, Gardiner Collection.

17. FW to Matthew Carey, 22 April 1819, Gardiner Collection. There is no record that *Altorf* was ever published in Scotland, and only one other reference to the possibility that it was considered for publication there.

18. Martha Wilson to Matthew Carey, 6 May 1819, Gardiner Collection.

19. Genesis 3:16. See Rosemary Agonito, *History of Ideas on Women* (New York: G. P. Putnam's Sons, 1977).

20. FW to Jefferson, 27 July 1820, *Thomas Jefferson Correspondence*, ed. Ford, p. 256.

21. RCM to FW, 19 Nov. 1818, 20 March, 17 April, 6 May, 10 July 1819, W Papers.

22. FW, Preface, *Altorf;* RCM to FW, n.d., W Papers.

23. FW to Thomas Abthorpe Cooper, n.d., negative photostat, Elizabeth Myers Autograph Collection, Library of Congress; FW to Matthew Carey, 29 Sept., 6 Oct. 1819, Gardiner Collection.

24. White House Farm is now preserved as the Buccleuch Mansion. See Cecilia Helena Payne-Gaposchkin, Introduction to "The Nashoba Plan for Removing the Evil of Slavery: Letters of Frances and Camilla Wright, 1820–1829," *Harvard Library Bulletin* 23 (Oct. 1975): 221–222; Payne-Gaposchkin, Introduction to *The Garnett Letters* (privately printed, 1979).

25. FW, *Views,* p. 31.

26. Ibid., pp. 37, 38.

27. Ibid., p. 63.

28. JG to J. C. L. de Sismondi, 3 Sept. 1827; FW to HG, n.d., G Letters.

29. FW, *Views,* p. 94.

30. Ibid., pp. 98–99.

31. RCM to FW and CW, n.d., W Papers.

32. FW to Matthew Carey, 4 Jan. 1820, Gardiner Collection; *Aurora General Advertiser,* 14 Jan. 1820; FW to Carey, 18 Jan. 1820, Gardiner Collection.

33. FW to Matthew Carey, 1 Feb. 1820, Gardiner Collection.

34. FW, *Views,* p. 261.

35. FW to JG and HG, 22 Nov. 1820, G Letters.

36. FW, *Views,* p. 267.

37. Ibid., pp. 269–270.

38. FW to JG and HG, 22 Nov. 1820, G Letters.

39. RCM to FW and CW, 28 Jan. 1820, W Papers; RCM to JG and HG, 21 June 1820, G Letters.

40. *National Intelligencer,* 11 Oct. 1820.

41. FW to Frances Campbell, 1820 (?), W Papers.

42. FW to JG and HG, 22 Nov. 1820, G Letters.

43. RCM to FW and CW, 28 Jan. 1820, W Papers; E. P. Thompson, *The Making of the English Working Class* (London: Penguin Books, 1976), p. 768.

44. Elie Halévy, *The Liberal Awakening, 1815–1830* (London: Ernest Benn, 1949), p. 95; FW to JG and HG, Oct. 1820, G Letters.

45. FW, *Views,* pp. 83, 13, 59, 261.

46. Ibid., p. 22.

47. Ibid., p. 201. See also Dangerfield, *The Awakening of American Nationalism,* pp. 72–96.

48. Ibid., pp. 97–140.

49. *The Correspondence of James Fenimore Cooper,* ed. James Fenimore Cooper (New Haven: Yale University Press, 1922), I, 151.

50. FW, *Views,* p. 187.

51. CW to James Mylne, Jr., 6 Feb. 1821, W Papers.

52. *A Letter to William Gifford, Esq., from William Hazlitt, Esq.* (London,

1819), pp. 5–6; *London Literary Gazette* 239 (18 Aug. 1821): 513–515; *Quarterly Review* 27 (April 1822): 72–73.

53. FW to JG and HG, 22 Nov. 1820, G Letters; *Scotsman* 5 (11 Aug. 1821): 249.

54. *North American Review* 5 (Jan. 1822): 15–26.

3. The Reckless Disciple

1. Jeremy Bentham to Richard Rush, 29 July 1821, Bentham MSS., University College, University of London; John Colls Diary, 13–29 Aug. 1821, Additional MSS., British Library.

2. Bentham to Sir Francis Burdett, 23 Sept. 1824, Burdett Collection, Bodleian Library, Oxford University. See *John Stuart Mill: Utilitarianism, On Liberty, Essay on Bentham,* ed. Mary Warnock (Cleveland: Meridian Books, 1970), pp. 78–125.

3. Robert Owen, *The Life of Robert Owen Written by Himself* (1857; reprint New York: A. M. Kelley, 1967), pp. 204–205. See *The Education of John Stuart Mill* (London, 1873).

4. Bentham, "Auto-icon," Bentham MSS., University College.

5. *Works of Jeremy Bentham,* ed. John Bowring (Edinburgh, 1843), X, 583; Colls Diary, 28 Aug. 1821, Add. MSS., British Library.

6. Bentham to Samuel Bentham, 13 April 1822, Bentham MSS., British Library.

7. FW to Lafayette, 16 July 1821, MSS. 304, University of Chicago Libraries.

8. Colls Diary, Add. MSS., British Library; Bentham, *Works,* X, 526.

9. Bentham, *Works,* X, 526.

10. Quoted in André Maurois, *Adrienne: The Life of the Marquise de la Fayette* (New York: McGraw-Hill, 1961), p. 468.

11. See FT, *Paris and the Parisians in 1835* (New York, 1836).

12. Albert Gallatin to FW (draft), 5 Sept. 1821; Lafayette to Gallatin, 26 Sept. 1821, Gallatin Papers, New York Historical Society; RCM to FW, 12 Oct. 1821, W Papers.

13. See Andreas Latzko, *Lafayette: A Life* (New York: Doubleday and Doran, 1936); Etienne Charavay, *Le Général La Fayette, 1757–1834* (Paris, 1898).

14. See René de Chambrun, *Les Prisons des La Fayette* (Librairie Académique Perrin, 1977).

15. Latzko, *Lafayette,* p. 340.

16. See Guillaume de Bertier de Sauvigny, *The Bourbon Restoration* (Philadelphia: University of Pennsylvania Press, 1966).

17. FW to Jeremy Bentham, n.d., *Works,* X, 527.

18. FW to Lafayette, 29 Dec. 1821, MSS. 304, University of Chicago; *Free Enquirer,* 5 Dec. 1829. See Bertier de Sauvigny, *Bourbon Restoration,* pp. 171–173 and 181–186.

19. FW, *Biography . . . of Frances Wright D'Arusmont,* reprinted in *Life, Letters and Lectures, 1834–1844* (New York: Arno Press, 1972), p. 19.

20. FW to Lafayette, 27 Dec. 1821, MSS. 304, University of Chicago.

21. See Jules Cloquet, *Recollections of the Private Life of General Lafayette* (New York, 1836), I, 161–206; *Lady Morgan in France*, ed. Elizabeth Suddaby and P. J. Yarrow (Newcastle upon Tyne: Oriel Press, 1971), pp. 139–145 and 184–194.

22. See Maurois, *Adrienne*, pp. 385–414.

23. FW to Lafayette, 29 Dec. 1821, MSS. 304, University of Chicago.

24. Cloquet, *Recollections of Lafayette*, II, 46.

25. *Views* was also translated into German and Dutch. The first American edition was published in 1821, the second British edition in 1822.

26. FW to Lafayette, 4, 11 Feb. 1822, W Papers.

27. RCM to FW, 31 Dec. 1821, W Papers.

28. FW to Lafayette, 15, 16 Feb., 15 March 1822, W Papers; Bentham to Samuel Bentham, 13 April 1822, Bentham MSS., British Library.

29. Anthony Trollope, *An Autobiography* (New York, 1883), pp. 19–20. See also Thomas Adolphus Trollope, *What I Remember* (New York, 1888); Eileen Bigland, *The Indomitable Mrs. Trollope* (London: Barrie and Jenkins, 1970).

30. FW to Lafayette, 20, 26 Feb. 1822, W Papers; General Guglielmo Pepe, *Memoirs of General Pepe* (London, 1846), III, 236.

31. FW to Lafayette, 16, 24 Feb. 1822, W Papers.

32. FW to Lafayette, 13, 15 Feb. 1822, W Papers.

33. FW to Lafayette, 4, 15, 23 March 1822, W Papers.

34. FW to Lafayette, 14 July 1822; RCM to FW, 2 Sept. 1822, W Papers.

35. FW to Lafayette, 20 Feb., 4 March 1822, W Papers.

36. FW, "To the Reader," *Altorf* (London, 1822).

37. Benjamin Flower to FW, 21 Dec. 1821, W Papers; FW, *Views of Society and Manners in America*, 2nd ed. (London, 1822), pp. 474–478, 90–91.

38. *Letters of Lafayette and Jefferson*, ed. Gilbert Chinard (Baltimore: Johns Hopkins University Press, 1929), pp. 422–423; Jefferson's Commonplace Book (Reel 5), Thomas Jefferson Papers, Library of Congress; *Letters of Lafayette and Jefferson*, p. 416.

39. FW to Lafayette, 20 Feb. 1822, W Papers.

40. FW, *A Few Days in Athens* (Boston, 1850), p. 56. The edition published in 1822 has twelve chapters. In 1826 Fanny wrote four additional chapters which were published in the *New Harmony Gazette*. She subsequently thought better of the four chapters and was angry when they were included in a later edition. Every subsequent edition of *A Few Days* has included the extra chapters, which are very different in tone and purpose from the original work.

41. FW, "To the Reader," *Altorf*; HG to JGP, 27 Jan. 1828, G Letters.

42. RCM to CW, 29 March 1822; FW to Lafayette, 15 March 1822, W Papers. Colls Diary, Add. MSS., British Library.

43. CW to James Mylne, Jr., 17 Dec. 1822, W Papers.

44. FW to Lafayette, spring-summer 1822, MSS. 304, University of Chicago; FW to Lafayette, Perkins' notes, W Papers.

45. FW to James Mylne, n.d. (740, f. 48v), National Library of Scotland; FW to Lafayette, n.d., W Papers.

46. FW to Lafayette, 14, 15 July 1822; JG to Lafayette, 19 July 1822, W Papers.

47. *Memoirs of General Pepe*, III, 239–240.

48. CW to James Mylne, Jr., 3 March 1823, W Papers.

49. FW, *Biography*, p. 19. See Bertier de Sauvigny, *The Bourbon Restoration*, pp. 186–193.

50. RCM to FW and CW, 16 March 1823, W Papers.

51. Lafayette to FW, May-June 1823(?), MSS. 304, University of Chicago; FW to Lafayette, n.d., W Papers.

52. FW to CW and RCM, 24 May 1824, W Papers.

53. Dupont de Nemours to FW and CW, 4, 6 April 1824, MSS. 304, University of Chicago. See Vincent Nolte, *Fifty Years in Both Hemispheres* (1854; reprint Freeport, N.Y.: Books for Libraries Press, 1972), p. 308.

54. Colls Diary, Add. MSS., British Library; FW to JG, 1 May 1824, G Letters.

55. FW to CW and RCM, 20, 24 May 1824, W Papers.

56. FW to CW and RCM, 24 May 1824, W Papers.

57. Ibid.

58. Seven years later Lafayette was still attracted to young women. In 1831 James Fenimore Cooper wrote Charles Wilkes: "It is my private opinion that the old man has been a good deal hunted this winter by sundry elderly ladies, who would fain attach the shreds of their charms to his great name, but his tastes are as juvenile as at twenty." (27 April 1831) *The Letters and Journals of James Fenimore Cooper*, ed. James Franklin Beard (Cambridge, Mass.: Harvard University Press, 1960), II, 72.

59. FW to CW and RCM, 24 May 1824; Lafayette to FW, 27 May 1824, W Papers. I have found no other references to a promise Lafayette made his wife as she lay dying.

60. FW to CW and RCM, 24 May 1824, W Papers.

61. FW to CW and RCM, 10 June 1824, W Papers.

62. Ibid.

63. FW to Garnier Pagès, 11 June 1824, microfilm copy, Louis Gottschalk Papers, University of Chicago.

64. CW to James Mylne, Jr., 20 July 1824, W Papers; Lafayette to Mme. Charles de Lasteyrie, 13 July 1824, microfilm copy, Gottschalk Papers.

65. Lafayette to JG and HG, 14 Aug. 1824, Dean Collection, Cornell University Libraries; Lafayette to Pagès, 12 Aug. 1824, microfilm copy, Gottschalk Papers.

4. The Lady Unattended by a Male Protector

1. See Edgar Ewing Brandon, ed., *Lafayette: Guest of the Nation* (Oxford, Ohio: Oxford Historical Press, 1950); Brandon, ed., *A Pilgrimage of Liberty* (Athens, Ohio: The Lawhead Press, 1944); J. Bennett Nolan, *Lafayette in America Day by Day* (Baltimore: Johns Hopkins University Press, 1934); Auguste Levasseur, *Lafayette in America in 1824 and 1825* (Philadelphia, 1829).

2. Brandon, *Guest of the Nation*, I, 36–38.

3. Washington *National Journal*, 16 Oct. 1824.

4. CW to James Mylne, Jr., 23 Sept. 1824, W Papers.

5. Brandon, *Guest of the Nation,* I, 204–208.

6. *New York Statesman,* 9 Sept. 1824.

7. Eleanor Parke Custis Lewis to Elizabeth Bordley Gibson, 15 Feb. 1825, MS. Collection, Mount Vernon Ladies' Association. See Donald Jackson, "George Washington's Beautiful Nelly," *American Heritage* 28 (Feb. 1977), 80–85.

8. Lafayette to Garnier Pagès, 14 Sept. 1824 (misdated Nov. 14), microfilm copy, Louis Gottschalk Papers, University of Chicago; *Letters of Lafayette and Jefferson,* ed. Gilbert Chinard (Baltimore: Johns Hopkins University Press, 1929), pp. 422–424.

9. Richard Peters to Nicholas Biddle, 30 Sept. 1824, microfilm copy, Nicholas Biddle Papers, Library of Congress.

10. FW to JG and HG, 12 Nov. 1824, G Letters.

11. Lafayette to his daughters, 10 Oct. 1824, Dean Collection, Cornell University Libraries; Auguste Levasseur to Pagès, 22 May 1825, microfilm copy, Gottschalk Papers.

12. See *Daily National Intelligencer* and *Daily National Journal,* 13–19 Oct. 1824.

13. Lafayette to Mrs. Eliza Custis, 20 Oct. 1824, Eliza Custis–Lafayette Correspondence (MS. 2408), Maryland Historical Society.

14. E. P. C. Lewis to E. B. Gibson, 22 Oct., 22 Nov. 1824, MS. Collection, Mount Vernon; Bernhard, Duke of Saxe-Weimar-Eisenach, *Travels through North America, during the Years 1825 and 1826* (Philadelphia, 1828), I, 41.

15. FW, *Views of Society and Manners in America* (1821; reprint Cambridge, Mass.: Harvard University Press, 1963), p. 219. See Barbara Welter, "The Cult of True Womanhood: 1820–1860," *American Quarterly* 18 (1966): 151–174; Barbara J. Berg, *The Remembered Gate: Origins of American Feminism* (New York: Oxford University Press, 1978), pp. 75–94.

16. FW to JG and HG, 30 Oct. 1824, G Letters.

17. FW to JG and HG, 12 Nov. 1824, G Letters; Lafayette to his daughters, 27 Oct. 1824, Dean Collection.

18. FW to JG and HG, 12 Nov. 1824, G Letters.

19. See Fawn Brodie, *Thomas Jefferson: An Intimate History* (New York: Bantam Books, 1975).

20. Jefferson to Edward Coles, 25 Aug. 1812, quoted in Brodie, *Thomas Jefferson,* p. 585; FW to JG and HG, 12 Nov. 1824, G Letters; *Notes on Virginia,* from *The Life and Selected Writings of Thomas Jefferson,* ed. Adrienne Koch and William Peden (New York: Modern Library, 1944), p. 256.

21. Brodie, *Thomas Jefferson,* p. 652; FW to M. J. Randolph, 4 Dec. 1824, Jefferson Papers, Library of Congress. On November 12 Lafayette left for Montpelier, James and Dolley Madison's home, but Camilla had caught a cold that kept her and Fanny at Monticello some days longer. The Madisons expected the Wrights as well, but Fanny wrote Dolley Madison that the lateness of the season forced them to cross the mountains to Washington as quickly as possible. FW to Dolley Madison, 4 Dec. 1824, Lafayette MSS., Lilly Library, Indiana University.

22. FW and CW to JG and HG, 21 Dec. 1824, G Letters; E. P. C. Lewis to E. B. Gibson, 15 Feb. 1824, MS. Collection, Mount Vernon; FW, *Biography . . . of Frances Wright D'Arusmont*, reprinted in *Life, Letters and Lectures, 1834–1844* (New York: Arno Press, 1972), p. 24; FT, *Domestic Manners of the Americans* (1832; reprint Gloucester, Mass.: Peter Smith, 1974), p. 226; FW, *Course of Popular Lectures II* (Philadelphia, 1836), p. 39.

23. Paul I. Wellman, *The House Divides: The Age of Jackson and Lincoln, from the War of 1812 to the Civil War* (Garden City, N.Y.: Doubleday, 1966), pp. 73–74. See also George Dangerfield, *The Awakening of American Nationalism, 1815–1828* (New York: Harper and Row, 1965), pp. 212–230.

24. FW to Dolley Madison, 23 Feb. 1825, Lafayette MSS., Lilly Library; quoted in Margaret Cole, *Robert Owen of New Lanark* (London: Batchworth Press, 1953), p. 96.

25. Ibid., p. 137.

26. *Daily National Journal*, 1 March 1825.

27. FW to JG, 8 June 1825, G Letters.

28. FW to JG and HG, (?) Jan. 1825; FW to JG, 8 June 1825, G Letters.

29. See Karl J. R. Arndt, *George Rapp's Harmony Society, 1785–1847* (Rutherford, N.J.: Fairleigh Dickinson University Press, 1972); Donald E. Pitzer and Josephine M. Elliott, "New Harmony's First Utopians," *Indiana Magazine of History* 75 (Sept. 1979): 225–300.

30. George B. Lockwood, *The New Harmony Movement* (1905; reprint New York: Dover, 1971), p. 27.

31. *The Diary of William Owen*, Indiana Historical Society Publications, vol. 4, no. 1 (Indianapolis: Indiana Historical Society, 1906), p. 128.

32. RDO, *Threading My Way* (1874; reprint New York: A. M. Kelley, 1967), p. 240. For Owen's financial commitment to Rapp see Arthur E. Bestor, *Backwoods Utopias: The Sectarian and Owenite Phases of Communitarian Socialism in America, 1663–1829* (Philadelphia: University of Pennsylvania Press, 1950), p. 180 (n. 74).

33. *Diary of William Owen*, p. 128; *The Diaries of Donald MacDonald, 1824–1826*, Indiana Historical Society Publications, vol. 14, no. 2 (Indianapolis: Indiana Historical Society, 1942), p. 246; FW to JG, 8 June 1825, G Letters.

34. CW to JG, 10 Jan. 1826, G Letters. See George Flower, *The History of the English Settlement in Edwards County, Illinois* (Chicago, 1882).

35. Mrs. Pickering to Edward Flower, 20 Aug. 1825, George Flower Papers, Chicago Historical Society; *Diary of William Owen*, p. 130; Bestor, *Backwoods Utopias*, pp. 219–220.

36. FW to JG and HG, 12 April 1825, G Letters.

37. Quoted in Brandon, *A Pilgrimage of Liberty*, p. 173; FW to JG and HG, 12 April 1825, G Letters.

38. FW to JG, 8 June 1825, G Letters.

39. FW to JG and HG, 12 April 1825, G Letters.

40. Quoted in Brandon, *A Pilgrimage of Liberty*, p. 210; FW to JG and HG, 12 April 1825, G Letters.

41. FW to JG, 8 June 1825, G Letters.

42. FW to JG, 1 Dec. 1825, G Letters.

43. Lockwood, *The New Harmony Movement*, p. 83.

44. FW to JG, 8 June 1825, G Letters.

45. Ibid. See also FW to Mme. Dupont (?), 26 Dec. 1825, pub. in *Le Globe* 4 (23 Jan. 1827): 369–370.

46. FW to JG, 8 June 1825, G Letters.

47. FW, *Biography*, pp. 22–29. Though Fanny wrote these pages almost twenty years later, they remain a fair statement of her assumptions in 1825.

48. FW to JG, 8 June 1825, G Letters.

49. Chase C. Mooney, *Slavery in Tennessee* (Bloomington: Indiana University Press, 1957), p. 69; FW to JG, 8 June 1825, G Letters.

50. FW, *Biography*, pp. 25–26.

51. FW to JG, 8 June 1825, G Letters.

52. Ibid.; CW to JG and HG, 11 June 1825, G Letters.

53. Ibid.; FW to JG, 8 June 1825; CW to JG and HG, 9 July 1825, G Letters.

54. FW to JG, 8 June 1825, G Letters.

55. *Diaries of Donald MacDonald*, p. 309; FW to JG, 8 June 1825, G Letters.

56. Lafayette to Garnier Pagès, 24 July 1825, microfilm copy, Gottschalk Papers; Lafayette to JG, 16 March 1826, Benjamin Franklin Collection, Yale University Library.

57. "Proposal for the Gradual Abolition of Slavery in the United States, Without Danger of Loss to the Citizens of the South," *New Harmony Gazette*, 1 Oct. 1825.

58. George Flower to Edward Flower, 22 Jan. 1826, Flower Papers.

59. *The Papers of Henry Clay*, ed. James F. Hopkins (Lexington: University of Kentucky Press, 1972), IV, 557; Lafayette to FW, 26 Aug. 1825, W Papers; *Correspondence of Andrew Jackson*, ed. John Bassett (Washington, D.C.: Carnegie Institution of Washington, 1926–1935), III, 290.

60. Lafayette to Garnier Pagès, 24 July 1825, microfilm copy, Gottschalk Papers.

61. FW to JG, 8 June 1825, G Letters.

62. E. P. C. Lewis to E. B. Gibson, 2 Oct. 1825, MS. Collection, Mount Vernon; FW to JG, 1 Dec. 1825, G Letters.

5. Nashoba and New Harmony

1. *The Writings of Thomas Jefferson*, ed. Paul Leicester Ford (New York, 1895), X, 343; CW to JG, 10 Jan. 1826, G Letters; George Flower to Edward Flower, 22 Jan. 1826, George Flower Papers, Chicago Historical Society.

2. George Flower, *History of the English Settlement in Edwards County, Illinois* (Chicago, 1882), p. 57. George and Jane Flower were finally divorced in Illinois on Jan. 15, 1836. *Laws of the State of Illinois, Passed by the Ninth General Assembly, at Their Second Session* (Vandalia, 1836), pp. 259–260. George and Eliza Andrews Flower were then married a second time on 18 March 1836, by which time they had had their twelfth and last child. I am indebted for these facts to Pauline Meyer of Edwardsville, Illinois.

3. George Flower to Frederick Rapp, 24 Oct. 1825, Arndt Archives, Worcester, Massachusetts. Alice Perkins described a book in the Guthrie trunk, which had sheets the size of legal paper and was called the Nashoba Book (W Papers). Its first entry was 8 Oct. 1825: "Frances Wright and George Flower arrived at Memphis by way of Nashville in search of land." According to Perkins, the entries say they left on Oct. 12 for Nashville, returning again on Nov. 18 to purchase 320 acres and contract for the building of two log cabins. The entry for Dec. 10 is "On or about this date George Flower left Memphis for Illinois." The Nashoba Book is lost with the trunk, but at least one of these dates conflicts with another apparently reliable source.

4. FW to JG, 1 Dec. 1825, G Letters; G. Flower to F. Rapp, 24 Oct. 1825, Arndt Archives.

5. FW to Mme. Dupont (?), 26 Dec. 1825, pub. in *Le Globe* 4 (23 Jan. 1827): 369–370; FW to JG, 30 Oct. 1824, G Letters.

6. CW to JG, 10 Jan. 1826, G Letters; Richard Flower to Edward Flower, 1 Dec. 1825, Flower Papers. The transaction was formally registered 11 Feb. 1826, Shelby County Register Office, Book B #405/6.

7. FW to Benjamin Lundy, 7 Nov. 1825, pub. in *Genius of Universal Emancipation*, 17 Dec. 1825.

8. G. Flower to F. Rapp, 24 Oct. 1825, Arndt Archives; Richard Flower to Edward Flower, 1 Dec. 1825, Flower Papers.

9. Lafayette to FW, 26 Aug. 1825, W Papers; *The Writings of Thomas Jefferson*, X, 343–345.

10. Lafayette to FW, 26 Aug. 1825, W Papers; *The Writings of James Madison*, ed. Gaillard Hunt (New York: G. P. Putnam's Sons, 1900–1910), IX, 224–229.

11. G. Flower to F. Rapp, 24 Oct. 1825, Arndt Archives; FW to Jeremiah Thompson, 9 Dec. 1825, W Papers.

12. *Genius of Universal Emancipation*, 10, 17 Dec. 1825; FW to Benjamin Lundy, 10 Jan. 1826, pub. in *Genius*, 12 Feb. 1826.

13. CW to JG, 10 Jan. 1826; FW to JG and HG, 20 June 1826, G Letters. Lafayette to JG and HG, 11 April 1826, Benjamin Franklin Collection, Yale University Library. See also Vincent Nolte, *Fifty Years in Both Hemispheres* (1854; reprint Freeport, N.Y.: Books for Libraries Press, 1972), pp. 325–342.

14. FW to JG, 1 Dec. 1825, G Letters.

15. See James E. Roper, "Marcus Winchester and the Earliest Years of Memphis," *Tennessee Historical Quarterly* 21 (1962): 326–351.

16. Ibid., p. 344.

17. RDO, *Threading My Way* (1874; reprint New York: A. M. Kelley, 1967), p. 301; FW to JG, 11 April 1826, G Letters. See James Richardson to RDO, 6, 17 May 1828, pub. in *New Harmony Gazette*, 4, 25 June 1828.

18. FW to Mme. Dupont (?), 26 Dec. 1825, pub. in *Le Globe* 4 (23 Jan. 1827): 369–370. See also Cecilia Payne-Gaposchkin, "The Nashoba Plan for Removing the Evil of Slavery: Letters of Frances and Camilla Wright, 1820–1829," *Harvard Library Bulletin* 23 (July 1975): 221–251; 23 (Oct. 1975): 429–461.

19. G. Flower to Edward Flower, 22 Jan. 1826; Mary Catherine Ronalds to Edward Flower, 15 Feb. 1826, Flower Papers.

20. Charles Wilkes to Lafayette, 30 Sept. 1826, Dean Collection, Cornell University Libraries; CW to JG, 10 Jan. 1826, G Letters.

21. See Arthur Bestor, *Backwoods Utopias: Sectarian and Owenite Phases of Communitarian Socialism in America, 1663–1829* (Philadelphia: University of Pennsylvania Press, 1950), pp. 160–201; J. F. C. Harrison, *Quest for the New Moral World: Robert Owen and the Owenites in Britain and America* (New York: Scribner, 1969).

22. George B. Lockwood, *The New Harmony Movement* (1905; reprint New York: Dover, 1971), pp. 94–97; Thomas Pears and Sarah Pears, *New Harmony: An Adventure in Happiness,* ed. Thomas Clinton Pears, Jr., (1933; reprint Clifton, N.J.: A. M. Kelley, 1973), p. 24.

23. William Owen to his father, 16 Dec. 1825, Robert Owen Papers, Cooperative Union, Manchester, England.

24. Richard Flower to Edward Flower, 1 Dec. 1825, Flower Papers; William Pelham to his son, 7 Sept. 1825, *New Harmony as Seen by Participants and Travellers,* pt. I (Philadelphia: Porcupine Press, 1975), n.p.; Pears and Pears, *New Harmony,* p. 35.

25. Bestor, *Backwoods Utopias,* pp. 120 (n. 92), 165.

26. CW to JG, 10 Jan. 1826, G Letters.

27. FW to JG, 11 April, 1826, G Letters; F Rapp to G Flower, 15 Dec. 1825, Arndt Archives.

28. See G. Flower to Lundy, 25 Aug. 1826, pub. in *Genius,* 30 Sept. 1826.

29. FW to JG, 11 April 1826, G Letters.

30. FW to F. Rapp, 4 March 1826; F. Rapp to FW, 14 April 1826, Series II— Accounts, Old Economy, Pennsylvania; FW to Lafayette, 30 March 1826, cited in Lafayette to FW, 27 July 1826, W Papers; Lafayette to JG, 19 June 1826, Benjamin Franklin Collection, Yale University Library.

31. FW to JG, 11 April 1826; RCM to JG, 2 Sept. 1826, G Letters; Jeremiah Thompson to FW, (?) 1826, W Papers.

32. FW to Lundy, 3 May 1826, pub. in *Genius,* 10 June 1826; RCM to JG, 2 Sept. 1826, G Letters.

33. FW to Lundy, 3 May 1826, pub. in *Genius,* 10 June 1826.

34. G. Flower to Lundy, 12 June 1826, pub. in *Genius,* 17 July 1826.

35. *Diaries of Donald MacDonald,* Indiana Historical Society Publications, vol. 14, no. 2 (Indianapolis: Indiana Historical Society, 1942), p. 341; *Genius,* 29 April 1826. See also Bernhard, Duke of Saxe-Weimar-Eisenach, *Reise Sr. Hoheit des Herzogs Bernhard zu Sachsen-Weimar-Eisenach durch Nord-Amerika in den Jahren 1825 und 1826* (Weimar, 1828), p. 140.

36. Lafayette to JG, 19 June 1826, Franklin Collection.

37. FW to JG and HG, 20 June, 7 July 1826; RCM to JG, 2 June 1827, G Letters.

38. *New Harmony Gazette,* 22 March 1826.

39. FW to JG and HG, 20 June 1826, G Letters; Maclure to Fretageot, 16

June 1826, MSS., Workingmen's Institute, New Harmony, Ind. See also Arthur Bestor, ed., *Education and Reform at New Harmony: Correspondence of William Maclure and Marie Duclos Fretageot*, Indiana Historical Society Publications, vol. 15, no. 3 (Indianapolis: Indiana Historical Society, 1948), pp. 285–417.

40. See William Maclure, *Opinions on Various Subjects* (1838; reprint New York: A. M. Kelley, 1971); Samuel G. Morton, *A Memoir of William Maclure, Esq.* (Philadelphia, 1844); Bestor, *Backwoods Utopias*, p. 146–159; "A Short Expose of the 'Improved Pestalozzian System of Education,' as Communicated by Mr. M'Clure to Silliman's Journal," *New Harmony Gazette*, 15 Feb. 1826; *American Journal of Science and Arts* 9 (June 1825): 163–164.

41. Maclure to Fretageot, 15 July 1825, 25 Aug. 1824, MSS., Workingmen's Institute.

42. Maclure to Fretageot, 11 Aug. 1826, MSS., Workingmen's Institute.

43. *New Harmony Gazette*, 17 May 1826. See also Bestor, *Backwoods Utopias*, pp. 182–201.

44. Bernhard, Duke of Saxe-Weimar-Eisenach, *Travels through North America, during the Years 1825 and 1826* (Philadelphia, 1828), II, 106–123.

45. CW to JG, 20 Aug. 1826, G Letters; Paul Brown, *Twelve Months in New Harmony* (Cincinnati, 1827), p. 118. It is uncertain when Fanny went to New Harmony or how long she stayed, as the primary sources conflict. According to Alice Perkins' notes from the Nashoba Book, Camilla and the three Flower children left Nashoba for Albion, Illinois, on April 10, and Camilla returned on April 30, while Fanny left for New Harmony on May 8 and returned on June 21. But none of Fanny's letters to the Garnetts suggests that Camilla left Nashoba at all, and every authenticated letter indicates that Fanny's visit to New Harmony was after mid-June and was much shorter than six weeks. Mrs. Perkins' notes must be in error.

46. Donald E. Pitzer and Josephine M. Elliott, eds., *New Harmony's Fourth of July Tradition* (New Harmony, Ind.: Raintree Books, 1976), pp. 9–13.

47. Quoted in CW to JG, 8 Dec. 1826, G Letters.

48. FW to JG and HG, 7 July 1826, G Letters.

49. CW to JG, 20 Aug. 1826, G Letters.

50. CW to HG, 12 Nov. 1826, G Letters.

51. CW to JG, 8 Dec. 1826, G Letters.

52. Flower to FW, 3 Oct. 1827, quoted in A. J. G. Perkins and Theresa Wolfson, *Frances Wright, Free Enquirer: The Study of a Temperament* (New York: Harper Bros., 1939), p. 156.

53. FT to HG, 7 Dec. 1828, G Letters.

54. Flower, *History of the English Settlement in Edwards County*, p. 276. A year later RCM wrote asking why Mrs. Flower had left her husband and whether she was likely to return (17 Jan. 1828, W Papers).

55. Maclure to Fretageot, 19 Dec. 1826, MSS., Workingmen's Institute.

56. Maclure to Fretageot, 21, 29, 30 Aug. 1826, MSS., Workingmen's Institute.

57. Fretageot to Maclure, 17 Jan. 1827, MSS., Workingmen's Institute.

58. *New Harmony Gazette*, 29 March 1826. The letter is signed "James" and datelined Memphis.

59. FW, *A Few Days in Athens* (Boston, 1850), pp. 153–213.

60. Ibid., p. 173.

61. FW, "Deed of the Lands of Nashoba, West Tennessee," MSS., Workingmen's Institute.

62. Maclure to Fretageot, 24 Feb. 1827, MSS., Workingmen's Institute.

63. *Robert Dale Owen's Travel Journal, 1827*, ed. Josephine M. Elliott, Indiana Historical Society Publications, vol. 25, no. 4 (Indianapolis: Indiana Historical Society, 1977), p. 23.

64. "Communication from the Trustees of Nashoba," *New Harmony Gazette*, 28 Feb. 1827.

65. *New Harmony Gazette*, 26 July 1826, 28 March 1827.

66. *Owen's Travel Journal*, p. 19.

67. J. C. L. de Sismondi to HG, 29 April 1827, G Letters.

68. *Owen's Travel Journal*, pp. 23–25.

69. Ibid., pp. 25–28; RDO to CW, 29 May 1827, W Papers.

70. *Owen's Travel Journal*, pp. 30–31. See also Grant Foreman, "Our Indian Ambassadors to Europe," *Missouri Historical Society Collections* 5 (1928): 109–128.

6. Cooperation Has Well Nigh Killed Us All

1. *Robert Dale Owen's Travel Journal, 1827*, ed. Josephine M. Elliott, Indiana Historical Society Publications, vol. 25, no. 4 (Indianapolis: Indiana Historical Society, 1977), pp. 33–34; Mary Shelley to FW, 12 Sept. 1827, G Letters.

2. *Genius of Universal Emancipation*, 18 Aug. 1827.

3. Ibid., 10 Nov. 1827; A. J. G. Perkins and Theresa Wolfson, *Frances Wright, Free Enquirer: The Study of a Temperament* (New York: Harper Bros., 1939), p. 171.

4. Nashoba Book, W Papers. Perkins and Wolfson include these passages in their account of what Benjamin Lundy published. They are mistaken.

5. Ibid.

6. George Flower to Lundy, 12 June 1826, pub. in *Genius*, 17 July 1826.

7. RDO, *Threading My Way* (1874; reprint New York: A. M. Kelley, 1967), p. 303. See Janet S. Hermann, *The Pursuit of a Dream* (New York: Oxford University Press, 1981).

8. Two decades later Fanny wrote of an "intriguing individual" who, in her absence, "had disorganized everything on the estate, and effected the removal of persons of confidence." Unless the reference is to Eliza Flower, the person in question must be James Richardson, but nothing about the description fits what we know happened at the time. FW, *Biography . . . of Frances Wright D'Arusmont*, reprinted in *Life, Letters and Lectures, 1834–1844* (New York: Arno Press, 1972), p. 31.

9. FW to JG and HG, 18 Aug. 1827, G Letters.

10. James Mylne to JG, 12 Aug. 1827, G Letters.

11. CW to Charles Wilkes, 13 Sept. 1827, W Papers.

12. FW to JG and HG, 25 July 1827; CW to JG and HG, 6 July 1827, G Letters.

13. *Owen's Travel Journal*, pp. 34–35; Mary Garnett to JG and Fanny Garnett, n.d., G Letters.

14. *Owen's Travel Journal*, pp. 36–43.

15. Ibid., pp. 38, 40, 42; RDO, "An Earnest Sowing of Wild Oats," *Atlantic Monthly*, July 1874, pp. 74–75; RDO, *Threading My Way*, p. 299.

16. FW to James Richardson, 18 Aug. 1827, W Papers; FW to JG and HG, 17, 18, 30 Aug., 1 Sept. 1827, G Letters.

17. FW to Richardson, 18 Aug. 1827, W Papers.

18. James Mylne to JG, 12 Aug. 1827, G Letters.

19. Wilkes to Lafayette, 27 June 1827, Dean Collection, Cornell University Libraries; Wilkes to CW, 15 Aug. 1827, W Papers.

20. Wilkes to JGP, 15 Oct. 1827, G Letters; Wilkes to Lafayette, 27 Feb. 1828, Dean Collection.

21. FW to Richardson, 18 Aug. 1827, W Papers.

22. FW to HG, 17 Aug. 1827, G Letters.

23. JG to J. C. L. de Sismondi, 3 Sept. 1827; FT to HG, 7 Dec. 1828, G Letters.

24. RDO to FW, 25 Aug. 1827, MSS. 304, University of Chicago; *The Life and Letters of Mary Wollstonecraft Shelley*, ed. Mrs. Julian Marshall (1889; reprint New York: Haskell House, 1970), II, 168–171.

25. Mary Shelley to FW, 12 Sept. 1827, G Letters.

26. *Letters of Mary Shelley*, II, 172–175; Mary Shelley to RDO, 9 Nov. 1828 (probably misdated: should be 1827), Dreer Collection, Pennsylvania Historical Society; FW to HG, 20 March 1828, G Letters.

27. FW to JG, 1 Sept. 1827; J. C. L. de Sismondi to JG, 9 Sept. 1827, G Letters.

28. The Theresa Wolfson Papers include a torn copy of this printed letter in an envelope addressed "Professor Mylne" and postmarked 28 Nov. 1827; FW to Sismondi, (?) Sept. 1827, G Letters.

29. RDO to FW, 6 Sept. 1827, W Papers; FW to Sismondi, (?) Sept. 1827, G Letters.

30. FT to JG, 17 May 1827; FT to JGP, 7 Oct. 1827, G Letters; Anthony Trollope, *An Autobiography* (New York, 1883), p. 23.

31. FW to RDO, 2 Oct. 1827, Dreer Collection; quoted in FW to JGP, 7 Oct. 1827, G Letters. Dr. Cecilia Payne-Gaposchkin concluded that the Frenchman to whom Fanny wrote was Henri Dutrone.

32. FW to HG, 8 Oct. 1827, G Letters; FW to Emily Ronalds, 16 Dec. 1827, C. E. French Papers, Massachusetts Historical Society; FW to RDO, 2 Oct. 1827, Dreer Collection; FT to JGP, 25 Nov. 1831, G Letters.

33. FW and FT to JGP, 26 Dec. 1827; FW to HG, 20 March 1828, G Letters.

34. FW to Emily Ronalds, 16 Dec. 1827, C. E. French Papers; FW to Jeremy Bentham, 3 Nov. 1827, Bentham MSS., British Library. Emily Sunstein, who is writing a biography of Mary Shelley, told me about the lock of hair.

35. FT to HG, 7 Dec. 1828, G Letters; FW, "Explanatory Notes on Nashoba,"

New Harmony Gazette, 30 Jan., 6, 13 Feb. 1828; published, in an attempt to discredit her, in *Fanny Wright Unmasked by Her Own Pen* (New York, 1830).

36. FT, *Domestic Manners of the Americans* (1832; reprint Gloucester, Mass.: Peter Smith, 1974), pp. 3–5; FW to JGP, 26 Dec. 1827, G Letters.

37. FT to HG, 7 Dec. 1828, G Letters; CW, 15 Dec. 1827, Nashoba Book, W Papers. The Shelby County Court records show that Whitby did not renounce his legal right to Camilla's modest fortune until after Fanny's return, for on March 1, 1828, he made Camilla's fortune over to Robert Dale Owen (Gholson-Kittredge Papers, Cincinnati Historical Society). Yet on Feb. 24, 1828, Camilla wrote Robert Jennings that her property remained under her own control (W Papers). Perhaps the discrepancy in dates can be explained by a simple lag in the legal process.

38. Maclure to Fretageot, 31 Dec. 1827, Chamberlain Collection, Boston Public Library.

39. FT, *Domestic Manners*, pp. 18–28.

40. Ibid., pp. 27–28; Sismondi to JG, 9 Sept. 1827, G Letters.

41. FT, *Domestic Manners*, pp. 27–28n.

42. FT to HG, 7 Dec. 1828, G Letters; FT to Lafayette, 1 Feb. 1829, Dean Collection.

43. FT to JGP, 26 Dec. 1827; FT to HG, 7 Dec. 1828, G Letters; FT to Wilkes, 14 Feb. 1828, Cincinnati Historical Society; FT, *Domestic Manners*, pp. 30–31; FW to HG, 20 March 1828, G Letters.

44. CWW to HG, 26 April 1828, G Letters; CWW to Robert Jennings, 24 Feb. 1828, W Papers; FT to HG, 27 April 1829, G Letters; FT to Wilkes, 14 Feb. 1828, Cincinnati Historical Society.

45. CWW to HG, 20 Nov. 1828; quoted in HG to JGP, 15 April 1828, G Letters.

46. Mary Carroll to FW, 4 Feb. 1828, W Papers; *Free Enquirer*, 24 June 1829.

47. Lafayette to James Madison, 27 Oct. 1827, Dreer Collection; Lafayette to JGP, postmarked June 1828, G Letters; *The Writings of James Madison*, ed. Gaillard Hunt (New York: G. P. Putnam's Sons, 1900–1910), IX, 310–311.

48. Lafayette to Wilkes, 28 Nov. 1827, Benjamin Franklin Collection, Yale University Library; Lafayette to JGP, postmarked June 1828, G Letters.

49. Nashoba Book, 29 Jan. 1828, W Papers.

50. "Communication from the Trustees of Nashoba," 1 Feb. 1828, pub. in *New Harmony Gazette*, 26 March 1828; HG to JGP, 1 July 1828, G Letters.

51. Nashoba Book; FW to Robert Jennings, 24 Feb. 1828, W Papers; *Free Enquirer*, 31 Oct. 1829. Fanny's letter to Jennings was later published in an attempt to discredit her: *Fanny Wright Unmasked by Her Own Pen* (New York, 1830); *Morning Courier and New York Enquirer*, 19 June 1830.

52. FW to Lafayette, 14 Feb. 1828, Dean Collection; FW to Jennings, 24 Feb. 1828, W Papers.

53. *The Writings of James Madison*, IX, 311; *Genius*, 26 April 1828; FW to HG, 20 March 1828, G Letters.

54. HG to JGP, 12 Dec. 1827; Sismondi to JGP, 13 Jan., 13 April 1828, G Letters.

55. RDO to FW, 18 March 1828, W Papers.

56. Otto Braun to FW, 14 March 1828, W Papers.

57. CWW to HG, 26 April 1828, G Letters.

58. FW to HG, 8 June 1828, cited in HG to JGP, 29 July 1828, G Letters; FW, *Biography,* pp. 32–33.

59. Ibid., p. 33.

7. The Latter-Day Saint Theresa

1. CWW to Lafayette, 23 June 1828, Dean Collection, Cornell University Libraries. Fanny and Robert Dale announced that they would raise the annual subscription rate from $2 to $3 to make it pay its own expenses.

2. See Elizabeth Anthony Dexter, *Colonial Women of Affairs* (Boston: Houghton Mifflin, 1924), pp. 166–179.

3. *Cincinnati Daily Gazette,* 15 April 1828.

4. Charles Hammond, "View of General Jackson's Domestic Relations, in Reference to His Fitness for the Presidency" (Washington, D.C., 1828), pp. 11, 20. See also Marquis James, *The Life of Andrew Jackson* (New York: Bobbs-Merrill, 1938), I, 51–77.

5. See George Flower, *History of the English Settlement in Edwards County, Illinois* (Chicago, 1882), pp. 174–177; FT, *Domestic Manners of the Americans* (1832; reprint Gloucester, Mass.: Peter Smith, 1974), pp. 75–81, 167–175; Bernard A. Weisberger, *They Gathered at the River* (1958; reprint New York: Farrar, Straus and Giroux, 1979).

6. FW, "Preface," *Course of Popular Lectures,* reprinted in *Life, Letters and Lectures, 1834–1844* (New York: Arno Press, 1972), pp. vii–viii.

7. Donald E. Pitzer and Josephine M. Elliott, eds. *New Harmony's Fourth of July Tradition* (New Harmony, Ind.: Raintree Books, 1976), pp. 23–26.

8. FT, *Domestic Manners,* pp. 70–73.

9. FW, "Preface," *Life, Letters and Lectures,* p. vi.

10. Ibid., pp. ix, 44. The dates given for Fanny's speeches are confusing. In the *New Harmony Gazette,* 27 August 1828, Robert Dale Owen wrote that she had delivered her first lecture on "Sunday the tenth of last month." August 10 was a Sunday; July 10 was not.

11. Gerda Lerner, *The Grimké Sisters from South Carolina* (New York: Schocken Books, 1974), p. 189; FW, *Life, Letters and Lectures,* p. 23. See Barbara Welter, "The Cult of True Womanhood: 1820–1860," *American Quarterly* 18 (1966): 151–174.

12. FW, *Life, Letters and Lectures,* pp. 31, 32.

13. Ibid., pp. 45, 18, 36.

14. Ibid., pp. 16–17.

15. Ibid., pp. 25, 51.

16. Lafayette to James Madison, 27 Oct. 1827, Dreer Collection, Pennsylvania Historical Society.

17. *New Harmony Gazette,* 27 Aug. 1828; *Cincinnati Evening Chronicle,* 26 July 1828.

18. *Cincinnati Daily Gazette,* 3 Sept. 1828.

19. *The Diaries of Donald MacDonald, 1824–1826,* Indiana Historical Society Publications, vol. 14, no. 2 (Indianapolis: Indiana Historical Society, 1942), p. 236; FT, *Domestic Manners,* pp. 43, 185n.

20. Ibid., pp. 58–59, 156.

21. Ibid., p. 75.

22. See William Bailie, *Josiah Warren: The First American Anarchist* (1906; reprint New York: Arno Press, 1972). In the summer of 1830 Fanny wrote of Warren and his Time Store: "Unaided by money, unbacked by influence, and unseconded save by his own conviction of the value of the principle he had seized and the beneficial consequences of the practice he was prepared to explore, he succeeded in exhibiting to the understandings, and bringing home to the worldly interests of thousands the perfect facility of living in plenty with one third of the labor and without any of the anxiety inseparable from the existing monied exchange of the world." FW, "Wealth and Money," *Free Enquirer,* 23 Oct. 1830.

23. *New Harmony Gazette,* 15 Oct. 1828.

24. CWW to HG, 20 Nov. 1828, G Letters.

25. FT to HG, 7 Dec. 1828; Charles Wilkes to JGP, 30 Sept. 1828; HG to JGP, 23 Sept. 1828; Anna Garnett Stone to JGP, 18(?) Sept. 1829, G Letters; Lafayette to JGP, 10 Nov. 1828, Benjamin Franklin Collection, Yale University Library; *Works of Jeremy Bentham,* ed. John Bowring (Edinburgh, 1843), XI, 4–5.

26. *New Harmony Gazette,* 6 Aug. 1828.

27. CWW to HG, 20 Nov. 1828, Garnett Letters.

28. Ibid.; FW to CWW, (?) Oct. 1828, W Papers.

29. FT to HG, 27 April 1829; CWW to HG, 20 Nov. 1828, G Letters.

30. FW, *Biography . . . of Frances Wright D'Arusmont,* reprinted in *Life, Letters and Lectures,* p. 43.

31. *Free Enquirer,* 17 Dec. 1828.

32. FW to CWW, 7 Dec. 1828, W Papers; FT to HG, 7 Dec. 1828, G Letters; Fretageot to Maclure, 5 Dec. 1828, MSS., Workingmen's Institute.

33. Quoted in *Life and Letters of William Barton Rogers,* ed. Emma Savage Rogers (Boston, 1896), I, 69–71; FW to CWW, (?)Dec. 1828, W Papers.

34. FW to CWW, 2 Jan. 1829, W Papers.

35. *Free Enquirer,* 3 Dec. 1828 (Library of Congress edition). The New York Public Library and the Library of Congress have different editions for the period when RDO was in New Harmony and FW was in New York.

36. FW, *Biography,* pp. 43–44. At this momentous point in Fanny's life, the autobiography ends.

37. FW to CWW, 5 Jan. 1829, W Papers; FW, 28 Jan. 1829, pub. in *Free Enquirer,* 29 Oct. 1828 (Library of Congress edition); *New York Commercial Advertiser,* 5 Jan. 1829.

38. FW to CWW, 5 Jan. 1829, W Papers.

39. *New York Commercial Advertiser,* 5 Jan. 1829.

40. Ibid., 6 Jan. 1829.

41. Ibid., 10 Jan., 1829.

42. Ibid., 12 Jan. 1829.

43. Ibid., 15, 20 Jan. 1829.

44. Ibid., 21 Jan. 1829.

45. Quoted in *Free Enquirer*, 11 Feb. 1829 (New York Public Library edition); *New York Evening Post*, 26, 12 Jan. 1829; *New York Enquirer*, 9 Jan. 1829.

46. FW, 15 Feb. 1829, pub. in *Free Enquirer*, 3 Dec. 1828 (Library of Congress edition).

47. FW, *Life, Letters and Lectures*, p. 1.

48. FW to Dr. Ducatel, 2 March 1829, Dreer Collection; FW to HG, n.d., G Letters.

49. Charles Wilkes to Lafayette, 30 April 1829, Dean Collection.

50. *New York Enquirer*, 12 Jan. 1829; *New York American*, 9 Jan. 1829; *Free Enquirer*, 25 Feb. 1829; New York *Correspondent* (5), pp. 58, 76.

51. Horace Traubel, *With Walt Whitman in Camden* (New York: Appleton, 1908), II, 45; I, 80; II, 204–205. Whitman paid Fanny the further compliment of borrowing from her. See F. O. Matthiessen, *American Renaissance* (New York: Oxford University Press, 1941), pp. 541–542n, 550n.

52. CWW to FW, 13 Feb. 1829, W Papers.

53. FW to CWW, 21 Feb., 5 Jan. 1829, W Papers.

54. FW to CWW, 21 Feb. 1829, W Papers.

55. FW, *Biography*, p. 40.

56. FW to CWW, 11 March 1829, W Papers; Fretageot to Maclure, 13 Feb. 1829, MSS., Workingmen's Institute, New Harmony, Ind.

57. RDO, "An Earnest Sowing of Wild Oats," *Atlantic Monthly*, July 1874, p. 73; FW to CWW, 11 March 1829, W Papers.

58. FW to CWW, 11 March 1829, W Papers; *Free Enquirer*, 8 April 1829.

59. FW, *Life, Letters and Lectures*, pp. 140–156; FT to Lafayette, 28 April 1829, Dean Collection.

60. RDO, "An Earnest Sowing," p. 73.

61. Simon A. O'Ferrall, *A Ramble of Six Thousand Miles through the United States of America* (London, 1832), pp. 15–16.

62. *Free Enquirer*, 29 April 1829.

63. Ibid., 6 May 1829.

64. FW, *Life, Letters and Lectures*, pp. 101–116; *Free Enquirer*, 8 July 1829.

65. CWW to JGP, 1 Aug. 1829, G Letters.

66. FT to JGP, 20 May 1829, G Letters; CWW to Richesson Whitby, n.d., 19 July 1829, W Papers.

67. *Free Enquirer*, 24 June 1829.

68. Ibid.; FW to CWW, 2 Jan. 1829, W Papers; *Free Enquirer*, 8 Feb. 1829 (New York Public Library edition).

69. *Free Enquirer*, 22 July 1829.

70. Ibid.; FW, *Life, Letters and Lectures*, pp. 126–140.

71. CWW to Whitby, 19 July 1829, W Papers.

72. CWW to JGP, 1 Aug. 1829, G Letters.

73. RDO, "An Earnest Sowing," p. 74; *Free Enquirer,* 3 July 1830.

74. Ibid., 12 Aug. 1829; Lyman Beecher, *Lectures on Political Atheism* (Boston, 1852), p. 93.

75. Quoted in *Free Enquirer,* 12 Aug. 1829.

76. Ibid., 1 July 1829.

77. CWW and FW to JGP, 19 Aug. 1829, G Letters.

78. CWW to Whitby, 6 Sept. 1829, W Papers.

79. Mary Carroll to William Maclure, 7 Nov. 1829, MSS., Workingmen's Institute.

80. *Free Enquirer,* 2 Sept. 1829.

81. Quoted in HG to JGP, 16 Feb. 1830, G Letters.

82. CWW to JGP, 1 Nov. 1829; HG to JGP, 12 Jan. 1830, G Letters.

83. HG to JGP, (?)April 1830, G Letters.

84. FW, *Life, Letters and Lectures,* pp. 169–183.

85. *Free Enquirer,* 23, 30 Sept. 1829.

86. Ibid., 23 Sept. 1829.

87. Ibid., 14 Oct. 1829.

88. Ibid., 31 Oct. 1829.

89. FW, *Life, Letters and Lectures,* pp. vii, viii; Lafayette to Garnier Pagès, 14 June 1829, microfilm copy, Louis Gottschalk Papers, University of Chicago.

90. FW to Richard Carlile, 16 Oct. 1829, Houghton Library, Harvard University.

8. Her Wisdom and Her Folly

1. Joseph Balthasar Inginac to FW, 15 June 1829, Dreer Collection, Pennsylvania Historical Society.

2. CWW to JGP, 1 Nov. 1829, G Letters; Lafayette to Garnier Pagès, 14 June 1829, microfilm copy, Louis Gottschalk Papers, University of Chicago; *Free Enquirer,* 31 Oct. 1829.

3. *Free Enquirer,* 21 Nov. 1829.

4. FW to CWW, 21 Feb. 1829, W Papers.

5. Amédée Dufour to the Count de Beauséjour, 11 Oct. 1829, quoted in *Gazette des Tribunaux,* 7 July 1841.

6. Maclure to Fretageot, 28 Nov. 1826; 8, 24 Feb. 1827, MSS., Workingmen's Institute, New Harmony, Ind.

7. *Free Enquirer,* 14, 21 Nov. 1829.

8. Ibid., 14 Nov. 1829.

9. *Works of Orestes A. Brownson,* ed. Henry F. Brownson (Detroit: T. Nourse, 1902), V, 57–59.

10. FW to the People of Pittsburgh, 5 Dec. 1829, pub. in *Free Enquirer,* 26 Dec. 1829.

11. Ibid., 19, 26 Dec. 1829; 30 Jan., 6 Feb. 1830.

12. Savage to FW, 13 Nov. 1829, W Papers.

13. FT to JGP, 12 March 1830, G Letters; FW to Maclure, 3 Jan. 1830, MSS., Workingmen's Institute.

14. Miscellaneous notes, W Papers.

15. RDO to Nicholas Trist, 3 Feb. 1830, Nicholas Trist Papers, Library of Congress; *Free Enquirer*, 20 Feb. 1830. At the time, Fanny wrote that she was taking thirty freed slaves to Haiti. Forty-five years later Robert Dale Owen, looking at the brig's manifest, discovered that there had been thirty-one people—thirteen adults and eighteen children. RDO, "An Earnest Sowing of Wild Oats," *Atlantic Monthly*, July 1874, p. 75. Fanny apparently added to the original Nashoba colony of nine adults and nine children, as William Leete Stone claimed to have seen bills of sale for ten adults and ten children whom she purchased in 1826. *Commercial Advertiser*, 2 June 1830. Nothing remains to suggest exactly when or by what process Fanny freed them.

16. FW to Lafayette, 15 March 1830, W Papers.

17. FW to Phiquepal, 19 March 1830, W Papers.

18. FW to Lafayette, 15 March 1830, W Papers; *Free Enquirer*, 1 May 1830.

19. RDO, *Threading My Way* (1874; reprint New York: A. M. Kelley, 1967), p. 283; RDO, "An Earnest Sowing," p. 75; Amos Gilbert, *Memoir of Frances Wright: The Pioneer Woman in the Cause of Human Rights* (Cincinnati, 1855), pp. 36, 53.

20. RDO to his father, 27 March 1830, Robert Owen Papers, Cooperative Union, Manchester, England.

21. *Free Enquirer*, 6, 13, 20, 27 Feb., 20 March, 17 April, 15 May 1830.

22. Lyman Beecher, *Letters on Political Atheism* (Boston, 1852), pp. 92–93; FW, *Life, Letters and Lectures, 1834–1844* (New York: Arno Press, 1972), pp. 184–197.

23. Ibid.; Bernard Weisberger, *They Gathered at the River* (1958; reprint New York: Farrar, Straus and Giroux, 1979), p. 151.

24. RDO to his father, 27 March 1830, Owen Papers.

25. Edward Pessen, *Jacksonian America: Society, Personality, and Politics* (Homewood, Ill.: Dorsey Press, 1969), pp. 285–293. For the Working Men's party, see also *Free Enquirer*, May 1829-winter 1830; Helen Sumner, "Working-men's Parties in New York," *History of Labour in the United States*, ed. John R. Commons (1918; reprint New York: Augustus M. Kelley, 1966), I, 231–284.

26. Quoted in *Free Enquirer*, 7 Nov. 1829; quoted in Sumner, *History of Labour*, I, 238.

27. *Free Enquirer*, 31 Oct. 1829; RDO to Trist, 18 Nov. 1829, Trist Papers.

28. *Free Enquirer*, 21 Nov., 5 Dec. 1829.

29. CWW to FW, 22 Nov. 1829, W Papers; quoted in William Randall Waterman, "Frances Wright," *Studies in History, Economics, and Public Law*, 256 (1924): 205–206.

30. *Free Enquirer*, 8 May 1830.

31. Quoted in *Free Enquirer*, 5 June 1830.

32. Ibid.; *Morning Courier and New York Enquirer*, 24, 28 May 1830.

33. *Free Enquirer*, 5 June 1830.

34. *New York Commercial Advertiser*, 28 May 1830.

35. Ibid., 2 June 1830; *Free Enquirer*, 12 June 1830; RDO, "An Earnest Sowing," p. 75.

36. Miscellaneous notes, W Papers.

37. *New York Commercial Advertiser,* 2 June 1830.

38. *Morning Courier and New York Enquirer,* 18 Feb., 8 May, 19 June 1830.

39. Ibid., 19 June 1830.

40. FW, *Life, Letters and Lectures,* pp. 198–205.

41. FT, *Domestic Manners of the Americans* (1832; reprint Gloucester, Mass.: Peter Smith, 1974), pp. 262–263; quoted in *Free Enquirer,* 19 June 1830.

42. FW, Last Will and Testament, MSS., Workingmen's Institute; FW, *Life, Letters and Lectures,* p. 220.

43. *The Diary of Philip Hone, 1828–1851,* ed. Allan Nevins (1927; reprint New York: Arno Press, 1970), I, 25–26, 9–10.

44. Quoted in Waterman, "Frances Wright," pp. 219–220; FT to JGP, 18 April 1831, G Letters.

9. Mixing with None but French Society

1. Richard Carlile to FW, 15 Sept. 1830, Dean Collection, Cornell University Libraries.

2. FW to Lafayette, n.d., quoted in A. J. G. Perkins and Theresa Wolfson, *Frances Wright, Free Enquirer: The Study of a Temperament* (New York: Harper Bros., 1939), p. 300.

3. RDO to Nicholas Trist, 1 Aug. 1830, Nicholas Trist Papers, Library of Congress; RDO to Caroline Dale Owen, 12 Aug. 1830, Robert Owen Papers, Cooperative Union, Manchester, England; RDO to Trist, 1 Nov. 1830, Trist Papers; quoted in *Free Enquirer,* 8 Jan. 1831.

4. See David H. Pinkney, *The French Revolution of 1830* (Princeton: Princeton University Press, 1972); Guillaume de Bertier de Sauvigny, *The Bourbon Restoration* (Philadelphia: University of Pennsylvania Press, 1966), pp. 440–456.

5. Bertier de Sauvigny, *Bourbon Restoration,* p. 449.

6. Pinkney, *French Revolution,* p. 162.

7. FW to Lafayette, "delivd 25th October 1830," W Papers. This letter is one of the few items among the Wolfson Papers that is not a copy by Alice Perkins. It seems to be in Camilla Wright's hand.

8. *Free Enquirer,* 27 Nov. 1830.

9. Ibid., 1 Jan. 1831.

10. Amos Gilbert, *Memoir of Frances Wright: The Pioneer Woman in the Cause of Human Rights* (Cincinnati, 1855), p. 19.

11. *The Letters and Journals of James Fenimore Cooper,* ed. James Franklin Beard (Cambridge, Mass.: Harvard University Press, 1960), II, 72.

12. HG to JGP, 12 Jan., 27 Feb. 1831, G Letters.

13. RDO to Trist, 23 Feb. 1831, Trist Papers; RDO to Robert Owen, 21 Feb. 1831, Owen Papers.

14. FW to Robert Owen, 16 March 1831, Owen Papers; HG to JGP, 25 March 1831, G Letters.

15. RDO, "An Earnest Sowing of Wild Oats," *Atlantic Monthly*, July 1874, p. 75.

16. FW to HG, n.d., G Letters.

17. RDO to Trist, 8 June 1831, Trist Papers; HG to JGP, 27 April 1831, G Letters.

18. Cited in Perkins and Wolfson, *Frances Wright*, pp. 312–313. Fanny had written, however, that "French law affords much protection to women." *Free Enquirer*, 29 April 1829.

19. HG to JGP, 2 Oct. 1831, G Letters; FW to Robert Owen, 10 Nov. 1831, Owen Papers.

20. HG to JGP, 26 Nov. 1831, G Letters.

21. Fretageot to Maclure, 25 Dec. 1831, MSS., Workingmen's Institute, New Harmony, Ind.

22. Ibid.; Fretageot to Maclure, 19 Aug. 1832, MSS., Workingmen's Institute.

23. Mary Shelley to FW, 30 Dec. 1830, Robert Dale Owen Collection, Indiana State Library; FW, "A Few Words," datelined 10 Nov. 1830, pub. in *Free Enquirer*, 8 Jan. 1831.

24. HG to JGP, 12 Jan., 21 March 1832; Maria Garnett to JGP, 5 May 1832, G Letters.

25. HG to JGP, 28 May 1832, 24 June 1833, G Letters.

26. HG to JGP, 25 July 1832, G Letters.

27. Mary Garnett to JGP, 29 June 1832, G Letters.

28. Richard W. Leopold, *Robert Dale Owen: A Biography* (Cambridge, Mass.: Harvard University Press, 1940), pp. 107–111; *Free Enquirer*, 20 Oct. 1832; RDO to Trist, 15 Oct. 1832, Trist Papers; *Free Enquirer*, 18 Feb. 1829 (New York Public Library edition).

29. *Free Enquirer*, 13 Oct. 1832.

30. Ibid.

31. RDO to MJO, 29 Sept.–1 Oct. 1832; MJO to RDO, 13–14, 19–25, 26–27 Sept. 1832, MSS., Workingmen's Institute.

32. MJO to RDO, 19–25 Sept. 1832; RDO to MJO, 26–27 Sept. 1832, MSS., Workingmen's Institute.

33. Perkins and Wolfson, *Frances Wright*, p. 317; MJO to RDO, 6–9, 14 Sept. 1832, MSS., Workingmen's Institute.

34. Ibid.

35. Ibid.; MJO to RDO, 19–25, 26–27 Sept., 8–18 Oct. 1832, MSS., Workingmen's Institute.

36. See FT, *Paris and the Parisians in 1835* (New York, 1836).

37. Lafayette to FW, 27 Sept. 1832, Lafayette MSS., Lilly Library, Indiana University; Gilbert, *Frances Wright*, p. 23.

38. FW to John Minter Morgan, 9 June 1833, MS. Collection, Public Library of Cincinnati and Hamilton County.

39. *Pioneer*, 5 July 1834; *Poor Man's Guardian*, 25 Oct. 1834.

40. Jules Cloquet, *Recollections of the Private Life of General Lafayette* (New York, 1836), II, 92.

10. The Woman Everybody Abuses

1. FW, *Course of Popular Lectures* (Philadelphia, 1836), II, xxi.

2. See Leonard L. Richards, *"Gentlemen of Property and Standing": Anti-Abolition Mobs in Jacksonian America* (New York: Oxford University Press, 1970). There were 115 incidents of mob violence recorded in the 1830s, as opposed to 21 in the 1820s. Ohio, when Fanny lectured there again, had more anti-abolitionist mobs than any other state. In New York and Pennsylvania, the violence reached its height in 1836–1837, when Fanny was there. See also *The Diary of Philip Hone, 1828–1851*, ed. Allan Nevins (1927; reprint New York: Arno Press, 1970), I, 168.

3. Many of their travels, as well as lists of their investments, are recorded in a pocketbook Phiquepal kept, now among the Frances Wright Papers at the Library of Congress.

4. See Alice Felt Tyler, *Freedom's Ferment* (1944; reprint New York: Harper and Row, 1962), pp. 463–547.

5. See Aileen S. Kraditor, *Means and Ends in American Abolition* (New York: Random House, 1969); Martin Duberman, ed., *The Antislavery Vanguard* (Princeton: Princeton University Press, 1968); Clifford S. Griffin, *Their Brothers' Keepers: Moral Stewardship in the United States, 1800–1865* (New Brunswick, N.J.: Rutgers University Press, 1960).

6. *Cincinnati Daily Gazette*, 26 Jan. 1836.

7. FW to the Gentlemen of the Committee, 24 Jan. 1836, Gratz Collection, Pennsylvania Historical Society.

8. *New York Evening Post*, 18 June 1836. See Gerda Lerner, "The Lady and the Mill Girl," *The Majority Finds its Past* (New York: Oxford University Press, 1979), pp. 15–30; Lerner, *The Female Experience* (Indianapolis: Bobbs-Merrill, 1977), pp. xxxv–xxxvi.

9. *Cincinnati Daily Gazette*, 28 May 1836; Poulson's *American Daily Advertiser*, 18 June 1836.

10. RDO to James M. Dorsey, 31 Jan. 1830, New Harmony Papers, Indiana Historical Society; FW to JG, 8 June 1825, G Letters.

11. Nor does the evidence prove Jackson the kindly master his followers made him out to be. Advertising for the return of an escaped slave, he offered $50 plus reasonable expenses if the slave were taken out of the state, plus $10 extra "for every one hundred lashes any person will give him to the amount of 300." Chase C. Mooney, *Slavery in Tennessee* (Bloomington: Indiana University Press, 1957), p. 52.

12. Amos Gilbert, *Memoir of Frances Wright: The Pioneer Woman in the Cause of Human Rights* (Cincinnati, 1855), pp. 48–49.

13. *Cincinnati Daily Gazette*, 28 May, 4 June 1836.

14. Ibid., 4 June 1836.

15. FW, *Popular Lectures*, II, x–xi, xv; *Pennsylvanian*, 12 July 1836.

16. FW, *Popular Lectures*, II, xv.

17. Ibid., pp. xvi–xxi; *Pennsylvania Sentinel*, 18 July 1836, quoted in *New York Journal of Commerce*, 19 July 1836; Pennsylvania *National Gazette*, 23 July 1836.

18. Ibid., 26 July 1836; FW, *Popular Lectures*, II, xx.

19. Ibid., pp. xxi–xxii.

20. Ibid., pp. xxi-xxiv.

21. *Cincinnati Daily Gazette*, 5 Aug. 1836; Richards, "*Gentlemen of Property and Standing*," pp. 92–100.

22. Catharine E. Beecher, *Letters on the Difficulties of Religion* (Hartford, 1836), p. 23.

23. FW, *Popular Lectures*, II, iii–iv.

24. *Cincinnati Daily Gazette*, 11 Nov. 1835.

25. Lafayette to JG, 31 Dec. 1825, Benjamin Franklin Collection, Yale University; FW, *Manual of American Principles*, p. 102; FW, *Popular Lectures*, II, 73–90.

26. FW, "Wealth and Money," *Free Enquirer*, 25 Sept., 2, 9, 16, 23 Oct. 1830.

27. Quoted in Arthur Schlesinger, Jr., *The Age of Jackson* (London: Eyre & Spottiswoode, 1946), p. 81; Phiquepal to FW, 1 June 1834, W Papers. See also Peter Temin, *The Jacksonian Economy* (New York: W. W. Norton, 1969).

28. FW, *Popular Lectures*, II, 60–62, 45; FW, *Manual of American Principles*, p. 56.

29. Quoted in Schlesinger, *The Age of Jackson*, pp. 317–318. See also James Parton, *Life of Andrew Jackson* (New York, 1861); Marquis James, *The Life of Andrew Jackson* (New York: Bobbs-Merrill, 1938); Robert V. Remini, *The Revolutionary Age of Andrew Jackson* (New York: Harper and Row, 1976).

30. See Edward Pessen, *Jacksonian America: Society, Personality, and Politics* (Homewood, Ill.: Dorsey Press, 1969), pp. 211–274.

31. FW, *Popular Lectures*, II, 62.

32. Ibid., pp. 63, 70.

33. FW to William Maclure, 16 June 1839, MSS., Workingmen's Institute, New Harmony, Ind.

34. FW to Sylva, 3 July, 10 Aug. 1836, W Papers.

35. Posey County Deed Book F, pp. 254–260, County Courthouse, Mount Vernon, Ind.; Alexander Maclure to William Maclure, 1 Oct. 1833; RDO to Richard Owen, 17 March 1836, microfilm copy, MSS., Workingmen's Institute.

36. *Boston Weekly Investigator*, copied in W Papers.

37. Ibid., 5 May 1837.

38. FW, *Biography . . . of Frances Wright D'Arusmont*; reprinted in *Life, Letters and Lectures, 1834–1844* (New York: Arno Press, 1972), p. 40; FW to RDO (?), 18 June 1845; RDO to W. R. Morris, 31 May 1845, W Papers.

39. *New Moral World*, 25 March 1837.

40. Joel Brown, unpub. memoir of FW, Public Library of Cincinnati and Hamilton County, p. 36.

41. *Morning Courier and New York Enquirer*, 19 Oct. 1836; *New York Commercial Advertiser*, 20 Oct. 1836.

42. FW, *Manual*, pp. 9–10; quoted in Poulson's *American Daily Advertiser*, 13 Jan. 1837.

43. FW, *Manual*, p. 3. See also Roderick S. French, "Liberation from Man and God in Boston: Abner Kneeland's Free-Thought Campaign, 1830–1839," *American Quarterly* 32 (1980): 202–221.

44. FW, *England the Civilizer: Her History Developed in Its Principles* (London, 1848), p. 18. See Fitzwilliam Byrdsall, *The History of the Loco-Foco or Equal Rights Party* (1842; reprint New York: Clement and Packard, 1967); Walter E. Hugins, *Jacksonian Democracy and the Working Class: A Study of the New York Workingmen's Movement, 1829–1837* (Stanford, Calif.: Stanford University Press, 1960), pp. 36–48, 172–202; Schlesinger, *The Age of Jackson,* pp. 190–209; Pessen, *Jacksonian America,* pp. 293–297.

45. FW, *Manual,* p. 9.

46. *The Diary of Philip Hone,* I, 253; RDO to his father, 15 May 1837, Robert Owen Papers, Cooperative Union, Manchester, England.

47. FW, *Manual,* pp. 3–4, 12, 24.

48. Ibid., pp. 45, 52.

49. Ibid., p. 82.

50. Sylva d'Arusmont Guthrie to Dr. W. S. Ruschenberger, 30 Aug. 1894, W Papers; [H. de Boinville] to FW, 20 May 1837, MSS., University of Chicago.

51. See Schlesinger, *The Age of Jackson,* pp. 221–241; Glyndon G. Van Deusen, *The Jacksonian Era, 1828–1848* (New York: Harper and Row, 1959), pp. 124–131.

52. *New York Daily Express,* 18 Oct. 1837.

53. *New York Evening Post,* 18 Oct. 1837; *Daily Express,* 20, 24 Oct. 1837.

54. Ibid., 17 Nov. 1837.

55. Ibid., 16 Dec. 1837; FW, *What Is the Matter?* (New York, 1838), p. 7; Phiquepal to FW, 5 Feb., 9 Oct., 28 Nov., 19 Dec. 1838, W Papers.

56. Lucy Say to William Maclure, 5 Nov. 1837, MSS., Workingmen's Institute.

57. *Cincinnati Chronicle,* 13 Jan. 1838.

58. See Schlesinger, *The Age of Jackson,* pp. 299–304.

59. FW, lecture datelined "New York, 23 Sept. 1838, at Masonic Hall." These fourteen lectures, which are among the Theresa Wolfson Papers, are handwritten in individual books Fanny carried with her onto the stage. Some of them have notations indicating when and where they were delivered, but on occasion these notations conflict with newspaper or other accounts at the time. Some of the speeches are fragmentary, but their sequence is reasonably clear. Only one speech, *What Is the Matter?,* was prepared for publication. They are available from Cornell University Libraries on microfilm #5216.

60. *New York Daily Express,* 28 Sept., 26 Oct. 1838.

61. Ibid., 1 Oct. 1838.

62. *New York Evening Post,* 8 Oct. 1838; *New York Daily Express,* 9 Oct. 1838.

63. *New York Evening Post,* 25 Oct. 1838.

64. FW, *What Is the Matter?,* pp. 13–16.

65. *New York Daily Express,* 26 Nov. 1838; *Selections from the Autobiography of Elizabeth Oakes Smith,* ed. Mary Alice Wyman (Lewiston, Me.: Lewiston Journal Co., 1924), p. 83; FW, lecture with headnote "New York Concert Hall 13th Jany 1836" (misdated); FW, lecture with headnote "Febry 3d, 1839," W Papers.

66. FW, lecture with headnote "New York, Concert Hall, 6th Jany 1839";

FW, lecture with headnote "New York Concert Hall 13th Jany 1836" (misdated), W Papers.

67. *Selections from the Autobiography of Elizabeth Oakes Smith*, pp. 83–85.

68. FW, lecture with headnote "New York Concert Hall 13th Jany 1836" (misdated), W Papers.

69. FW, first untitled lecture; lecture with headnote "New York, 17th Feby, 1839," W Papers.

70. FW, lecture with headnote "March."

71. Sylva to Ruschenberger, 30 Aug. 1894, typescript copy, W Papers; FW to William Maclure, 16 June 1839, MSS., Workingmen's Institute.

72. *The Diary of Philip Hone*, I, 402.

11. The Last Drops of Bitterness

1. FW, *Biography . . . of Frances Wright D'Arusmont*, reprinted in *Life, Letters and Lectures, 1834–1844* (New York: Arno Press, 1972), p. 37.

2. Ibid., pp. 8n, 34.

3. Ibid., pp. 32, 37–38.

4. Ibid., pp. 29–30.

5. FW, *Political Letters of Frances Wright D'Arusmont*, reprinted in *Life, Letters and Lectures, 1834–1844*, p. 16.

6. *Reasoner* 2.51 (1847): 277.

7. *Reasoner* 2.52 (1847): 287.

8. Ibid., p. 288.

9. Ibid.; *Reasoner* 2.54 (1847): 313; FW to George Jacob Holyoake, n.d.; Holyoake to FW, 15 June 1847, Holyoake Papers, Cooperative Union, Manchester, England.

10. *Reasoner* 3.57 (1847): 349–351.

11. Holyoake to Isaac Ironside, n.d., Holyoake Papers.

12. *Reasoner* 3.57 (1847): 348–349; FW to Holyoake, n.d.; Ironside to Holyoake, 18 June 1847, Holyoake Papers.

13. FW, *England the Civilizer: Her History Developed in Its Principles* (London, 1848); FW to Richard Rush, 4 April 1848, GK Papers.

14. *Reasoner* 4.98 (1848): 275; unknown addresser to FW, 30 Jan. 1849, GK Papers.

15. *England the Civilizer*, pp. 359, 72.

16. Ibid., pp. 11–13, 22.

17. Ibid., pp. 376, 414.

18. Ibid., p. 469.

19. Ironside to Holyoake, 18 June 1847, Holyoake Papers.

20. Virginia Woolf, *Three Guineas* (New York: Harcourt, Brace & World, 1966); FW, *Life, Letters and Lectures*, p. 1. See also Carol Gilligan, *In a Different Voice* (Cambridge, Mass.: Harvard University Press, 1983).

21. Leonard N. Beck, "The Library of Susan B. Anthony," *The Quarterly*

Journal of the Library of Congress 32 (1975): 333; Paulina W. Davis, *A History of the National Woman's Rights Movement for Twenty Years* (New York, 1871), p. 10.

22. See Barbara Berg, *The Remembered Gate: Origins of American Feminism* (New York: Oxford University Press, 1978), p. 224.

23. FW, *Life, Letters and Lectures*, p. 1.

24. *Reasoner* 2.54 (1847): 315.

25. See General Register of Sasines, #RS/3/2286/1–67, Scottish Record Office.

26. Phiquepal's complaint to the court, 1850, W Papers; *Reasoner* 2.52 (1847): 288.

27. FW to Watson, 6 May 1846, W Papers; *Reasoner* 2.55 (1847): 317–318.

28. See Particular Register of Sasines for Forfarshire, #RS35/298, #RS35/308, Scottish Record Office. The Trust Deed was recorded 20 Sept. 1847 in Deed Book A, p. 75, Office of the Recorder, Hamilton County Courthouse, Cincinnati, Ohio.

29. Alexis d'Arusmont to Phiquepal, 22 Dec. 1847; FW to William R. Morris, 3 Dec. 1847; Phiquepal to Alexis, 5 Feb. 1848, W Papers.

30. Copy of FW's complaint to the court, Frances Wright Papers, Library of Congress. The first two pages of this document are missing.

31. FW to Gholson, n.d., GK Papers.

32. Copy of FW's complaint to the court, Frances Wright Papers; "D'Arusmont v. D'Arusmont and Others," *Western Law Journal* 8 (Oct. 1850–Oct. 1851): 548–562.

33. Phiquepal to FW, 1 Oct. 1850, GK Papers.

34. Robert Walsh to Phiquepal, 12 Oct. 1850, GK Papers.

35. Shelby County Clerk's copy of "Frances Wright d'Arusmont vs. Phiquepal d'Arusmont," 22 Jan. 1851; FW to William Green, 1 Feb. 1851, GK Papers; Amos Gilbert, *Memoir of Frances Wright: The Pioneer Woman in the Cause of Human Rights* (Cincinnati, 1855), pp. 39–40.

36. FW to sheriff of Shelby County, 21 April 1851, GK Papers.

37. "D'Arusmont v. d'Arusmont and Others," pp. 560–561.

38. Diary of Sylva d'Arusmont, Frances Wright Papers; FW to Gholson, 13 Nov. 1851, GK Papers.

39. Sylva to Dr. Ruschenberger, 25 April 1896, typescript copy, W Papers; Frances Sylva Guthrie d'Arusmont, *Memorial on Suffrage*, 3 Feb. 1874, W Papers.

40. Joel Brown, unpub. memoir of Frances Wright, Public Library of Cincinnati and Hamilton County, p. 6.

41. Ibid., p. 8.

42. RDO, "An Earnest Sowing of Wild Oats," *Atlantic Monthly*, July 1874, p. 75; quoted in CW to JG, 8 Dec. 1826, G Letters; Phiquepal to FW, 1 Oct. 1850, GK Papers.

43. See G. J. Barker-Benfield, "Sexual Surgery in Late-Nineteenth-Century America," *Seizing Our Bodies*, ed. Claudia Dreifus (New York: Random House, 1978), pp. 13–41.

44. W. Y. Gholson to Thomas Todd, 25 April 1852, GK Papers. The details of Fanny's last months come from miscellaneous letters, bills, notes, and checks in the GK Papers.

45. E. J. Howze to FW, 1 Jan. 1852, GK Papers.

46. FW to Gholson, n.d. and 6 June 1852, GK Papers.

47. FW, Last Will and Testament, GK Papers.

Index